Transformation Dynamics in FinTech

An Open Innovation Ecosystem Outlook

Open Innovation: Bridging Theory and Practice

ISSN 2424-8231

Series Editors: Anne-Laure Mention *(Global Business Innovation, RMIT, Australia)*
Marko Torkkeli *(Lappeenranta University of Technology, Finland &
INESC TEC, Portugal)*

The series aims to contribute to knowledge creation and more importantly, to knowledge accumulation, through the combination of multiple streams, perspectives, disciplinary approaches and diverse backgrounds. In doing so, it departs from the current body of literature adopting a purely academic perspective on Open Innovation, and thus restates the importance of anchoring Open Innovation research into the reality, practices, challenges facing firms and policymakers. This book series covers multiple perspectives, such as measuring and assessing the impact of Open Innovation, dealing with organizational matters and culture, designing strategies, policies, incentives and measures to support and implement Open Innovation, and discussing the advantages and limitations of adopting Open Innovation strategies.

Published

Transformation Dynamics in FinTech

An Open Innovation Ecosystem Outlook

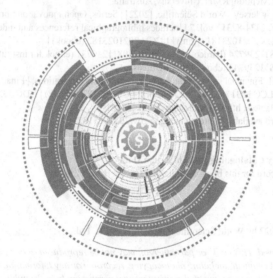

Editors

Dimitrios Salampasis
Swinburne University of Technology, Australia

Anne-Laure Mention
RMIT University, Australia

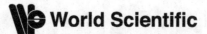 **World Scientific**

NEW JERSEY · LONDON · SINGAPORE · BEIJING · SHANGHAI · HONG KONG · TAIPEI · CHENNAI · TOKYO

Published by

World Scientific Publishing Co. Pte. Ltd.

5 Toh Tuck Link, Singapore 596224

USA office: 27 Warren Street, Suite 401-402, Hackensack, NJ 07601

UK office: 57 Shelton Street, Covent Garden, London WC2H 9HE

Library of Congress Cataloging-in-Publication Data

Names: Salampasis, Dimitrios, editor. | Mention, Anne-Laure, editor.
Title: Transformation dynamics in FinTech : an open innovation ecosystem outlook /
    editors, Dimitrios Salampasis, Swinburne University of Technology, Australia,
    Anne-Laure Mention, RMIT University, Australia.
Description: New Jersey : World Scientific, [2022] | Series: Open innovation : bridging theory
    and practice, 2424-8231 ; vol. 7 | Includes bibliographical references and index.
Identifiers: LCCN 2021023181 (print) | LCCN 2021023182 (ebook) |
    ISBN 9789811239724 (hardcover) | ISBN 9789811239731 (ebook for institutions) |
    ISBN 9789811239748 (ebook for individuals)
Subjects: LCSH: Financial services industry--Technological innovations. | Finance--Data processing.
Classification: LCC HG173 .T74 2022 (print) | LCC HG173 (ebook) | DDC 332.10285--dc23
LC record available at https://lccn.loc.gov/2021023181
LC ebook record available at https://lccn.loc.gov/2021023182

British Library Cataloguing-in-Publication Data
A catalogue record for this book is available from the British Library.

For any available supplementary material, please visit
https://www.worldscientific.com/worldscibooks/10.1142/12355#t=suppl

Desk Editors: Balamurugan Rajendran/Yulin Jiang

Typeset by Stallion Press
Email: enquiries@stallionpress.com

Printed in Singapore

About the Editors

Dimitrios Salampasis is an educator, writer, academic researcher, and globally recognized emerging leader in financial technologies innovation. Dimitrios serves as the Director, Master of Financial Technologies and Lecturer of FinTech Innovation and Entrepreneurship at the AACSB Internationally-Accredited Swinburne Business School, Swinburne University of Technology in Melbourne, Australia. Dimitrios is a Visiting Professor of FinTech at the University of Québec at Rimouski, Canada, a Blockchain and FinTech Fellow at the Singapore University of Social Sciences and Visiting Faculty at the School of Management Fribourg, Switzerland. Dimitrios is an MAICD (Australian Institute of Company Directors) and a FINSIA (Financial Services Institute of Australasia) Senior Associate and Mentor.

Dimitrios has more than 16 years of international professional working experience in the private, public, and NGO sectors having served in different functions and career levels. Prior to joining academia, Dimitrios worked in the management consulting industries being involved in global advisory and consulting activities on emerging market investing, assisting companies in developing long-term strategic focus and sustainable market business strategies. Dimitrios publishes in international peer-reviewed academic journals and books and his work is presented in major international conferences and invited keynote speeches and lectures around the world.

Dimitrios' research interests revolve around the organizational, human, technological, and societal sides of innovation and open innovation in financial services and FinTech innovation. His areas of specialist expertise, research, teaching, industry engagement, and advisory work revolve around the emergence and development of FinTech-enabled business models, blockchain-based business models and sustainable development, quantum computing in financial services, digital transformation in banking, and FinTech education, together with the relevant global FinTech-related regulatory and policy interventions.

Dimitrios is a very passionate advocate of the need of bridging the communication gap between business/financial services managers and technologists/data scientists. He is actively contributing, both in Australia and globally, to the curation of the best-in-class FinTech talent that is able to grasp both business and technology through his interaction with policy-making, political, regulatory, industrial, and academic stakeholders around the globe. Through his work, Dimitrios is developing novel, immersive, and experiential learning models to encourage the shaping of the emerging young talent together with the perpetual and renewable upskilling of professionals and executives by inspiring, nurturing, and curating the next generation of best-in-class FinTech talent and supporting the mentorship and growth of an effective and successful Australian and global FinTech innovation ecosystem.

Anne-Laure Mention is the Director of the Global Business Innovation Enabling Capability Platform at RMIT, Melbourne, Australia. She is also a Professor at the School of Management at RMIT, Melbourne; Visiting Professor at Université de Liège, Belgium; Visiting Professor at Tampere University of Technology, Finland; and a Fintech and Blockchain Visiting Fellow at Singapore University of Social Sciences. She holds several other visiting positions in Europe and Asia. Anne-Laure is one of the founding editors of the *Journal of Innovation Management*, and was the Deputy Head of the ISPIM Advisory Board (2012–2018). She is the co-editor of a book series on *Open*

Innovation, published by World Scientific/Imperial College Press. Her research interests revolve around open and collaborative innovation, innovation in business-to-business services, with a particular focus on financial industry and FinTech, technology management, and business venturing. She has been awarded the prestigious IBM Faculty Award twice for her research on innovation.

About the Contributors

Omar Abdelhakim is a CEMS Master's in Management graduate. He is currently based in Prague working as a corporate accountant for US IT services and solutions company.

Magne S. Angelshaug is a PhD Research Scholar at the Norwegian School of Economics (NHH). He holds a Master in Cybernetics from the Norwegian University of Science and Technology (NTNU) and an MBA in Management control from NHH. He has extensive experience from management and management consulting, and currently holds positions within the finance industry of Norway.

Finn C. Arctander is a Digital Consultant at OMMAX, focusing on digital transaction advisory and digital strategy development for leading European companies. He is primarily advising private equity clients, supporting with due diligence work and digital value creation. Prior to OMMAX, Finn studied in Norway, US, Spain, and Australia and gained professional work experience from Spain and Germany. Finn holds a double Master's degree: MSc in Business Administration and Economics and Master in International Management (CEMS MIM) from Norwegian School of Economics (NHH).

Wajeeha H. Awadh is a FinTech and digital banking expert. At Al Baraka Banking Group, she is a Section Head of Digital Banking and FinTech, where she is currently engaged with digital transformation strategies and projects. Wajeeha has also been part of Strategic Planning Department and Sustainability and Social Responsibility Department, where she worked on projects, including the establishment of a new Islamic bank in Morocco, group-wide product intelligence system, group-wide sustainability reporting, and integrating United Nations' Sustainable Development Goals (SDGs) with Al Baraka Sustainable Development Goals. Wajeeha is currently pursuing a doctoral program at Asia Pacific University of Technology and Innovation. Her research focuses on the adoption of *Shariah*-compliant financing-based crowdfunding platforms by Micro, Small and Medium Enterprises (MSMEs). Wajeeha is also a member of Bahrain Women in FinTech Initiative and is part of FinTech Ecosystem and Talent workgroups in Bahrain FinTech Bay, the largest FinTech Hub in MENA region. She was also the Head of Bahrain Tech Awards for the year 2019 and was listed in Top 50 Most Influential Women in Islamic Business and Finance by Cambridge IFA. Wajeeha is an international speaker and has both academic and non-academic publications in the area of FinTech.

Thomas K. Bennett has a Bachelor of Commerce (Finance, Economic & Commercial Law) and a Graduate Certificate in Data Science from the University of Sydney. Whilst pursuing his studies he has undertaken policy, research, and financial services internships in Washington D.C., Shanghai, and Sydney. Most recently, Thomas has been a Research Assistant and Business Manager at the Australian Payments Network. He is currently working on the Cambridge Centre for Alternative Finance's RegSimple project as both a data and regulatory analyst.

Suraj Bhattarai is an IT professional from Bhutan. Suraj graduated from Leiden University, the Netherlands, in the field of Business & Management in 2017 (MSc ICT in Business, Business-IT Alignment) for which he was awarded a full Netherlands Fellowship Programme (NFP) scholarship by the Dutch government.

Meredith Bowden is a futures thinker, facilitator and psychologist based in Melbourne, Australia. She has over 20 years of professional experience in the public and private sectors, including public affairs, psychology, health promotion, leadership, management, and strategic planning. Meredith completed her Masters in Strategic Foresight at Swinburne University of Technology in 2018. She co-established FuturesPlanner, a strategic foresight and risk and opportunity consultancy, in 2016. FuturesPlanner helps individuals and organizations find ways forward in uncertain and complex times. Meredith's areas of interest are emergent strategy-making, strategic conversation, systems thinking, and futures-focused leadership development.

Caroline E. Braastad is a consultant with two years' experience, working for the Oslo-based Management Consulting firm Sprint Consulting. Caroline holds a CEMS Master's in International Management and Financial Economics from the Norwegian School of Economics (NHH) and the National University of Singapore (NUS). She is passionate about innovation and new technology and specializes in helping organizations improve their ability to innovate through methods like lean start-up and design thinking.

Jörn Bühring is an Assistant Professor at The Hong Kong Polytechnic University, School of Design. He earned a BA-equivalent degree in the field of Tourism Management (Hotelfachschule Hamburg), an MBA (Victoria University) majoring in Entrepreneurship and Innovation, and a PhD in futures Consumer Engagement Innovation at Swinburne University of Technology (SWIN) in Australia. In his current position, he is developing a collaborative approach (Design Economies, Ignite Innovation) that brings academia, designers, and business stakeholders together to develop high-impact design knowledge, concepts, and solutions. His research explores Design Foresight, Vision, and Fiction techniques as emerging processes within Strategic Design and Innovation Management.

Nolwenn Camps-Leysour de Rohello is a Finance consultant holding a BAA in Finance, Economics and Mathematics from HEC Montreal, as well as an MSc in International Business from Ivey Business School at Western University. Skilled in both Business Strategy and Corporate Finance, Nolwenn has extensive experience working with leading global organizations in the financial services area across North America. She primarily focuses on developing Finance strategies, improving processes and deploying large-scale business transformation programs.

Fiona Carter is a client experience and marketing specialist who has significant experience working across complex global and local organizations. Currently, Fiona is the Head of Marketing at an Australian technology company focused on telecommunications and solving complex business challenges. Regarded as a natural leader who can bring large teams together to create achievable strategic plans and execute outcomes, Fiona has a talent for engaging stakeholders and keeping them accountable. Fiona is passionate about helping individuals and businesses reach their full potential and is a certified business coach. Fiona is currently completing her MBA at UNSW. Work-life balance is important to Fiona, she enjoys hiking on the weekend, walking her Groodle, and spending time with friends and family.

Crag Carttling is passionate about driving innovative approaches to solving "wicked problems" and creating economic, social, and environmental value for everyone. Crag has a diverse multidisciplinary background in business, environmental management, and community development, underpinned by a double degree in Environmental and Social Sciences and a double Masters in Entrepreneurship and Innovation and Business Administration (Executive). Crag has worked across the not-for-profit, government and private sectors in areas, including tourism and hospitality, event management and the arts, and environmental management and community development. Crag is motivated by the belief that with open, engaging, and innovative approaches, solutions can be found which bring together mainstream business approaches with community needs to achieve economic, social, and environmental sustainability and prosperity.

Noel Finck has a background in accounting and trustee services with 30 years of professional experience. After completed his Bachelor of Business (Accounting), Noel worked as an accountant in the publishing and travel industries in Australia and in the UK. Upon returning to Australia, Noel has primarily worked in the trustee industry in management roles. Noel's core area of expertise is the provision of Executorial and Trustee services. Additional qualifications include a Graduate Diploma in Corporate Management from Deakin University. Noel is a Fellow of the Association of Chartered Certified Accountants. Noel is currently a Senior Manager in the Family Office team at Pitcher Partners Melbourne working with private family clients.

Leila Fourie is Group CEO of the Johannesburg Stock Exchange (effective 1/10/19). Prior to this, Dr Fourie served as Executive responsible for Commercial Lending at Commonwealth Bank Australia & previously CEO of the Australian Payments Network. Leila has served on multiple boards and held senior roles in banking, capital markets, and payments in South Africa and Australia. Before moving to Australia, Leila served on the Board of the JSE as Executive Director. Prior to that, Leila worked for Standard Bank, first as Global Director Credit and Capital and previously as Card Division Managing Director. Leila has a PhD in Economic and Financial Sciences. Her PhD thesis investigated Sovereign Rating Contagion and her Master's thesis covered procyclicality in banking through the economic cycle. Dr Fourie won the Economic Society South Africa prize for the best Masters' thesis and published several articles in academic journals.

Harry Fulgencio currently doing his PhD on Information Systems. His theoretical research output includes the following topics: living labs, business model, e-health and social innovation, He specializes in qualitative design research method and scholarly understanding of emerging technological innovations that help companies and the society.

Rachid Ghilal is Professor of Finance at the Department of Management Sciences at UQAR, Lévis Campus. After a degree in civil engineering and an MBA, Professor Ghilal obtained his PhD in finance from the joint doctoral program in administration of Montreal (UQAM, HEC, McGill, Concordia). Professor Ghilal has produced several publications and presented his research in several Canadian provinces, the US, and Europe. His research and teaching interests revolve around the following themes: international portfolio diversification, exchange traded funds, responsible investment performance, financial risk management, machine learning in finance, blockchain, and FinTech.

Alexander Kaiser is a Member of the Board of Vicenda Asset Management Ltd, Switzerland, in addition to his position of Managing Director of Vicenda Australia. Alexander has more than 20 years of experience in the financial services/capital markets industry. From 2001 to 2012, he held a variety of management positions at Credit Suisse's Clariden Leu unit. He has in-depth knowledge of corporate financial management, business development, structured finance, and equity research. Alexander is also an Adjunct Professor/Industry Fellow of Corporate Finance at the University of Applied Science Western Switzerland and at Swinburne University of Technology, Melbourne. Furthermore, he served until the end of 2014 as Honorary Consul of the Commonwealth of Australia for German-speaking Switzerland. Alexander continues to provide services through his consulting company in Zug/Switzerland and Melbourne with a focus on strategy, corporate finance and M&A, predominately for family offices, asset managers, and pension funds, including a global property investor. Alexander has an undergraduate honours degree in Finance & Accounting from UAS Western Switzerland, an MBA from Monash University and MLaw (Commercial Law) from Deakin University.

Tamer Khraisha holds a PhD in Network Science from the Central European University, and he is currently working in the IT industry as a Software and Data Developer. Research interests of Tamer include financial data science, machine learning, and technological innovation. He authored a variety of papers on topics like fitness landscape, innovation on networks, and finance.

Volkmar J. Klausser is a Digital Project Lead at Finanz Informatik Solutions Plus GmbH. He has more than eight years of professional working experience in intrapreneurial teams in the financial services industry. As Project Lead, Volkmar is responsible for IT projects ranging from B2C brokerage applications to the digitization of processes. Volkmar has previously completed his studies in Technology and Innovation Management, writing a master thesis on the "Development of a Smart Lending Process for Private Customers in Germany." He further completed his Master's in Business Administration (Executive) and Entrepreneurship and Innovation at Swinburne University of Technology. Volkmar's research is focused on how emerging technologies can improve the services provided by the financial industry.

Hans LeFever currently Lectures at the MBA program of The Hague University of Applied Sciences, The Netherlands. Dr. Hans Le Fever obtained a PhD in experimental physics at Leiden University and this early experience with the application of computers for scientific purposes landed him a job at Shell, where he spent 22 years in a variety of planning and IT Management functions. He has worked in areas with diverse cultures and levels of IT maturity, always focused on creating tangible and intangible value for the organization from the application of IT. Since 2003, he is an Independent Academic and Professional Educator in the field of managing IT and scientific innovation. He was an Academic Program Director for the Leiden University ICT in Business MSc curriculum and still lectures and supervises a variety of thesis research. On the innovation side, he focuses on the development of innovative start-ups in the life sciences.

Vincenzo Lorefice in the 22 years after graduating as a Mechanical Engineer from RMIT University, Melbourne, has honed his engineering experience in Toyota automotive manufacturing and logistics facilities, learned and applied lean manufacturing fundamentals/methodologies, and developed a specialty and great reputation in planning, process, layout, and value stream design. Since Toyota, Vince's journey has led him to graduating with a Master of Entrepreneurship and Innovation from Swinburne University, Melbourne, through which he has developed new business thinking and a more mature understanding/appreciation for manufacturing business. In his latest position at Swinburne University, Vince is consulting to manufacturing businesses with a goal to help them become more cost-competitive, resilient, and sustainable by leveraging Industry 4.0 digital technologies and business model innovation to find new ways of creating value for their business and customers, and improve business outcomes.

Avni Misra is a Researcher at RMIT University, College of Business. Her research focuses on innovation management with interest on digitalized innovation, business networks, and industrial marketing. Her qualitative research capabilities extend toward another key area of research that deals with the issues and management of gender equality. Additionally, Avni is a Lecturer of product innovation and management and B2B Marketing at RMIT University, key work integrated learning courses as a part of the Bachelor of Business degree. Some of her current research is toward examining role of business networks in technology commercialization. Furthermore, in the gender equality space, she is involved in multiple projects investigating the impact of gender as key variable that influences decision-making in different organizational operations in different industries. Avni has presented at several innovation and marketing conferences in Australia and internationally. She received her PhD in innovation and industrial marketing from RMIT University. She received her second Master's degree in Business Marketing from RMIT University and her Master's in Biotechnology from India. Apart from academia,

Dr. Misra is also a marketing consultant working on several service-oriented projects in the technology industry and has over 6yrs of experience working for different marketing firms in India and clients in Australia.

Hamid Nach is Professor of Information Systems (IS) at the University of Quebec at Rimouski, Lévis Campus. He is the Business Technology Management (BTM) Area Coordinator, Co-Founder and Co-Chair of the FinteQC and Co-Founder of "Accent Numérique" Lab. He has 10 years experience in the private sector, particularly in the telecom industry. He has served in different functions and corporate levels. His earlier research focused on the impact of IT on identities. The results of his work appear in journals such as *Computers in Human Behavior* and *Management Research Review* and were presented in several international conferences. In the last few years, he has been interested in investigating FinTech's adoption, use, and impact. His focus is on the business use of artificial intelligence and blockchain and the emerging FinTech's business models. Dr. Nach is speaker, trainer and coach. He developed a BAA major program in BTM at UQAR, and his teaching covers a wide range of BTM related areas such as, e-Business, IT architecture, and e-commerce.

Erin B. Taylor is an Associate at the Institute for Culture and Society, Western Sydney University, and Principal Consultant at Canela Consulting, The Hague. Her research specialization is financial behavior, including service use, decision-making, and financial inclusion. Erin is the author of the book *Materializing Poverty: How the Poor Transform Their Lives* (2013, AltaMira). She has contributed chapters to books including *Women, Consumption and Paradox: Towards A More Humanistic Approach to Consumption* (2020, Routledge), *Money at the Margins: Global Perspectives on Technology, Financial Inclusion and Design* (2018, Berghahn), and *Design Anthropology: Object Cultures in Transition* (2017, Springer). Erin is also co-author of the report *Female Finance: Digital, Mobile, Networked* (with Anette Br-løs, 2020, EWPN/Keen Innovation).

Jeffrey Vanderveen having graduated as an Electrical and Electronic Engineer from Victoria University, spent his early career as a Process Engineer in the manufacturing industry. He was especially focused on problem-solving and implementing lean manufacturing methodologies. After completing a diploma in ORMS from The University of Melbourne, he transitioned into a career in engineering and maintenance management. Now having completed a double Masters in Advanced Manufacturing Engineering and Entrepreneurship and innovation he helps manufacturing businesses modernize and streamline their processes and operations.

Percy Venegas is the Chief Scientist at Economy Monitor, where he conducts research and advises businesses and investors on Risk Forecasting and Automated Intelligence (Evolutionary Algorithms). He is a Former Intel Engineer, where he was the Chair of Statistical Process Control at a global automation and robotics group. Percy was awarded an MBA in International Business from MIB Trieste School of Management, Italy; attended the MIT Sloan China Program, Lingnan University College at Sun Yat-Sen University in Guangzhou; earned an Executive Master in Sustainable Development and Corporate Responsibility from EOI Business School, Campus Universidad Complutense de Madrid; and completed the Artificial Intelligence Programme from the Said Business School, University of Oxford. He was in the Founding Advisory Board of the *Social Venture Capital Conference*, Latin America, Caribbean, and South Florida, and is currently a member of the New England Complex Systems Institute, and, the International Institute of Forecasters. Percy Venegas pioneered the study of Asymmetric Trust and Fields Finance in economics and has published and presented on the topic at the University of Cambridge and MIT, among others. Percy is currently engaged in initiatives at the Oxford Centre for Innovation to promote the responsible transition to Post-Quantum & Decentralized Artificial Intelligence.

Contents

https://doi.org/10.1142/9789811239731_0001

Chapter 1

Negotiating the Sweet Spot of Open Innovation: Engaging with Global Ecosystem Catalysts Reimagining FinTech Transformation

Dimitrios Salampasis,[*,§] *Anne-Laure Mention*[†,¶] *and Avni Misra*[‡,||]

[*]*School of Business, Law and Entrepreneurship, Swinburne University of Technology, Hawthorn VIC 3122, Australia*

[†]*Royal Melbourne School of Technology, Melbourne VIC 3000, Australia*

[‡]*School of Economics Finance and Marketing/School of Management, Royal Melbourne School of Technology, Melbourne VIC 3000, Australia*

[§]*dsalampasis@swin.edu.au*

[¶]*Anne-Laure.Mention@rmit.edu.au*

[||]*avni.misra@rmit.edu.au*

1. Advances in FinTech Industry

The magical, dynamic, and novel blend of emerging technologies and traditional financial principles and instruments, known as FinTech, has given rise to "a new financial industry that applies technology to improve financial activities" (Schueffel, 2016, p. 45). FinTech is gradually becoming a tactical approach for the development of financial services companies. Technology revolution and digitalization have been providing several digital alternatives to financial institutions worldwide. The financial services landscape is continuously evolving (Goasduff, 2019; Ruddenklau, 2020), generating numerous smart and data-led innovations in the product, service, and process landscape. Financial organizations are investing a great deal (resources, capabilities, organizational transformation, mergers and acquisitions, and partnerships) in managing and anticipating the challenges that are constantly being created by new technologies and changing consumer needs. They are doing so by incorporating technology-based partnerships, training employees to understand new technologies, adapting to new business models, designing data management strategies, employing agile ways of working across different business functions, and restructuring operating models to make efficient advancements (Ruddenklau, 2020; Ernst and Young, 2020).

The financial service industry is highly reliant on information and data from its consumers and affiliated business sources. Integrating emerging technologies into the processes that help manage such services aid in translating the potential of data and information into monetary benefits. A survey with financial services experts conducted in 2019 by Accenture, in collaboration with Oxford Economics, reported that 90% of respondents had put together long-term strategies for technology-based innovation. One-third of the respondents advocated integrating digital technologies in internal operations as a critical tactic of the long-term plan. Digitalization strongly influences the financial service industry (Lee and Shin, 2018; Puschmann, 2017). In collaboration with information technology experts, financial services organizations have focused on digital augmentation of current business models, product development methods, process management, and improving customer experiences (Goasduff, 2019). Integration of digitalized self-service platforms, customer relationship management platforms, big data, and artificial intelligence (AI) implementation for different operational processes have amplified the outputs delivered by financial service organizations. Moreover, open data is gradually being utilized within a number of financial services sectors as an enabler of digital transformation (Nicoletti, 2019). Integration of websites, social media platforms, search engine optimization and search engine marketing management, and digitalized storytelling approaches for marketing-based activities have helped prepare the financial firms to manage customer acquisition, engagement, interaction, and retention, while improving reach at a consumer level (Wright, 2019; Ernst and Young, 2020).

Financial organizations have incorporated digital technology into their regular business practices. Some examples include large organizations, such as Commonwealth Bank of Australia, which has developed i-bond, a blockchain operating new debt system, which allows sharing and lending money between large organizations and fund managers worldwide via an online process bond trading (Eyers, 2018). On the other hand, medium-sized organizations or SMEs are not far behind. Xero, an accounting-based technology firm from New Zealand, provides business owners with real-time visibility of their financial position using a smart online accounting platform. Robinhood, a US-based firm, has developed a subscription-based e-trade software for its customers to buy and sell stocks. In Europe, wefox, a Berlin-based firm provides a digital service platform for insurance broker insurers and end-customers. This explains the rising need for FinTech innovations and practices in the financial service industry.

In the same vein, the growth and transformational and multidisciplinary nature of FinTech and its associated advancements have drawn the interest of academic scholars (Mention, 2011, 2019, 2020; Mention and Torkkeli, 2012, 2014; Lee and Shin, 2018;

Salampasis *et al.*, 2020; Salampasis *et al.*, 2019; Salampasis and Mention, 2018; Palmié *et al.*, 2020; Puschmann, 2017; Boratyńska, 2019) who have published their recent academic research that focuses on examining FinTech using different scholarly positions, based on the multidimensional nature of FinTech. Some have emphasized understanding it from a digitalized evolution point of view, where they investigated the impact of digital makeover of the financial service industry on developing value (Palmié *et al.*, 2020), disruptive innovations (Varga, 2017; Boratyńska, 2019), and development of new business models (Lee and Shin, 2018). Others have used the ecosystem approach as a frame of reference to understand the evolution of FinTech (Imerman and Fabozzi, 2020), the entrepreneurial FinTech ventures (Spigel, 2019), entrepreneurial finance (Salampasis *et al.*, 2020), innovation relationships (Still *et al.*, 2016), and FinTech innovation management (Still *et al.*, 2016). A critical article discussing the "Future of Fintech," authored by Mention (2019), has highlighted the increasing interest of academic journals that have introduced special issues on the topic related to FinTech innovation and management, such as *Journal of Management Information Systems'* "Financial Information Systems and the FinTech Revolution" (Gomber *et al.*, 2018), *International Journal of Entrepreneurship and Management*'s "Innovation for Financial Services" (Mention *et al.*, 2012), *Technological Forecasting & Social Change* on 'Capital Markets in the 21st Century: Transformation Through Technological Change, Regulatory Reform and Financial Innovation" (Diaz-Rainey *et al.*, 2015), *International Journal of Business Innovation and Research* on "Innovation for Financial Services" (Mention and Torkkeli, 2014), and *Philosophy and Technology*'s "Towards a Philosophy of Financial Technologies" (Coeckelbergh *et al.*, 2018). Although previous studies have explored the advancement in FinTech from different perspectives, there is still a need for gaining a deeper understanding of the FinTech ecosystems and their involvement and contributions in digitalized open innovation (OI) processes that are implemented for developing potential FinTech innovations.

As a result, it is vital to acknowledge the efforts made to compile the knowledge that provides a panoramic view of the FinTech industry, its innovation ecosystem, implementation of a digital approach in its innovation processes, and the future exploration of the FinTech landscape. Pavel (2021), in his book *FinTech Strategy*, explored SMEs. New firms with limited resources can compete with large organizations and other financial institutions by discussing and implementing different growth strategies and business models. The book chapters use a case-based approach to gather discussions and provide a strategic view using an entrepreneurial perspective. The book, *The Future of FinTech* by Nicoletti (2017) discusses the rise of the FinTech sector, different business models, innovation strategies, and success factors for FinTech initiatives, emphasizing the understanding of technologies, products, processes, and business models in a FinTech environment. Liermann and Stegmann (2019) and Lynn *et al.* (2019), in their books *The Impact of Digital Transformation and FinTech on the Finance Professional* and *Disrupting Finance*, respectively, have discussed the impact of digitalization on financial management and explore technologies in the finance sector. All four publications have discussed the advancements in FinTech and the evolving role of technologies and their contributions to the finance industry. However, these works paid limited attention to ecosystems' role in FinTech, and, in particular the foundational role of OI as a vehicle for FinTech-led value creation, capture, extraction, and dissemination both from an organizational and ecosystemic standpoint (Fasnacht, 2009, 2018; Mention and Torkelli, 2014; Salampasis, 2014).

Scholars have identified the need for a concerted effort, involving scholars and practitioners from different disciplines to understand the links between different innovation approaches in FinTech (Lee and Shin, 2018; Puschmann, 2017; Svensson *et al.*, 2019; Boratyńska, 2019; Palmié *et al.*, 2020) and the links between different approaches. Such research endeavors have also put emphasis on identifying the needs of other inter-organizational and intra-organizational players and their relationships within the FinTech ecosystem, and how it impacts the different innovation management activities.

To address the need of the growing future research areas, this book has been conceptualized and structured to understand the different FinTech ecosystems' different levels and their management using a digitalized OI perspective. This book aims to do so by first identifying FinTech research scope to understand the FinTech industry's momentum in Chapter 1, and then exploring the organizational innovation approaches and their implementation in developing future FinTech innovations in Chapters 2–4. The combined chapters aim to understand the FinTech innovation and development from the standpoint of an individual, as well as organizational decision-making approach in the first half of the book. Chapters 5–7 adopt an ecosystem lens to FinTech innovation, value creation, and wealth management tactics. In the latter half of the book, Chapters 8–11 discuss the integration of digital advancements in FinTech for improved data management and explore the role of AI and block-chain technologies for developing enhanced financial services. Towards the end of the book, Chapter 12 aims to provide a deeper understanding of the developing financial landscapes. The range of subjects discussed across the different book chapters indicates that FinTech innovations and ecosystem management are gaining attention and have a broader implication in innovation, information technology development, business ecosystem, and organizational management. This book also discusses the digitally integrated FinTech OI approach and the dynamics of inter-organizational and intra-organizational relationships supporting the innovation process. It further extends into understanding the contributions of different organizational and individual actors within the FinTech ecosystems.

The introductory chapter is structured as follows. Section 2 discusses the intersection of OI and the FinTech industry and delves into FinTech ecosystems' discussion and digitalization of the FinTech OI process. This leads to the section that provides an overview of the book chapters and contributions to the management of FinTech advancement.

2. Intersection of the Three Key Dimensions: OI, FinTech Ecosystem, and Digital Integration Framework

Growing knowledge around Fintech innovation and the evolution of an effective ecosystem that assists in developing the innovative solutions have made it necessary to observe the phenomena by using an integrated approach. It is important to understand the role and points of intersections of the three key dimensions, which include OI approach, the role of the ecosystem, and the digital tools that influence such developments. The framework in Figure 1 shows the application of an integrated approach to understand the key points of influence, where a diverse and digitalized ecosystem comprising different stakeholders and technologies influences the stages of an OI process. The framework indicates that the stakeholders within the ecosystem can operate at different levels — at an industry level, where the interactions happen between multiple networks constituting of multiple organizational entities; at a dyadic level, where interactions are limited to one or two entities; at a cross-functional team level within the organizations, where different teams internally collaborate and also externally cross-function with teams of other partnering organizations; and lastly at individual levels, where actions of individual entities influence the OI process. The knowledge and resource exchange are strongly influenced by the integration of different digital tools. These tools influence, manage, and initiate the exchange and output during the process. To recognize the role of each dimension and its contribution to these phenomena, it is important to understand all three dimensions individually.

2.1. *Growing FinTech OI trends*

Over the last decade, there has been rapid growth in the financial service industry's technological developments. Digital technologies have disrupted how businesses operate within the financial sector's large ecosystems and have led to the evolution of FinTech

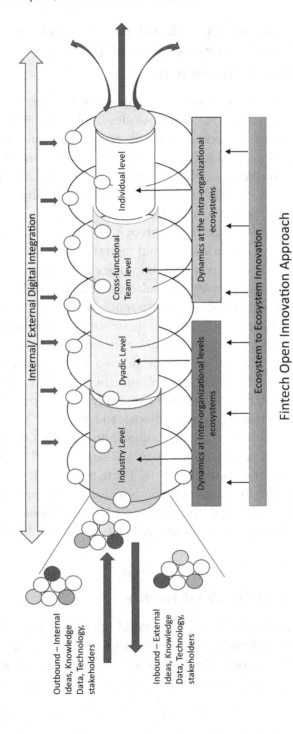

Figure 1.   Integrated Framework showing the intersection of OI approach, role of the ecosystems, and the integration of the digital tools.

(Karagiannaki *et al.*, 2017). The evolution and growth of FinTech have led to the development of new business models and market opportunities, improving customer and stakeholder experiences (Karagiannaki *et al.*, 2017). Scholars such as Chesbrough (2010) and Mina *et al.* (2014) have explored how companies evolve their innovation approaches and align them with service-oriented approaches using digitalized platforms to break the innovation monotony and gain competitive advantage. Financial firms have relied on different innovation approaches to develop potential FinTech innovations to keep up with the industry's evolving nature.

The OI approach has been identified as a suitable method for financial firms to innovate new potential products and services, as OI allows the business to recognize the needs of the changing business environment and utilize the involved stakeholders to become competitive in the market. The OI paradigm assumes that firms can innovate advanced technologies using external and internal ideas and paths to market (Chesbrough, 2003). Previously established research has explored the blend of OI and FinTech using different perspectives, such as Fasnacht (2009), who studied the incorporation of open platforms in the fund management process. Martovoy *et al.* (2015) and Vermeulen (2004) studied the pros and cons of OI in financial service development and management. In an empirical study, Salampasis *et al.* (2014) identified the external drivers for OI in the financial service sector and the role of trust (Salampasis *et al.*, 2015; Mention *et al.*, 2014). At the same time, practitioners within the financial sector across the globe have been applying OI-based methods to meet the changing financial service innovation trends. For example, BBVA, a Spanish bank's OI unit, has worked consistently to stay updated with the latest FinTech innovations and acquired an online bank to gain deeper consumer insights who prefer operating online for their banking activities. Bank of America innovated the "Keep the Change" savings program in collaboration with different retailers. It helped consumers manage their saving accounts with a rounding-up calculator integrated into their card payments.

Scholars and practitioners have attempted to provide a more in-depth understanding of the future of FinTech and how OI presents itself as a potential tool for future growth. It is worth noting that the successful implementation of OI approaches for the advancement of FinTech is possible because of the contribution of multiple stakeholders that participate in the process and the ecosystem to which they belong. Thus, it is important to use an ecosystem(ic) lens to examine the intersection of FinTech and OI approaches.

2.2. *FinTech ecosystems and stakeholder perspective*

A steady interdependent FinTech ecosystem contributes to the growth of the FinTech industry (Lee and Shin, 2018). A FinTech ecosystem comprises FinTech start-ups, technology developers, government, financial customers, traditional financial institutions (Lee and Shin, 2018; Diemers *et al.*, 2015), as well as financial services authorities and regulatory bodies and sandboxes (Alaassar *et al.*, 2020). These different entities in the FinTech ecosystem contribute to developing innovations, facilitating resource accessibility and management, and contributing to various ecosystem activities. Financial ecosystems transform how FinTech has evolved. FinTech companies are transforming using OI as the modus operandi, which depends on a deeper involvement of diverse inter-organizational and intra-organizational ecosystems that feed the innovating organizations of the FinTech ecosystem with the required complementary assets for inventing successfully.

Recently, a lot of attention is being paid to understand and explore the concept of FinTech ecosystems from different dimensions. It provides evidence that FinTech innovations are an outcome of the OI approach adopted by various financial firms that interact with other financial and non-financial firms within an ecosystem. Lee and Shin (2018) studied the FinTech ecosystems by examining the different business model approaches and investment decisions. Alongside this, the paper also discusses the managerial challenges for various FinTech stakeholders. In addition to that, Svensson *et al.*

(2019) added knowledge to the FinTech ecosystem management theory by understanding the relationships and alliances and their role in shaping the FinTech ecosystems. Castro *et al.* (2020) examined the evolution of FinTech ecosystems by understanding the role of social, technological, and organizational actors in the evolution process. They also applied the service innovation perspective to understand the dynamics of FinTech evolution.

Many practitioners and consulting firms have collected data and developed reports to understand the FinTech ecosystems fully. For example, Pollari and Teper (2019) from KPMG invested in creating a visualization of the Australian FinTech landscape and demonstrated the range and diversity of the precipitously developing sector. The Alliance for Financial Institutions produced a detailed report on understanding regulators' role in developing enabling FinTech ecosystems (AFI, 2020). It also explored the characteristics of existing FinTech ecosystems, key stakeholders, and areas where regulators can contribute to FinTech ecosystems' development. The FinTech ecosystem's phenomena and the need to understand its relevance is a general requirement as the studies and reports are not limited to one country. Still, it has become a global phenomenon under observation. An example that aligns well is the development of a global regulatory sandbox (Alaassar *et al.*, 2020). A regulatory sandbox plays a key role in facilitating knowledge exchange for financial entrepreneurial activities. Another good example would be the comprehensive report published by Diemers *et al.* (2015) on behalf of Strategy&, a consulting firm, which explained the role of the four critical elements — business environment, regulatory support, access to capital, and financial expertise — that support the development of a FinTech ecosystem and how it can be applied to build a successful FinTech ecosystem in Gulf regions. Understanding the implementation of an ecosystem and its functioning for facilitating OI to develop FinTech is evident, as has been emphasized in academia and practice. It is still an evolving field that calls for developing more comprehensive research to fully understand all its different dimensions and how they can be strategically applied. However, there is one dimension that is simultaneously emerging, that is the integration of digital tools for developing financial technologies and the advanced management of the FinTech OI processes and ecosystems.

2.3. *Digitally integrated FinTech OI approach*

The ever-changing nature of digital technology, development, and advancement is a complex phenomenon. On the one hand, it provides financial organizations the capabilities and aligning ecosystems to operate in a fast-paced and flexible environment. It generates new possibilities and modifies the value offerings and supply chain of financial intermediation, disrupting the existing business models. At the same time, it accompanied challenges related to uncertainty, safety, and controllability (Nylén and Holmstrom, 2015). The different levels of the neo-ecosystems within the financial sector comprise not only a consortium of organizations and individual entities but also digital technologies that assist the interactions between different levels of the FinTech ecosystem by acting as mediating services (Latour, 2005; Chen and Hung 2016; Jacobides *et al.*, 2018), thus making it difficult to control the impact of ecosystem interactions on OI. Therefore, FinTech firms are continually looking for gaining a deeper understanding of the role of integrating digital technologies for openly innovating as well as managing the ecosystem interactions that are pertinent for the stakeholders of the financial sector (traditional and non-traditional).

To address the need for attention, academics have recently started investing their interests in understanding the role of digital integration in managing FinTech OI. Boratyńska (2019) studied the impact of economic and financial characteristics of digital financial technology on value creation for financial services with the aim to gain insights regarding the types of tools that can enable stakeholders create value on FinTech. Breidbach *et al.* (2020) identified user-inspired research agendas to direct scholars and managers to conduct relevant research in a field of digital financial service systems, orchestration of value creation with FinTech, and development of flexible infrastructures. Previously established research also laid some foundations for developing future research agendas for gaining further understanding of the digital transformation of the financial service sector through OI approach. For example, Riasanow *et al.* (2018) conducted extensive research to identify the different inter-organizational innovation patterns of digital transformation in the financial sector and examined the influence of the blockchain technologies

Additionally, there is a plethora of research examining the involvement of digitalization in the FinTech innovation process conducted by practitioners and government and financial institutions to understand the applications of the same. For example, the report published by Deutsche Bank written by Dapp and Slomka (2015) outlined the issues related to the digital ecosystems in the banking sector and the structural changes required to manage them effectively. Riemer *et al.* (2017) studied the Australian B2C FinTech landscape and existing financial services to understand how the FinTech has been successful in harnessing digital technologies. It uses a customer perspective to provide ways in which FinTech can offer value to its consumers by integrating digital technologies. In an OECD 2019 roundtable, the key topic of discussion was digital and BigTech disruption in financial markets using a regulatory management perspective.

Although this topic is attracting global attention from academia and industry, it is still not well grounded. Moreover, aligning with the very volatile nature of technologies and consumer needs, there is always a need for gaining further understanding about the realms of FinTech evolution from all three perspectives — OI, ecosystems, and digital integration. The chapters in this book have attempted to assemble the knowledge regarding all three dimensions systematically to provide a much-needed understanding of the trends of FinTech. The next section unfolds the details of each chapter to provide a stronger picture of the prospects this book.

3. Unfolding the Dimensions of FinTech

In this book, Nach, Salampasis, and Ghilal have reviewed the current FinTech research and suggested a FinTech research agenda in

Chapter 2. Their chapter analyzes six major databases and provides their observations regarding FinTech research scholarships' growing scope, thereby providing meaningful insights to shape the future research agenda. In addition, they have also identified FinTech as being associated with several evolving technologies and their applications. Such innovative solutions are a result of a diverse ecosystem in which the financial service organizations operate.

This discussion is further extended in Chapters 3, 4, and 5 of this book, where the authors provide a different take on FinTech by applying a unique perspective of OI. In Chapter 3, Taylor has explored the relationship between innovation, mobility, and change, and how it impacts the development and management of consumer relationships. The author examines the positive and negative impact of the increased access to financial products using mobility as an analytical tool — this allows us to identify the different types of outcomes that emerge financial innovations within different populations. It sheds light on the different types of risks that are associated with evolving financial innovations. This provides food for thought for organizations to strategize ways to manage the complexities associated with innovating new FinTech innovations.

Complementing Taylor's findings in Chapter 3, Bühring in Chapter 4 provides a detailed review of the challenges resulting from ever-evolving business environments. Bühring uses the financial services landscape lens to identify financial firms' issues and uncertainties due to interruptions caused by FinTech and associated new business model approaches. It pushed organizations to think about new strategic organizational decision-making skills in innovation. In Chapter 5, Klausser, Salampasis, and Kaiser provide an overview of how banking organizations utilize OI mechanisms to develop services that are adapted to the changing market environment. With the use of multiple case studies based on the type of OI approach (inside out, outside in, and coupled OI) applied by the company, they examine the factors that enable or hinder the successful application of the OI approaches in the context of banking services. Their work further expands on understanding the usefulness of an OI approach for financial institutions.

An essential foundation of FinTech development is the ecosystem in which it operates. In Chapter 6, Awadh discusses the role of the ecosystem in supporting FinTech through OI. The chapter elaborates on different stakeholders such as FinTech start-ups, traditional financial institutions, governments, financial customers, technology providers, human capital, supporting platforms, associations, and international profile in the FinTech innovation. It further suggests how the OI approach allows multiple players from within the ecosystem to work collaboratively to ensure the development of FinTech.

In the same vein, Braastad, Rohello, Arctander, Abdelhakim, and Angelshaug in Chapter 7 discuss how stakeholders can reinforce value creation within the FinTech cluster. The chapter identifies the motivation of different stakeholder groups, and the commonalities and challenges between them, influencing value creation. It further suggests how organizational collections enhance the value creation process by applying and participating in effective collaboration mechanisms. It also recommends ways to overcome challenges related to cluster management by developing common cultures for value creation, adapting business models to suit the OI approach, communicating the progress for capitalizing on success, building knowledge management processes, and creating formal agreements for common projects. The authors emphasize that such a mechanism can create beneficial spillover effects on all actors in the ecosystems.

To advance the discussion, Finck, Bowden, Carter, Carttling, Lorefice, and Vanderveen in Chapter 8 identify the challenges and prospects that wealth managers need to foresee and respond to for being successful. They then suggest ways by which the organizations can be ready for the anticipated changes in their findings. The chapter discusses the role of changing business models, emerging market needs, and consumer segments; incorporating digitalized tools for advancement; understanding the lean methodology; and exploring the changing culture and value. It attempts to widen the knowledge of wealth managers regarding the influence of different elements of an OI approach on the development of FinTech as an industry. It is interesting how a dominant part of the chapter discusses the role of different digital technologies that provide wealth management incumbents advice and considerations for disruptive technology readiness.

The role of digital integration in OI has been explored in depth by several scholars and practitioners. A majority of stakeholders in a FinTech ecosystem are reliant on digital processes and technologies for innovating successfully. Chapter 9 of this book, authored by Fourie and Bennett, extends this discussion by using open banking regimes. The chapter assesses the impact of open banking on the financial services sector and the economy in Australia. Open banking is an example of the digital transformation of financial services. It indicates a shift in the digitalized financial services and provides a competitive landscape. The authors' efforts have been directed toward providing a clear description of the emerging business models within this landscape, the outcomes, and challenges associated with open banking, and discusses the principles for practicing safe innovation. The chapter provides a detailed overview of the open banking system and its essential attributes that need to be considered by the FinTech ecosystem stakeholders to ensure and expand a successful implementation of OI in the financial sector.

The financial sector's digital transformation is discussed more specifically in Chapter 10 of this book. Bhattarai, Fulgencio, and LeFever have added detailed knowledge about blockchain's role as one of the most disruptive digital tools for managing financial transactions. The chapter examines the advantages of blockchain, its business applications, and the business models within the context of FinTech through OI. In doing so, the chapter identified a critical gap in applying blockchain business models within FinTech organizations. The discussion offers an exciting perspective toward implementing blockchain technology and its alignment with the business models in FinTech to discover new business opportunities.

Blockchain is not the only digital technology integrated into FinTech that grabs scholars and practitioners' attention. In Chapter 11 of this book, Venegas goes further to explain the growing interest of wealth managers in FinTech, AI, as well as blockchain as investable technologies. The findings suggest that FinTech is considered a mature investment vertical, as several investors are increasingly financing FinTech companies. The predictive modeling approach also indicated that the convergence of adjacent technologies such as AI and blockchain is also drawing interest from an investor with experience in FinTech. Based on the analysis in the chapter, Percy predicts that the investment front will significantly impact different aspects of FinTech, current or emerging, in the long run.

With the increasing advancement of FinTech and changing business models due to ever-increasing digitalization, there is bound to be complexities that may barricade the development of FinTech. It is crucial to anticipate and identify solutions to tackle such complexities with potential solutions. The book wraps up with Khraisha's Chapter 12, which uses an interesting approach of fitness landscapes to model both the space of solutions to a financial problem and the search heuristics adopted by FinTech firms to explore such areas. The findings offer critical insights into the different dimensions of FinTech innovation complexities. It further adds engaging offerings for policy-makers and firms to understand the right regulatory solutions to tackle financial complexities. It also discusses the part that OI plays in generating collaborations, which is another complexity that needs to be well regulated.

Overall, this book provides a holistic view of FinTech OI with digital integration using multiple lenses. Different FinTech ecosystem members can adapt this understanding to strategies virtually for developing successful FinTech innovations.

4. Contributions

In conclusion, this volume contributes managerially and theoretically to the emerging discussion about the advancement of FinTech and the management of FinTech OI using resourceful ecosystems. The book shares knowledge regarding different perspectives of FinTech development by applying a diverse range of contextual settings to understand how it can be a beneficial approach for all stakeholders involved in the FinTech ecosystem. However, it cannot exemplify all available and examined contexts regarding FinTech developments. Still, we aim to provide sufficient reportage of the topics to instigate further discussion and encourage practitioners and academics to push boundaries.

From an academic perspective, it provides information regarding the overlap between three key business concepts — OI, digital integration, and ecosystems. It establishes a narrative using financial services and its applications as a context that can be applied to interlink and examine the different phenomena related to the multidisciplinary concepts. It is expected that the multidisciplinary approach linking the concepts of the FinTech ecosystem, OI, and digital integration will assist in understanding the intersections between the disciplines and help in laying the foundations for future research. The chapters' research findings and outcomes in this book can be interpreted and applied to different settings for identifying techniques and approaches that assist in designing better organization strategies for managing FinTech. The chapters extend the discussion broadly, aligning with FinTech innovation and management (Gomber *et al.*, 2018; Mention, 2019) to start with and then leading up to the discussion of future FinTech landscapes (Holmes and King, 2019; Pollari and Teper, 2019). The findings from the chapters extend the theoretical knowledge by laying a specific focus on understanding the role of different stakeholders and digital technologies involved in the process of FinTech development.

Managerially, the book explores strategic avenues employed by incumbent financial managers to organize their innovation processes. The implementation of FinTech applications in traditional and non-traditional financial organizations can lead to the development of new business models that align with the changing needs and demands of the customers and end-consumers of the emerging and existing financial markets. It also opens areas for vigorous discussion for financial and wealth management organizations to identify compatible ecosystems and benefit from the skills, resources, systems, and capabilities associated with that ecosystem using the strategic approach outlined in this book's chapters. First, from a digital integration perspective, it defines a clear picture of how digital tools and technologies can be implemented to develop FinTech innovations using the OI process. Second, it suggests how digital tools can be used for managing interactions at different levels for different stakeholders of the FinTech ecosystem.

Different studies in this book all contribute, in their own way, to further enhance this knowledge on how to develop an openly innovative FinTech future. Some chapters extend the discussion, while some review the information while adding a new foundation for future growth. We want to thank all the authors for contributing their ideas and knowledge in this book, further supporting the notion that the area of FinTech OI and ecosystems is a rising field of research and practice with beneficial outcomes and that it needs more attention. Overall, this book provides intriguing postulations for FinTech as a crucial financial service management solution, yet acknowledges its opposition regarding regulations and practical applications. We hope that the book's insights are potential, pertinent, and possible approaches for better managing FinTech OI processes and that this collection of chapters opens avenues for future research and discussion for FinTech management.

References

Alaassar, A., Mention, A. L., & Aas, T. H. (2020). Exploring how social interactions influence regulators and innovators: The case of regulatory sandboxes. *Technological Forecasting and Social Change*, 160, 120257.

Alliance for Financial Inclusion (AFI). (2020). Creating Enabling FinTech Ecosystems: The Role of Regulators. Special Report. Available online at https://www.afi-global.org/sites/default/files/publications/2020-01/AFI_FinTech_SR_AW_digital_0.pdf (Accessed on 4 June 2021).

Boratyńska, K. (2019). Impact of digital transformation on value creation in fintech services: An innovative approach. *Journal of Promotion Management*, 25, 631–639.

Breidbach, C. F., Keating, B. W., & Lim, C. (2020). Fintech: Research directions to explore the digital transformation of financial service systems. *Journal of Service Theory and Practice*, 30(1), 79–102. https://doi.org/10.1108/JSTP-08-2018-0185.

Castro, P., Rodrigues, J. P., & Teixeira, J. G. (2020). Understanding FinTech Ecosystem Evolution through Service Innovation and Socio-technical System Perspective. In *International Conference on Exploring Services Science*, February, Springer, Cham, pp. 187–201.

Chen, P. C., & Hung, S. W. (2016). An actor-network perspective on evaluating the R&D linking efficiency of innovation ecosystems. *Technological Forecasting and Social Change*, 112, 303–312.

Chesbrough, H. W. (2003). *Open Innovation: The New Imperative for Creating and Profiting from Technology* (Harvard Business School Press, Boston Massachusetts).

Chesbrough, H. (2010). Business model innovation: Opportunities and barriers. *Long Range Planning*, 43(2–3), 354–363.

Coeckelbergh, M., DuPont, Q., & Reijers, W. (2018). Towards a philosophy of financial technologies. *Philosophy & Technology*, 31(1), 9–14.

Dapp, T., & Slomka, L. (2015). Fintech reloaded–Traditional banks as digital ecosystems. Deutsche Bank Research, pp. 261–274.

Diaz-Rainey, I., Ibikunle, G., & Mention, A. (2015). The technological transformation of capital markets. *Technological Forecasting and Social Change*, 99, 277–284.

Diemers, D., Lamaa, A., Salamat, J., & Steffens, T. (2015). Developing a FinTech ecosystem in the GCC: Let's get ready for take-off. Strategy&. Available online at https://www.strategyand.pwc.com/m1/en/reports/developing-a-fintech-ecosystem-in-the-gcc.pdf (Accessed on 4 June 2021).

Ernst & Young (2020). How digitalization impacts financial services companies and their audits. Retrieved from: https://www.ey.com/en_au/assurance/how-digital-transformation-impacts-financial-services-companies-and-their-audits (Accessed on 4 June 2021).

Eyers, J. (2018). "World Bank appoints CBA for first bond deal on blockchain." Australian Financial Review. Available online at https://www.afr.com/companies/financial-services/world-bank-appoints-cba-for-first-bond-deal-on-blockchain-20180809-h13qji (Accessed on 4 June 2021).

Fasnacht, D. (2009). *Open Innovation in the Financial Services: Growing Through Openness, Flexibility and Customer Integration* (Springer Science & Business Media).

Fasnacht, D. (2018). Open Innovation in the Financial Services. In *Open Innovation Ecosystems* (Springer, Cham), pp. 97–130. https://doi.org/10.1007/978-3-319-76394-1_4.

Goasduff, L. (2019). Top Trends on the Gartner Hype Cycle for Artificial Intelligence, 2019, September 12. Retrieved from Gardner: Smarter with Gardner. https://www.gartner.com/smarterwithgartner/top-trends-on-the-gartner-hype-cycle-for-artificial-intelligence-2019/ (Accessed on 4 June 2021).

Gomber, P., Kauffman, R. J., Parker, C., & Weber, B. W. (2018). On the fintech revolution: Interpreting the forces of innovation, disruption, and transformation in financial services. *Journal of Management Information Systems* 35(1), 220–265.

Holmes, C., & King, R. (2019). The evolution of business-to-business FinTech: What the future holds. *Journal of Payments Strategy & Systems*, 13(3), 217–225.

Imerman, M. B., & Fabozzi, F. J. (2020). A conceptual framework for FinTech innovation. Available at SSRN 3543810.

Jacobides, M. G., Cennamo, C., & Gawer, A. (2018). Towards a theory of ecosystems. *Strategic Management Journal*, 39(8), 2255–2276.

Karagiannaki, A., Vergados, G., & Fouskas, K. G. (2017). The impact of digital transformation in the financial services industry: Insights from an open innovation initiative in Fintech in Greece. In Mediterranean Conference on Information Systems (MCIS) Proceedings. Association For Information Systems. http://aisel.aisnet.org/mcis2017/2 (Accessed on 4 June 2021).

Latour, B. (2005). *Reassembling the social: An introduction to actor-network-theory* (Oxford University Press, New York).

Lee, I. & Shin, Y. J. (2018). FinTech: Ecosystem, business models, investment decisions, and challenges. *Business Horizons*, 61, 35–46.

Liermann, V., & Stegmann, C. (eds.) (2019). *The Impact of Digital Transformation and FinTech on the Finance Professional*. (Palgrave Macmillan, Cham, Switzerland).

Lynn, T., Mooney, J. G., Rosati, P., & Cummins, M. (2019). *Disrupting Finance: Fintech and Strategy in the 21st Century* (Springer Nature), p. 175.

Martovoy, A., Mention, A. L., & Torkkeli, M. (2015). Inbound open innovation in financial services. *Journal of Technology Management & Innovation*, 10(1), 117–131.

Mention, A. L. (2011). Innovation for financial services. *Innovation Management*. Retrieved from: https://innovationmanagement.se/2011/09/13/innovation-for-financial-services/ (Accessed on 4 June 2021).

Mention, A. L., Torkkeli, M., & Huizingh, E., (eds.) (2012). Special Issue: Innovation for Financial Services. *International Journal of Entrepreneurship and Innovation Management* 16(1/2).

Mention, A.-L. (2019). The future of FinTech. *Research-Technology Management*, 62, 59–63.

Mention, A.-L. (2020). The age of FinTech: Implications for research, policy and practice. *The Journal of FinTech*, 1(1) (online).

Mention, A. L., & Torkkeli, M. (2012). Drivers, processes and consequences of financial innovation: A research agenda. *International Journal of Entrepreneurship and Innovation Management*, 16(1–2), 5–29.

Mention, A. L., & Torkkeli, M. (eds.) (2014). *Innovation in Financial Services: A Dual Ambiguity* (Cambridge Scholars Publishing).

Mention, A. L., Martovoy, A., & Torkkeli, M. (2014). Open innovation in financial services: What are the external drivers? *International Journal of Business Excellence*, 7(4), 530–548.

Mina, A., Bascavusoglu-Moreau, E., & Hughes, A. (2014). Open service innovation and the firm's search for external knowledge. *Research Policy*, 43(5), 853–866.

Nicoletti, B. (2017). *Future of FinTech: Integrating Finance and Technology in Financial Services. Palgrave Studies in Financial Technology* (Palgrave Macmillan, Basingstoke, UK).

Nicoletti, B. (2019). Digital Transformation via Open Data in Insurance. Digital Innovation. In *Open Innovation: Bridging Theory and Practice Digital Innovation*, Mention, A.-L. (ed.) (World Scientific Publishing), pp. 113–149.

Nylén, D., & Holmström, J. (2015). Digital innovation strategy: A framework for diagnosing and improving digital product and service innovation. *Business Horizons*, 58(1), 57–67.

Pavel R. M. (2021). FinTech Strategy: Linking Entrepreneurship, Finance, and Technology. In *Palgrave Studies in Democracy, Innovation, and Entrepreneurship for Growth*. Carayannis, E. G. (ed). (Palgrave Macmillan, Cham, Switzerland).

Palmié, M., Wincent, J., Parida, V. & Caglar, U. (2020). The evolution of the financial technology ecosystem: An introduction and agenda for future research on disruptive innovations in ecosystems. *Technological Forecasting and Social Change*, 151, 119779.

Pollari I., & Teper D. (2019). Australian Fintech Landscape. KPMG. Retrieved from: https://home.kpmg/au/en/home/insights/2017/08/australian-fintech-landscape.html

Puschmann, T. (2017). Fintech. *Business & Information Systems Engineering*, 59, 69–76.

Riasanow, T., Flötgen, R. J., Setzke, D. S., Böhm, M., & Krcmar, H. (2018). The generic ecosystem and innovation patterns of the digital transformation in the financial industry. In *PACIS*, p. 77.

Riemer, K., Hafermalz, E., Roosen, A., Boussand, N., El Aoufi, H., Mo, D., & Kosheliev, A. (2017). *The Fintech Advantage: Harnessing Digital Technology, Keeping the Customer in Focus* (University of Sydney, Business School and Capgemini).

Ruddenklau A. (2020). Tech giants in financial services. KPMG. Retrieved from: https://home.kpmg/xx/en/home/insights/2018/02/tech-giants-in-financial-services-fs.html

Salampasis, D. (2014). Organizational readiness for open innovation in the financial services sector: The missing element of trust. In *Innovation in Financial Services: A Dual Ambiguity*, Mention, A.L. & Torkkeli, M. (eds.) (Cambridge Scholars Publishing, Newcastle), pp. 295–336.

Salampasis, D. and Mention, A. L. (2018). FinTech: Harnessing innovation for financial inclusion. In *Handbook of Blockchain, Digital Finance, and Inclusion*, Vol. 2 (Academic Press), pp. 451–461.

Salampasis, D. Mention, A-L., and Kaiser A. (2019). Age of discovery: navigating the balance between human and machine. In *WealthTech: Wealth and Asset Management in the FinTech Age*, Schueffel, P. (ed.) (Information Age Publishing, Charlotte, NC), pp. 167–174.

Salampasis, D., Mention, A. L., & Torkkeli, M. (2014). Open innovation and collaboration in the financial services sector: Exploring the role of trust. *International Journal of Business Innovation and Research*, 8(5), 466–484.

Salampasis, D. G., Mention, A. L., & Torkkeli, M. (2015). Trust embeddedness within an open innovation mindset. *International Journal of Business and Globalisation*, 14(1), 32–57.

Salampasis, D., Pickering, M., and Klausser, V. (2020). Blockchain-enabled entrepreneurial financial funding and investments: The new era of ICOs. In *Blockchain for Data Analytics*, Ahmed, M. (ed.) (Cambridge Scholars Publishing), pp. 145–184.

Schueffel, P. (2016). Taming the beast: A scientific definition of FinTech. *Journal of Innovation Management*, 4(4), 32–54.

Spigel, B. (2019). Joining Fin and Tech: Examining the Cohesiveness and Nestedness of Fintech Entrepreneurial Ecosystems. Available at SSRN: https://ssrn.com/abstract=3511120 or http://dx.doi.org/10.2139/ssrn.3511120

Still, K., Huhtala, T., & Saraniemi, S. (2016). FinTech as business and innovation ecosystems. Paper was presented at the ISPIM Innovation Summit, Kuala Lumpur, Malaysia on 4–7 December 2016.

Svensson, C., Udesen, J. & Webb, J. (2019). Alliances in financial ecosystems: A source of organizational legitimacy for FinTech startups and incumbents. *Technology Innovation Management Review*, 9, 20–32.

Varga, D. (2017). FinTech, the new era of financial services. *Vezetéstudom ny-Budapest Management Review*, 48(11), 22–32.

Vermeulen, P. (2004). Managing product innovation in financial services firms. *European Management Journal*, 22(1), 43–50.

Wright G. (2019). The best financial service brands' digital strategies include these 4 things. Mo Agency. Retrieved from: https://www.mo.agency/blog/best-financial-services-digital-strategies

Chapter 2

A Scoping Review Toward Framing a Research Agenda

Hamid Nach,[*,‡] *Dimitrios Salampasis*[*,†,§] *and*
Rachid Ghilal[*,¶]

[*]*University of Quebec at Rimouski, 1595, boul. Alphonse-Desjardins,*
Lévis (Qc), Canada
[†]*School of Business, Law and Entrepreneurship, Swinburne University*
of Technology, Hawthorn VIC 3122, Australia
[‡]*hamid_nach@uqar.ca*
[§]*dsalampasis@swin.edu.au; Dimitrios_Salampasis@uqar.ca*
[¶]*Rachid_Ghilal@uqar.ca*

Abstract. FinTech, the rapidly evolving new breed of technology-driven financial offerings, generates a renewed momentum by bringing together disconnected trends challenging incumbent financial services firms. In response to the increasing FinTech-enabled forces of technology innovation, process disruption, and services transformation, along with the fact that FinTech is gradually becoming an area of academic research, this chapter contributes to the innovation and technology management literature by (1) providing a mapping of current FinTech research and (2) suggesting a FinTech research agenda. A scoping review across six major databases has been conducted, leading to an $N = 92$ sample chosen and analyzed based on pre-determined selection criteria and according to the developed theoretical framework. The review illuminates observations with regards to the scope, conceptualization, topical themes, and research approaches revolving around extant FinTech scholarship, while providing novel and comprehensive knowledge on the underlying technology aspects, FinTech-enabled business models, and value-creation outcomes.

Keywords. FinTech, information technology; financial services; digitalization; scoping review.

1. Introduction

The last few years have been marked by a rapid development and a high-level sophistication of information technology (IT). The trend had contributed to the emergence of a new type of companies that are bringing breakthrough processes, services, and products to market. In the financial sector, particularly, new players, termed FinTechs — short of Financial Technology — are applying technology to create innovative banking services that are in tune with the digital age. FinTech is an umbrella term that refers generally to the use of technology to deliver innovative financial solutions (Arner *et al.*, 2016). A growing number of start-ups are spearheading projects that aim to lower costs and entry barriers to finance services such as payment, loans, money transfers, and investments.

The financial services industry has always been at the forefront of seizing IT innovations (Kutler, 2013). The industry has been experiencing rapid and profound changes driven by pervasive data-oriented and smart technologies, including cloud and mobile computing, artificial intelligence (AI), blockchain, Application Programming Interfaces (APIs), and big data. These game-changing technologies enable the emergence of new business models that are, in many instances, disruptive and transformative, fundamentally changing the financial services landscape (Puschmann, 2017). FinTechs are bringing breakthrough processes, services, and products to market. They are applying technology to create innovative banking services that are in tune with the digital age.

FinTech-driven business models are customer-centric and, in many instances, disruptive. Innovating both in digital technologies and financial services is increasingly conferring FinTech companies a key place in the financial ecosystem (Chishti and Barberis, 2016). Their growth, however, can also be considered as a threat to the traditional financial services business models. Indeed, it is estimated that, by 2020, the traditional financial services industry is likely to lose more than 20% of their business due to financial technology (PwC, 2016). In the meantime, investment in FinTech is soaring — rising from US$1.8 billion in 2010 to US$19 billion in 2015 (Hutt, 2016). The drive for FinTech continues as worldwide funding hit US$15 billion by mid-August 2016 (Bakker, 2015). This surge connotes a high interest in this particular wave of digitalization. It also provides a fertile ground for practitioners and researchers as there are so many, yet-to-be answered questions on FinTech systems and their impact on individuals, organizations, and society.

In 2018, global investment in FinTech companies reached US$111.8 billion across 2,196 deals (KPMG, 2018). Moreover, 88% of incumbents are increasingly concerned over revenue loss against innovators (PwC, 2017). FinTechs have a distinct competitive advantage in terms of customer-centricity, agility, flexibility, transparency, inclusion, and efficiency compared to incumbents (Lee, 2015; Nicoletti, 2017). These emerging financial and non-financial players leverage technological breakthroughs toward developing technologically diversified products, services, and processes, redefining the current financial services norms and narratives.

Undoubtedly, there is a great amount of research conducted in the field of financial services and banking sector, however, very few studies have focused on the particular case of FinTechs (Zavolokina *et al.*, 2016). FinTech's focused scientific research in the field of information systems, particularly, is scarce. Only a handful of papers in the literature discuss the phenomenon from the Information Systems (IS) perspective. For example, Foster and Heek (2013) examined how a Kenyan mobile money system M Pesa reached millions of poor consumers. Burtch *et al.* (2013) studied the link between crowdfunding and social influence, and later, they examined the role of cultural differences in online peer-to-peer lending (Burtch *et al.*, 2014). Yet, FinTechs are on the rise and rigorous scientific studies are needed to develop an understanding of the phenomenon. The technology has already induced a digital transformation and will, in a near future, have a strong impact on the financial services which is likely to lead to a fundamental reorganization of the whole industry (Puschmann, 2017).

Research scholarship has only paid scant attention to this FinTech phenomenon, with a number of studies providing an overview of the current state of FinTech research employing various research methods, including bibliometric citation meta-analysis (Wu, 2017), systematic literature review (Gomber *et al.*, 2017), and analysis of media and press outlets (Vergne and Swain, 2017; Zavolokina *et al.*, 2016a). Notwithstanding the contributions of these studies, our knowledge on how FinTech is addressed in the scientific literature is, so far, limited.

Research on the FinTech phenomenon is still in its infancy, and the opportunities are very open today (Zavolokina *et al.*, 2016b). This research contributes by suggesting a research agenda to IS scholars to delve into this under-researched area. We call on IS theorists to bring FinTechs, as systems, into the mainstream of the IS discipline. More particularly, we urge them to develop a sharper eye for the diverse and fine-tuned ways in which FinTechs may impact the financial ecosystem. This agenda, however, is not intended to be seen as offering a complete account of what is to be pursued as there may be other opportunities in addressing the issue. Rather, it exposes some promising research domains that appear to have been neglected in IS research so far, and that would seem to deserve greater attention. The remainder of this chapter is structured as follows: Section 2 outlines the research method used to review the literature and the steps taken to ensure rigor and systematicity. Section 3 presents the main findings. In Section 4, the authors discuss the main finding, while Section 5 presents promising avenues for further research.

2. Research Method

This research adopts the Arksey and O'Malley's (2005) and Levac *et al.*'s (2010) scoping review guidelines. As suggested by Paré *et al.* (2016), the method maximizes both systematization and transparency, ensuring a high level of rigor, reliability, and trustworthiness.

Scoping reviews are highly systematic in nature, yet they are different from traditional systematic reviews (Li *et al.*, 2018). Systematic reviews attempt to integrate prior empirical findings on a mature topic in order to provide answers to questions like "what works" and "what works best." Scoping reviews seek to (1) provide an initial indication of the size and nature of available literature on an emerging topic, (2) identify gaps, and (3) propose a future research agenda (Paré *et al.*, 2015). Therefore, "the focus in scoping reviews is more on-what has been done-than on-what has been found. The main idea is to map the territory, which is why scoping reviews are also called mapping reviews" (Li *et al.*, 2018, p. 4475).

2.1. *Developing a review protocol*

As suggested by Levac *et al.* (2010), a formal and detailed review protocol was developed and followed throughout the entire review process: (1) identifying the research question; (2) identifying relevant studies; (3) studying selection; (4) charting the data; and (5) collating, summarizing, and reporting results. The broad questions included in the protocol are:

(1) Which issues and questions have been investigated by extant FinTech literature?
(2) What are the main gaps?
(3) Which are the promising research avenues?

2.2. *Identifying relevant studies*

This stage involves identifying the relevant studies and developing a decision plan for where to search, which terms to use, which sources are to be searched, and setting the time span and language (Levac *et al.*, 2010). As FinTech research spans across several disciplines, including finance, management, IT, engineering, law, data, and computer science, the authors decided to adopt a broad approach. Six databases were searched: ABI/INFORM Collection (ProQuest), Business Source Premier (EBSCO), Emerald Fulltext, Scopus, and

Web of Science (WoS). Since these databases include a rich yet complementary collection of publishers and journals, the in-depth search allowed for a comprehensive coverage and minimized the risk of selection bias. The authors searched the databases using the two following descriptors: "FinTech" or "FinTechs." The terms could appear anywhere in the paper, including the title, the abstract, the keywords, or the full text. Every database was independently searched using the same keywords and search criteria. The authors did not specify any timeframe during but limited the search into the peer-reviewed papers (excluding editorials, forwards, magazines, book titles and reviews, commentaries, news, and reports). The search was conducted on December 18, 2018, yielding a total of 893 papers ($N_{ABI/INFORM} = 398$; $N_{EBSCO} = 55$; $N_{EMERALD} = 28$; $N_{SCOPUS} = 261$; $N_{WoS} = 151$). A total of $N_{DPL} = 220$ duplicates was found, bringing to $N_{ISR} = 673$ papers (Figure 1).

2.3. *Study selection*

Study selection involves post-hoc inclusion and exclusion criteria. To ensure that we consistently screened and selected the relevant papers for our study, 25 out of the 673 papers were randomly chosen for training purposes. The authors held multiple meetings and developed and applied the inclusion and exclusion criteria in order to have a shared understanding. The authors decided to focus on the business technology literature. Papers solely exploring technical or regulatory aspects of FinTech were excluded. All $N_2 = 673$ were independently screened by the authors who excluded non-English ($n = 59$), Law and Regulation ($n = 50$), and Software Engineering ($n = 15$) publications (Figure 1). Further, 15 paper titles were excluded (Abstracts $n = 3$, Research proposals $n = 5$, and not available Conference Proceedings $n = 5$).

At this stage, the sample consisted of $N_3 = 534$ papers, which afterwards was screened by the authors based on the title, the abstract, and when necessary, the full article. On completion of this step, $N = 442$ papers were excluded (no FinTech focus and/or relevance). The authors perceive FinTech as a process of transformation, which lies on the intersection of financial and digital innovations that create or

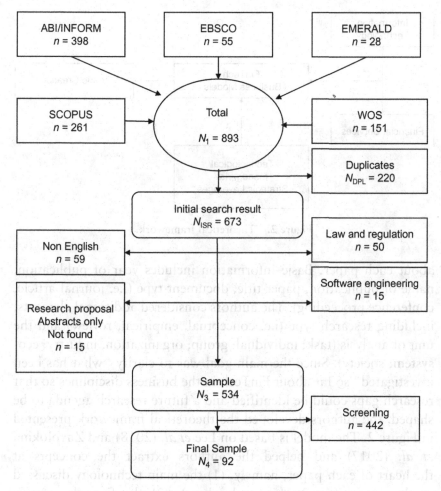

Figure 1. Initial search result.

challenge existing business models, which ultimately allows to offer innovative financial products or services (Zavolokina *et al.*, 2017). The final sample consisted of $N_4 = 92$ papers.

2.4. Charting the data

During this step, a coding sheet was created for extracting data from the 92 papers. The coding form contains basic and core information

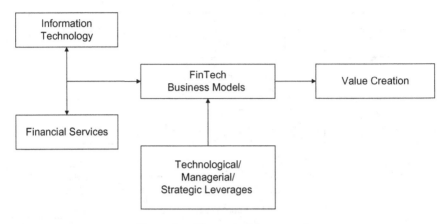

Figure 2.   Theoretical framework.

about each paper. Basic information includes year of publication, name of publication, paper title, document type (i.e. journal article, conference proceeding). The authors considered additional elements, including research type (i.e. conceptual, empirical, review) and the unit of analysis (task; individual; group; organization, industry; ecosystem; society). Since the main goal was to clarify "what has been investigated" so far about FinTech in the business disciplines so that research gaps could be identified and a future research agenda to be shaped, the authors developed the theoretical framework presented in Figure 2. The model is based on Lee *et al.* (2018) and Zavolokina *et al.* (2017) and helped the authors extract the concepts at the heart of each paper, namely, (1) the main technology discussed in the paper, (e.g. mobile technology); (2) the financial service (e.g. payment); (3) the business model (e.g. mobile payment); (4) technological, managerial, and strategic leverages (e.g. strategic alliance); and (5) the value creation (e.g. financial inclusion). The model allowed us to make sense of the data and to provide an overview of the breadth of the literature (not a synthesis).

The authors randomly selected 10 papers and sat together to extract data based on the value. The goal was to develop a shared understanding of the coding framework and coding process. The authors found that the empirical and conceptual papers fitted well with the framework despite the fact that some papers used a generic term for technology while others were more specific (e.g. mobile technologies). Unsurprisingly, the review papers did not fit with models because their main objective is to make sense of existing literature, as explained later. So, the authors independently screened the papers for which they were responsible. The papers from which information was not easily extracted were discussed and verified. When necessary, the papers for which no consensus was reached were screened by another researcher. This cross-checking process maximized the validity of the screening process. Similar to most scoping reviews (Li *et al.*, 2018; Ngai and Wat, 2002), a numerical and descriptive analysis of the extent and nature of studies using tables and charts was computed in order to elucidate the nature and scope of the extant literature, which will be presented in the following section.

3. Results

3.1. *Publication year and type*

All included papers were published after 2016, a sign that interest in FinTech research is quite recent. A total of 16 papers (17.4%) were published in 2016; 22 in 2017 (23.9%), which is a 37.5% increase; and 54 (58.7%) in 2018, which is a 145% increase from 2017 to 2018. The exponential growth of publications reflects the intensity of interest in FinTech over the last three years (Figure 3). In terms of

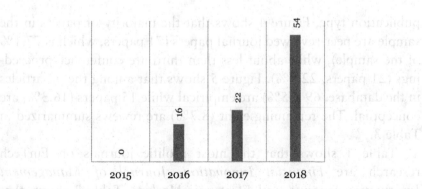

Figure 3.   Number of publications per year.

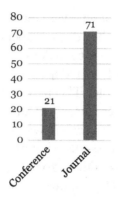

Figure 4.   Type of publication.

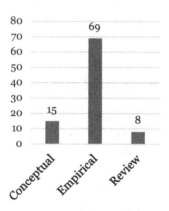

Figure 5.   Nature of studies.

publication type, Figure 4 shows that the majority of papers in the sample are peer-reviewed journal papers (71 papers, which is 77.1% of the sample), while about less than third are conference proceedings (21 papers, 22.9%). Figure 5 shows that among the 92 articles in the database, 69 (75%) are empirical while 15 papers (16.3%) are conceptual. The remaining eight (8.7%) are reviews summarized in Table 3.

Table 1 shows that the most prolific journals on FinTech research are *Financial Innovation*, *Journal of Management Information Systems*, and *Electronic Markets*. Table 2 shows that

Table 1. Publications by journal (more than 3).

Journals	# of pub.	Papers
Financial Innovation	4	Chen *et al.* (2017); Jui-Long and Luo (2016); Li *et al.* (2017); Zavolokina *et al.* (2016c)
Journal of Management Information Systems	3	Gomber *et al.* (2018); Gozman *et al.* (2018); Jiang *et al.* (2018)
Electronic Markets	3	Gimpel *et al.* (2018); Jung *et al.* (2018b); Stoeckli *et al.* (2018)

Table 2. Publications by conference (more than 2).

Conferences	# of pub.	Papers
International Conference on Information Systems (ICIS)	4	Eickhoff *et al.* (2018); Muthukannan *et al.* (2018); Ng *et al.* (2018); Zavolokina *et al.* (2016b)
ACM International Conference Proceeding Series	3	Fermay *et al.* (2018); Hsueh and Kuo (2017); Mathur *et al.* (2018)
Americas Conference on Information Systems (AMCIS)	2	Kuhlmann *et al.* (2018); Wang and Chang (2018)

out of the 21 conferences papers, 9 come from three conferences, namely, the *International Conference on Information Systems* (ICIS), the *ACM International Conference Proceeding Series* (ICPS),[1] and the *Americas Conference on Information Systems* (AMCIS).

3.2. *Level of analysis and focus of inquiry*

As shown in Figure 6, the level of analysis of the papers is distributed unevenly. Indeed, 23.8% papers (excluding the review papers which were flagged as N/A) in the sample focus on the industry

---

[1]International Conference Proceeding Series (ICPS) publishes conference proceedings that are mainly sponsored by Association for Computing Machinery (ACM) Special Interest Groups (SIGs).

Table 3.   The review papers.

Authors	Description
Schueffel (2016)	The author used a comprehensive literature review to provide a definition of the term FinTech
Zavolokina *et al.* (2016b)	The authors reviewed how the press and other popular media understand and frame FinTech, discussing definitions that represents its meaning
Zavolokina *et al.* (2016c)	The authors used English and German popular press to study the factors that influence the perception of FinTech through the lens of the media
Gomber *et al.* (2017)	This article reviewed the state of research in Digital Finance and FinTech and gave an outlook on potential future research directions
Wu (2017)	The author conducted a bibliometric citation to review scholarly research on FinTech trends
Cai (2018)	The author conducted a systematic review of influential publications among 402 papers published between 2010 and 2018 regarding two applications of FinTech: crowdfunding and blockchain
Martínez-Climent *et al.* (2018)	By looking into the documents published in the Thomson Reuters WoS on the field of financial return crowdfunding, this research studied crowdfunding as a financial instrument, specifically crowdfunding that generates a financial return, i.e. peer-to-peer lending (P2P) and equity crowdfunding (EC)
Eling and Lehmann (2018)	Based on a dataset of 84 papers and industry studies, the authors analyzed the impact of digital transformation on the insurance sector using Porter's Value Chain and Berliner's Insurability Criteria

level, followed by the ecosystem (16.7%), the task (15.5%); the organization and the group (14.3% each), the individual (11.9%), and society (3.6%). It should be noted that few papers had more than one level of analysis (e.g. Gomber *et al.*, 2018; Shim and Shin, 2016). It is important to mention that we decided not to consider "multi-level" as a coding variable, opting for the most salient level of analysis.

As previously explained, the papers in the sample were coded according to the theoretical framework presented in Figure 2. With regards to the first element IT, 25 papers used "Information Technology" as a generic term with no reference to a particular

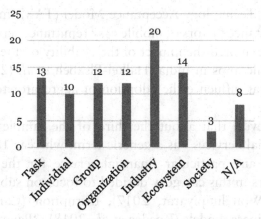

Figure 6. Levels of analysis.

Table 4. Most discussed technologies.

Information Technology	25
Non specified	17
Mobile Technology	16
P2P Platforms	15
Blockchain Technology	5
Robo-adviser	4
Artificial Intelligence	4
Frugal Technologies	2
Web Technologies	2
Internet of Objects	1
Aggregators	1

technology, and 17 papers made little or no reference to technology. This cohort of papers has mainly dealt with FinTech-related business issues (e.g. Teja, 2017; Varga, 2018). The technologies that attracted the most research interest are "mobile technologies" and "P2P platforms," well ahead of other technologies such as "Blockchain" (e.g. Larios-Hernandez, 2017; Raikwar *et al.*, 2018), "Artificial Intelligence" (e.g. Day *et al.*, 2018; Riikkinen *et al.*, 2018), and "Internet of Objects" (Marafie *et al.*, 2018) (Table 4). Examples of authors who considered mobile technologies are Jeong *et al.* (2018),

who used the Technology Acceptance Model (TAM) model to analyze the acceptance factors of mobile easy remittance service. Mathur
et al. (2018) explored the impact of the usability on the adoption of
FinTech mobile apps in India. Haikel-Elsabeh *et al.* (2016) discuss
the factors that influence the adoption of aggregator tools for personal finance.

Results reveal that about the third of the sample (29 papers)
used "Financial Services" as a generic term, whereas 18 papers did
not consider any particular financial service for the purpose of
study. Authors in this category decided to focus on subjects such as
innovation (Wonglimpiyarat, 2017), disruption (Cai, 2018), or
emerging business models (Roeder *et al.*, 2018). "Payment" ranked
high on the list of the most discussed financial services in FinTech
research, followed by "Lending," "Investment," and "Funding"
(Table 5).

An interesting observation in Table 6 is that, out of the 55 papers
that discuss issues related to business models, 14 papers addressed
"Mobile Banking," which has captured most researchers' attention,
followed by "Crowdlending" with 9 papers (e.g. Hsueh and Kuo,
2017; Lee, 2017; Stern *et al.*, 2017), "Robo-Advising" within a total

Table 5.   Most discussed financial services.

Financial services	29
Non specified	18
Payment	12
Lending	9
Investment	7
Funding	6
Insurance	4
Personal finance	2
Wealth management	2
Microloan	1
Donation	1
Remittance	1

Table 6. Most discussed FinTech-enabled business models.

Non specified	37
Mobile banking	14
Crowdlending	9
Robo-advising	7
Crowdfunding	6
e-payment	5
Smart contract	4
Digital investment	2
Internet-only bank	2
InsurTech	2
e-loan provider	1
Fincare	1
Information aggregation	1
Insurance chatbot	1

of 7 papers (e.g. Jung *et al.*, 2018a; Phoon and Koh, 2018), and "Crowdfunding" in 6 papers (e.g. Jiang *et al.*, 2018; Wonglimpiyarat, 2018). As Table 7 reveals, most of "value creation" addressed so far by FinTech research is "Investment efficiency" (18.5%), "FinTech adoption and use" (16%), "Financial inclusion" (12%), and "FinTech innovation" (10.9%).

Figure 7 supports the visualization of the different aspects of flows, the complexity of the data, and the level of detail projected by the scoping review and the analysis. It provides a visual understanding of the theoretical framework and helps out the mapping of the different components required to provide meaningful research outcomes, insights, and suggestions on the hybrid approaches between technology and financial services and the value-creation outcomes across the different sub-sectors of the financial services sector. The cohort of technological, managerial, and strategic leveragers accentuate the multifaceted nature of financial technologies innovation and the impact they have both individually and collectively within

Table 7.   Most discussed FinTech value creation outcomes.

Investment efficiency	17
FinTech adoption and use	15
Financial inclusion	11
FinTech innovation	10
Bank digitization	5
FinTech development	3
Automation	2
Competitive advantage	2
FinTech integration	2
Fundraising efficiency	2
Customer experience	1
FinTech design	1
FinTech growth	1
Firm valuation	1

the different industrial sectors of financial activity. The dearth of these leveragers spans across the individual, team, organizational, institutional, industry, and ecosystem landscape, providing numerous value-creation mechanisms that can further be mobilized redefining the nature of the relationship between technological advancements and financial services principles.

4. Discussion

The outcomes of the above-mentioned scoping review provide a number of very interesting observations worth noting that contribute to the current understanding of FinTech within the extant research scholarship, along with helping toward shaping a future FinTech-related research agenda.

FinTech is gradually becoming an area of academic scholarship. In this context, the majority of extant literature has been focusing

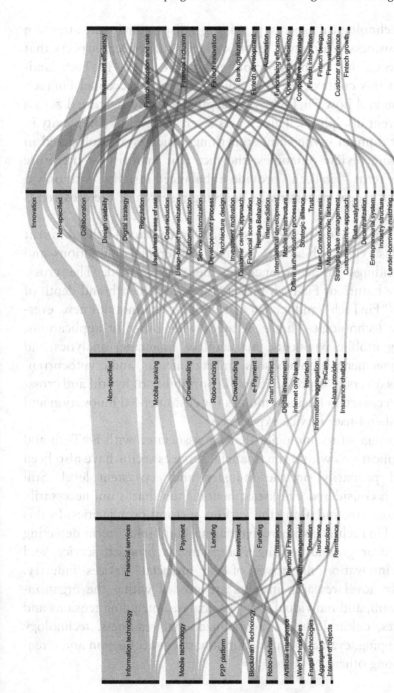

Figure 7.   Sankey diagram of FinTech research focus.

on the technological aspects, providing a disproportionate attention to the business, economic, legal, societal, and ethical aspects that are projected in the multidisciplinary nature of the FinTech landscape. In this context, there is still not a widely accepted FinTech definition and how FinTech is conceptualized and perceived across the different disciplines. This creates a certain level of complexity in terms of domain ownership, something which is also observed in the scoping review outcomes; the fact that majority of literature using the term "FinTech" provide unbalanced insights, with only a handful of recent papers really enabling research at the crossroads of FinTech.

The FinTech *neologism* is strongly spread across the different financial services sub-sectors receiving different connotations and understandings in accordance to the related field. The cross-discipline nature of FinTech reflects the sheer breadth and depth of the term "FinTech" and its association with a number of new, ever-changing technologies that generate a wide range of applications, including mobile payments, marketplace financing, analytics and risk management, robo-advisors, smart contracts, and cryptocurrencies. This diversity is projected in the portability of hybrid and cross-industry/ecosystem business models for customer-led innovation and improved end-user service experience.

The range of technologies that are associated with FinTech and their applications within the financial services sector have also been analyzed primarily on the industry and ecosystem level. Still FinTech is considered a holistic phenomenon that is not necessarily clustered across and along the various sectoral peculiarities. In this context, FinTech is also perceived as an "umbrella" term depicting disruptive or groundbreaking change in the product, service, and process innovation narratives of the financial services industry. Definitely novel research insights are needed within the organizational, team, and individual levels of analysis, including tensions and paradoxes, cultural shift and organizational readiness, technology road mapping, evaluation and adoption, talent acquisition and retention, among others.

Another very interesting aspect is related to the emergence of numerous technology-enabled financial services business models, which are highly associated to the respective sectors. The related technological developments create cross-sectorial applications leading to the development of innovations within incumbent business models aimed at generating value (additionality, creation, multiplication). This means that the same technology can be applied across different financial services sub-sectors leading to associated, similar, or completely different FinTech innovations.

We present FinTechs using Alter Steven's work system framework (Alter, 2013), which is based on a genuine system perspective that focuses on IT-reliant systems in organizations as opposed to the prevailing system-as-technical-artifact perspective; therefore, treating human participants and business processes as part of the systems, not just as users of technology and as the context in which technology is used. According to Alter (2013), a work system is a dynamic system in which human participants perform work (processes and activities) using information technologies, and other resources to produce specific products and services for specific customers. A work system is a combination of nine interacting elements: (1) participants who are people who perform work and interact with the system, including both users and non-users of Information Technology; (2) Technologies that refer to all the hardware and software resources on which the operation of a business is based; (3) Information which, in the context of work system, is expressed as informational entities that are processed; (4) Processes and activities occur in a work system to produce (5) products and services for designated (6) customers; These six components are supported by three elements, namely, (7) the environment, which includes the relevant organizational, competitive, and regulatory environment within which the work system operates, and that affects the work system's effectiveness and efficiency; (8) the infrastructure that includes the human and technical infrastructure, all of which can be essential to a work system's operation; and finally (9) the strategies which comprises, particularly, the enterprise strategy within which the work system exists.

4.1. *Participants*

Various players are turning to FinTechs to drive forward the reinvention of banking and finance. Among these players, there are entrepreneurs, investors, computer scientists, academia, regulators, and policy-makers. Investors, from angels to specialist venture capitalists, are pumping in a good deal of money in FinTechs. Policymakers and regulators are catching up, albeit slowly, with the realities of the Fintech's fast-emerging new landscape by providing the necessary regulation to foster the development of the FinTech companies and prevent the movement of money by criminals and fraudsters (Pollari, 2016). The academic community and universities are increasingly offering curricula to focus on digital technologies and finance and they are contributing to creating channels for FinTech innovations (Cockerton, 2016).

4.2. *Technologies*

Typically, banks use centralized legacy technologies and rely heavily on interconnected systems which makes their adaptation to the new digital landscape a challenging endeavor (Gonzalez, 2016). FinTechs, on the other hand, are not bound to any legacy system; they are tech-driven and explore every opportunity provided by new technologies (Chishti and Barberis, 2016). FinTechs' early offers were relatively simple, such as online payment and money transfer, with little impact on established banks' operations. But today, FinTechs use a new generation of digital technologies such as blockchain, cryptocurrencies, and mobile-based technologies and applications to design breakthrough products and services which may alter banking as we know it.

In particular, blockchain, also known as Distributed Ledger Technology (DLT), is a decentralized and distributed digital ledger of transactions that is cryptographically enabled and tamper-proof. It is the underlying technology enabling cryptocurrencies such as bitcoin (Fowler and Fytatzi, 2016a). Blockchain is peer-to-peer based technology. It can be public or private, as blockchain networks are being developed by companies and consortiums for private use. Blockchain is immutable, transparent, and trustworthy (Underwood, 2016). Indeed, blockchain technology creates trust by enabling people to perform a transaction without having to go through a neutral central authority to ensure its integrity (Schwab, 2016). Because it enables trust without the need for an outside third party, blockchain increases the risk of disintermediation of banks as the value it creates is taken away from banking institutions and put in the hands of end consumers (Arsov, 2016).

Furthermore, the proliferation of mobile technologies and the Internet of Things (IoT) provides emerging FinTechs with an unprecedented ability to reach to even a larger clientele and the possibility to scale up at a lower cost (Fowler and Fytatzi, 2016b). The IoT is best described by a network linking heterogeneous devices (e.g. products, objects, etc.). Smaller, cheaper, and smarter sensors are being installed in homes, clothes, cars, watches, and other accessories (Schwab, 2016). Today the number of things connected to the Internet is growing at a rapid pace. In this respect, they are having a transformative impact in the financial sector as more devices are joining the realm of payment and insurance services. By way of illustration, usage data originated from cars, smart thermostats, and other devices can be leveraged by insurance companies to offer tailored products and services to their customers.

Another highly regarded technology in the FinTech scene is the robot-adviser. Robot-advisers are fully automated machines which make investment decisions without any human interaction and may fully replace professionals providing advisers to benefit investors (Sironi, 2016, p. 21). These technologies are still in their infancy but are game changers of personal finance. "Robo-advisory" algorithms and their corresponding apps provide advisory services and portfolio tools at a fraction of traditional banks' transaction cost, thereby threatening a segment of the current financial industry (Schwab, 2016).

What's more, modern finance is becoming an industry where the main players are no longer entirely human (Lin, 2014). The use of artificial intelligence and machine learning has dramatically accelerated and it provides high-end processing capabilities to assess risk, for example, to manage investments or analyze trading opportunities (Lin, 2014). Chatbots, particularly, are one of the opportunities offered by AI. Chatbots are becoming the bridge between consumers and businesses. They appears to be a good answer for financial institutions to manage millions of one-to-one conversations with their customers (Horton, 2017).

4.3. *Product and services*

Traditionally, people use financial services to exchange money, to save, to invest, to finance, or to insure against risk (Kashyap and Weber, 2016). The technologies described above provide FinTechs with the ability to reshape how these needs are addressed by delivering innovative financial products and services that are secure, frictionless, and inexpensive, anytime, anywhere.

Payment through the Internet and mobile technologies has been around for quite some time (e.g. PayPal). The widespread adoption of tap-to-pay enabled devices and the rise of smartphone-compatible, small, and low-fee card-reader devices (e.g. Square), have enabled people to make digital payments. But the rise of blockchain-based wallets is spurring a new wave of payment methods between individuals and even between companies. The technological advance of cryptocurrencies lays in their ability to process transactions over a distributed network without a central node functioning as a bank or clearinghouse (Luther, 2016). Processing transactions using the blockchain is also considered less costly than the traditional approach of payment.

Peer-to-Peer (P2P) Lending is another fast growing segment of the FinTech's spectrum. It is likely that it will continue to take market share from banks as millennials embrace convenient alternatives to bank financing. *P2P Lending* refers to loan origination between private individuals or companies on online platforms (Davis and Murphy, 2016). For borrowers, online P2P lending is a way to receive an inexpensive and greater conditions loan comparatively to traditional financial institutions. For lenders, *P2P*

Lending is as an investment tool where the risk is mitigated by the credit rating of borrowers (Bachmann *et al.*, 2011). In terms of *credit scoring*, FinTech companies have many advantages over traditional competitors as they gather real-time data about their customers.

FinTechs are also in position to take *risk management* by storm. A wide range of solutions based on algorithms and behavioral analysis are offered to detect the risk of fraud (Fowler and Fytatzi, 2016a). FinTechs are harnessing the power of digital technologies to redefine how *asset and wealth management* are undertaken too. In this regard, the wealth manager's role is at risk of being replaced by technology whose promise is to ensure stronger investment performance. Besides, the proliferation of mobile and the IoT allows the creation of tailored insurance products based on highly personalized data. *Insurtech*, which best describes this category of products and services, affects virtually every aspect of the finance industry. A growing number of FinTech and incumbent financial institutions are offering, for example, auto insurance where the pricing is partially based on driving behavior as monitored by a device or a mobile application.

4.4. *Processes and activities*

Fintech leverage new technologies to perform tasks which otherwise would have been impractical with traditional methods (Medeiros and Chau, 2016). New advancements in technology empower FinTech firms to deliver frictionless experiences by automating many processes. In this regard, automation is a key process for the FinTech operations and it fuels, in this way, the disintermediation of many work layers in traditional banking models. For example, the credit decision process can be automated and executed within minutes, instead of days when the process is based on paperwork (Horton, 2017). Automation is also considered to give clients self-service capabilities for routine requests (e.g. account opening, document management, etc.) (Welsh, 2017).

FinTechs also rely on sophisticated data analytics (e.g. behavioral and predictive algorithms) to make informed decisions, tailor products and services, or unlock insights (Sironi, 2016). Some are also applying ingredients of games to real-world financial situations, such as saving, investing, and retiring. Gamification sits at the crossroads of digital technology, behavioral finance, and motivation theory. For FinTechs, it provide customers with engaging user experiences to improve their investment behavior, create stickiness, and enhance profitability (Sironi, 2016).

4.5. *Information*

FinTech firms rely on data-powered business models. They have the ability to tap into multiple sources of data (from personal to behavioral data). The availability of vast amounts of data (big data) and affordable technology allows the companies to create novel opportunities and drive more impactful results for clients (Schwab, 2016). Data is captured in various forms (e.g. social media, remote devices, customers' accounts, data from APIs, imagery, sensors, wearables, connected homes, etc.) and allow to obtain a granular view of customers preferences and usage.

4.6. *Customers*

We concur with Pollari (2016) as he argues that changing consumer behavior and preferences are playing a key role in the development of FinTechs. Customers are embracing new technologies, seeking information from alternative sources, and demanding greater levels of personalization and immediacy. Consumers, particularly millennials, have also become empowered with instant access to information and the ability to manage their financial information on their mobile devices.

In addition to the "young," the "wealthy," and the "connected" customer, FinTechs are also targeting the "unbanked" people who were long considered by traditional banking institutions as "nonprofitable." Many incumbent banks believe the low-income people were too low marginal to be an attractive customer group (King, 2012). FinTechs are addressing these "long tail customers," who are not serviced or reached by traditional banks. This was the case in

Kenya where the four Big Banks shared a 3.5-million customer pool, while M-Pesa, the mobile payment solution, reached 17 million customers in less than 6 years (King, 2012).

4.7. *Environment*

Finance is a highly regulated industry, but to strive, FinTechs have to cope with the highly demanding regulatory framework (Apfelbacher, 2016). On the other hand, regulators are being challenged to an unprecedented degree. For example, because there is no central issuer for cryptocurrencies, some FinTech startups are likely to grow outside of established regulatory structures unless regulation addresses such issues. Thus, regulators have to cope with the speed of technological change and understand its impact on the industry. Amid these challenges, regulators and policymakers will need to support technological development and remove barriers to market developments while preserving the interest of the consumers and the public at large (Schwab, 2016).

4.8. *Infrastructure*

FinTechs are propelled by the convergence of multiple advances in technology. Leong *et al.* (2017) argue that these emerging companies are taking advantage of the availability and affordability of IT infrastructure (e.g. Internet, mobile, social media), the maturity of computing platforms (e.g. big data, cloud-computing), and business operations (on-demand services economy). The opening up and reuse of Application Program Interface (APIs) has also granted FinTech with a fertile ground to speed up innovation and development. P2P (peer-to-peer) platforms are now dismantling barriers to entry and lowering costs.

4.9. *Strategies*

Innovation is in the heart of most FinTech's strategies. But to ensure their growth, FinTechs rely on other strategies such as developing partnerships, networks, and collaboration with various stakeholders. An increasingly frequent type of collaboration is between FinTechs and banks who can work together to build combined offers (Mariotto, 2016), and depending on their partnerships types, FinTechs can still offer their services under their brand (Juengerkes, 2016). Also, promising Fintech startups can be selected by business accelerators and incubators to be mentor, fund and even partner with (Vandenreydt, 2016). Otherwise, collaboration between complementary Fintechs and/or across various Fintechs communities is a strategy that would also enable sharing of experiences and learning (Vandenreydt, 2016). Besides, consolidation through mergers and acquisitions will likely to be considered as the industry continues to mature.

5. FinTech, a Research Agenda

One area of research that investigators may want to focus on is the FinTech value chain. It is a timely issue to understand how FinTechs create value. Processes such as research and development, innovation, and inter-firm collaboration, in the context of FinTechs, need to be depicted. We presented in the previous section a high-level view of FinTechs' work system. What could be a promising research opportunity is to gain a more granular view of the FinTech's different work systems that generate business results. There are also several questions that remain open as how information systems are functioning and managed in these organizations. Moreover, the role that modern technologies — e.g. blockchain — play in designing digital products and services is yet to be examined and fully understood. Particularly, identifying the IT affordances that support developmental tasks of designers need to be tackled and demystified (Table 8). As presented above, Fintech is a dynamic phenomenon which can have significant impact on individuals, organizations and society. Yet, Fintech's focused scientific research in the field of information systems is still scarce. The goal of this section is to suggest research opportunities to IS scholars to delve into this promising area.

Table 8. The FinTech: A work system's perspective.

Customers	Products/services
• Changing customers' preferences • Long tail customers • SMEs • Banks	• Payment • Investment • P2P lending • Mobile wallets • Crowdfunding • Credit scoring • Insurtech • Chatbot • Robot advisor

Major activities and processes
• Automation • Gamification of customer service processes • Advisory automated processes

Participants	Information	Technologies
• Entrepreneurs • Computer scientists • Academia • Investors • Regulators • Policymakers	• Personal data • Behavioral data • Financial data	• Artificial intelligence • Machine learning • Cryptocurrencies • Blockchain • Mobile • Wearable technologies • Data analytics • Predictive algorithms

Infrastructure	Environment	Strategies
• Cloud computing • APIs • Big data • Mobile technologies • Internet of things • Social media • DLT	• Regulation • Compliance • Governance • Ethics	• Acquisition • Partnership • Investment funding • Collaboration • Growth

5.1. *FinTech adoption*

It is noteworthy that some FinTech products and services have already reached millions of users, particularly in the sector of mobile payments. Others are in their early phases of development and use, e.g. AI-based advice services and cryptocurrency-based wallets. Future research may focus on the factors that drive the wide use of FinTech's banking services, such as payment. Another area of research may address questions like how and why clients (e.g. individuals, SMEs) may adopt and use FinTech solutions that are offered by nontraditional banks and insurance companies. Further, it remains unclear how consumers may adopt emerging services offered by Insurtech and how far people are willing to share their data. Furthermore, some FinTech technologies, such as the blockchain, decentralize the notion of trust. It is relevant to examine how the literature on trust (Jarvenpaa *et al.*, 2004; Söllner *et al.*, 2016) can inform to develop a more nuanced conceptualization of "decentralized trust."

Among the topics that can also be investigated is identifying salient affordances and their interaction and dependencies as provided by FinTech technologies and how they are actually enacted by customers. Recognizing the social forces that can enhance or constrain the actualization of such affordances can also improve our understanding of how users or group of users enact those affordances and solve practical problems.

5.2. Business impact of FinTechs

As we have argued previously, FinTechs are inducing a dramatic shift in the financial sector. They have implications for various stakeholders such as established banking institutions, insurance companies, rating agencies, and audit and accounting firms (Medeiros and Chau, 2016). As the IT transformation occurs, the financial institutions have to reposition themselves (Pollari, 2016). The shift requires incumbents to revise their organizations, business models, and information systems in order to meet FinTechs' challenges and expectations. In this regard, academics have a plethora of new research avenues to shed light on this digital transformation.

It should be noted that banks have long integrated the digital in their distribution channels which has contributed, over the time, to shrinking the number of their physical branches. Yet, the impact of

FinTechs may be even bigger. Fast-moving FinTechs provoke a disaggregation of the established financial value chains. As things go, they are in position to disintermediate the existing relationship between banks and their customers. The trend is forcing financial institutions to reorganize their strategies and operations. Some banks, for example, are considering partnership or collaboration with FinTech companies. Others see FinTech as an integral part of their innovation strategy to bring new services to their consumers (Vandenreydt, 2016).

Among the perennial topics in IS research is the investigation of the impact of IT on individuals, groups, organizations, and industries (Markus and Silver, 2008; Pinsonneault and Kraemer, 1997). Accordingly, IS researchers can investigate the impact of FinTechs on financial institutions (e.g. business models strategies, organizational structure, culture, etc.). They can also explore how the financial ecosystem evolves in light of the FinTech trend. FinTech also raises questions as how the IT function within banking and insurance institutions will evolve. It appears to be necessary to look into how IT governance, IT management, and IT operations would adapt as it is becoming critical to balance flexibility, innovation, and standardization (Tallon and Pinsonneault, 2011; Vega-Jurado *et al.*, 2008).

5.3. *Societal impact of FinTechs*

Another possible direction of research to pursue is understanding the societal impacts of FinTechs. Research that investigates the impact of FinTechs on the work of professions, particularly, is much needed. Indeed, some particular jobs may be partly or completely automated (e.g. wealth manager, credit risk specialist, etc.). IS scholars can examine the impact of FinTech on employment and on the job market (Lacasse *et al.*, 2016). Besides, identifying the new skills to be developed in these professions regarding the rise of robot-advisors is another issue that deserves further investigation.

As FinTechs have facilitated the proliferation of mobile banking solutions, particularly in developing countries (Fowler and Fytatzi, 2016b), large populations and low-income families throughout the world are able to benefit from banking services and perform transactions in a secure and convenient manner. In this regards, there are interesting enquiries to conduct that may shed light on the dynamics of social inclusion, digital inequality, and digital divide (Wei *et al.*, 2011; Zhao *et al.*, 2014).

It is noteworthy that it is still difficult to predict the future of cryptocurrencies as there is still an ongoing debate at whether cryptocurrencies can actually function as a substitute for standard currencies and become a "global" currency (Ciaian *et al.*, 2016). There are roughly two opposing camps in this regard — those who believe cryptocurrencies, particularly the bitcoin, do not behave as a real currency, but rather resembles speculative investments, and those who believe that the cryptocurrencies can deliver on its promise as a global virtual currency (Ciaian *et al.*, 2016; Harwick, 2016; Luther, 2016). The outcome may be somewhere in the middle. The question, therefore, is to examine what FinTech's stakeholders (participants) can do to foster a positive outcome of cryptocurrencies for better service inclusion and accessibility.

5.4. Cybersecurity

As a matter of fact, FinTech raises concerns about cybersecurity as well. It is a timely issue to ensure that FinTech advances continue to be made and directed toward the best possible outcomes. Data theft, darknet, and financial malwares are only a fraction of the threats to the Fintech's value chain. IoT is also exposing organizations to unpredicted level of vulnerabilities and threats. Cybersecurity researchers can investigate cybercrime challenges and best practices for securing data and ensuring the integrity of financial transactions.

5.5. Regulation

Banking is a highly regulated industry. This provides banks, at least until now, with competitive advantage against new players such as FinTechs who are required to comply with regulations in order to offer a secure, trustworthy service, regardless of geography and legislation (Wendenburg, 2016). However, regulators are increasingly challenged as they are called to come forward with an effective regulation framework that removes barriers to FinTech market developments and preserves the interest of the consumers and the public at large. Academics can address the question of how regulation can affect FinTech's innovation and development. The other way around is also critical to investigate. In another words, how policymakers and regulators can understand, adapt, and shape the necessary digital transformation to the benefit of society. Uber and Airbnb business models have initiated such questions (Henten and Windekilde, 2016) and they are likely to persist with the rise of FinTechs.

5.6. *Privacy and ethics*

In the era of FinTech, customer potential monetization of their own data (personal, behavioral, financial), and user profiling through big-data analysis and inference techniques are opening the way for new, much more customized and personalized services, which can benefit users and consumers. However, these also raise important concerns when it comes to user privacy and individual autonomy, which encompass how data privacy and confidentiality meanings will evolve through this digital transformation, and what will be the social impact. In addition, although many FinTech startups are marketing themselves as better, cheaper, and more ethical alternatives to traditional finance, their ethics seems not to be their main concern (Trieu, 2016); survival is. Therefore, how ethics in the new world of finance will evolve and will this new world repeat the mistakes of traditional finance are unknowns that could provide interesting research avenues to follow.

6. Conclusion

The aim of this scoping review has been to map the current FinTech research scholarship landscape, provide meaningful insights, and facilitate the shaping of a future research agenda. While this chapter contributes to the understanding of the FinTech landscape within the extant research scholarship, the authors acknowledge that results of the present scoping review must be interpreted with caution due to some limitations worth noted. The first limitation is related to the search strategy and more specifically to the language restriction. As mentioned earlier, the authors considered only papers written in English, excluded "regulation papers" and "software engineering papers." The second limitation is related to the risk of selection bias. While the papers in the sample were retrieved from five databases that are commonly used across the social sciences disciplines, there is still a possibility that the authors did not take into account papers that might have been relevant to the study.

However, the authors believe that the sampling, within the realms of a scoping review, has been conducted so as to ensure a wide range of analytical generalizations. The authors are confident that this research opens up avenues for further research that are of interest to be explored in the future, contributing to the understanding of FinTech in the context of academic research, industry and policymaking. The proposed theoretical framework and the data visualization can serve as a basis for further empirical investigations, specifically considering diverse perceptions from multiple disciplines and streams of research. Future FinTech scholars may wish to draw much more from interdisciplinary research, engage into various data collection techniques, along with embracing alternative methodological approaches including qualitative, quantitative, simulations, experiments, and longitudinal. Moreover, future research endeavors need to explore the association of FinTech to different major management, business, and finance-related theories, providing novel insights and solid theoretical foundations of FinTech as an emerging field of research and study.

References

Alter, S. (2013). Work system theory: Overview of core concepts, extensions, and challenges for the future. Business Analytics and Information Systems. Paper 35. Available online at http://repository.usfca.edu/at/35 (Accessed on 5 June 2021).

Apfelbacher, A. (2016). The Future of Financial Services. in *The Fintech Book* (John Wiley & Sons Ltd).

Arksey, H. & O'Malley, L. (2005). Scoping studies: Towards a methodological framework. *International Journal of Social Research Methodology*, 8(1), 19–32.

Arner, D. W., Barberis, J., & Buckley, R. P. (2016). The evolution of fintech: New post-crisis paradigm. *Georgetown Journal of International Law*, 47(4), 1271–1320.

Arsov, A. (2016). Bitcoin as an Innovative Payment Currency in Germany: Development of the E-Gold Standard. Varazdin: Varazdin Development and Entrepreneurship Agency (VADEA), pp. 300–317.

Bachmann, A., Becker, A., Buerckner, D., Hilker, M., Kock, F., Lehmann, M., Tiburtius, P., & Funk, B. (2011). Online peer-to-peer lending — A literature review. *Journal of Internet Banking and Commerce*, 16(2), 1–18.

Bakker, E. (2015). The FinTech Ecosystem Report: Measuring the Effects of Technology on the Entire Financial Services Industry. BI Intelligence. Available online at https://edoclogic.com/wp-content/uploads/2018/01/Technology-changing-FinTech-Markets-J.Jefferys-and-Randy.pdf (Accessed on 4 June 2021).

Burtch, G., Ghose, A., & Wattal, S. (2013). An empirical examination of the antecedents and consequences of contribution patterns in crowd-funded markets. *Information Systems Research*, 24(3), 499–519.

Burtch, G., Ghose, A., & Wattal, S. (2014). Cultural differences and geography as determinants of online prosocial lending. *MIS Quarterly*, 38(3), 773.

Cai, C. W. (2018). Disruption of financial intermediation by Fintech: A review on crowdfunding and blockchain. *Accounting and Finance*, 58(4), 965–992.

Chen, Z., Li, Y., Wu, Y., & Luo, J. (2017). The transition from traditional banking to mobile internet finance: An organizational innovation perspective-a comparative study of Citibank and ICBC. *Financial Innovation*, 3(1), 1–16.

Chishti, S., & Barberis, J. (2016). *The Fintech book: The financial technology handbook for investors, entrepreneurs and visionaries* (John Wiley & Sons, West Sussex, United Kingdom).

Ciaian, P., Rajcaniova, M., & Kancs, D. A. (2016). The digital agenda of virtual currencies: Can bitcoin become a global currency? *Information Systems and eBusiness Management*, 14(4), 883–919.

Cockerton, C. (2016). Nurturing new Fintech communities. In *The Fintech Book: The Financial Technology Handbook for Investors, Entrepreneurs and Visionaries*, Chishti, S., & Barberis, J. (eds.) (John Wiley & Sons, West Sussex, United Kingdom), pp. 42–44.

Davis, K., & Murphy, J. (2016). Peer-to-peer lending: Structures, risks and regulation. *JASSA*, 3, 37–44.

Day, M. Y., Lin, J. T., & Chen, Y. C. (2018). Artificial intelligence for conversational robo-advisor. *Proceedings of the 2018 IEEE/ACM International*

Conference on Advances in Social Networks Analysis and Mining, ASONAM 2018, pp. 1057–1064.

Eickhoff, M., Muntermann, J., & Weinrich, T. (2018). What do fintechs actually do? A taxonomy of Fintech business models. *ICIS 2017: Transforming Society with Digital Innovation.* https://aisel.aisnet.org/icis2017/EBusiness/Presentations/22/ (Accessed on 6 June 2021).

Eling, M., & Lehmann, M. (2018). The impact of digitalization on the insurance value chain and the insurability of risks. *Geneva Papers on Risk & Insurance,* **43**(3), 359–396.

Fermay, A. H., Santosa, B., Kertopati, A. Y., & Eprianto, I. M. (2018). The development of collaborative model between Fintech and bank in Indonesia. *ACM International Conference Proceeding Series.*

Foster, C., & Heeks, R. (2013). Innovation and scaling of ICT for the bottom-of-the-pyramid. *Journal of Information Technology,* **28**(4), 296–315.

Fowler, S., & Fytatzi, K. (2016a). Blockchain to lead next tech revolution. *Oxford Analytica Daily Brief Service,* pp. 1-n/a.

Fowler, S., & Fytatzi, K. (2016b). Prospects 2017-22: Fintech. *Oxford Analytica Daily Brief Service.* p. 1.

Gimpel, H., Rau, D., & Roglinger, M. (2018). Understanding Fintech start-ups — A taxonomy of consumer-oriented service offerings. *Electronic Markets,* **28**(3), 245–264.

Gomber, P., Koch, J. A., & Siering, M. (2017). Digital finance and FinTech: Current research and future research directions. *Journal of Business Economics,* **87**(5), 537–580.

Gomber, P., Kauffman, R. J., Parker, C., & Weber, B. W. (2018). On the Fintech revolution: Interpreting the forces of innovation, disruption, and transformation in financial services. *Journal of Management Information Systems,* **35**(1), 220–265.

Gonzalez, R. (2016). Lending (capital) in the 21st century. In *The Fintech Book: The Financial Technology Handbook for Investors, Entrepreneurs and Visionaries,* Chishti, S., & Barberis, J. (eds.) (John Wiley & Sons, West Sussex, United Kingdom), pp. 25–27.

Gozman, D., Liebenau, J., & Mangan, J. (2018). The innovation mechanisms of Fintech start-ups: Insights from Swift's Innotribe competition. *Journal of Management Information Systems,* **35**(1), 145–179.

Haikel-Elsabeh, M., Nouet, S., & Nayaradou, M. (2016). How personal finance management influences consumers' motivations and behavior regarding online banking services. *Communications & Strategies,* **103**(15–34), 213–214.

Harwick, C. (2016). Cryptocurrency and the problem of intermediation. *The Independent Review,* **20**(4), 569–588.

Henten, A. H., & Windekilde, I. M. (2016). Transaction costs and the sharing economy. *Info: The Journal of Policy, Regulation and Strategy for Telecommunications, Information and Media,* **18**(1), 1–15.

Horton, D. (2017). Fintech in 2017: Automation will rule. *American Banker*, 182(5), 1.

Hsueh, S. C., & Kuo, C. H. (2017). Effective matching for P2P lending by mining strong association rules. *ACM International Conference Proceeding Series*, pp. 30–33.

Hutt, R. (2016). What does the rise of FinTech mean for banking? World Economic Forum Agenda. Available online at https://www.weforum.org/agenda/2016/04/what-does-the-rise-of-fintech-mean-for-banking/ (accessed on 4 June 2021).

Jarvenpaa, S. L., Shaw, T. R., & Staples, D. S. (2004). Toward contextualized theories of trust: The role of trust in global virtual teams. *Information Systems Research*, 15(3), 250–267.

Jeong, Y. J., Jeon, H. M., Ock, Y. S., & Jeong, S. C. (2018). A study on the acceptance factors to use mobile easy remittance service. *ICIC Express Letters, Part B: Applications*, 9(1), 61–67.

Jiang, Y., Ho, Y. C., Yan, X. B., & Tan, Y. (2018). Investor platform choice: Herding, platform attributes, and regulations. *Journal of Management Information Systems*, 35(1), 86–116.

Juengerkes, B. E. (2016). FinTechs and Banks–Collaboration is Key. In *The FinTech book: The financial technology handbook for investors, entrepreneurs and visionaries*, Chishti, S., & Barberis, J. (eds.) (John Wiley & Sons, West Sussex, United Kingdom), pp. 179–182.

Jui-Long, H., & Luo, B. (2016). Fintech in Taiwan: A case study of a bank's strategic planning for an investment in a Fintech company. *Financial Innovation*, 2(1), 1–16.

Jung, D., Dorner, V., Glaser, F., & Morana, S. (2018a). Robo-Advisory. *Business & Information Systems Engineering*, 60(1), 81–86.

Jung, D., Dorner, V., Weinhardt, C., & Pusmaz, H. (2018b). Designing a robo-advisor for risk-averse, low-budget consumers. *Electronic Markets*, 28(3), 367–380.

K. Kashyap, M., & Weber, G. (2016). How emerging technologies will change financial services. In *The FinTech Book: The Financial Technology Handbook for Investors, Entrepreneurs and Visionaries*, Chishti, S. & Barberis, J. (eds). (John Wiley & Sons, West Sussex, United Kingdom), pp. 226–228.

King, B. (2012). *Bank 3.0: Why Banking Is No Longer Somewhere You Go but Something You Do* (John Wiley & Sons, Singapore).

KPMG (2018). The pulse of Fintech 2018: Biannual global analysis of investment in Fintech. Retrieved from: https://assets.kpmg/content/dam/kpmg/au/pdf/2018/pulse-of-fintech-h1-2018.pdf

Kuhlmann, M., Roth, F. M., Becker, C., & Theissen, E. (2018). Fincare — A digital spending conscience or "do you really need a flamethrower?" *Americas Conference on Information Systems 2018: Digital Disruption, AMCIS 2018*.

Kutler, J. (2013). Fun, gamification and finance. *Institutional Investor*, 47(4), 5.

Larios-Hernandez, G. J. (2017). Blockchain entrepreneurship opportunity in the practices of the unbanked. *Business Horizons*, 60(6), 865–874.

Lacasse, R., Berthe Lambert, B., & Osmani, E. (2016). Fintech arena and creative disruption in financial services. *7th International Research Meeting in Business and Management* (Nice, France).

Lee, M. R., Yen, D. C., & Hurlburt, G. F. (2018). Financial technologies and applications. *IT Professional*, 20(2), 27–33.

Lee, P. (2015). The Fintech entrepreneurs aiming to reinvent finance. *Euromoney (UK)*, 46(552), 42–48.

Lee, S. (2017). Evaluation of mobile application in user's perspective: Case of P2P lending apps in fintech industry. *KSII Transactions on Internet and Information Systems*, 11(2), 1105–1115.

Leong, C., Tan, B., Xiao, X., Tan, F. T. C., & Sun, Y. (2017). Nurturing a Fintech ecosystem: The case of a youth microloan startup in China. *International Journal of Information Management*, 37(2), 92–97.

Levac, D., Colquhoun, H., & O'Brien, K. (2010). Scoping studies: Advancing the methodology. *Implementation Science*, 5(69), 1–9.

Li, Y., Marier-Bienvenue, T., Perron-Brault, A., Wang, X., & Paré, G. (2018). January. Blockchain technology in business organizations: A scoping review. In Proceedings of the 51st Hawaii International Conference on System Sciences. Conference paper available online at https://scholarspace.manoa.hawaii.edu/handle/10125/50454 (accessed on 4 June 2021).

Li, Y., Spigt, R., & Swinkels, L. (2017). The impact of FinTech start-ups on incumbent retail banks' share prices. *Financial Innovation*, 3(1), 1–16.

Lin, T. C. W. (2014). The new financial industry. *Alabama Law Review*, 65(3), 567–623.

Luther, W. J. (2016). Bitcoin and the future of digital payments. *The Independent Review*, 20(3), 397–404.

Marafie, Z., Lin, K. J., Zhai, Y., & Li, J. (2018). Proactive fintech: Using intelligent IoT to deliver positive Insurtech feedback. *Proceeding — 2018 20th IEEE International Conference on Business Informatics, CBI 2018*, pp. 72–81.

Mariotto, C. (2016). Competition for lending in the Internet era: The case of peer-to-peer lending marketplaces in the USA. *Communications & Strategies*, 103, 35–58.

Markus, M. L., & Silver, M. S. (2008). A foundation for the study of IT effects: A new look at Desanctis and Poole's concepts of structural features and spirit. *Journal of the Association for Information Systems*, 9(10–11), 609–632.

Martínez-Climent, C., Zorio-Grima, A., & Ribeiro-Soriano, D. (2018). Financial return crowdfunding: Literature review and bibliometric analysis. *International Entrepreneurship and Management Journal*, 14(3), 527–553.

Mathur, N., Karre, S. A., Mohan, S. L., & Reddy, Y. R. (2018). Analysis of Fintech mobile app usability for geriatric users in India. *ACM International Conference Proceeding Series*, pp. 1–11.

Medeiros, M., & Chau, B. (2016). Fintech — Stake a patent claim? *Intellectual Property Journal*, 28(3), 303–314.

Muthukannan, P., Tan, F. T. C., Tan, B., & Leong, C. (2018). The concentric development of the financial technology (fintech) ecosystem in Indonesia. In *ICIS 2017: Transforming Society with Digital Innovation*.

Ng, E., Muthukannan, P., Tan, B., & Leong, C. (2018). Fintech platform development: A revelatory case study of a Chinese microloan startup. In *ICIS 2017: Transforming Society with Digital Innovation*.

Ngai, E. W. T., & Wat, F. K. T. (2002). A literature review and classification of electronic commerce research. *Journal of Information Management*, 39(5), 415–429.

Nicoletti, B. (2017). *The Future of Fintech: Integrating Finance and Technology in Financial Services* (Palgrave, Rome).

Paré, G., Tate, M., Johnstone, D., & Kitsiou, S. (2016). Contextualizing the twin concepts of systematicity and transparency in information systems literature reviews. *European Journal of Information Systems*, 25(6), 493–508.

Paré, G., Trudel, M.-C., Jaana, M., & Kitsiou, S. (2015). Synthesizing information systems knowledge: A typology of literature reviews. *Information & Management*, 52(2), 183–199.

Phoon, K., & Koh, F. (2018). Robo-advisors and wealth management. *The Journal of Alternative Investments*, 20(3), 79–94.

Pinsonneault, A., & Kraemer, K. L. (1997). Middle management downsizing: An empirical investigation of the impact of information technology. *Management Science*, 43(5), 659–679.

Pollari, I. (2016). The rise of Fintech: Opportunities and challenges. *JASSA*, 3, 15–21.

Puschmann, T. (2017). Fintech. *Business Information Systems Engineering*, 59(1), 69–76.

PwC (2017). Redrawing the lines: Fintech's growing influence on financial services. Global Fintech Report. Retrieved from: https://www.pwc.com/jg/en/publications/pwc-global-fintech-report-17.3.17-final.pdf

Raikwar, M., Mazumdar, S., Ruj, S., Sen Gupta, S., Chattopadhyay, A., & Lam, K. Y. (2018). A blockchain framework for insurance processes. *2018 9th IFIP International Conference on New Technologies, Mobility and Security, NTMS 2018 — Proceedings*, pp. 1–4.

Riikkinen, M., Saarijärvi, H., Sarlin, P., & Lähteenmäki, I. (2018). Using artificial intelligence to create value in insurance. *The International Journal of Bank Marketing*, 36(6), 1145–1168.

Roeder, J., Cardona, D. R., Palmer, M., Werth, O., Muntermann, J., & Breitner, M. H. (2018). Make or break: Business model determinants of Fintech venture success. *MKWI 2018 — Multikonferenz Wirtschaftsinformatik*, pp. 1221–1232.

Schueffel, P. (2016). Taming the beast: A scientific definition of Fintech. *Journal of Innovation Management*, 4(4), 32–54.

Schwab, K. (2016). The Fourth Industrial Revolution. Agenda, World Economic Forum.

Shim, Y., & Shin, D.-H. (2016). Analyzing China's Fintech industry from the perspective of actor–network theory. *Telecommunications Policy*, 40(2–3), 168–181.

Sironi, P. (2016). *Fintech Innovation: From Robo-Advisors to Goal Based Investing and Gamification* (John Wiley & Sons, West Sussex, United Kingdom).

Söllner, M., Hoffmann, A., & Leimeister, J. M. (2016). Why different trust relationships matter for information systems users. *European Journal of Information Systems*, 25(3), 274–287.

Stern, C., Makinen, M., & Qian, Z. X. (2017). Fintechs in China — With a Special Focus on Peer to Peer Lending. *Journal of Chinese Economic and Foreign Trade Studies*, 10(3), 215–228.

Stoeckli, E., Dremel, C., & Uebernickel, F. (2018). Exploring characteristics and transformational capabilities of Insurtech innovations to understand insurance value creation in a digital world. *Electronic Markets*, 28(3), 287–305.

Tallon, P., & Pinsonneault, A. (2011). Competing perspectives on the link between strategic information technology alignment and organizational agility: Insights from a mediation model. *MIS Quarterly*, 35(2), 463–486.

Teja, A. (2017). Indonesian Fintech business: New innovations or foster and collaborate in business ecosystems? *The Asian Journal of Technology Management*, 10(1), 10–18.

Trieu, H. (2016). Ethics in Fintech? In *The Fintech Book* (John Wiley & Sons Ltd).

Underwood, S. (2016). Blockchain beyond bitcoin. *Communications of the ACM*, 59(11), 15–17.

Vandenreydt, F. (2016). Fintech trends from the frontline — Building collaborative opportunities for start-ups, market infrastructures, and wholesale banks. In *The Fintech Book* (John Wiley & Sons Ltd).

Varga, D. (2018). Triple-bottom-line impact analysis framework of Fintech companies. *A hármas optimalizálás hatásának vizsgálati keretrendszere fintech cégek esetében*, 11, 24–34.

Vega-Jurado, J., Gutiérrez-Gracia, A., & Fernández-de-Lucio, I. (2008). Analyzing the determinants of firm's absorptive capacity: Beyond R&D. *R & D Management*, 38(4), 392.

Vergne, J. P., & Swain, G. (2017). Categorical anarchy in the UK? The British media's classification of bitcoin and the limits of categorization. In *From Categories to Categorization: Studies in Sociology, Organizations and Strategy at the Crossroads* (Research in the Sociology of Organizations, Vol. 51), Durrand, R., Granqvist, N. & Tyllström, A. (eds.) (Emerald Publishing Limited, Bingley, United Kingdom), pp. 185–222.

Wang, M., & Chang, Y. (2018). Technology leadership, brand equity, and customer loyalty towards fintech service providers in China. *Americas Conference on Information Systems 2018: Digital Disruption, AMCIS 2018*.

Wei, K.-K., Teo, H.-H., Chan, H. C., & Tan, B. C. Y. (2011). Conceptualizing and testing a social cognitive model of the digital divide. *Information Systems Research*, 22(1), 170–187, 208, 210–211.

Welsh, T. (2017). 5 predictions for advisor Fintech in 2017. *Investment Advisor*, 37(2), 5.

Wendenburg, J. C. (2016). Global compliance is key. In *The FinTech Book: The Financial Technology Handbook for Investors, Entrepreneurs and Visionaries*, Chishti, S. & Barberis, J. (eds.) (John Wiley & Sons, West Sussex, United Kingdom), pp. 22–24.

Wonglimpiyarat, J. (2017). Fintech banking industry: A systemic approach. *Foresight: The Journal of Futures Studies, Strategic Thinking and Policy*, 19(6), 590–603.

Wonglimpiyarat, J. (2018). Challenges and dynamics of Fintech crowd funding: An innovation system approach. *Journal of High Technology Management Research*, 29(1), 98–108.

Wu, P. S. (2017). Fintech trends relationships research: A bibliometric citation meta-analysis. *Proceedings of the International Conference on Electronic Business (ICEB)*, pp. 99–105.

Zavolokina, L., Dolata, M., & Schwabe, G. (2016a). Fintech — What's in a name? *2016 International Conference on Information Systems, ICIS 2016*.

Zavolokina, L., Dolata, M., & Schwabe, G. (2016b). Fintech — What's in a name? *Thirty Seventh International Conference on Information Systems*, Dublin, Ireland.

Zavolokina, L., Dolata, M., & Schwabe, G. (2016c). The Fintech phenomenon: Antecedents of financial innovation perceived by the popular press. *Financial Innovation*, 2(1), 16.

Zavolokina, L., Dolata, M., & Schwabe, G. (2017). Fintech transformation: How IT-enabled innovations shape the financial sector. In *Enterprise Applications, Markets and Services in the Finance Industry*, Feuerriegel, S. & Neumann, D. (eds.) (Springer International Publishing, Cham), pp. 75–88.

Zhao, F., Collier, A., & Deng, H. (2014). A multidimensional and integrative approach to study global digital divide and e-government development. *Information Technology & People*, 27(1), 38–62.

Chapter 3

The Human Impact of Financial Innovation: Mobility, Choice, and Risk

Erin B. Taylor

Western Sydney University, Sydney, New South Wales, Australia
erin@canela-group.com

Abstract. Innovation in financial technology is often conceptualized as centering upon technological developments or novel applications of technology to undertake financial transactions. Yet the drivers of innovation often lie in the global mobility of people, organizations, ideas, skills, capital, and technology (Armano and Javarone, 2017). While mobility is increasingly in the reach of ordinary people, such as through migration, access to technology, or education, the ability to produce innovation or consume innovative products is unevenly distributed. Moreover, new products on the market are more likely to cause problems or risks to consumers as their potential impacts have not yet been fully tested. This is especially true of the new range of financial products, commonly known as "FinTech," that are emerging in the consumer market. Today, there are far more financial services available to consumers, and they are provided by a wide range of companies, many of whom are not traditional financial service providers. The availability of financial services through the Internet, and their use on mobile devices, means that consumers can access a far wider and more specialized array of financial products from companies located around the world. This greater level of access and choice in financial products has the potential to deliver both positive and negative effects for consumers. On one hand, it can expand consumer choice, increase access to product information, assist with financial literacy, and decrease transaction costs. On the other hand, it may exacerbate certain social and economic issues, such as fraud, user errors, learning difficulties, ineffective UX, stress, and financial mismanagement. Within this context, "mobility" is a useful analytical tool to identify the different kinds of effects that emerge from financial innovation within different populations, and in different use-cases. In this chapter, I explore the relationship between innovation, mobility, and change, and how this relationship affects consumers. I discuss a range of issues that increased access to financial products presents for consumers, particularly in the areas of product mobility, human mobility, and information mobility. I draw upon the "mobilities turn" (Schiller and Salazar, 2013; Sheller and Urry, 2006), which has addressed the various ways, both positive and negative, in which the increased mobility of people, things, and information around the world affects people's lives and social relationships. I end with a discussion of the challenges researchers face in keeping up-to-date with the social effects of financial transformation.

Keywords. Finance; innovation; impact; mobility; choice; risk.

1. Introduction

Consumer finance practices are undergoing a transformation worldwide, resulting from the increased mobility of people, products, and information. While mobility has always been an inherent feature of financial innovation and behavior, the digitization of financial services and the near-universal penetration of the Internet means that consumers now have access to a vast array of financial products and services from providers who are located around the globe (Taylor, 2017a, 2017b; Vacheron, 2015).[1]

---

[1]Credit transfers, direct debits, and card payments account for 92.26% of payments, but we are likely to see a sizeable shift in the products people use and how

Moreover, people are using financial products while on the move. A person can pay their credit card debt while riding in a train, do their grocery shopping online as they sit in a café, bet on a football match while perched on a public toilet, or buy illicit drugs using bitcoins. Along with people and products, information is also far more mobile. People can find extensive product information online, and they can share their personal information far more easily.

The rise of FinTech, i.e. new financial services often offered by non-traditional providers, has been accompanied by a great deal of hype, with its supporters claiming that the greater choice, competition, and personalization that new financial services deliver is a sea change for consumers who were formerly dependent on a monopolistic banking industry that did not serve the interests of individual consumers (OECD, 2011). While digital financial services (such as online banking), began the shift away from bricks-and-mortar banks and payments point to online transactions, the entry of non-traditional providers into the market significantly altered the landscape.

The promise of FinTech is to offer customer-centric services that solve a far wider range of problems than simply completing successful, one-off economic transactions (Nicoletti, 2017). Products such as budget trackers, payments apps, robo-advisors, and personalized pension videos may (to some degree) improve information quality, boost literacy, provide for disadvantaged groups, and increase overall efficiency while decreasing transaction costs (Broløs and Taylor, 2020; Gomber *et al.*, 2017; Taylor and Broløs, 2020). Financial innovation is also currently being applied to combat problems of poverty and socio-economic development, such as through the development of microfinance and mobile money services around the world (Maurer *et al.*, 2018; Maurer, 2015).

However, while new financial services certainly hold social and economic promise, they also increase certain risks, such as fraud, user errors, learning difficulties, stress, and financial mismanagement.

---

they use them. These include e-wallets, near field communication (NFC) technology, cryptocurrencies, person-to-person (P2P) insurance, and non-bank providers of credit, insurance, and currency conversion services.

For some people, financial services such as mobile money prove more of a curse than a blessing when they place increased social demands on highly limited incomes (Kusimba *et al.*, 2018; Horst and Taylor, 2018). Similarly, too much information, the circulation of incorrect information, or being on the wrong side of the "digital divide" can pose a burden to the consumer (Dodgson *et al.*, 2013; Pippa, 2000). Negative effects can also occur with monetary remittances, which are often used to strengthen family ties but which can also limit an individual's autonomy over their income due to pressure from family members to send more money (Singh, 2016). It can also increase the "financial divide" between those who receive remittance and those who do not (Hobbs and Jameson, 2012). The movement of capital through new, smaller providers may also present problems, such as security and privacy risks (Lee and Shin, 2018), as well as challenges for anti-money-laundering initiatives (*Ibid.*).

The fast-changing nature of innovation in financial services makes it difficult for policy-makers and regulators to work fast enough to protect consumers. In Europe, regulators are adjusting by developing programs to reduce the burden of compliance such as the Better Regulations Package, which provides scope for self-regulation and co-regulation, and the Regulatory Fitness and Performance Programme (REFIT), which aims to simplify EU laws that can particularly burden small and medium-sized enterprises (SMEs).[2] Within these programs, rules-based regulation is giving way to principles-based regulation as the latter grants businesses greater space to innovate (Black, 2008). However, some researchers have criticized this approach, claiming that it can stimulate a regulatory "race to the bottom" that needs to be countered by global cooperation between regulators (Frantz and Instefjord, 2018). Given that financial services are increasingly offered across jurisdictions, more

---

[2]See the European Commission pages https://ec.europa.eu/info/law/law-making-process/evaluating-and-improving-existing-laws/refit-making-eu-law-simpler-and-less-costly_en and https://ec.europa.eu/digital-single-market/en/news/principles-better-self-and-co-regulation-endorsed-better-regulation-package

emphasis on global regulatory coordination would indeed seem timely.

Identifying the issues facing consumers now and in the future is a complex task. Financial products and needs vary from place to place, and people use financial products in diverse ways depending upon their needs, preferences, and the context in which they live. In this chapter, I attempt to begin this task by building a framework that breaks mobility down into three key areas: product mobility, human mobility, and information mobility. This framework is not intended to be all-encompassing, rather it is a basis upon which to ask further questions. First, I give a brief overview of the history of mobility in consumer finance. Second, I explore the relationship between mobility and innovation. Third, I review recent research on the benefits and risks of financial transformation. Finally, I map out a rough agenda for future research that may be of benefit to both companies developing financial products, and researchers and policy-makers who wish to keep abreast of consumer issues.

2. A Brief History of Innovation in Consumer Finance

Innovation in consumer finance has a long and varied history pre-digitization that is intimately tied to mobility. Indeed, this history begins with the invention of money itself. Money, whether in the form of coins, shells, banknotes, tally sticks, or promissory notes, must be transportable if it is to be used as a means of payment between geographically distant markets. For this to occur, money must be light and durable, and we must also agree on its value (say, one dollar, five Euro, and so on). When this combination of material and symbolic properties fails, money becomes less mobile. This is clearly seen in cases of hyperinflation, in which money's value drops so much that people are forced to carry it around in bulk, such as by piling up packets of banknotes in wheelbarrows. These kinds of events make everyday trade difficult and slow down entire economies.

Making money mobile, then, has been a central quest in humanity's history of toolmaking. As people have migrated around the world, they have taken their monetary technologies with them. By the early 20th century, the coins and banknotes that we recognize today had come to dominate over alternative forms of money, such as shells, livestock, and precious metals. By this time, currencies had also undergone a process of centralization, with privately created currencies being replaced by coins and notes minted by states.

In the Netherlands, for example, the Dutch Central Bank has been issuing centralized currency for over 200 years (and replaced 14 different mints). This was just one of a series of financial innovations that emerged in North Holland during the 17th and 18th centuries to increase the liquidity of money and markets (Ferguson, 2008). In fact, so many market technologies emerged here that financial historian Simon Lelieveldt refers to Amsterdam as a "money laboratory," since it was the testing ground for the development of dozens of financial products that were subsequently adopted around the globe (cited in Taylor, 2013). The Dutch East India Company (1602) was the first company in the world to issue stocks, an invention that helped it to raise far more capital than its competitors and grow much faster than had previously been possible. Amsterdam also became a major center for the trade of grain and tax revenues, which benefited the development of the city and its markets.

These new market technologies were important because they generated ways to manage money and to move it around. Global trade propelled the development of telecommunications systems, such as the trans-Atlantic telegraph, which were used to wire money. For the first time, monetary values no longer needed to be moved in the form of tangible material things, such as paper or metal, but instead could be sent in the form of an electric current. Hence the basis for digitization was born.

Consumer finance products were simultaneously undergoing a revolution. In Victorian England, few individuals had bank accounts. Instead, as sociologist Liz McFall (2014) describes in her book *Devising Consumption*, insurance and credit agents would walk from household to household offering their products. This all changed during the 20th century as having an account with a formal bank became more accessible and more necessary.

In the second half of the 20th century, consumer finance in wealthy countries underwent a process of centralization as people came to rely on banks to supply all their financial needs, including savings accounts, checks, personal loans, mortgages, and life insurance. Thus retail banks took up a prominent role in the development of financial products. Perhaps unsurprisingly, it was the US that led the way, building upon technologies they had imported from the UK. However, a major reason why the US was an early innovator was because they needed to find ways to cope with their fractured banking system. From the early 20th century, various US-based companies invented precursors to credit cards. In 1921, Western Union began to issue charge cards that were printed on paper, and in 1934, American Airlines issued Air Travel Cards. The 1950s saw the development of Diners Club, Carte Blanche, and American Express cards. At first, these products were mostly used by elites, but banks began to encourage their usage by mailing credit cards to people unsolicited. The democratization of access to mobile consumer finance grew with the installation of the first automatic teller machine in New York City in 1961 by the City Bank of New York. However, paper checks continued to dominate transactions in the US until December 2004, when electronic transactions finally overtook checks (Thoma, 2005).

The dominance of retail banks as service providers continued until late in the 20th century. A combination of regulation and efficiency of scale meant that it was difficult for smaller players to establish a foothold in the market, and so retail banking in any individual country tended to be dominated by a few major players. As a result, banks became platforms for most financial services that people used. Bank cards (debit and credit) were one of the most important developments, since they relieved consumers of the burden of having to withdraw cash. Later, this advantage was augmented by a trend toward employers depositing employees' salaries directly in their bank accounts. This made it theoretically possible for consumers to avoid cash altogether.

Yet, even as the foundations were being laid for retail banks to dominate consumer finance, conditions necessary for the diversification of providers were developing. From the 1980s onward, a series of deregulation movements around the world aimed to lessen the monopoly of banks and open up the playing field for smaller providers (such as account switching regulation in the UK). From the 1990s onward, the spread of computers and the Internet made it much easier for small companies to develop financial tools at low cost and deliver them to consumers.

It should also be noted that even at the height of the reign of the banks, their dominance was not universal. There are many countries with sizeable populations that were never "banked" and have instead depended upon alternative formal and informal products, including moneylenders and savings associations (Collins, 2009). Far from being behind the rest of the world, these countries are now often at the forefront of financial innovations, with services such as microfinance and mobile money pushing the boundaries of how consumer finance products are offered and who offers them (Roodman, 2012). Thus we are not only seeing a shift from banks to a wide variety of financial service providers, we are also (to a certain extent) witnessing a shift in *where* these services are produced. Financial innovation today is a vastly different experience for both producers and consumers as each have greater access to the market, and therefore also to the benefits and risks that come with innovation.

When assessing financial innovation we should keep in mind that, in terms of volume, finance is very much a consumer-oriented market. While the public image of finance often centers around Wall-Street–style investment banks, mundane consumer finance actually accounts for the majority of transactions worldwide via both formal and informal services. Annual retail banking revenues amount to around US$3.4 trillion (McKinsey, 2013), and according to the World Bank, global remittances reached US$401 billion in 2012 (World Bank, n.d.). The World Payments Report 2018 states that rates of non-cash transactions grew by 10.1% during 2015–2016, reaching a total of US$482 billion.

There are around five billion adults around the world using financial services. While many people continue to depend upon locally provided financial services (such as a bank in their town), they can now potentially choose from a dizzying array of financial providers and products. As a result, there is a shift away from "high street" banking to multichannel access. Bank branches and other locality-based services are disappearing, and financial service providers are finding that they must compete in a global market. In the more traditional retail sector, consumers are provided for by retail banks, credit unions, mortgage brokers, and payday loans companies, among others. Newer, non-bank industries include remittance services, payments services, mobile banking, mobile money, e-wallets, and microcredit.

At a national level, the digitization of finance has resulted in an increase of domestic products and providers, such as transport cards, online payment systems, and digitized parking meters and applications. At a global level, consumers can access a wide range of monetary and finance tools, including Google Wallet, PayPal, bitcoin, money transfer services, insurance products, and investment advice. While many of the product innovations carried out by companies emanate from the US, their global reach means that their services have the potential to affect consumers from all around the world. Just as PayPal provided a means for consumers around the globe to transact among themselves swiftly and inexpensively, so do providers such as Google Wallet and Apple Pay have the potential to significantly alter how we use consumer finance products and services.

In countries with large "unbanked" populations,[3] the technologization of finance is helping people to skip the transition from retail banks to other service providers altogether. Approximately 2.5 billion adults are without a formal bank account (Demirjuc-Kunt, 2012). Instead of extending banking networks, which require a great

---

[3]The term "unbanked" should not be interpreted to mean that people have no financial services whatsoever, since other formal and informal services are generally on offer.

deal of infrastructure and investment, basic financial services are being offered through microfinance agencies and mobile phone-based systems. Mobile phones are particularly useful because they give people access to a range of services under the one platform, including domestic and international transfers, merchant payments, savings accounts, insurance, and credit (Maurer, 2015). These services replace or complement a wide array of informal services, speeding up transactions and reducing costs.

Services such as these are integral to the transformation of consumer finance from something that happens within domestic market and is defined by national borders, to a practice that integrates people, providers, and regulatory bodies around the globe. Yet we have little idea what directions these transformations will take, or what issues consumers will encounter in the near future. These problems are likely to materialize in ways we do not expect, and there may well be other problems on the horizon that we have not foreseen. We can anticipate many potential issues based on what we already know, but it is also important to actively scrutinize new products and practices in order to stay abreast of new issues that arise. Consumer finance researchers are faced with the task of tracking these diverse and complex changes and predicting their effects.

To date, no systematic attempt has been made to identify the potential issues generated by increasing mobility in consumer finance. This is partially due to the novel nature of many consumer finance products, services, and practices, but it is also because institutions and researchers tend to focus on particular areas or topics. Indeed, most research on digital finance and well-being has focused on countries with limited financial infrastructure and large "unbanked" populations (e.g. microfinance and mobile money research), yet digital finance also stands to impact the well-being of "banked" consumers from across a wide range of social strata. Some risks to well-being are specific to vulnerable populations (e.g. literacy, device access) but others pose a general risk to the population (e.g. fraud, choice). While researchers investigate many of these consumer issues, there is no integrated framework for surveying them as a whole or anticipating future issues.

3. A Mobility Framework

I propose that a focus on mobility can help us to assess the human impacts of financial services. The effects of mobility on society and the economy have been widely recognized by social scientists and economists, and have been variously discussed in terms of globalization (e.g. Ang, 1994; Mintz, 1986; Polanyi, 1944), modernity (Bauman, 2013; Giddens, 2013; Miller, 1994), the network society (Castells, 1996; Castells and Cardoso, 2006), migration (Brettell and Hollifield, 2013, 2014; Glick Schiller and Caglar, 2010) and, more recently, the "mobilities turn" (Schiller and Salazar, 2013; Sheller and Urry, 2006).

The promise of mobility is that it improves people's lives by giving them greater choice as consumers, increasing their access to markets, and widening their scope to create a life of their choosing (Taylor, 2018). Among other things, it augments people's ability to move (migration), send objects (trade and gift-giving), and swap information (communications and education). Information mobility can act as a leveler of difference, such as when people have access to useful information via mobile phones and the Internet (Horst and Miller, 2006; Wyatt *et al.*, 2000). Mobility, we are told, can increase life options, flatten hierarchies, increase social capital, and increase wealth overall.

These forms of mobility can also have positive effects on people's financial lives. The mobility of material or financial objects, such as gifts, trade stock, social security payments, remittances, or loans, can provide a safety net, a source of capital, and social connection (Appadurai, 1988; Singh, 2016). Greater access to products and providers means more consumer choice and more competition. When financial services are available over the Internet, customers are not obliged to buy services from local providers and can access far more information about the products and services they are considering. Customers can shop around for a product with the right features to suit them, at a reasonable price, and from a trusted provider. In their own time, they can check reviews and ratings by other customers to help them make a decision based on "social proof." If they are not satisfied with what they are being offered, they can take their business elsewhere. The availability of financial services on mobile phones also saves time and money. It is often far easier to complete financial transactions digitally using a mobile device than, say, going into a bank branch to make a payment or transfer money. However, increased mobility also brings disadvantages.

Mobility's effects are not always positive. For many people, mobility is not a free choice, but a "choice of the necessary" (Bourdieu, 1984) to sustain their livelihood, such as in the case of refugees fleeing a war zone (Simich and Andermann, 2014). Moreover, humans on the move frequently encounter systematic discrimination based on their appearance, dress, and perceived cultural identity. Digital mobility does not circumvent discrimination; as is now well documented, people also encounter discrimination in their interactions with algorithms and digital systems (Fry, 2018). As I will describe in the following section, increased mobility can also produce a range of negative effects in financial innovation and application.

The question of who benefits from the movement of people, things, and information depends very much on what choices are available to people, how they are able to combine them, and whether those choices can be successfully deployed to meet the goals they have set. The things that make mobility possible or shut it down are not always what we would expect. Whether mobility is beneficial or harmful depends upon the extent to which people have control over it, how they use it, and how it is deployed by others. Differential access to mobilities can exacerbate social differences based on race, class, nationality, gender, financial position, health, and many other factors. States and their actors also play roles in permitting or limiting mobility and choice (Kalir and Wissink, 2015).

Researchers and commentators have also closely associated innovation with mobility. This includes capital mobility (Archibugi *et al.*, 1999), labor mobility (Felsenstein, 2011), innovation networks (Bullinger *et al.*, 2004; Dhanaraj and Parkhe, 2006), the movement of knowledge and knowledge workers (Miguélez and Moreno, 2013; Rooney *et al.*, 2012), and the movement of skilled workers (Gorin, 2017; OECD, 2001). As with mobility generally, the capacity to engage with innovation is unevenly distributed by a wide range of intersecting factors. This is true for both creating and consuming innovation, since they equally depend upon the accessibility of resources, knowledge, and skills. The producers of innovation do not always take consumers' needs or use-cases into account either, so even if innovative products are accessible, they may not have high functionality or may pose risks (Hellström, 2003). This is especially true with respect to technological and financial innovation: data security and privacy are major ongoing issues and the onus has often been put on the individual consumers to protect themselves rather than on companies designing security into products ("security by design").

When thinking about mobility and innovation, we therefore need to understand how the power to enable or constrain mobility is harnessed, distributed, and enacted. In whose interest is it to restrict or facilitate innovation? Why might some people choose *not* to use the financial innovations available to them, even when it may well bring them social and economic benefits? How might these considerations affect how we think about financial innovation and its human impact overall?

One way to approach this set of problems is to examine how personal, collective, and structural factors affect the outcomes of mobility. Migration scholars have been asking these kinds of questions for some time with respect to the movement of people (Brettell and Hollifield, 2014). More recently, the mobilities turn has shifted to a broader discussion of mobility in terms of people, things, and ideas. According to Sheller and Urry (2006), the mobilities turn challenges "sedentarist theories," i.e. the idea that staying put is normal and that migration is an exception. It focuses on "the myriad ways in which people and their cultural practices are not confined to a fixed territory but are part of multiple spatial networks and temporal linkages" (Schiller and Salazar, 2013, pp. 185–86).

Importantly, the mobilities turn goes beyond migration to study the mobility of people, things, information, and the networks by which they move. It acknowledges multidirectional flows, not just of people but also of the goods and information that travel *with* them and separately *from* them. It also pays attention to how different kinds of mobilities are intertwined. Mobility of one thing can also be used as a proxy for another, such as when people are able to send money via a mobile phone rather than travel themselves (Horst and Taylor, 2018). Similar to Amartya Sen's (2014) observation that freedom begets other freedoms, mobility begets other forms of mobility. Without knowing something of the conditions of life in another place, one is unlikely to move there. Without the means to transport one's self, goods, and information (trucks, motorbikes, feet, containers, mobile phones), mobility cannot occur.

Breaking down mobilities into people, things, and information and examining the relationships between them is useful because different kinds of mobility have varying consequences for people and society. To analyze these effects in financial innovation, I discuss mobility in terms of three types: product mobility, human mobility, and information mobility.

With respect to *product mobility*, there is considerable scholarship in anthropology, sociology, and economics on how the mobility of consumer products can increase life quality and lower costs in some circumstances, but decrease well-being and exacerbate inequalities when people cannot access the objects and resources they need (Gupta and Ferguson, 1997; Isherwood and Douglas, 1979; Miller, 1987).

Similarly, *human mobility* can enhance access to financial services and sources of income, such as better wages or remittances of money from family who have migrated (Bastia, 2013; Hobbs and Jameson, 2012; Norris, 2001; Vertovec and Cohen, 1999). Conversely, immigrants may find themselves socially ostracized or financially excluded.

Information mobility (Dodgson *et al.*, 2013; Gathergood, 2012) has critical implications for decision-making, choice, and life chances, such as choosing the right products or complaining about a service. However, too much information, the circulation of incorrect information, or a lack of information can pose a burden or increase the gap between those who benefit and those who do not.

Information mobility has been examined with respect to the resurgence of the "sharing economy" (e.g. P2P insurance), the effects of too much information on product choice, misinformation or incorrect information, privacy issues, the rise of financial education applications on smartphones, and being on the wrong side of the "digital divide."

3.1. *The impacts of financial mobility*

I now turn to how these forms of mobility can impact consumers of financial services. Table 1 presents a range of issues that can occur due to increased mobility. Note that this list is by no means exhaustive; its purpose is to simply illustrate some of the effects of financial mobility.

Table 1. Benefits and risks of increasing mobility in consumer finance.

	Rewards	Risks
Product mobility	More product choice More provider choice Ease of transactions	Difficult to regulate products across jurisdictions Increased risk of fraud Potential increase in the "digital divide"
Human mobility	Human migration has increased remittances, a significant component of GDP in many countries Human mobility can encourage product uptake	Security risks in managing finances while on the move domestically and internationally Living across national borders can complicate household financial management, e.g. taxes, pensions, etc.
Information mobility	Greater ability to compare products Access to peer reviews of products Assist to financial literacy	Too many choices can make decisions harder Product information can be misleading or false Inadequate financial literacy can cancel positive effects

Moreover, we need to take into account how these mobilities intersect. As I mentioned earlier, at times mobility along one axis might counter immobility along another axis, such as when a person is able to send remittances rather than travel themselves (Horst and Taylor, 2018). At other times, forms of mobility combine to increase risk, such as experiencing credit card fraud while traveling. For this reason, I have detailed some of the major problems that arise from these mobilities, indicating where the intersections occur.

3.1.1. *Information and choice*

As I have mentioned, part of the promise of FinTech is giving consumers more information and more options. Yet many research studies show that an abundance of information or options can work against consumers' interests (Thompson *et al.*, 2005). When faced with many options or too much information, consumers often decide to make no choice at all: they will walk away empty-handed. This "decision fatigue" or "information fatigue" also affects consumers of financial products. Insurance companies have long been well acquainted with this conundrum. Consumers' assessments of insurance products heavily depend on a few key pieces of information, especially price and the general purpose of the coverage (e.g. travel) (Mayer, 2007). However, Mayer notes that consumers in the US who search for insurance online find it difficult to compare what different insurance companies are offering and may abandon their search or delay purchase. As a result, many insurance companies prefer to call customers to finish the sale as this results in a greater rate of sales success.

A similar effect is found with respect to pensions. Pensions communications are of high volume, and consumers receive them through multiple channels: newsletters, annual reports, websites, mobile apps, videos, and many other media. Research shows that a high number of customers fail to find the pensions information they need. In the Netherlands, legislation requires pensions communications to be layered in a format called "Pensions 1-2-3." Communications are broken up into three levels of complexity. When a customer joins a pensions provider, they are sent basic information about their pension plan. This is the first layer. The second and third layers contain more detailed and complex information, and customers can access this through multiple channels. However, some researchers have found that this layering is not helping customers to find information. Researcher Louise Nell (2017) argues in her PhD thesis on Dutch consumers that the problem is not the layering itself, but that customers are struggling to navigate through the layers. She says that the menus and interfaces are generally not easy to use, and that consumers are given access to far too much information. Each individual channel or media must provide a good user experience, and the entire multichannel environment needs to be designed with the customer journey in mind. It is also important to "push" information to consumers (bringing it to their attention through emails, social media, calls, and so on) rather than rely on them to "pull" it (making information available and expecting consumers to find it).

Today, consumers are using a much greater variety of financial tools than in the past, and we receive information about them through multiple channels. In many ways, this "multichannel banking" fits with consumers' behavior: we tend to use multiple devices and communicate on multiple channels, so it makes sense to provide services and information through a range of platforms. However, it is difficult for people to understand their overall financial position when their information is stored in different places (e.g. multiple investments, debts, savings, etc.). As a result, in the financial world there is a shift toward centralizing information is one of the most promising ways to help people find information. Financial service providers are investing heavily into dashboards, applications, and websites to aggregate information from different providers, with insurance and pensions leading the way. However, to date there is very little research done on how effective these aggregators are overall for people's financial well-being. More research is needed in the area.

3.1.2. *Making quality decisions*

Closely related to the problem of choice is the problem of decision-making. Having instant access to global financial services can be great for consumers, but it can also be dangerous. What happens when people can use instant payments to make purchases from home at any time of the day? What about when people can apply for credit online? Many people consistently make sensible decisions, but some find themselves with purchases that they regret, or worse, burdened with unmanageable debt (Davies *et al.*, n.d.; Deville, 2015).

Closely related to choice is the issue of transaction costs. Even if people have the technical capability to learn to use new products, they may not be willing to invest the time and energy needed. As I have argued elsewhere (Taylor and Lynch, 2014), there are many reasons why people are not motivated to learn to use new products. People lead busy lives and simply do not feel that the benefits of adopting a new product will be worth the time and effort. They may already feel overloaded with products and prefer to simplify their financial management. Switching providers might save money, but it can drastically increase transaction costs. Moreover, many people have personalized, trusting relationships with their financial service providers. Buying financial services from a number of providers can lower consumer confidence in the product's value and quality.

3.1.3. *Exclusion*

The reverse of this problem is a lack of access to digital devices and the Internet. A large portion of the world's population is still excluded from most financial services because they lack access to hardware or telecommunications infrastructure. It is estimated that smartphone penetration will reach 30.5% in 2017,[4] which means that most of the world's population do not have ready access to most financial services. Instead, mobile money has been promoted as a way to solve this problem, since it does not rely on smartphones or the Internet (Maurer, 2015). People can use any ordinary mobile handset to make a range of transactions. This is a compelling example of how "digital finance" can benefit from relatively low-tech solutions. However, infrastructural problems mean that, in many

---

[4]Smartphone user penetration as percentage of total global population from 2014 to 2019, Statista, http://www.statista.com/statistics/203734/global-smartphone-penetration-per-capita-since-2005/

countries, maintaining a phone can be unreliable, such as when people do not have electricity at home (Taylor *et al.*, 2007).

3.1.4. *Usability and literacy*

Another issue for consumers is learning to use new products and services, especially digital ones. Finances are notoriously confusing for non-specialists. Pre-digital, most people already struggled to make budgets, remember their bank card PINs (also an information issue), understand loan terms, or make informed decisions about their pension schemes. Post-digital, financial management becomes even more complex, especially for people with low levels of technological literacy (Taylor and Horst, 2017).

This "digital divide" was made evident with the shift to multichannel banking. In the UK, for example, many customers are slow in adopting multichannel banking, engage in low levels of account switching, and prefer to do their banking in person in high street branches.[5] However, the UK also boasts large numbers of early adopters and acts as a testing ground for innovative products.[6] The first group tend to be the elderly and those with less education; the latter tend to be younger, educated professionals. This wide gulf has some interesting by-products, including a boutique bank in Harrods that emphasizes its personal, in-branch service. However, such boutique services are marketed to wealthy, urban elders, not to the majority.

Many of these tools have the potential to improve financial literacy. For example, wealth calculators and investment tools can help people to learn about budgeting, interest rates, and so on. Other financial tools may render financial literacy less necessary — e.g. robo-advice and pension dashboards can help consumers make

---

[5] According to the Competition and Markets Authority, rates of account switching for UK current accounts are just 3%: Personal current accounts and SME banking, CMA, 18 July 2014.

[6] Some of these are bank-specific, such as Barclays Pingit. Others are used by multiple banks, such as Paym, which was developed by the UK Payments Council. Yet others are offered by non-bank providers, including SumUp, Intuit Pay, and the World First Money Transfer App.

decisions without understanding the financial calculations that undergird them. However, the new generation of financial tools also brings the concept of "financial literacy" into question. Given that new products and services are appearing on the market every day, our definition of "financial literacy" should also measure whether people adequately understand the products and services they are using. Given that few people read products' terms and conditions, most likely they do not. In a sense, then, this move toward automation and rapid solutions in FinTech may be reducing overall financial literacy.

3.1.5. Security and fraud

Security and fraud are two more issues that are complicated by digital finance. Digital finance certainly decreases the risk of robbery and fraud compared to cash as it adds extra layers of security and ties accounts to personal identities. Yet there are also plenty of avenues for theft or fraud. One well-known phenomenon is having one's credit card "swiped" and the details used for other transactions. In some countries, mobile money has also been a target of fraud and theft in various guises (Matinde, 2014; Ogwal, 2014). The simplest kind of theft occurs when an agent asks a customer to hand over their phone to complete a transaction on their behalf, and instead sends money to their own account.

Financial fraud is not limited to mainstream formal services. Bitcoin, the best-known cryptocurrency, has been subject to fraud on more than one high-profile occasion (Chester, 2016). As technology grows more complex, so do the means by which fraud is conducted. But many of the old problems remain, such as people storing their PINs in their wallets along with their bank cards. In fact, this kind of problem increases when people have more products, since they have more login details to remember. At the end of the day, technological sophistication cannot outrun ordinary human fallacy — and more choices can make it worse.

3.1.6. Infrastructure and regulation

While many financial products are now made to operate across borders, infrastructure remains surprisingly inadequate. Most international travelers will have encountered problems using bank cards when outside their home country. This problem is exacerbated for people who live on (and across) national borders. For example, Limburg, one of the first official Euro zones, includes parts of Belgium, The Netherlands, and Germany. Many people in the area commute daily across the borders, perhaps living in one country, working in a second, and sending their children to school in a third. This can create problems with all kinds of consumer finance products and services, such as paying taxes, using transport cards, and managing pension funds.

The accessibility of financial services across international borders can also make the industry difficult to regulate and police, since consumers often make purchases from outside their national legal jurisdiction. It is impossible for a regulatory body in, say, France, to regulate a product emanating out of the US, and vice versa, unless international agreements are in place. Even when cooperation between governing bodies is well established, regulation can be difficult, since new products and providers are entering the market all the time. It is also difficult for consumers to seek redress if there is a problem with their product or service.

4. Moving Forward

These are just a few of the many real and potential risks facing consumers of digital finance products today. We must also consider who is most at risk. We have already noted that most people struggle to understand finances, even when all their products and services come from one single provider. To a certain extent, then, we should treat everybody as at-risk. However, there are certainly social groups who will face greater risks than others when engaging new products and services.

First, there are the early adopters. They may seem like a strange group to identify as at-risk, since they are technologically savvy and would seem to be one of the groups least at risk. However, they are at the frontline of adoption and are therefore the first to engage with new products and services that may not have been properly tested, assessed, or regulated. Second, there are people who have limited literacy of some kind, such as textual, numerical, financial, or tech-nological. These include groups that are not technologically savvy, such as the elderly; people whose first language is not the national language; and people who have low levels of education. A third group is those who are exposed to risk due to a higher level of socio-economic marginalization. This includes people who take on debt to cope with poverty, or who purchase financial products from uncerti-fied providers because they cannot afford more expensive products. This is just a small selection of possible at-risk groups, and who is "at risk" will differ from place to place. Given the complexity of digital services and their adoption, we cannot assume that we know who will face the highest level of risk.

How can we stay abreast of the issues that consumers face in an increasingly mobile world of money and finance? The digitization of consumer finance presents methodological issues for tracking changes in consumer behavior. New financial products are appear-ing every day, meaning that data are not up-to-date. Furthermore, diversity in product use is not accurately reflected in statistics, since "traditional" modes of payment such as a credit card are used to purchase further consumer finance products (e.g. buying online insurance, sending money, depositing money in an e-wallet). We therefore need to be prepared to draw upon multiple methods from our research toolboxes (Taylor and Lynch, 2020).[7] We cannot assume that either qualitative or quantitative methods will give us the answers we need. Data analysis can be a wonderful way to spot big-picture trends and tell us *what* is happening, while qualitative research can tell us *why* people are behaving in certain ways, or pro-vide early information about changes in the market.[8]

---

[7]See also the Consumer Finance Research Methods Project, Institute for Money, Technology and Financial Inclusion (IMTFI), University of California Irvine, http://www.imtfi.uci.edu/cfrmp.php
[8]Central banks and other financial institutions routinely compensate for "data lag" by conducting qualitative research, especially in times of rapid change (Holmes, 2013).

Moreover, research needs to be future-facing. We need to both generate insights into changing consumer behavior and keep a bird's-eye view on the development of the market overall. This will assist us to build a picture of the risks likely to arise in the near future. Researchers, practitioners, and regulators need to be aware that consumer finance product consumption today is taking place in a complex global market and design their research and policy accordingly to protect consumers. Solid research will inform us of what kinds of interventions are needed, how regulation and policy might respond, and in what ways we need to accommodate people's existing practices.

Acknowledgments

This chapter partially draws upon work carried out between 2011–2017 while the author was a post-doctoral researcher at the Instituto de Ciências Sociais, University of Lisbon, Portugal. The research was supported by a Research Fellow grant from the Fundação para a Ciência e a Tecnologia. The chapter builds on a working paper published with the Community Development Investment Centre at the Reserve Bank of San Francisco. The author would like to thank Alexia Maddox for her excellent comments on a draft version.

References

Ang, I. (1994). Globalisation and culture. *Continuum*, 8(2), 323–325.
Appadurai, A. (ed.) (1988). *The Social Life of Things: Commodities in Cultural Perspective* (Cambridge University Press, Cambridge).
Archibugi, D., Howells, J., & Michie, J. (eds.) (1999). *Innovation Policy in a Global Economy* (Cambridge University Press, Cambridge).
Armano, G., & Javarone, M. A. (2017). The beneficial role of mobility for the emergence of innovation. *Scientific Reports*, 7(1), 1781.
Bastia, T. (ed.) (2013). *Migration and Inequality*. Vol. 100 (Routledge, London and New York).
Bauman, Z. (2013). *Liquid Modernity* (John Wiley and Sons, Hoboken, NJ).

Black, J. (2008). Forms and Paradoxes of Principles Based Regulation. LSE Law, Society and Economy Working Papers 13/2008. London School of Economics and Political Science.

Bourdieu, P. (1984). *Distinction: A Social Critique of the Judgement of Taste.* (Routledge, London and New York).

Brettell, C. B., & Hollifield, J. F. (eds.) (2014). *Migration Theory: Talking Across Disciplines* (Routledge, London and New York).

Brettell, C. B., & Hollifield, J. F. (eds.) (2013). Theorizing migration in anthropology: The social construction of networks, identities, communities, and globalscapes. In *Migration Theory* Brettell, C.B. and Hollifield, J.F. (eds.) (Routledge, London and New York), pp. 121–168.

Broløs, A., & Taylor, E. B. (2020). Female finance: Digital, mobile, networked. EWPN and Keen Innovation.

Bullinger, H. J., Auernhammer, K., & Gomeringer, A. (2004). Managing innovation networks in the knowledge-driven economy. *International Journal of Production Research*, 42(17), 3337–3353.

Castells, M. (1996, 2nd edn. 2009). *The Rise of the Network Society, The Information Age: Economy, Society and Culture*, Vol. I (Oxford, Malden, MA; Blackwell, UK).

Castells, M., & Cardoso, G. (eds.) (2006). *The Network Society: From Knowledge to Policy* (Johns Hopkins Center for Transatlantic Relations, Washington, DC), pp. 3–23.

Chester, J. (2016). Dealing with fraud in the bitcoin world. *Forbes*, 16 March. Retrieved from: http://www.forbes.com/sites/jonathanchester/2016/03/16/dealing-with-fraud-in-the-bitcoin-world/#102ac2711b40 (Accessed on 7 July 2021).

Collins, D., Morduch, J., Rutherford, S. & Ruthven, O. (2009). *Portfolios of the Poor: How the World's Poor Live on $2 a Day* (Princeton University Press, Princeton, NJ).

Deville, J. (2015). *Lived Economies of Default: Consumer Credit, Debt Collection and the Capture of Affect* (Routledge, London and New York).

Demirjuc-Kunt, A. (2012). Measuring financial exclusion: How many people are unbanked? CGAP, 24 April. Retrieved from: http://www.cgap.org/blog/measuring-financial-exclusion-how-many-people-are-unbanked

Dhanaraj, C., & Parkhe, A. (2006). Orchestrating innovation networks. *Academy of Management Review*, 31(3), 659–669.

Dodgson, M., Gann, D., Wladawsky-Berger, I., & George, G. (2013). *From the Digital Divide to Inclusive Innovation: The Case of Digital Money* (RSA, Singapore).

Felsenstein, D. (2011). Human capital and labour mobility determinants of regional innovation. In *The Handbook of Regional Innovation and Growth* (Edward Elgar, Cheltenham), pp. 119–131.

Ferguson, N. (2008). *The Ascent of Money: A Financial History of the World* (Penguin, London).

Frantz, P., & Instefjord, N. (2018). Regulatory competition and rules/principles-based regulation. *Journal of Business Finance and Accounting*, 45(7–8), 818–838.

Fry, H. (2018). *Hello World: How to be Human in the Age of the Machine* (Random House, New York).

Gathergood, J. (2012). Self-control, financial literacy and consumer over-indebtedness. *Journal of Economic Psychology*, 33(3), 590–602.

Giddens, A. (2013). *The Consequences of Modernity* (John Wiley and Sons, Hoboken, NJ).

Glick Schiller, N., & Caglar, A. (2010). *Locating Migration: Rescaling Cities and Migrants* (Cornell University Press, New York).

Glick Schiller, N., & Salazar, N. B. (2013). Regimes of mobility across the globe. *Journal of Ethnic and Migration Studies*, 39(2), 183–200.

Gomber, P., Koch, J. A., & Siering, M. (2017). Digital finance and FinTech: Current research and future research directions. *Journal of Business Economics*, 87(5), 537–580.

Gorin, C. (2017). Skilled mobility, networks and the geography of innovation, Doctoral dissertation, Université de Lyon.

Gupta, A., & Ferguson, J. (eds.) (1997). *Culture, Power, Place: Explorations in Critical Anthropology* (Duke University Press, Durham, NC).

Hellström, T. (2003). Systemic innovation and risk: Technology assessment and the challenge of responsible innovation. *Technology in Society*, 25(3), 369–384.

Horst, H. A., & Taylor, E. B. (2018). Objects of mobility: The role of the mobile phones on the border of Haiti and the Dominican Republic. In *Linguistic and Material Intimacies of Cell Phones*, Bell, J. A. and Kuipers, J. C. (eds.) (Routledge, London and New York), pp. 52–68.

Horst, H., & Miller, D. (2006). *The Cell Phone: An Anthropology of Communication* (Berg, Oxford).

Hobbs, A. W. and Jameson, K. P. (2012). Measuring the effect of bi-directional migration remittances on poverty and inequality in Nicaragua. *Applied Economics*, 44(19), 2451–2460.

Holmes, D. R. (2013). *Economy of Words: Communicative Imperatives in Central Banks* (University of Chicago Press, Chicago, IL).

Isherwood, B., & Douglas, M. (1979). *The World of Goods: Towards an Anthropology of Consumption* (Routledge, London and New York).

Kalir, B., & Wissink, L. (2016). The deportation continuum: Convergences between state agents and NGO workers in the Dutch deportation field. *Citizenship Studies*, 20(1), 34–49.

Kusimba, S., Kunyu, G., & Gross, E. (2018). Social networks of mobile money in Kenya. In *Money at the Margins: Global Perspectives on Technology, Financial*

Inclusion, and Design, Vol. 6, Maurer, B., Musaraj, S., & Small, I. (eds.) (Berghahn, New York), pp. 52–68.

Lee, I., & Shin, Y. J. (2018). Fintech: Ecosystem, business models, investment decisions, and challenges. *Business Horizons*, 61(1), 35–46.

Matinde, V. (2014). Mobile money fraud 'on the rise' in Kenya. *IT Web Africa*. Retrieved from: http://www.itwebafrica.com/security/515-kenya/233054-mobile-money-fraud-on-the-rise-in-kenya; https://itweb.africa/content/KWEBbvyZgVz7mRjO (Accessed on 7 July 2021).

Maurer, B. (2015). *How Would You Like to Pay? How Technology is Changing the Future of Money* (Duke University Press, Durham, NC).

Maurer, B., Musaraj, S., & Small, I. (eds.) (2018). *Money at the Margins: Global Perspectives on Technology, Financial Inclusion, and Design* (Berghahn, New York).

Mayer, R. N. (2007). Online insurance. In *Handbook of Consumer Finance*, Xiao, J. J. (ed.) (Springer, New York), pp. 52–68.

McFall, L. (2014). *Devising Consumption: Cultural Economies of Insurance, Credit and Spending* (Routledge, London and New York).

McKinsey (2013). The triple transformation: Achieving a sustainable business model. Retrieved from: http://www.mckinsey.com/industries/financial-services/our-insights/the-search-for-a-sustainable-banking-model (Accessed on 7 July 2021).

Miguélez, E., & Moreno, R. (2013). Research networks and inventors' mobility as drivers of innovation: Evidence from Europe. *Regional Studies*, 47(10), 1668–1685.

Miller, D. (1994). *Modernity: An Ethnographic Approach* (Berg, Oxford).

Miller, D. (1987). *Material Culture and Mass Consumption* (Blackwell, Oxford).

Mintz, S. W. (1986). *Sweetness and Power: The Place of Sugar in Modern History* (Penguin, London).

Nell, L. (2017). Multichannel pension communication: An integrated perspective on policies, practices, and literacy demands. PhD thesis, Utrecht University.

Nicoletti, B. (2017). *Future of FinTech* (Palgrave Macmillan, London).

Norris, P. (2000). The worldwide digital divide. In *Paper for the Annual Meeting of the Political Studies Association of the UK, London School of Economics and Political Science* (pp. 10–13).

Norris, P. (2001). *Digital Divide: Civic Engagement, Information Poverty, and the Internet Worldwide* (Cambridge University Press).

Ogwal, I. (2014). Survival of the fittest: The evolution of frauds in Uganda's mobile money market (Part-I). MicroSave. Retrieved from: http://blog.microsave.net/survival-of-the-fittest-the-evolution-of-frauds-in-ugandas-mobile-money-market-part-i/

Pippa, N. (2000). The worldwide digital divide: Information poverty, the Internet and development. In Annual Meeting of the Political Studies Association of the UK, London School of Economic and Political Science (pp. 10–13).

Polanyi, K., & MacIver, R. M. (1944). *The Great Transformation*, Vol. 2 (Beacon Press, Boston), p. 145.

Sen, A. (2014). Development as freedom (1999). *The globalization and development reader: Perspectives on development and global change*, 525.

Sheller, M. and Urry, J. (2006). The new mobilities paradigm. *Environment and planning A*, 38(2), 207–226.

Singh, S. (2016). *Money, Migration, and Family* (Palgrave Macmillan, New York).

Simich, L., & Andermann, L. (eds.) (2014). *Refuge and Resilience: Promoting Resilience and Mental Health Among Resettled Refugees and Forced Migrants*, Vol. 7 (Springer, Berlin).

Rooney, D., Mandeville, T., & Kastelle, T. (2013). Abstract knowledge and reified financial innovation: Building wisdom and ethics into financial innovation networks. *Journal of Business Ethics*, 118(3), 447–459.

Roodman, D. (2012). *Due Diligence: An Impertinent Inquiry into Microfinance* (CGD Books, London).

Taylor, E. B. (2018). Mobility, inequality and choice: Circulation on the border of Haiti and the Dominican Republic. *Transitions: Journal of Transient Migration*, 2(1), 65–80.

Taylor, E. B. (2017a). Money in a mobile age: Emerging trends in consumers' financial practices. Community Development Investment Centre, Reserve Bank of San Francisco, Working Paper 2017-03.

Taylor, E. B. (2017b). Consumer finance in a mobile age: Methods for researching changing user behaviour. *EPIC: Perspectives*, 197–215.

Taylor, E. B. (2015). Mobile money: Financial globalization, alternative, or both? In *MoneyLab Reader: An Intervention in Digital Economy*, Lovink, G., Tkacz, N., & de Vries, P. (eds.) (Institute of Network Cultures, Amsterdam). pp. 244–256.

Taylor, E. B. (2013). Amsterdam: A money laboratory for centuries. Retrieved from: https://erinbtaylor.com/entry/amsterdam-a-money-laboratory-for-centuries (Accessed on 7 July 2021).

Taylor, E. B., Baptiste, E., & Horst, H. A. (2011). *Mobile Banking in Haiti: Potentials and Challenges* (IMTFI, University of California Irvine, Irvine, CA).

Taylor, E. B., & Brøløs, A. (2020). Financial technology and the gender gap: Designing & delivering services for women. In *Women, Consumption and Paradox: Towards A More Humanistic Approach to Consumption*, de Waal Malefyt, T., & McCabe, M. (eds.) (Routledge, London and New York), pp. 103–128.

Taylor, E. B., & Horst, H. A. (2017). Designing financial literacy in Haiti. In *Design Anthropology: Object Cultures in Transition*, Clarke, A. J. (ed.) (Springer, New York).

Taylor, E. B., & Lynch, G. (2020). *Consumer Finance Research Methods Toolkit* (Institute for Money, Technology and Financial Inclusion, Irvine, CA).

Taylor, E. B., & Lynch, G. (2014). *Global Consumer Finance: Sharing Knowledge for Better Research* (IMTFI, University of California Irvine, Irvine, CA).

Thoma, M. (2005). How fast are debit and credit cards replacing checks? *Economist's View*, 11 September. Retrieved from: http://economistsview.type-pad.com/economistsview/2005/09/how_fast_are_de.html (Accessed on 7 July 2021).

Thompson, D. V., Hamilton, R. W. & Rust, R. T. (2005). Feature fatigue: When product capabilities become too much of a good thing. *Journal of Marketing Research*, **42**(4), 431–442.

Vacheron, P. A. (2015). Instant payments at Point of Sale: Overcoming customer and merchant barriers. *EPC Newsletter*, 27.

Vertovec, S., & Cohen, R. (eds.) (1999). *Migration, Diasporas, and Transnationalism* (Edward Elgar Publishing, Cheltenham).

World Bank. Topics in Development: Migration, Remittances, and Diaspora. Retrieved from: http://www.worldbank.org/en/topic/migrationremittances diasporaissues (Accessed on 7 July 2021).

Wyatt, S., Henwood, F., Miller, N., & Senker, P. (2000). *Technology and Inequality: Questioning the Information Society* (Psychology Press, London).

Chapter 4

Innovation with Foresight: Anticipating Alternative and Creative Responses in Strategic Organizational Decision-making

Jörn Bühring

*School of Design, The Hong Kong Polytechnic University,
Hung Hom, Kowloon, Hong Kong*
joern.buehring@polyu.edu.hk

Abstract. This chapter provides a review on key issues and their implications caused by rapidly changing business environments which have prompted a call for new strategic organizational decision-making capabilities in innovation. Looking at the problem through the lens of the financial services (FS) landscape, thematic analysis points toward traditional FS players that are faced with uncertainty and disruptions triggered by technology-enabled financial solution providers (FinTech) and their new business models devised for 21st-century client-integrated ecosystems. The analysis highlights that, amid accelerating environmental complexity, business leaders and educators are called upon to become more forward thinking and to develop their creative and strategic innovation capabilities. Considering the foresight and design literature, the hypothesis is that a systematic and collaborative futures thinking function can improve the strategic innovation direction of the enterprise. This chapter is divided into five sections that describe, at a high level, the FS landscape in the context of China; introduce the role of strategic foresight and design in innovation; and outline the four stages of integrating their synergies, which are exemplified by stories of real-case scenarios derived from FS futures studies over the medium-term time horizon.

Keywords. Forecasting; futuring; futures thinking; foresight; strategic design; scenario planning; decision-making.

1. Introduction

Over the past two decades, the financial services (FS) industry, comprising banking, payments, capital markets, insurance, wealth management, and real estate, has been experiencing major forces of change, including changing consumer and user behaviors, technological advances, and disruptive business models (Beckett *et al.*, 2000; Diaz-Rainey *et al.*, 2015; Salampasis *et al.*, 2017). Meanwhile, technology-based businesses that compete against, enable, or collaborate with traditional financial institutions (i.e. FinTech) are experiencing rapid growth worldwide. In fact, globalization and decades of banking deregulations have resulted in the blurring of banking, insurance, and capital market boundaries, which are further causes of innovations that create uncertainty and other complications. Indeed, legacy players in the FS industry are showing signs of losing their competitive edge, while FinTech companies are deploying advanced technologies, innovative business models, and value created for a social consumer to disrupt and fundamentally change the way FS are being delivered (Chishti and Barberis, 2016). Against this backdrop of inevitable change, stakeholders responsible for the growth and indeed survival of their organizations have to anticipate alternative and creative responses alongside these evolving trends and spot the early signs (weak signals) that may inform discontinuities, which could jeopardize an organization's strategic direction (Saritas and Smith, 2011).

The need for innovation and growth is widely reported across all sectors of the economy, and the axiom is that organizations have to respond to change and uncertainty in fundamentally new ways if they are to be successful in the future. Globalization, digitization, commoditization, and politicization are among the forces playing out in the firm's external business environment; amid accelerating environmental complexity and uncertainty, a more strategic approach to innovation is needed in order to anticipate rapid social, technological, and environmental change (Buehring and Liedtka, 2018; Buhring and Koskinen, 2017).

Such major hurdles have prompted a call for business leaders and educators to become more forward-thinking and to develop the organization's innovation and creative capabilities to remain viable in the long term (Koen *et al.*, 2002; Kock *et al.*, 2015; van der Laan and Yap, 2016; Meroni, 2008). As scholars who have studied innovation success factors emphasize, being successful in the long term requires an active innovation culture, a robust and disciplined planning approach, and powerful tools that are commonly understood by diverse specialist teams (Hoorn, 2014; Kumar, 2004; Godet and Roubelat, 1996). Areas deeply concerned with these challenges, in both theory and practice, are foresight and design. In each field, scholars who focus on thinking about the future are devoting increased attention to exploring the important question of what constitutes the most effective organizational processes for crafting a successful long-term direction (Hamel, 2002; Hofer and Schendel, 1978; Heskett, 2009; Slaughter, 2002; Rohrbeck *et al.*, 2015; Wilkinson *et al.*, 2014).

Looking across the foresight and design literature, the hypothesis is that a new strategic and collaborative futures thinking function can improve the strategic decision-making capabilities of the enterprise by combining foresight and design in ways that embrace their synthesis (Buhring and Koskinen, 2017; Buhring, 2017; Liedtka, 2017). Similarly, while design and innovation approaches more often focus on solving problems in today's world and the immediate future, strategic foresight is applied when developing alternative scenarios for the longer-term future in which these solutions will exist (Slaughter, 2002; Bishop *et al.*, 2007). Indeed, building common grounds between design, innovation, and foresight and their respective theoretical and practical applications has been identified as an important strategic collaboration in business (Margolin, 2007).

This chapter aims to provide a high-level introduction to strategic foresight and design principles relevant to the innovation conversation, and translating these from abstract ideas into practical techniques and approaches. To this end, this chapter is complimented with stories from design-inspired foresight research and futures applications that offer the reader thought-provoking insights into FS futures scenarios to the year 2030.

The chapter is structured in four major sections; it begins with a brief overview (Section 2) of the FS, wealth management, and private banking landscape and the challenges faced by rapidly evolving 21st century ecosystems. Contextually, the overview is purposely placed within the Asian Century phenomena (Mahbubani, 2008) and informed by the China perspective. In Section 3, the role of strategic foresight and design is introduced, and how the integration of both disciplines can provide the organization with capabilities to anticipate alternative and creative responses in strategic innovation decision-making. From this stance, in Section 4, the integration of foresight with design principles is presented through four stages of conceptual factors that can inform strategic decision-making in innovation: (1) insights and alignment around current reality; (2) facilitating the design with foresight conversation; (3) thinking of and specifying alternative and desirable futures; and (4) active experimentation to gather new knowledge and learning. In Section 5, an understanding of ways in which innovation can benefit from applying the synergies between strategic foresight and design is further demonstrated through stories (case study exemplars) from FS futures research.

2. FS Landscape and 21st-century FinTech Ecosystems (China)

Globalization and decades of banking deregulations have resulted in the blurring of banking, insurance, and capital market boundaries, resulting in legacy players in the FS industry losing their competitive edge (Shiller, 2009).

In many countries, the main features (products and services) of the FS industry in general, and the banking sector in particular, comprise the central bank and depository organizations such as banks, building societies, credit unions, general financiers, and others involved in asset management. These can be summarized into four segments:

- Financial enterprises or institutions (i.e. banks, private banking, insurance companies)
- Regulatory bodies — financial markets (i.e. bonds, equities, and currency markets)
- Participants (i.e. issuers and investors)
- Payment systems (i.e. check, cash, and online payment and its participants).

The interrelations of these four FS segments are the facilitation of funds available for different activities such as investment, transactions, personal use, and savings. Fundamentally, the FS industry engages in financial transactions and creates, liquidates, purchases, and sells financial assets (insurance, bonds, securities, etc.). Some of the inherent comparative advantages that have sustained these institutions in their dominant position over the past several decades are being eroded due to globalization and the declining entry barriers; post–2008 Global Financial Crisis (GFC) regulatory changes; advances in information and delivery technologies; and factors that have brought about strategic objectives by the banks themselves. For example, while investment-related services were previously handled by investment banks, just as insurance-related services were facilitated by insurance banks, this was due to higher restrictions and regulations imposed on banks, securities firms, and insurance companies that prevented them to engage in more than one of these three lines of business within the same organization.

In the US, the introduction of the Gramma–Leach–Bliley Act of 1999 had these barriers that once disassociated different services removed, and an integrated banking system came into existence (Collinsa et al., 2003). Conversely, rapid urban population growth and development, which in turn drove increasing demands for FS, have encouraged many established financial institutions to alter in terms of size and geographic expansions.

China's financial system, compared with those of developed countries, has experienced fundamental changes to its once single bank structure, which was the People's Bank of China (PBOC). The Chinese government owned the PBOC during the period from 1950 to 1978, which, under the Ministry of Finance, controlled approximately 93% of the total financial assets of the country (Allen et al., 2007). China's remarkable growth from one of the world's poorest countries to the second largest economy in just 30 years, was fundamentally reformed by its market, legal, and financial systems, which have since provided considerable expansion into specialized banking businesses and banking and non-banking financial intermediaries. From the inception of China's stock market in the 1990s, to China's entry into the World Trade Organization (WTO) in late 2001, a new era of financial reforms has been instrumental in China's relaxing of restrictions on foreign ownership of its FS institutions, which was announced by the China Banking and Insurance Regulatory Commission in August of 2017 (CBRC, 2017).

The accelerated economic growth in China has given way to wealth management (personal investment, financial advisory, and planning) and private banking (highly personalized banking relations) services. Though the concept of private banks has deep roots in Western countries, and are operated based on very well-developed business models, in the Chinese FS industry, however, private banking is a relatively new value proposition. Developing private banking services for wealthy individuals was first initiated by the Bank of China in the mid-2000s, thereafter, it was adopted by other domestic banks. With the growth of wealth, Chinese High-Net-Worth Individuals (HNWIs) were demanding more wealth management services, which encouraged further growth of private banking systems.

Financial technology is the combination of FS and information technology, or FinTech, which has a long history dating back to the first period of financial globalization when transatlantic transmission cables were introduced in the 19th and 20th centuries. In the 21st century, a new era of FinTech has emerged from the aftermath of the 2008 GFC, which gave rise to end-to-end processing of transactions enabled through the Internet and the use of cloud services. Consumers of FinTech services have since come to expect seamless onboarding to allow, for example, digital loan approvals, free person-to-person payments, and online, cashless transaction solutions. Consequently, such innovative new approaches have posed considerable challenges to regulators and traditional market players alike.

Similarly, traditional banking businesses were significantly impacted by the rapid technological developments in the non-bank, high-tech industries, which further accelerated after China's joining of the WTO. Although the Bank of China started to extend its business to the Internet in 1996, online and telephone banking services rapidly expanded throughout the Mainland, which, resulting from its WTO membership, allowed foreign banks to leverage their competitive advantages they had built through information and network technologies. In present-day China (in 2019), client-integrated ecosystems are provided by key players such as Baidu, Alibaba, and Tencent (BAT), each offering multipurpose services across interconnected platforms that are increasingly expanding beyond its shores. In China alone, there are nearly 800 million active monthly users reliant on such services platforms, and their numbers are growing. The notion of interconnected ecosystems is a relatively recent phenomenon; since 2011, capabilities from various aspects, e.g. ride-sharing, messaging, directions, and medical services, have been aggregated and integrated into single-entry-point applications, such as WeChat™. China's AliPay™, a third-party payment and lifestyle platform operated by Ant Financial (Alibaba Group), is able to process more than 10 billion transactions per day without being a bank (Kshetri, 2016; Arner *et al.*, 2016).

The possibilities for ecosystem-driven incumbents (exemplified by BAT) to engage and facilitate client access to these ecosystems are almost unparalleled to anywhere else in the world as it manifests itself in the many aspects of consumers' daily lives. Such are the disruptions for traditional banks — they have to contend with multiple challenges and uncertainties tied to regulations, legacy systems, emerging technology enablers, new market entrants and their disruptive business models, along with consumers seeking *anytime, anywhere, anyhow* financial and wealth management services.

Disciplines deeply concerned with addressing these challenges, in both theory and practice, are strategic foresight and design. As Section 3 will highlight, scholars in foresight and design and practitioners in strategic planning and innovation are devoting increased attention to exploring the important question of what constitutes the most effective organizational processes for crafting a successful long-term direction (Hamel, 2009; Hofer, 1978; Heskett, 2009; Slaughter, 2002; Rohrbeck *et al.*, 2015).

3. The Role of Strategic Foresight and Design in Innovation

Across all sectors of the economy, the axiom is that organizations have to respond to change in fundamental new ways if they are to be successful in the future. Driven by globalization, digitization, commoditization, and politicization, business leaders are operating in an ever-more interconnected world, where few can retain a competitive edge independently of others. In this fast-past environment, however, many traditional companies in the FS sectors are still operating on the assumption of stability, despite the exponential growth and disruption caused by rapidly advancing information technologies (Reeves, 2011).

Consequently, as the business environment becomes more uncertain, the ability to monitor and make sense of change may directly impact the leader's ability to articulate a clear and compelling vision and strategy for the future of the organization (Groves, 2006). In other words, failure to anticipate the future business environment could possibly be disastrous for corporations. Equally, as companies age and grow, businesses must now continuously innovate and reinvent themselves. Reinventing, however, becomes harder as prevailing operating models and practices become deep-seated into the organizational ways of doing (Doppelt, 2017); it is this complexity which indeed becomes the barrier to change.

The organizations' innovation focus most often is directed toward short-term product and service propositions aimed at meeting current market needs (Koen *et al.*, 2002), whereas the motivation of using strategic foresight and design applied to innovation decision-making is about anticipating change in the medium- to longer-term future. Just as futurists and strategic foresight consultants conduct environmental scanning to detect new events and drivers of change over the 10-year time horizon (Day, 2006), government policy-makers and large corporations in durable goods and process industries rely on even longer-range futures thinking in their strategic planning and decision-making processes (Fuerth, 2009).

Thus, addressing the reported lack of systematic futures thinking at the strategic front end of innovation (Koen *et al.*, 2002; Eling and Herstatt, 2017), the creative use of strategic foresight with design synthesis (i.e. design foresight) (Wilkinson, 2014; Buehring and Liedtka, 2018) can better prepare organizations to deal with uncertainty over the medium time horizon (5–15 years), as Figure 1 illustrates.

3.1. *Defining strategic foresight*

The main purpose of strategic foresight is to understand the organization's environment, the driving forces behind environmental change, and the consequences of such changes that need to be

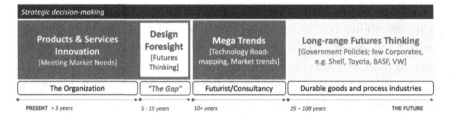

Figure 1. "Design Foresight" — addressing the systematic futures thinking gap across the medium time horizon relevant in strategic innovation decision-making.

considered in order to survive and thrive (Martin, 1995; Marsh *et al.*, 2002; Heger and Rohrbeck, 2012; Vecchiato, 2015; Adegbile *et al.*, 2017). The foresight discipline encompasses a wide range of approaches and activities designed to help business stakeholders deal with uncertainty (Inayatullah, 2008). As such, foresight is the process of systematically attempting to look into the longer-term future of science, technology, the economy, and society, which Martin (1995) considered as critical for identifying the areas of strategic research and emerging technologies capable of yielding the greatest economic and social benefits.

One of the objectives in foresight is to consider different ways in which the external environment may evolve over the medium term (5–15 years), or even longer (Slaughter, 2002; Voros, 2003; Dator, 2009). Decision-makers often start with a leading question: "what would our response to uncertainty have to be if a future were to unfold that was distinctively different from the one anticipated in the current strategic innovation plan?" To this end, researchers and foresight practitioners deploy methodologies and techniques not to better predict the future, instead, they practice foresight to become better prepared for different, or alternative futures. They express these types of inquiries in the form of futures scenario statements that help prepare for or actively shape the future (Bishop *et al.*, 2007).

The practice of foresight is effective when decision-makers expand beyond subjective views of reality and consider more closely the relationship between objective reality (fact-based, measurable, and observable) and possible futures (Mietzner and Reger, 2005). Foresight activities play an important role in the strategic decision-making processes designed to help shape the desired future. Here, Tsoukas and Shepherd (2009) propose to adopt a language and mindset that favors invention rather than navigation, which they defined as the "foresight-as-invention" paradigm. Developing a structured future thinking approach can help organizations to envision how seeds of change from today's fringes might make way into the mainstream and how, conversely, the elements from today's mainstream might fall to obsolescence. Thinking about different possibilities through futures scenario building allows decision-makers to imagine alternative futures (Figure 2) and classify them into possible (might happen), plausible (could happen), probable (likely to happen), and preferable or desirable as " wanting to happen" (Hancock and Bezold, 1993; Voros, 2001).

Consequently, the systematic approach to futures thinking is based on future scenarios that explore holistic, integrated, and alternative futures that contain tangible images of how preferable and desirable futures might be shaped.

When comparing the similarities and distinctions between strategic foresight and strategic planning, critics have pointed out weaknesses in traditional planning processes, which do not sufficiently

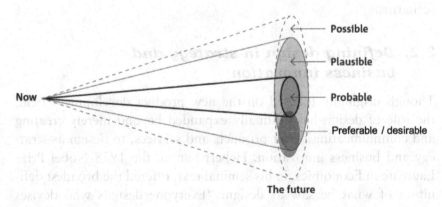

Figure 2. "Future Cone."
Source: Adapted from Voros (2003) and Hancock and Bezold (1994).

handle the complexity, discontinuities, and rapid changes in today's disruptive business environment (Marsh *et al.*, 2002; Miller and Cardinal, 1994). Both they and Vaara and Whittington (2012) highlight several important emerging areas in need of the development of better theory and practice: (1) strategy as emergent rather than planned a priori; (2) the involvement of broader groups of stakeholders in planning processes; and (3) the failure to translate strategic plans into organizational outcomes (Buehring and Liedtka, 2018).

More recently, foresight approaches have called for broader inclusion of more "non-expert" stakeholders (Cuhls, 2003), which is highly relevant to the FS industry as changing consumer and user behaviors, new technological enablers, and disruptive business models are among the major drivers of change in this traditionally conservative field of business. While preferable or desirable futures are more emotional than cognitive, Inayatullah (2007) argues for practicing futures thinking to enhance employees' confidence that they can create the future that they desire. Similarly, Wilkinson *et al.* (2014) describe a highly participatory, multi-stakeholder process they term "transformational foresight." Both they and Hines and Zindato (2016) explicitly call for greater integration of design practices in foresight work, by highlighting its more empathetic, experiential, and participatory approaches in the development of scenarios.

3.2. *Defining design in strategy and business innovation*

Though originally focused on the new product development field, the role of design has gradually expanded beyond merely creating and communicating better products and services, to design as strategy and business innovation. Hebert Simon, the 1978 Nobel Prize Laureate in Economics, in his seminal text, offered the broadest definition of what he saw as design: "Everyone designs who devises courses of action aimed at changing existing situations into preferred ones" (Simon, 1955, p. 67). Largely due to the popularity of "design thinking," a term and process propagated in the early 2000s by the innovation consultancy IDEO, design is increasingly positioned as an organizational competence, where its totality of activities spans the entire innovation ecosystem, involving interdisciplinary stakeholder teams responsible for creating sustainable value propositions that ensure the organization's future (Buhring, 2017; Lojacono and Zaccai, 2004; Bohemia *et al.*, 2004; Heskett, 2001; Boztepe, 2016; Mozota, 1998).

Design is also strategy, or strategic design, which Meroni (2008, p. 31) noted is about conferring to social and market bodies a system of rules, beliefs, values, and tools to deal with the external environment; this is especially needed for those having to deal with strategic design decisions in uncertain and turbulent times (Manzini and Meroni, 2007). Consequently, strategic design can be seen as an activity, which takes into account collective interests and values, defines strategic orientations through scenarios, and offers learning opportunities about the external environment (Cagnin, 2018).

The favorable use of design as a problem-solving approach has sparked the use of processes and applications toward transformative innovations in a global economy (Dunne and Martin, 2006; Oster, 2008; Liedtka, 1998), with the further potential for unifying interdisciplinary stakeholder conversations that enhance a collective's ability to align, learn, and change together (Liedtka, 2017). While it has been argued that design has not yet reached the same status of science, art, technology, and economics (Jonas, 2001, p. 65), Sanders (2008) later acknowledged that the design landscape in recent times has been subjected to a great deal of exploration and growth, which has contributed to conflict and confusion as to its evolving role, meaning, and identity in both practice and research. At risk of being seen as banal and inconsequential, John Heskett's (2017, p. 18) response to "what is design" was:

"… if considered seriously and used responsibly, design should be the crucial anvil on which the human environment, in all its detail, is shaped and constructed for the betterment and delight of all."

Confusion about design exists primarily on two levels: first, the wide spectrum of activities and practices to which the word is attached, and second, the varied levels at which design is practiced. As the role of design in business expands, high levels of creativity are needed to deal with complex systems and the degree to which sub-systems can be improved or rethought entirely; such complexities will determine the degree of coded knowledge and methodology required in utilizing design principles at a strategic level (Figure 3).

In dealing with complexity in theory and applications, and the context where its potential is understood and well managed, design as a strategic and professional business activity can be a powerful tool for adapting to new circumstances, and a considerable economic asset.

There are several similarities and distinctions between strategic foresight and strategic design. While each discipline has its ways of identifying and dealing with the future, strategic foresight's broad perspectives of possible, probable, and plausible futures do not get into the design of solutions, just as the focus in design is much more immediate, taking a human-centered approach which informs problem-solving from the user (needs) perspective. The overlapping

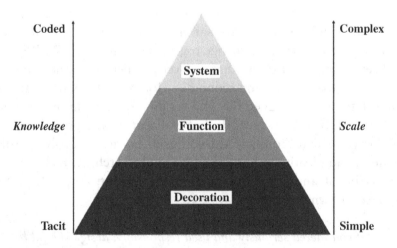

Figure 3.   Knowledge and scale of complexity in design.
Source: Heskett (2017).

considerations are most obvious in the strategic planning and visioning context, where the focus is to foster strategic innovation by
detecting early warning signs of change and giving deeper insights
into the phenomenon behind these signs.

3.3. *Anticipating alternative and creative responses in strategic organizational decision-making*

Looking across the foresight and design literature, the hypothesis is
that a new strategic and collaborative futures thinking function can
improve the strategic decision-making capabilities of the enterprise
by combining foresight and design in ways that embrace their synthesis applied to innovation (Buhring and Koskinen, 2017; Buhring,
2017; Liedtka, 2017). Specifically, the purpose of applying foresight
to strategic innovation decision-making is to develop alternative scenarios for the longer-term future in which these solutions will exist
(Slaughter, 2002; Bishop *et al.*, 2007). Building common grounds
between the strategic use of design and foresight and their respective
theoretical and practical applications, has been identified as an
important collaboration in business (Margolin, 2007; Andersen
and Andersen, 2014). Foresight provides the future context for
design and design embodies ideas and concepts by visualizing alternative and desirable futures for foresight, thus complimenting each
other to envision, inspire, experiment and communicate the direction
of where to go.

The integration of foresight with design offers the promise of
helping decision-makers deal more effectively with anticipating
change in the macro-level environments. Based on different possibilities, decision-makers can select and integrate the most preferable and
desirable future, and, looking backwards from that future to the
present, the use of backcasting (Vergragt, 2011) helps strategize a
plan for how this can be achieved (Figure 4).

In Section 4, the synergistic value of integrating strategic foresight with design is presented as starting points for entry into the
futures innovation conversation.

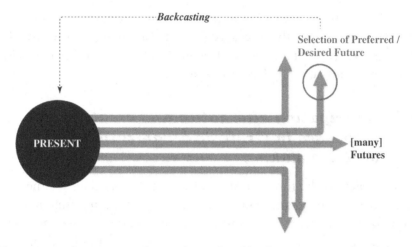

Figure 4.   Backcasting — selecting from plausible alternatives a preferred future, and developing a plan of how this can be achieved.

4. Four Stages of Integrating Foresight with Design in Strategic Organizational Decision-making

In Section 3, the linkages between strategic foresight and design, and their respective roles in business strategy and innovation, were introduced. A primary focus was placed on the need for systematic futures thinking as a transformational approach and organizational capability for producing visions of preferable/desirable futures. The integration of strategic design with foresight in decision-making can also be articulated in a four-stage conversation process, which is identified by conceptual "high-level" futures thinking factors (Figure 5).

4.1. Stage 1 — Achieving insight and alignment around current reality

The main focus in this stage is on both gaining deep and novel insights into today's challenges and customer pain points and establishing alignment across critical stakeholders about key elements of

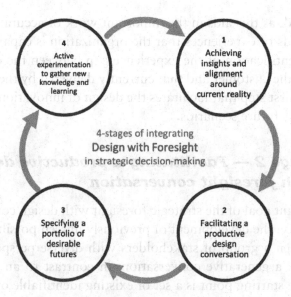

Figure 5. Four-stages of integrating design with foresight in strategic decision-making. *Source*: Buehring and Liedtka (2018).

the present situation (Wilkinson *et al.*, 2014; Gabrielli and Zoels, 2003). Here, both strategic design and foresight principles can provide important contributions, as they encourage the grounding of discussions of the future in the reality of today. This aims to accomplish two ends: first, to facilitate reframing of the initial question, by challenging decision-makers to examine the assumptions they are bringing into the definition of the problem itself, hence, opening up wider human-centric perspectives. And second, to work toward aligning the views of key stakeholders around critical innovation criteria that describe the ideal (or preferable/desirable) future, thus ensuring coherence and commitment in a more inclusive conversation across a broader group of stakeholders.

Design tools, for example, encourage innovators to pursue deeper insights into current reality (Bucolo and Matthews, 2011). This is best facilitated though first-hand ethnographic data collection techniques, as this leads to an empathetic understanding of the experiences of those to be served. Organizational capability mapping can be deployed, as this aids in the important work of accurately assessing the kinds of experiences that the organization is capable of producing. Identification of the experience gap between the experience desired by the customer and that currently delivered by the organization is the first step that facilitates the design of innovation strategies that address future scenarios.

4.2. Stage 2 — Facilitating a productive design with foresight conversation

An important goal of the strategic foresight with design conversation is emergence: the development of previously unseen possibilities that emerge when a group of stakeholders with diverse perspectives are involved in a generative conversation, in contrast to an evaluative one (whose starting point is a set of existing identifiable options). In order to accomplish this, the conversation must achieve two things: (1) find a blend of inquiry and advocacy and (2) leverage the diversity within the conversation to produce higher-order solutions rather than divisive debates (Buehring and Liedtka, 2018). The two are closely related.

An essential aspect of successful strategic foresight with design work is the engagement of critical players in the larger ecosystem, outside of the organization itself. It is through mutual learning and cooperation among these players that shaping behaviors, aimed at making preferred scenarios a reality in the future, is coordinated. However, turning the theoretical diversity these players bring into the formulation of more creative, shared scenarios requires changing the nature of the conversation itself to incorporate an increasing role for dialogue as well as debate, and for inquiry as well as advocacy. Participants in such conversations must listen to understand rather than defend, and search for possibilities rather than weaknesses. These conversations must also occur at different levels: the industry, the market, the consumer, and the organization itself, and the functional and local levels within it. It is these nested and coordinated conversations that make possible the translation of abstract strategies into actionable new ways of thinking and behaving.

4.3. Stage 3 — Specifying a portfolio of desirable futures

Whereas in strategic foresight, scenario building might tend to focus on possible and plausible futures, strategic foresight with design conversation brings a strong emphasis on specifying a set of preferred or desirable futures. As highlighted in previous sections, the intent lies more with shaping or inventing the future than merely responding to it. The emphasis here is on optionality — specifying a range of different future options, which are the "alternative futures." Strategic design tools can assist decision-makers to construct a portfolio of alternatives with an eye toward time horizons. This approach helps assumptions to surface, and the impact of developing solutions relative to ease of their implementation, with capability development a critical factor.

Strategic design also suggests that new futures, in order to become realities, must be experienced, rather than merely thought; more than cognitive, they must be vivid, personally meaningful, and compelling to the members of the organization who must adopt new behaviors in order to execute them. The idea of experiencing a new future in an emotional as well as cognitive way is grounded in an interpretive, socially constructed perspective, rather than an objectively rational one (Andrews, 2012). In other words, how to make new ideas tangible? Architects build models, and product designers construct prototypes (Buhring and Koskinen, 2017) — but prototyping a new future is more challenging to envision. This is where design's emphasis on visualization tools like storytelling and journey mapping contribute to foresight work (Sametz and Maydoney, 2003; Eggink and de la Bruheze, 2015).

4.4. Stage 4 — Active experimentation to gather new knowledge and learning

In stage 4, the conversation centers on design's emphasis on learning in action, which offers a final and powerful contribution to enhancing the strategic innovation process when used in conjunction with foresight. Specifically, assumptions underlying the future scenarios can be surfaced and tested through experiments (i.e. artefacts, prototypes, enactment, etc.) in the present. In engaging stakeholders or ecosystem players, at different levels, in the design and execution of these experiments, learning becomes ongoing and scenarios can be adjusted as real-world feedback informs the process.

5. Stories (Case Study Exemplars) of Strategic Foresight and Design Practices Relevant to Organizational Decision-making

As mentioned earlier, there is a growing awareness that business organizations, regardless of industry or size, are faced with unprecedented uncertainties over social analyses, globalization, and technology revolutions, as observed by the increasing interest in future studies. Simultaneously, a fundamental shift has emerged where access and value attributed to information is cause of an emerging social structure that presents fundamental challenges for organizations and their understanding of markets and new users within them. Against this changing business environment, organizations are required to transform themselves, rethink their business models, innovate, and envisage possible, probable, and preferable futures (see Figure 2) in order to adapt their approach to business, and indeed the ways they engage with now vastly empowered consumers.

To be successful, however, organizations must learn new management practices that enable them to look beyond the horizon and interpret trends, drivers of change, wild cards, and discontinuity, amid a constant lookout for weak signals that are often the first important indicators of looming issues and probable change. As ancient wisdom suggests, "there is no favorable wind for the man who knows not where he is going" (Seneca, 4 BC–A.D. 65).

In Sections 3 and 4 of this chapter, strategic foresight and design principles where introduced, such as crafting material visions of preferable/desirable futures. Furthermore, a four-stage conceptual process of integrating strategic foresight with design was presented to purposefully construct awareness, and conversations, of the long-term challenges and opportunities for more immediate decision-making. Consequently, organizations practicing futures thinking will have developed the capacity to identify emerging problems before they occur, hence gaining a solid understanding of complex forces driving exponential change in their respective industry (Bevolo and Brand, 2003). Over time, they have adopted a process of organizational learning to consider the impacts of alternative futures.

In the next sections, stories of FS futures (2030) are derived from the author's empirical and applied research in wealth management and private banking futures studies. The four stories presented are case study exemplars, each related to one of the four conceptual stages of integrating foresight with design in strategic organizational decision-making.

5.1. Stage 1 — Achieving insights and alignment around current reality

5.1.1. Story 1: FS Futures, current reality — A Delphi study

Method: To engage in foresight and issue identification, researchers often must rely on the opinions of experts who are better aware of what is going to happen in the future (Rowe and Wright, 2001). Since experts possess tacit knowledge over specific business aspects, they can identify and judge the most critical uncertainties (Linstone and Turoff, 1975). In this case study, the Delphi method was used as the basis of foresight (Altschuld, 1993).

In a 2030 futures study involving a heterogeneous group of industry experts in the FS sector (Buhring, 2017), the Delphi survey was to ignite a conversation around the prevailing innovation system, and probe deeper into what defines the current "status quo" from four different perspectives: industry, market, organization, and the consumer. Data analyzed at the end of the first survey round provided important insights as to which products and services were considered as drivers of continuous growth. With the focus on innovation, the data highlighted that the primary objective was to address current customer needs. Due to the diversity of participants in their backgrounds, perspectives, and experiences, a broad range of opinions were recorded as to what are the signs of change that would have impact on the organization. Defining the current reality (see Figure 5, Stage 1), in the context of the market (China) perspective, the Delphi produced the following insights:

> In the current Private Banking (PB) market, services are intended to identify, protect, and grow diversified valuables and values of clients. PB localization (China) provides continuous advantages and the ability on differentiating itself from other PBs through client-centric advisory capabilities. Amidst ongoing regulatory complexity and the lack of clarity (e.g. segregation of banks and securities, varying regional/local policy, rule-sets, foreign ownership restrictions, license requirements), successful players in PB continue to defend, or look for opportunities, which protect the interests against new FS entrants (e.g. FinTech) and other non-banking players.

The main focus in this stage is on both gaining deep and novel insights into today's challenges, while establishing alignment across a diverse group of stakeholders about key elements of the present situation, and the early signs of change that loom over the medium-term time horizon.

5.2. Stage 2 — Facilitating a productive design conversation

5.2.1. Story 2: FS futures — Preferable futures 2030 — A Delphi study

Resultant from the aforementioned FS futures study, a series of futures scenario statements to the year 2030 were produced as consensus toward the Delphi panels' combined vision of preferable or desirable futures. From this research, the strategic foresight and design conversation expanded from information gathering, to processing the inherent cues for specific potential new futures. A key observation in this study phase was noticed by designers and inter-disciplinary innovation practitioners who questioned the dominant business logic, which in context of the traditional FS business and operating model, was considered in conflict between the embedded present and these imagined futures. Facilitating a productive design conversation (cf. Figure 5, Stage 2), in the context of the industry 2030 (Greater China) perspective, the Delphi produced the following insights:

> In 2030, the Private Banking (PB) industry in Greater China is operating in a much more deregulated and democratized market environment with reduced authorities extended to bank licensees. This forces PBs to adapt business models alleviated of non-core systems/services (e.g. via outsourcing of data mining, automation, artificial intelligence assistance) to reduce the need for human interactions across non-critical touch-points. Continued investments in revenue-producing innovation drivers lead to higher profit margins and further evolvement of the client advisory model. The PB of 2030 follows new sources of revenues via bespoke Ultra high-net-worth Individual (UHNW) advisory services, while digital customer experiences have greatly improved through the elimination of language barriers via systems translation (e.g. Baidu^{TM}, BabelFish^{TM}). Additional revenue streams have been created through client segmentation based on "needs," which allows for services to be intelligently switched between robo-advisory automation and bespoke human advisory services.

As introduced in Section 4, an important goal in this stage of the conversation is the development of previously unseen possibilities that emerge when a group of stakeholders with diverse perspectives are involved. The outcome is one that brings to light new opportunities outside of the current business logic (or mindset), and by anticipating the consequences of sociotechnological change factors over the relevant time horizon (i.e. 2030), new possibilities of value creation may emerge. For example, how would wealth management services need to evolve, if the meaning of individual wealth is challenged by the motivation and behaviors attributed to social value creation instead?

5.3. Stage 3 — Specifying a portfolio of desirable futures

5.3.1. *Story 3: Financial services futures — Consumer and organizational perspectives*

An overarching objective of the four stages of integrating design with foresight in strategic decision-making is to encourage participants and stakeholders to take an important first step toward continuously thinking about the future. Therefore, stakeholders become mindful that choices made today (i.e. actions) will have consequences in the future, and, for these choices to be made responsibly and wisely, they need to select among many alternative futures and determine which future is desired (see Figure 4, Section 4). Realizing this opportunity — that stakeholders can only influence what is "yet to be," while having to live with "what has already been" — the determination in this stage of the conversation is to spark a mindset of action-oriented foresight that are manifested in business practices, which seek to move merely possible futures into the realm of plausibility, while generating knowledge that will bring them about as reality.

In 2030, for example, the Chinese consumer is most probably living through mobile lifestyle choices, moving family and investments autonomously. Among the findings derived from the Delphi consumer perspectives were evolving behavioral consumption patterns that will see consumer preferences shift toward lifestyle-inspired services and experiences, surpassing the interests of accumulating material products and goods. Moreover, the Chinese consumer in 2030 is anticipated to favor Private Banking that develop trust through their values as a corporate citizen, and the community support that impacts the overall brand reputation. Taking a portfolio approach toward identifying and analyzing the likely implications of desired and alternative futures will prepare the organization to deal with uncertainties and be better prepared for the future.

5.4. Stage 4 — Active experimentation to gather new knowledge and learning

5.4.1. Story 4: Financial services futures — Consumer and organizational perspectives visualized

In this particular example of a design foresight futures study, insights and new knowledge provided the platform for a visioning approach, which forms an important part of disseminating the research findings. For example, utilizing storytelling narratives and imaginary creations is an effective way to engage with the intended readership of a design foresight study in entertaining, informing, and energizing ways. Stories can change or enhance readers' perceptions of futures, seeing themselves in different perspectives, and identifying their "self" by interpreting and completing the story in his or her head (Sametz and Maydoney, 2003). In this 2030 futures study, personas were created that embodied the essence of futures scenario statements in verbal and non-verbal communications intended to connect the reader on both analytical and emotional levels. Illustrating the scenario based on "actors" in the story, in this example (Figure 6), the fiction writer and design team had the opportunity to introduce an added layer to the narrative story-telling: generational and stakeholder perspectives.

The four-stage process step, as described in Section 4, highlights the assumptions underlying future scenarios that can be surfaced and tested through experiments (i.e. artefacts, prototypes, enactment) in formats that effectively extend the research results and new knowledge gained by non-expert audiences. While a chapter of a book can deliver a large amount of information to the person who sits down and studies it, the number of readers might be smaller. Books are not passive entertainment — they have to be actively read by participants who have to be willing to do the

ELENI ZHAO LAL

She IS the zeitgeist, which makes her their best chance of seeing the future

FRANK CASTOR

Node chief Frank is a plugged-in bank boss like no other

PAMELA XI CHEN

Pamela has her finger on the pulse of the world's biggest economy

AH–LUM LO

Tech-chief Ah-Lum switches seamlessly between humans and AI

ADITI DAS

The data miner knows whom to sign up in partnership deals

Figure 6.   Futures scenarios in verbal and non-verbal communications — cross-generational persona and stakeholder perspectives.

Source: Bühring, J. H. (2021, p. ix).

work, so readers are self-selected enthusiasts for the material. This stands in contrast to movies, which are more easily accessible, can find wider audiences, and if well put together, can have as much impact as books (Ma *et al.*, 2012). The adage that a picture speaks a thousand words (Magill, 1989) is valid even in its most literal interpretation. Here, portions of the findings can also be produced in form of an animated video — thus making the most salient findings "consumable" by a larger and more varied group of staff and internal stakeholders. To this end, futures scenarios can be brought to life, while at the same time, project stakeholders must be willing to move away from a literal transmission of the print work toward a thematic one, as the process flow and storyboard examples (Figure 7) illustrate.

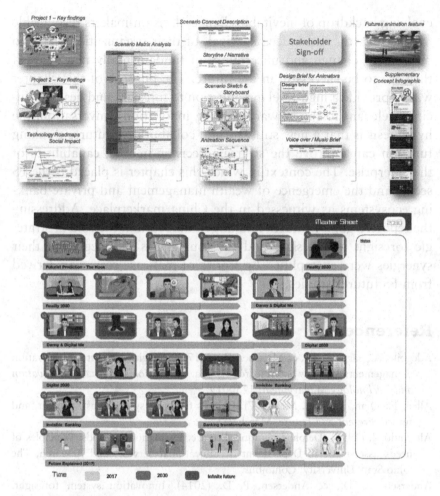

Figure 7. A high-level visualization of the actual production design activity flow applied in video animation research dissemination, and the animation video high-level scene sequencing story master board.

6. Conclusion

FS players over the past two decades have been experiencing major forces of change, while technology-based businesses (FinTech) that compete against, enable, or collaborate with traditional financial institutions are experiencing rapid growth globally. Against this evolving backdrop of inevitable change, decision-makers responsible for the growth, and indeed survival, of their organizations have to respond to change and uncertainty in fundamentally new ways if they are to be successful in the future. The purpose of this chapter was to provide a high-level introduction to foresight and design principles relevant to the forward-looking innovation conversation; the hypothesis is that a new strategic and collaborative futures thinking function can improve the strategic decision-making capabilities of the enterprise. The context in which this chapter is placed is the FS sector and the emergence of wealth management and private banking ecosystems as witnessed in the China marketplace. Addressing the reported gap of futures thinking in innovation, the role of strategic foresight and design, and the four stages of integrating their synergies were exemplified by stories of real-case scenarios derived from FS futures studies.

References

Adegbile, A., Sarpong, D., & Meissner, D. (2017). Strategic foresight for innovation management: A review and research agenda. *International Journal of Innovation and Technology Management*, 1750019.

Allen, F., Qian, J., Qian, M. (2007). China's financial system: Past, present, and future. *Present and Future*, March 28.

Altschuld, J. (1993). Delphi technique. Lecture. Evaluation methods: Principles of needs assessment II, Department of Educational Services and Research, The Ohio State University, Columbus.

Andersen, A. D., & Andersen, P. D. (2014). Innovation system foresight. *Technological Forecasting and Social Change*, **88**, 276–286.

Andrews, T. (2012). What is social constructionism. *Grounded Theory Review*, 11(1), 39–46.

Arner, D. W., Barberis, J., & Buckley, R. P. (2016). The evolution of fintech: New post-crisis paradigm. *Georgetown Journal of International Law*, 47(4), 1271–1320.

Beckett, A., Hewer, P., & Howcroft, B. (2000). An exposition of consumer behaviour in the financial services industry. *International Journal of Bank Marketing*, 18(1), 15–26.

Bevolo, M., & Brand, R. (2003). Brand design for the long term. *Design Management Review*, 14(1), 33–39.

Bishop, P., Hines, A., & Collins, T. (2007). The current state of scenario development: An overview of techniques. *Foresight*, 9(1), 5–25.

Bohemia, E., Rieple, A., Liedtka, J., & Cooper, R. (2014). *Proceedings of the 19th DMI: Academic Design Management Conference: Design Management in an Era of Disruption*, Introduction to the Special Issue, Design Management Institute.

Boztepe, S. (ed.) (2016). Design expanding into strategy: Evidence from design consulting firms. *DRS 2016* International Conference, Design Research Society, Brighton, UK.

Bucolo, S., & Matthews, J. H. (2011). A conceptual model to link deep customer insights to both growth opportunities and organisational strategy in SME's as part of a design led transformation journey. In *Design Management: Towards a New Era of Innovation: Proceedings of the 2011 Tsinghua-DMI International Design Management Symposium*. Ip, A., Cai, J., Liu, J., & Tong, G. (eds.), Innovation and Design Management Association Ltd., Hong Kong, pp. 243–250.

Buehring, J. H., & Liedtka, J. (2018). Embracing systematic futures thinking at the intersection of Strategic Planning, Foresight and Design. *Journal of Innovation Management*, 6(3), 134–152.

Buehring, J., & Liedtka, J. (2018). Foresight by design: Supporting strategic innovation with systematic futures thinking. *Cumulus Paris 2018*, 11–13 April, Paris, France, pp. 330–346.

Buhring, J. (ed.) (2017). Design-inspired foresight: Strategic foresight techniques for preferable futures. Design Management Academy, 7–9 June 2017, Hong Kong, China; London, UK.

Buhring, J. & Koskinen, I. (eds.) (2017). Beyond forecasting: A design-inspired foresight approach for preferable futures. *International Association of Societies of Design Research*, 31 October–3 November, Cincinnati, Ohio, USA.

Bühring, J. H. (2021). *Private Banking and Wealth Management Futures 2030: Greater China Perspectives*. Springer Briefs in Finance Series. Springer, Singapore.

Cagnin, C. (2018). Developing a transformative business strategy through the combination of design thinking and futures literacy. *Technology Analysis & Strategic Management*, 30(5), 524–539.

China Banking and Insurance Regulatory Commission. CBRC Sets to Further Open up the Banking Sector https://www.cbirc.gov.cn/en/view/pages/ItemDetail.html?docId=163819 (Accessed on 7 July 2021).

Chishti, S., & Barberis, J. (2016). *The FINTECH Book: The Financial Technology Handbook for Investors, Entrepreneurs and Visionaries* (John Wiley & Sons, Hoboken, New Jersey, USA).

Collinsa, M. C., Kwagb, S.-W. A, & Yildirimc, H. S. (2003). The effects of the Gramm-Leach-Bliley Act on bank stockholders' returns and risks. *Journal of Economic Literature, Financial Institutions and Services, JEL Classifications G21, G28* (American Economic Association, Nashville, TN, USA).

Cuhls K. (2003). From forecasting to foresight processes — New participative foresight activities in Germany. *Journal of Forecasting*, **22**(2–3), 93–111.

Dator, J. (2009). Alternative futures at the Manoa School. *Journal of Futures Studies*, **14**(2), 1–18.

Day, G. S., & Schoemaker, P. J. (2006). *Peripheral Vision: Detecting the Weak Signals That Will Make or Break Your Company* (Harvard Business School Press, Boston MA, USA).

Diaz-Rainey, I., Ibikunle, G., & Mention, A.-L. (2015). *The Technological Transformation of Capital Markets* (Elsevier).

Doppelt, B. (2017). *Leading Change Toward Sustainability: A Change-Management Guide for Business, Government and Civil Society* (Routledge).

Dunne, D., & Martin, R. (2006). Design thinking and how it will change management education: An interview and discussion. *Academy of Management Learning & Education*, **5**(4), 512–523.

Eggink, W. & de la Bruheze, A.A.A. (2015). Design storytelling with future scenario development; envisioning" the museum." In Summer cumulus conference 'The virtuous circle', Milan, 3–7 June 2015. Available online at https://research.utwente.nl/en/publications/design-storytelling-with-future-scenario-development-envisioning- (Accessed on 7 July 2021).

Eling, K., & Herstatt, C. (2017). Managing the front end of innovation — Less fuzzy, yet still not fully understood. *Journal of Product Innovation Management*, **34**(6), 864–874.

Fuerth, L. S. (2009). Foresight and anticipatory governance. *Foresight*, **11**(4), 14–32.

Gabrielli, S., & Zoels, J.-C. (eds.). Creating imaginable futures: Using human-centered design strategies as a foresight tool. *ACM Proceedings of the 2003 Conference on Designing for User Experiences*.

Godet, M., & Roubelat, F. (1996). Creating the future: The use and misuse of scenarios. *Long Range Planning*, **29**(2), 164–171.

Groves, K. S. (2006). Leader emotional expressivity, visionary leadership, and organizational change. *Leadership & Organization Development Journal*, **27**(7), 566–583.

Hamel, G. (2002). *Leading the Revolution: How to Thrive in Turbulent Times by Making Innovation a Way of Life* (Harvard Business School Press).

Hancock, T., & Bezold, C. (1993). Possible futures, preferable futures. *The Healthcare Forum Journal*, **37**(2), 23–29.

Heger, T., & Rohrbeck, R. (2012). Strategic foresight for collaborative exploration of new business fields. *Technological Forecasting and Social Change*, **79**(5), 819–831.

Heskett, J. (2001). Past, present, and future in design for industry. *Design Issues*, **17**(1), 18–26.

Heskett, J. (2009). Creating economic value by design. *International Journal of Design*, **3**(1).

Heskett J. (2017). *A John Heskett Reader: Design, History, Economics* (Bloomsbury Publishing, London), Book: ISBN: HB: 978-1-4742-2125-2.

Hines, A., & Zindato, D. (2016). designing foresight and foresighting design: Opportunities for learning and collaboration via scenarios. *World Future Review*, 8(4), 180–192.

Hofer, C. W. & Schendel, D. (1978). Strategy formulation: Analytical concepts. 7(2) *International Studies of Management & Organization* (West Publishing, St. Paul, Minnesota, USA).

Hoorn, J. F. (2014). *Creative Confluence* (John Benjamins Publishing Company).

Inayatullah, S. (2008). Six pillars: Futures thinking for transforming. *Foresight*, 10(1), 4–21.

Jonas, W. (2001). A scenario for design. *Design Issues*, 17(2), 64–80.

Koen, P. A., Ajamian, G. M., Boyce, S., Clamen, A., Fisher, E., Fountoulakis, S. et al. (2002). *Fuzzy Front End: Effective Methods, Tools, and Techniques* (Wiley, New York, NY).

Kock, A., Heising, W., & Gemünden, H. G. (2015). How ideation portfolio management influences front-end success. *Journal of Product Innovation Management*, 32(4), 539–555.

Kshetri, N. (2016). Big data's role in expanding access to financial services in China. *International Journal of Information Management*, 36(3), 297–308.

Kumar, V. (ed.) (2004). Innovation planning toolkit. *Proceedings of the Futureground Design Research Society International Conference*, Melbourne, Australia.

Liedtka, J. (ed.) (2017). Beyond better solutions: Design thinking as a social technology. Design Management Academy, 7–9 June 2017; Hong Kong, China; London, UK.

Liedtka, J. (1998). Linking strategic thinking with strategic planning. *Strategy & Leadership*, 26(4), 30.

Linstone, H., & Turoff M. (1975). *The Delphi Method: Techniques and applications* (Addison-Wesley Pub. Co., Advanced Book Program).

Lojacono, G., & Zaccai, G. (2004). The evolution of the design-inspired enterprise. *MIT Sloan Management Review*, 45(3), 75.

Ma, K.-L., Liao, I., Frazier, J., Hauser, H., & Kostis, H.-N. (2012). Scientific storytelling using visualization. *IEEE Computer Graphics and Applications*, 32(1), 12–9.

Magill, F. N. (1989). *Masterpieces of World Literature* (HarperCollins Publishers).

Mahbubani, K. (2008). The case against the West: America and Europe in the Asian century. *Foreign Affairs*, 87(3), 111–124.

Manzini, E., & Meroni, A. (2007). Emerging user demands for sustainable solutions, EMUDE. *In Design Research Now* (pp. 157–179). Birkhäuser. https://doi.org/10.1007/978-3-7643-8472-2.

Margolin, V. (2007). Design, the future and the human spirit. *Design Issues*, 23(3), 4–15.

Marsh, N., McAllum, M., & Purcell, D. (2002). *Strategic Foresight: The Power of Standing in the Future* (CrownContent).

Martin, B. R. (1995). Foresight in science and technology. *Technology Analysis & Strategic Management*, 7(2), 139–168.

Meroni, A. (2008). Strategic design: Where are we now? Reflection around the foundations of a recent discipline. *Strategic Design Research Journal*, 1(1), 31–38.

Mietzner, D., & Reger, G. (2005). Advantages and disadvantages of scenario approaches for strategic foresight. *International Journal of Technology Intelligence and Planning*, 1(2), 220–239.

Miller, C. C., & Cardinal, L. B. (1994). Strategic planning and firm performance: A synthesis of more than two decades of research. *Academy of Management Journal*, 37(6), 1649–1665.

Mozota, B. B. (1998). Structuring strategic design management: Michael Porter's value chain. *Design Management Review*, 9(2), 26–31.

Oster, G. W. (2008). Practitioners corner: Derailing design thinking. *International Journal of Leadership Studies*, 4(1), 107–115.

Reeves, M., & Deimler, M. (2011). Adaptability: The new competitive advantage. *Harvard Business Review*, 39, 135–141.

Rohrbeck, R., Battistella, C., & Huizingh, E. (2015). Corporate foresight: An emerging field with a rich tradition. *Technological Forecasting and Social Change*, 101, 1–9.

Rowe, G., & Wright, G. (2001). Expert opinions in forecasting: the role of the Delphi technique. In *Principles of forecasting* (Springer, Boston, MA), (pp. 125–144).

Salampasis, D., Mention, A. -L., & Kaiser, A. O. (2017). Wealth management in times of robo: Towards hybrid human-machine interactions. Available at SSRN 3111996.

Sametz, R., & Maydoney, A. (2003). Storytelling through design. *Design Management Journal (Former Series)*, 14(4), 18–34.

Sanders, L. (2008). An evolving map of design practice and design research. *ACM Interactions*, 15(6), 13–17.

Saritas, O., & Smith, J. E. (2011). The big picture–trends, drivers, wild cards, discontinuities and weak signals. *Futures*, 43(3), 292–312.

Shiller, R. J. (2009). *The New Financial Order: Risk in the 21st Century* (Princeton University Press).

Slaughter, R. (2002). *New Thinking for a New Millennium: The Knowledge Base of Futures Studies* (Routledge).

Simon, H. A. (1955). A behavioral model of rational choice. *The Quarterly Journal of Economics*, 69(1), 99–118.

Tsoukas, H., & Shepherd, J. (2009). *Managing the Future: Foresight in the Knowledge Economy* (John Wiley & Sons).

Vaara, E., & Whittington, R. (2012). Strategy-as-practice: Taking social practices seriously. *Academy of Management Annals*, 6(1), 285–336.

Van der Laan, L., & Yap, J. (2016). *Foresight & Strategy in the Asia Pacific Region* (Springer).

Vecchiato, R. (2015). Strategic planning and organizational flexibility in turbulent environments. *Foresight*, 17(3), 257–273.

Vergragt, P. J., & Quist, J. (2011). Backcasting for sustainability: Introduction to the special issue. *Technological Forecasting and Social Change*, 78(5), 747–755.

Voros, J. (2001). Reframing environmental scanning: An integral approach. *Foresight*, 3(6), 533–551.

Voros, J. (2003). A generic foresight process framework. *Foresight*, 5(3), 10–21.

Wilkinson, A., Mayer, M., & Ringler, V. (2014). Collaborative futures: Integrating foresight with design in large scale innovation processes-seeing and seeding the futures of Europe. *Journal of Futures Studies*, 18(4), 1–26.

Chapter 5

Driving the Future of FinTech-led Transformation in Financial Services: Business Trends and the New Face of Open Innovation

Volkmar J. Klausser,[*,‡] *Dimitrios Salampasis*[†,§] *and Alexander Kaiser*[†,¶]

[*]*Finanz Informatik Solutions Plus GmbH*
Wilhelm-Pfitzer-Straße 1, 70736 Fellbach, Germany
[†]*School of Business, Law and Entrepreneurship,*
Swinburne University of Technology, Hawthorn VIC 3122,
Australia
[‡]*volkmar.klausser@f-i-sp.de*
[§]*dsalampasis@swin.edu.au*
[¶]*akaiser@swin.edu.au*

127

Abstract. The emergence of the most recent FinTech phase resulted in multidimensional challenges, putting pressure on the traditional modus operandi within the financial services industry. Whilst incumbents initially responded to this FinTech phase by waiting out or attacking the new market entrants, the environment more recently shifted toward a more collaborative approach built on open innovation. The transition is further encouraged through regulatory initiatives (e.g. open banking), paving way for the development of FinTech-enabled ecosystems. Based on a review of publicly available information, this research is founded on academic and industry literature and aims at illuminating how banking organizations utilize open innovation as a vehicle for strategic intervention in order to respond to the changing market environment. Several cases that correspond to the attributes and characteristics of the three main types of open innovation (inside out, outside in, and coupled open innovation) are investigated, and common determinants contributing to the success of those initiatives derived in order to provide an outlook on future developments within the industry.

Keywords. Open innovation; financial services; FinTech ecosystems; open banking; strategies for disruption; value co-creation.

1. Introduction

Applying technology within the financial services sector to deliver novel solutions has a long history. As early as 1866, the first successful transatlantic cable was laid, providing the necessary infrastructure for the first major period of financial globalization (Arner *et al.*, 2016). One century later, the product and services spectrum within the banking industry is one of the most diverse in the market (Brunner, 2009), enabling FinTech, as "a new financial industry that applies technology to improve financial activities" to surface (Schueffel, 2017, p. 45).

The current FinTech phase emerged in 2008 (Alt *et al.*, 2018) at a time where the European short-term money markets were drying up, thus negatively impacting entrepreneurial finance (Paulet, 2018).

The FinTech phase builds on innovation, customer orientation, and entrepreneurial spirit (Alt *et al.*, 2018), creating an environment that enables new players from the non-banking sector to enter the financial market. These new players introduce novel digital solutions, differentiating themselves from traditional banks and enabling new forms of financing (Alt *et al.*, 2018; Dapp, 2017; Lee and Shin, 2018).

In recent years, this FinTech phase evolved at a rapid pace (Lee and Shin, 2018), and the newly created FinTech-enabled business models are putting pressure across the different sectors of financial services, with banking being at the forefront of transformation and change. Numerous reports consider banks being part of the first wave of disruption, along with being the breakwater against disruption.

Incumbents have gradually started to recognize and acknowledge the relevance of the FinTech ecosystem and the need to undergo fundamental business transformations (Nonninger and Mekebeb, 2018). In this context, different strategies of either proactive or reactive nature are utilized. To that respect, incumbents can respond to the newly evolving competitors by taking the three positions of waiting, joining, or beating them (Gans, 2016):

Waiting

The first strategy is about analyzing what the new market entrants lack. Incumbent organizations usually possess value chain elements that are difficult to replicate.

Joining

The second alternative is to actively approach start-up organizations and to engage in partnerships. Deutsche Bank, for example, founded Innovation Labs (2020), which thrive on collaboration and partnerships with technology start-ups.

Beating

The third strategy is about bettering new competitors. The incumbent organization waits until it becomes clear which technologies are becoming dominant in the market. Next, the business acts to protect its market position by aggressively investing in the new technology. The objective is to control the technology toward achieving mainstream adoption.

When opting for one of the strategies, incumbent organizations have to consider that FinTechs are introducing disruptive technologies to the marketplace to reduce the friction which is associated with today's financial services (King, 2018).

As a result, the atmosphere between FinTechs and incumbent organizations is transforming. Whilst a few years ago, the talks were about who is going to beat whom, the discussion shifted toward engaging in more collaborative efforts (King, 2018) and building ecosystems to replace bilateral partnerships between incumbents and challengers (Hatch *et al.*, 2019).

This transition is encouraged by Banking as a Service and open banking, through which financial data is made more accessible on a global scale (Hallsworth and Robert, 2019) while banking becomes a service model for the development of new products and services.

Banking as a Service is about providing access to functionality, enabling bank-like services outside of a bank-owned channel (BBVA, 2019). The underlying ecosystems, created by incumbents, turn FinTechs into customers, supporting the development of novel business models and monetization strategies (Nonninger and Mekebeb, 2019).

Through open banking, on the other hand, access to data is democratized, and the EU and UK have taken the lead in passing regulations accordingly (Hallsworth and Robert, 2019). Whilst this movement is reshaping financial services and winning strategies (Davis, 2019) and has seen significant activity in the second half of 2019 (Innopay, 2019), it is considered being only 1% complete (Davis, 2019).

In this context, this book chapter explores how banking organizations utilize open innovation as a vehicle for strategic intervention in relation to FinTech transformation and change. Several cases that correspond to the attributes and characteristics of the three main types of open innovation (inside out, outside in, and coupled open innovation) are analyzed.

2. Open Innovation

To some extent, innovation had always been open (West and Gallagher, 2016). Open innovation has been recognized as one of the most important paradigms in innovation management. It caters to the opening and democratization of the innovation lifecycle and the reaching out beyond the organizational boundaries to capitalize on internal and external knowledge, ideas, and pathways to market.

Initially, open innovation was defined as "the use of purposive inflows and outflows of knowledge to accelerate internal innovation, and expand the markets for external use of innovation, respectively" (Chesbrough *et al.*, 2006, p. 1) that is "systematically relying on a firm's [...] capabilities of internally and externally carrying out the major technology management tasks [...] along the innovation process" (Lichtenthaler, 2008, p. 148).

Open innovation assumes that firms should utilize external as well as internal ideas and paths to market as they advance their innovations (Bogers *et al.*, 2018). Chesbrough and Bogers (2014, p. 17) further define open innovation as "a distributed innovation process based on purposely managed knowledge flows across organizational boundaries, using pecuniary and non-pecuniary mechanisms in line with the organization's business model." Open innovation is betting on the power of "crowd wisdom" to find the right solution (Simanis and Hart, 2019). It is worth mentioning here the definition that Chesbrough himself is using to describe open innovation; a porous business model joining sides to the notion of transparency, openness, and sharing (Chesbrough, 2003), or the fact that the boundaries of the firm become permeable (Lichtenthaler, 2011).

The underlying philosophy of open innovation is grounded in the complementarity between the inflows and outflows of knowledge while bringing economic value to creativity and knowledge (van der Meer, 2017). Within an open knowledge era, experiencing a profound abundance and a non-stop flow of information, where the transferring of knowledge inflows and outflows and access to information is beyond understanding, collaboration becomes the new business-as-usual mindset that can facilitate success within this constantly changing business world characterized by high competition and volatility.

As a concept, open innovation has been of complementary nature to previous concepts of employees' cumulative innovation (Scotchmer, 2004; Reuter, 1977; Chandler, 1962), the supplier and user innovation paradigm (Von Hippel, 1986, 1988, 2005a, 2005b, 2009), open source (West and Gallagher, 2006), user co-creation (Franke and Piller, 2004), user-centered innovation and customer integration (Baldwin and Von Hippel, 2011; Baldwin *et al.*, 2006; Oliveira and Von Hippel, 2011), peer-to-peer innovation (Satzger and Neus, 2010), distributed innovation (Sawhney and Prandelli, 2000; Bogers and West, 2012) and the early supplier involvement process (Bidault *et al.*, 1988) by bringing on board the competitors as a potential external source of innovation, opening up the innovation process.

The core of open innovation model is grounded in the infusion of external ideas and knowledge into new product development (Laursen and Salter, 2006; Chesbrough and Appleyard, 2007), denoting an emerging shift from a closed to an open innovation paradigm (Chesbrough *et al.*, 2006; Dahlander and Gann, 2010). This propensity to the open paradigm is illustrated into the fact that "closed innovation springs entirely from internal company innovation activity, largely in the form of organized R&D" (Helfat, 2006, p. 86). On the other hand, the open innovation model advances its emergence from "sources external to the company in combination with supplementary internal company innovation activity" (*Ibid.*).

In the process of understanding the functionality of these knowledge inflows and outflows, Gassmann and Enkel (2004) identified three processes within the structure of the open innovation paradigm: inside-out (outbound), outside-in (inbound), and coupled (bidirectional) process, which are illustrated in Figure 1.

The three processes are based on a porous boundary between the business and its environment. The inside-out process allows for

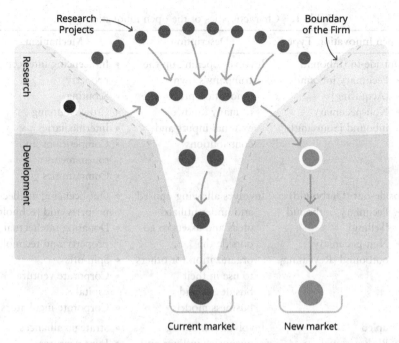

Figure 1. The model of open innovation.
Source: Adapted from Chesbrough (2003) upon author's written permission.

in-house developed research projects to be brought to market outside of the boundaries of the firm. Meanwhile the outside-in process allows for the business to acquire external knowledge in order to advance its research projects. The coupled process, meanwhile, is a combination of the inside-out and outside-in processes (Chesbrough, 2003). Table 1 summarizes the key attributes and mechanisms of the different processes.

2.1. *Outside-in (inbound)*

The outside-in open innovation process builds upon the opening of the companies' boundaries to cooperate with external sources, such as suppliers and customers (Gassmann and Enkel, 2005; Gassmann, 2006). The environment is monitored by companies to source knowledge from stakeholders (Inauen *et al.*, 2011).

Table 1.   Characteristics of the open innovation types.

Open Innovation Type	Description	Mechanisms
Outside-in (Inbound) ➢ Pecuniary inbound [Acquiring] ➢ Non-pecuniary inbound [Sourcing]	Involves opening up the company's own innovation processes to many kinds of external inputs and contributions	• In-licencing intellectual property • Scouting • Crowdsourcing • Intermediaries • Competitions and tournaments • Communities
Inside-out (Outbound) ➢ Pecuniary outbound [Selling] ➢ Non-pecuniary outbound [Revealing]	Involves allowing unused and under-utilized ideas and assets to go outside the organization for others to use in their businesses and business models	• Out-licencing intellectual property and technology • Donating intellectual property and technology • Spin-offs • Corporate venture capital • Corporate incubators
Coupled ➢ Bi-directional ➢ Interactive collaboration in form of joint production	Involves combining purposive inflows and outflows of knowledge to collaboratively develop and/or commercialize an innovative	• Strategic alliances • Joint ventures • Consortia • Networks • Ecosystems • Innovation platforms

Source: Salampasis (2015).

2.2. *Inside-out (outbound)*

Inside-out open innovation is defined as the process, "whereby a business places some of its assets or projects outside its own walls" (Chesbrough, and Garman, 2009, p. 3). By doing so, R&D cost can be reduced, whilst not giving up growth opportunities (*Ibid.*). However, the process results in cultural, organizational, and political challenges (*Ibid.*). Inside-out innovation is common in many present-day banking practices (Manning and Bodine, 2012). To adapt to new technologies, some financial institutions take technological innovation so seriously that new ventures are spun out (Yurcan and

Robert, 2015). Salampasis and Mention (2019) delineate outbound open innovation into two sub-modes: inward and outward, along with elucidating the role of outbound open innovation as a vehicle for unrelated diversification and enabler of intrapreneurial aptitude within technology-driven ecosystems.

2.3. *Coupled innovation*

The coupled process combines the outside-in with the inside-out approach for joint development in innovation networks, alliances, and joint ventures. A majority of companies aim to set industry standards or introduce a dominant design for their products (Gassmann and Enkel, 2005).

Within the financial services industry, the three different processes of open innovation are applied in a range of different scenarios ranging from hackathons via strategic alliances and joint ventures to spin-offs.

3. Financial Services and Open Innovation

Recent large-sample surveys on the adoption of open innovation in large firms indicate that outside-in open innovation hereby is being practiced more often than inside-out innovation (Brunswicker and Chesbrough, 2018). However, it "has had a limited impact upon the broader disciplines of management and economics" (West *et al.*, 2014, pp. 809–810). Further, the concept is still being scarcely practiced in the financial services sector, with the most prominent barriers being organizational structure, including "a lack of consistency among managers' instructions and their failure to implement and support innovations" (Schueffel and Vadana, 2015, p. 43); cultural inertia; as well as related costs to open innovation (Schueffel and Vadana, 2015). Nonetheless, studies show that 55% of digital commercial banking services were initially implemented by non-bank firms (Oliveira and Von Hippel, 2011), thus illustrating the relevance of external sources to the financial services sector.

Financial institutions usually reflect an extensive lack of innovation and, needless to say, open innovation. However, there are existing examples of financial institutions that have adopted open innovation practices, such as DBS (experimentation as a service), Bank of America (FinTech Start-ups — Silicon Valley), Thomson Reuters (Catalyst Fund), Wells Fargo (Mentoring Program for Start-ups), BNP Paribas (Leveraging Open Innovation to build the Bank of Tomorrow), CIBC and MaRs (Open Innovation Space for Financial Technology Start-ups), and BBVA, along with the establishment and development of innovation centers and labs by many banking and financial services institutions (Standard Bank, Capital One, Commonwealth Bank, Citi, Visa, Chase Bank, etc.). These examples illuminate the shift of the financial services sector in terms of embracing new ways of value creation, developing new learning mechanisms, and sharing best practices with other industries.

4. Cases

In order to embrace this transition, the following cases utilized different strategies in order to create new value propositions.

4.1. *Open banking — Nordea Bank and MasterCard*

Open banking is burgeoning at a time when the retail banking sector is beginning to recognize the robustness and the importance of data in innovation, entrepreneurship, and growth and its utilization for the development of new business models, alternative and cutting-edge value propositions, and the establishment of new ways to connect across multiple sectors and data sources.

The access to data has always been considered as one of the main hurdles FinTech ventures face to test, develop, and commercialize new products and services. For years, such organizations have been solely relying on controversial, unstable, and expensive screen scraping and reverse engineering methods to obtain valuable information from bank accounts upon customer authorization and sharing of online banking credentials. FinTechs and other financial services players do leverage on such data to price risk, validate income, and acquire insights on spending patterns and behaviors. Such methods come with numerous disadvantages, particularly around the storing of users' credentials by third-party providers: the fact that they indirectly legitimize the revealing of user passwords to third-party providers; the inability of users to have any control over the scope, the purpose, and the duration of the access to the data and information; and that consumers are vulnerable against fraud and misuse of data.

In this context, the pivotal introduction of open banking in a number of jurisdictions globally aims at putting together harmonized frameworks by means of a mandated data-sharing regime around effective management of data inflows and outflows, enabling an "ecosystemic" view around data sharing across multiple parties. Open banking primarily emerged from the Second Payment Services Directive (PSD2), an EU banking regulation instrument that is emphasizing innovation, security, and sound market competition. PSD2 regulation has been serving as an example for other jurisdictions, including the US, China, and Australia, that have been taking similar initiatives and approaches toward open banking (Botta *et al.*, 2018).

The main philosophy behind open banking is the transition of data ownership from the banking institution to the consumer, opening up competition, innovation and collaboration (Ramdani *et al.*, 2020), while reducing the significant power that banks have by being the custodians' data and the guardians of trust. In this context, the delivery of financial services is shifting from vertically integrated to unbundled architectures, resulting in banking institutions no longer not having the exclusive privilege, and now non-bank third parties being part of the value and delivery chain. By utilizing Application Programming Interfaces (APIs), banks facilitate the standardized means of sharing[1] customer-permissioned data, small business data, and services to authorized third-party providers (TPPs), upon

---

[1]Depends on the jurisdiction and the ad hoc legal and regulatory open banking requirements.

customer consent, either directly or via the customer's banking institution, opening up new ways and horizons around the understanding of data potentialities and data utilization, the creation of augmented value of data, the provision of new (or alternative) products and services, and the institutionalization of greater transparency and freedom of choice (Supervision BCoB, 2019). Moreover, the opening up of competition aims at lowering the barriers to entry for more players to participate in the space. Standaert *et al.* (2020) have branched open banking into five strategic dimensions: product innovation, customer experience integration, ecosystem competition, datascape, and geographical scope. In this context, the purpose of open banking is twofold: on the one hand, providing consumers with more control over the management and usage of their data, and on the other hand generating substantial potential for businesses active within the financial services industry to innovate, compete, and strategize using customer and small business data (Wadsworth, 2020).

By definition, APIs are secure channels of communication which provide tokenized authentication methods that banks and accredited third parties use to transmit data (or in general proprietary data and analytics) upon customer consent and without human intervention. The underlying logic behind API functionality is interactivity between different applications, data, and devices, creating connectivity across the ecosystem stakeholders allowing them to "talk" to each other (Zachariadis, 2020). In broader terms, the philosophy behind APIs is grounded on the ability to expose a certain functionality in ways that it can be accessible to other users.

Banking institutions are utilizing a variety of architectural designs in terms of structure and deployment of APIs. In principle, APIs are branched into three main categories:

(1) **Private,** which serves the purpose of sharing information internally among the different siloed business systems of a bank;
(2) **Partner,** which serves the purpose of sharing customized data only with contracted partners and for specific business models; and

(3) **Open,** which serves the purpose of sharing data securely with accredited third parties without the need for prior and/or formalized contractual or business relationship.

Even though the open banking regime has been initially considered as a substantial threat to incumbents, being at the same time associated with complexity, ambiguity, and obstacles, several players worldwide employ customized and innovative digital banking and innovation strategies to leverage on this opportunity to diversify their business models and reposition themselves within the new generation of financial services ecosystems (Guibaud, 2016). The key attributes of open banking can be positioned at the intersection between inside-out (outbound) and coupled open innovation since financial services organizations can monetize API in different ways and benefit from the open banking regime, paving the way to more trusted and consumer-oriented innovation narratives (Courbe, 2018). For the purpose of this analysis, the cases of two forward-looking financial services institutions, Nordea Bank and MasterCard, are explored. Both organizations approach the changes that open banking brings differently but proactively and in relation to their organizational innovation strategies, compared to competitors. Both organizations leverage on internal and external capabilities, tools, and opportunities to strategically position themselves within the open banking ecosystem by fostering and supporting the creation of new business models.

4.1.1. *Nordea Bank*

Nordea Bank is a 200-year-old Nordic Bank that has its headquarters in Finland. At the end of 2017, the bank became an early mover within open banking by launching a future-oriented platform, the Nordea Open Banking Developer Portal,[2] aimed at providing access to developers, customers, and FinTechs to register and test Nordea's APIs. The rationale behind this movement was grounded on the

---

[2]The Nordea Open Banking Developer Portal has won the 2017 Banking Technology Award for Top Digital Innovation.

capitalization of the foundational changes the PSD2 would bring to the European payments space. The vision behind Nordea is not simply to meet the requirements posed by the PSD2 Directive but to leverage open banking and open APIs to develop and create better financial solutions and innovate open banking business models by making available real customer data to PSD2 licensed third parties. This vision is in line with extant research looking at ways to develop API ecosystems to support the growth of open-banking APIs beyond the minimum regulatory requirements (Farrow, 2020). Test data is available to everyone that is registered in Nordea's developer portal. What is interesting from a strategic intervention point of view is that an incumbent is leveraging compliance for co-creation of products and services with FinTech companies and other external developers aspiring to become a leader within the open banking regime. In that respect, Nordea is orchestrating a dynamic ecosystem of innovation by opening up its APIs to everyone, even its competitors, enabling interaction with other systems without compliance issues.

4.1.2. *MasterCard*

MasterCard is a multinational financial services corporation, leader in global payments, and a technology company. In 2019, the company launched the MasterCard Open Banking Solutions with the vision to enable innovation and competition within the financial services landscape. This launch accelerates MasterCard's open banking strategy by offering a suite of comprehensive open banking solutions in Europe that include (1) open banking connect, (2) open banking protect, (3) open banking resolve, and (4) open banking consulting.

The portfolio of these applications and services aims at supporting the open banking ecosystem, gaining momentum along with the growth of the digital economy. These solutions facilitate the interaction between financial institutions and TPPs, helping the stakeholders of the open banking ecosystem better navigate across the requirements of the regime while contributing to the adoption of open banking globally.

The launch of the MasterCard Open Banking Solutions leverages the global expertise that MasterCard has been developing concerning the operation and support of global banking and payments systems. During 2020, MasterCard already established strong and strategic partnerships with Aion,[3] DiPocket,[4] Modulr,[5] and Finicity[6] to better harness and support the growth of the open banking ecosystem by positioning itself as a trusted intermediary within the financial services landscape.

Jim Wadsworth, MasterCard SVP, Open Banking, stated that "Collaboration is key to building a resilient open banking market [...] as we work to create an even safer system for all participants. This is a significant milestone for the wider ecosystem and opens the door to even greater adoption of open banking across Europe" (Finextra, 2020). The overall venture aims at developing a connectivity hub that will support trustworthy and legitimate communication and exchange between banks, start-ups, and TPPs.

The cases of Nordea Bank and MasterCard illuminate some interesting observations worth noting, also concerning the adoption of open innovation practices. Allowing and empowering external developers and organizations to leverage on cutting-edge capabilities fosters competition while putting together a distributed architecture grounded on collaboration among incumbents, FinTechs, and TPPs. The creation and development of new products, services, and user experiences foster stronger integration, harnessing the potential of open banking. Both Nordea Bank and MasterCard harness the advantages of a competitive "as-a-service" and "platform-enabled" competitive business model by fitting the broader institutional strategies and capabilities to the digital ecosystem and the customer needs. By adopting open innovation practices, both Nordea Bank and MasterCard have managed to diversify their existing business models, repositioning themselves within the

---

[3]Digital banking platform.
[4]Provider of cashless payment solutions via a mobile app.
[5]Digital payment account for businesses.
[6]Provider of real-time access to financial data and insights.

financial services sector as enablers and ecosystem orchestrators, leveraging internal capabilities and a trustworthy brand along with establishing innovative partnerships and strategic acquisitions to gain access to networks and other consortia to improve digital platforms and capabilities and create value both for the organizations and for the ecosystem, while adopting a holistic open banking approach.

The emergence of new business models due to open banking is creating greater and promising opportunities gradually paving the way for an open finance (also known as Open X) regime that will cater to the next wave and generation of innovation of tech-enabled smart financial services created, deployed, and disseminated through collaborative open platforms and digital value chains. Moreover, open banking is accelerating innovation by moving beyond banking and services, providing opportunities and a robust foundation for further connectivity with other data-driven sectors of the economy, creating an integrated marketplace architecture, facilitating the exchange of services and data, and resulting in solid, innovative and competitive customer experiences.

4.2. *Visa*

Visa is a global payments technology company connecting different stakeholders to fast, secure, innovative, and reliable payment solutions. In November 2020, Visa launched the FinTech Partner Connect Program in Europe, intending to support and curate the next generation of global, digitally enabled payment experiences. The program is grounded on the combinatory integration and deployment of in-house and carefully selected external FinTech expertise and capabilities. This initiative aims at providing a suite of value-added capabilities and tools to merchants and financial institutions in Europe.

The combinatory forces of Visa and the selected FinTech partners[7] reflect numerous elements of open innovation principles and

---

[7]13 leading European FinTechs.

mechanisms aimed at the acceleration of the development of the new generation of digital solutions. Visa clients can gain access to a portfolio of solutions spanning consumer credit insights, buy-now-pay-later, and transaction compliance, to sustainable banking, digital identity verification, and personalized customer engagement tools.

4.3. *Goldman Sachs*

Goldman Sachs is an American multinational investment bank and a global leader in financial services. In 2014, a group of financial institutions got together under the leadership of Goldman Sachs and created Symphony, a collaboration and chat platform project that came to life as a joint effort in the field of secure and compliant financial services enterprise messaging, aiming at providing seamless internal collaboration and communication, along with, a channel of communication with external stakeholders and data integration tools.

David Curle, the CEO of Symphony Communication, believes that Symphony is "a consortium by necessity and by choice" (Su, 2019), developing a market-driven rather than an enterprise-driven solution.

Goldman Sachs launched the internal project "Babel," building an instant messaging platform to unify internal communication tools (Williams-Grut, 2019). When Wall Street banks discovered in 2014 that Bloomberg reporters could see limited information on their terminal users' activity (*Ibid.*), Goldman Sachs spun-out the project, founding the business Symphony Communication Services Holdings LLC together with 13 partners (LaCapra, 2014). The newly formed business merged the "Babel" project with the technologies developed by the encrypted messaging start-up Perzo (Williams-Grut, 2019), and upon launching in September 2015, became an alternative to the platform found on Bloomberg terminal's chat function (Alloway, 2014) and Slack.

Within the first year after being released, Symphony raised US$170 million by its founders and partners, such as Google

Alphabet (Finextra, 2016). Further, it built a user base of 116,000 paying customers and announced a Webhooks API, which enables other companies to integrate into Symphony, extending its functionality through bots, apps, and integrations (Williams-Grut, 2016).

The business raised in 2019 an additional US$165m, being valued at a unicorn level at US$1.4bn (Aravindan, 2019), bringing the total amount of money raised to date to US$461m (McNulty, 2020). Key strategic investors backing Symphony are Goldman Sachs, BNP Paribas, J.P. Morgan, Mitsubishi UFJ Financial Group, HSBC, UBS, Société Générale, and Standard Chartered. The platform had built a base of more than 450,000 licensed users, compared to the 325,000 clients of Bloomberg (Noonan and Szalay, 2019), aiming to target profitability by 2021 or 2022 (Aravindan, 2019).

Symphony is the outcome of a collaborative endeavor aiming at becoming an organization that can be trusted by its clients who are seeking a secure business communication and messaging tool that is cost-effective, broader, and alternative to Bloomberg that start-ups and smaller technology firms (not only limited to financial services) can afford.

4.4. *BBVA*

Being born out of the merger of two major Spanish banking institutions, BBVA is a global financial services group, which was founded in 1857 (BBVA, 2020). The business aspires to achieve a more sustainable and inclusive society (*Ibid.*). To achieve this, the bank was a pioneer in building an omnichannel vision and strategy, shifting away from product-centric toward customer-centric models, putting the customer at the front and center of the business (Bey *et al.*, 2013). As a result, systems are initially developed as ideal future solutions for customers, followed by finding "a way to make that system work for the bank" (Manning and Bodine, 2012, p. 83).

With technology rapidly evolving in the past decades, customers, as well as their requirements and how they can be reached, have changed (González, 2015). Starting in 2008, BBVA adapted to this technological transformation by rebuilding its technology platform from scratch and doubling its system investments from €1.2 billion in 2006 to €2.4 billion in 2013 and shifting "the proportion of funds spent to keep systems operational ("run") to funds invested in new development ("change"), moving from the industry standard of 80%/20% to a new standard of 60%/40%" (González, 2015, p. 12). This overhaul enabled the business to launch several innovative offerings by the end of 2012, such as online personal finance management in late 2008, a next-generation ATM, an app allowing money to be withdrawn from a BBVA cash machine with an SMS code, a video conference platform to connect customers and employees, a virtual banking assistant that can perform banking tasks, and a personal advisor which combines personal advice with remote channels (Ensor, 2012).

The cost associated with the continuous development of novel offerings has paid off for BBVA. The strong push on customer-focused digital capabilities has shown a clear impact on the growth of the bank's customer base (Genç, 2019), with almost 40 million customers digitally interacting with the business (Davenport and Andrew, 2019). Also, BBVA has become one of the leaders in terms of profitability, ahead of its European peers (Genç, 2019). Having developed the "self-driving bank account," the bank's AI Factory is dedicated to further personalizing customer financial advice (Davenport and Andrew, 2019).

4.5. *Paydirekt*

With technologies constantly evolving, the financial industry is subject to disruption by new companies that specifically invest in the monetization of disruptive digital solutions (Huch, 2016). The market for e- and m-Payment was disrupted by PayPal, which was founded in December 1998. Their open digital payments platform counts 325 million active users and is available in 200 markets worldwide, supporting receiving funds in 100 currencies (PayPal, 2020).

Whilst PayPal has become one of the world's largest online payment systems, German banks responded in 2014 with the founding of Paydirekt. Since April 2016 the functionality of Paydirekt is available to around 1,400 banks. The platform positions itself as not being a start-up idea, but a customer-centered service and counts over 3.5 million users (Paydirekt, 2020).

As an entire industry joined forces to develop the new service, Paydirekt faced challenges in regards to collaboration which required complex governance structures that ultimately prevented quick business decisions (Hasselwander, 2019; Nestler, 2020).

When banks started offering Paydirekt in 2016 (Paydirekt, 2020), PayPal was already established in Germany, having built strong and significant partnerships. The switching cost for integrating Paydirekt into commerce-platforms was therefore initially not worthwhile for many customers (Hasselwander, 2019).

Today, Paydirekt has 3.5 million registered users (Paydirekt, 2020), and the number of transactions on the Paydirekt platform is not meeting the expectations of the German banking industry (Atzler, 2020a), resulting in 12 private banks (including ING, Santander, and Targobank), leaving the initiative and selling their shares in the platform to Deutsche Bank and Commerzbank (Atzler, 2020b).

Moving forward, experts from the major German lobby associations in the banking industry, as well as from the largest banks, are involved in launching the project "#DK." The objective of the project is to merge the payment-methods Paydirekt, Giropay, Girocard, and Kwitt into one platform under the working title "X-Pay" (Schreiber, 2019; Atzler, 2019a; Atzler, 2019b).

In August 2020, the initiative announced that Paydirekt GmbH is taking over Giropay GmbH, and the services of Paydirekt and Giropay will be merged under the brand of Giropay. In the next step, Kwitt is expected to be integrated under the brand as well (Nestler, 2020).

5. Bringing the Cases Together

The above-mentioned cases highlight several key elements of the role of open innovation as a vehicle of business model innovation, as an enabler of ecosystem innovation, and as a lubricant of a successful

Figure 2. Timeline of when the cases went to market.

data-driven cultural shift within the financial services sector. Figure 2 shows when the examined cases went to market.

The first to adopt open innovation practices was BBVA. The bank started rebuilding its technology platform in 2008. Since then, core banking functions have been digitized, new digital products and services developed, and either partnerships or acquisitions of start-ups conducted. Further, BBVA is transforming its organizational structure aiming to become a software company (Buvat and Khadikar, 2016). Overall, these initiatives resulted in the company building one of the leading open banking ecosystems (Semple, 2019).

A similar path toward orchestrating a dynamic ecosystem of innovation has been pursued by Nordea Bank since 2017, when it opened its APIs to everyone. Similar to BBVA, the bank has hereby positioned itself as one of the leading open banking ecosystems.

MasterCard and Visa, which have launched initiatives in FinTech more recently, act as a gateway between banks such as Nordea Bank or BBVA and authorized TPPs.

Meanwhile, when Goldman Sachs and its partners developed the instant messaging service symphony in 2015, a Webhooks API was integrated in order to allow TPPs to integrate their solutions with the symphony platform. Hereby, similar to open banking, an ecosystem approach was utilized.

Paydirekt, which launched in 2016 as a competitor to rising online payment systems in Germany, did not pursue an ecosystem approach. The business utilizes its APIs to allow merchants to connect their shop-system.

Regarding the technologies utilized, it can be concluded that BBVA, Nordea Bank, MasterCard, and Visa embrace current trends and are shaping a new market environment by embracing the coupled approach to open innovation.

Symphony, on the other hand, utilizes modern technologies in order to compete with established players within the industry. The business was founded utilizing the inside-out open innovation approach and took advantage when the industry lost trust in the messaging platform offered by Bloomberg. Symphony entered the marketplace by offering a cheaper and more secure product than its competitor, thus differentiating itself in key areas.

Whilst Paydirekt resulted from a similar inside-out approach, the number of participants involved resulted in complex governance structures. Upon release of the new platform, the market environment had already matured and the offering failed to sufficiently outperform its competitors in order to see a strong adoption.

Overall, the cases illustrate the importance of adopting open innovation practices within the financial services industry. Hereby the relevance of data, as well as the foundation of ecosystems has increased in recent years and is further accelerated by legislation, Open Banking, and Banking as a Service.

Data is providing numerous opportunities for innovation and change. Data-driven business applications and business models have rewritten the competitive forces within the financial services industry and its value chain. The resulting transition within the industry calls for stronger collaboration, focused and strategic partnerships, as well as smart leveraging and deployment of internal and external capabilities, competencies, and resources.

The democratization of data, which caters to stronger data accessibility, aims at fostering and driving trust within the various financial services ecosystems by bringing a new context of transformation, erasing communication and capacity boundaries, and encouraging the development of hybrid business models, structures, and architectural designs to support the pivotal nature of a data-driven financial services regime.

The above-mentioned organizations, by taking advantage of a variety of open innovation practices, have managed to rethink and reposition their strategies, restructure their governance, and orchestrate new ecosystems and strategic partnerships to remain at the forefront of innovation and nurture positive outcomes of data-driven financial services projects and solutions, along with instilling and curating the next generation data-driven culture of entrepreneurship in financial services.

Ecosystems are positioned at the heart of open innovation practices adopted by financial services organizations capitalizing on several emerging trends such as open banking, emerging technologies and technological evolutions, customer centricity, and regulatory requirements and provisions.

These trends gradually lead financial services organizations to become more open and outward looking and establish strategic partnerships with key stakeholders in terms of business model innovation initiatives and repositioning within existing or emerging ecosystems. In particular, the deployment of APIs enables new horizons of connectivity and frictionless data transferability and portability, along with a new breed of culture and mindset of innovation.

The emergence and adoption of "as-a-service" business models within financial services cater for co-development, co-creation, and co-commercialization practices, bringing additional levels of agility and first-to-market potentialities. The adoption of ecosystemic approaches to innovation also drives the importance of setting up, maintaining, and governing strategic partnerships (internal and external) with the focus on value creation both for the partners and the ecosystem as a whole, along with the illumination of the roles the key stakeholders have and their contribution toward the future evolution of such ecosystems (Castro *et al.*, 2020).

6. Concluding Remarks

Adopting open innovation practices within the financial industry can empower and foster collaboration between financial institutions, representing a better chance for survival rather than trying to get by based on a proprietary basis and existing legacy.

The analysis of the cases has shown that the role of open innovation within the financial industry is primarily perceived as a tool for finding and providing solutions to complex problems (streamlining operations, capturing new market niches, and establishing a competitive advantage) and meeting business needs and objectives while safeguarding trust through human branding and operational transparency (Salampasis *et al.*, 2014).

Furthermore, open innovation fosters stepping change and simplicity for customers, while at the same time nurturing activity, legitimacy, and responsiveness. Similarly, open innovation facilitates actions of addressing human behavior in terms of integrating processes and simplifying in terms of making it easier to do business. Simplicity is cognitive and is related to action-taking, while ease is the amount of effort required to take that particular action. The adoption of open innovation practices opens up sourcing and tapping on creativity and executional capabilities from people with new sets of skills that can exist outside the financial industry too. In this framework, this adoption puts a structure, objective, coaching, and expertise around the inherent talent in the financial industry by providing guidance, focus, and deliverables. Furthermore, open innovation caters to the development of new sorts of experiences for the financial industry, while empowering differentiation. Last but not least, open innovation is seen as a vehicle and opportunity of building trustworthiness by using authority from the outside to verify hypotheses of new innovative product and service development.

The adoption of open innovation practices in financial services constitutes a new type of strategic innovation leadership epitomizing interconnected and interrelated elements that cover a wide spectrum of multidimensional attributes, as described in the cases above. Open innovation in financial services is positioned at the core strategic DNA being responsible for infusing and diffusing an innovation culture within the organization. Apart from the acceleration and the new face of digital transformation, open innovation is responsible for creating value and competitive advantage by allowing organizations to reach out and systematically identify and commercialize new products and services developed with external partners, safeguarding market and customer relevance, while creating an integrated open innovation capability within financial services institutions.

The adoption of open innovation practices in financial services allows for embracing competition for frictionless financial services navigating the new global financial architecture and building for the long term.

The financial industry failed to adapt to a dynamic changing environment on a global scale, and this failure accelerated its nearly total destruction. This financial meltdown has completely rewritten the rules of business and capital management and has pointed toward the direction of changing mentality and dominant culture (Dahrendorf, 2010).

Learning from the overall failure case of the financial system, financial institutions gradually begin to establish a managerial culture that helps them learn the why, the how, and the when to adapt and adopt an open and collaborative approach toward innovation. This critical approach to open innovation addresses the question of what the actual benchmark for success is for the financial industry per se. In this frame of reference, open innovation in the financial industry also calls for expulsion of ignorance, irresponsibility, and information asymmetries regarding the consequences of employing risky behaviors both by financial institutions and individuals.

The future is unpredictable and the only certainty is disruption, especially in the eyes of the shaping and developments of global FinTech innovation labs and entrepreneurial activities in the technology start-up scene (mobile payments, money transfers, loans, fundraising, asset management, alternative forms of finance, big data, etc.), showcasing emerging disruptions of trans-disciplinary nature, along with the associated reworking of financial regulations, transparency, customer behavior, and sustainable growth.

The emerging FinTech ecosystems that are driven by competition and diversity aim at fostering and promoting stability, efficiency, and accessibility, along with the orchestration of all the relevant and interrelated stakeholders. As seen, the cases discussed hereby enable an evolutionary path of open innovation in financial services by following patterns driven by competitive forces, regulatory interventions, and business models that are designed to hedge systemic risk. The deployment of open innovation practices, as portrayed by the cases, reconceptualizes the very nature of competition and innovation, gradually altering the topology of financial services, ultimately leading to the disruption of the traditional business model of financial services institutions.

Unlike in other sectors (e.g. biotech sector), where capital is provided from the beginning and further payments aligned with milestones, it is not uncommon in the financial services sector to start with a commercial partnership (consisting often of in-kind contributions or a mandate) followed by an investment round where the bank takes a stake if a Proof-of-Concept (POC) is provided. These means that such deals would start basically as non-pecuniary deals. It is also common that a large group of FinTechs quietly partner as suppliers of the big banks (especially in RegTech/risk/compliance space and in the investment advice/portfolio management sector). If the model is successful and scalable and provides a Unique Selling Proposition (USP) or a complementary offering, then banks may take over a FinTech (pecuniary inbound). Our observations indicate that such a process is not binary, but rather fluid.

The above-mentioned cases illuminate that the adoption of open innovation practices in the financial industry can help financial institutions reach out beyond the existing and prevailing narrative of innovation and look far ahead of the traditional industrial and organizational boundaries. The nurturing of collaboration and openness can help financial institutions maintain and leverage on their market leadership by utilizing technologies, know-how, talent, values, and norms from different industries but also from organizations within the financial industry itself, so as to develop and lead significant breakthroughs.

Open innovation introduces terms such as connectivity, mobility, and experimentation. Tapping into a multitude of disciplines that financial institutions traditionally overlook leverages the true meaning and purpose of innovation within the financial industry that will not only lead to financial value but also primarily create an ecosystem architectural design of transformative FinTech innovation.

References

Alloway, T. (2014). Goldman's symphony of babble. *Financial Times*. Retrieved from: https://ftalphaville.ft.com/2014/08/06/1916472/goldmans-symphony-of-babble/ (Accessed on 4 June 2021).

Alt, R., Beck, R., & Smits, M.T.(2018). Fintech and the transformation of the financial industry. *Electronic Markets*, 28(3), 235–243.

Atzler, E. (2019a). Paydirekt Vor Dem Aus: Deutsche Banken Wollen Zahlungssysteme Zusammenlegen: Handelsblatt. Retrieved from: https://www.handelsblatt.com/finanzen/banken-versicherungen/arbeitstitel-x-pay-paydirekt-vor-dem-aus-deutsche-banken-wollen-zahlungssysteme-zusammenlegen-/24976628.html (Accessed on 4 June 2021).

Atzler, E. (2019b). Deutsche Banken Forcieren Prüfung Ihrer Zahlungsdienstleistungen: Handelsblatt. Retrieved from: https://www.handelsblatt.com/finanzen/banken-versicherungen/paydirekt-giropay-und-kwitt-deutsche-banken-forcieren-pruefung-ihrer-zahlungsdienstleistungen/24446396.html (Accessed on 4 June 2021).

Atzler, E. (2020a). Deutsche Banken Kommen Bei Der Bündelung Ihrer Zahlungsangebote Nur Langsam Voran: Handelsblatt. Retrieved from: https://www.handelsblatt.com/finanzen/banken-versicherungen/bezahlen-im-internet-deutsche-banken-kommen-bei-der-buendelung-ihrer-zahlungsangebote-nur-langsam-voran/25639912.html (Accessed on 4 June 2021).

Atzler, E. (2020b). Deutsche Bank Und Commerzbank Übernehmen Mehr Anteile an Schwächelndem Bezahldienst Paydirekt: Handelsblatt. Retrieved from: https://www.handelsblatt.com/finanzen/banken-versicherungen/online-bezahlen-deutsche-bank-und-commerzbank-uebernehmen-mehr-anteile-an-schwaecheln-dem-bezahldienst-paydirekt/25391266.html (Accessed on 4 June 2021).

Aravindan, A. (2019). Goldman-backed chat platform symphony raises $165 million in new funds. *Reuters*. Retrieved from: https://www.reuters.com/article/us-symphony-funding/goldman-backed-chat-platform-symphony-raises-165-million-in-new-funds-idUSKCN1TD1RB (Accessed on 4 June 2021).

Arner, D. W., Barberis, J., & Buckley, R. P. (2016). The evolution of fintech: New post-crisis paradigm. *Georgetown Journal of International Law*, 47(4), 1271–1320.

Baldwin, C. & Von Hippel, E. (2011). Modeling a Paradigm Shift: From Producer Innovation to User and Open Collaborative Innovation. *Organization Science*, 22(6), 1399–417.

Baldwin, C., Hienerth, C. & Von Hippel, E. (2006). How user innovations become commercial products: A theoretical investigation and case study. *Research Policy*, 35(9), 1291–1313.

BBVA (2019). How does banking-as-a-service differ from open banking? BBVA. Retrieved from: https://www.bbva.com/ndb/en/article/how-does-banking-as-a-service-differ-from-open-banking/ (Accessed on 4 June 2021).

BBVA (2020). BBVA in Brief. Retrieved from: https://shareholdersandinvestors. bbva.com/bbva-group/bbva-in-brief/factsheet/ (Accessed on 4 June 2021).

Bey, A. B., Reyes, C., Vanesa, F., Luz, G., Antonio, H., Israel, J., Marta, M., Luz, M., Manolo, P., Carlos, S., Javier, S., Elena, V., Ignacio, V., Gustavo, Y., & "Phil" Sang, G. (2013). BBVA Innovation Edge. Customer Experience (English): Omnichannel. BBVA Innovation Center.

Bidault, F., Despres, C., & Butler, C. (1998). The drivers of cooperation between buyers and suppliers for product innovation. *Research Policy*, 26(7–8), 719–732.

Bogers, M., & West, J. (2012). Managing distributed innovation: Strategic utilization of open and user innovation. *Creativity and Innovation Management*, 21(1), 61–75.

Bogers, M., Chesbrough, H., & Moedas, C. (2018). Open innovation: Research, practices, and policies. *California Management Review*, 60(2), 5–16.

Botta, A., Ulissi, T.J., Sasia, E., Digiacomo, N., Höll, R., Jain, R. *et al.* (2018). PSD2: Taking advantage of open banking disruption. McKinsey & Company (Global Banking Practice). Retrieved from: https://www.mckinsey.de/~/media/ McKinsey/Industries/Financial%20Services/Our%20Insights/PSD2%20 Taking%20advantage%20of%20open-banking%20disruption/PSD2-Taking-advantage-of-open-banking-disruption.pdf (Accessed on 4 June 2021).

Brunner, F. (2009). *Wertstiftende Strategien Im Bankgeschäft* (Physica-Verlag HD, Heidelberg).

Brunswicker, S., & Chesbrough, H. (2018). The adoption of open innovation in large firms. *Research-Technology Management*, 61(1), 35–45.

Buvat, J., & Khadikar, A. (2016). Bbva: Rebooting banking for a digital economy: Capgemini Consulting. Retrieved from: https://www.capgemini.com/consulting-no/wp-content/uploads/sites/36/2017/08/bbva_pov_v6_03-03-16.pdf (Accessed on 4 June 2021).

Castro, P., Rodrigues, J. P., & Teixeira, J. G. (2020). Understanding Fintech Ecosystem Evolution through Service Innovation and Socio-Technical System Perspective. Exploring Service Science. *Lecture Notes in Business Information Processing* (Springer International Publishing), pp. 187–201.

Chandler, A. D. (1962). *Strategy and Structure: Chapters in the History of the Industrial Enterprise* (MIT Press, Cambridge).

Chesbrough, H. W. (2003). The era of open innovation. *MIT Sloan Management Review*, 44(3), 35–41.

Chesbrough, H. W., & Appleyard, M. M. (2007). Open innovation and strategy. *California Management Review*, 50(1), 57–76.

Chesbrough, H., & Bogers, M. (2014). Explicating open innovation: Clarifying an emerging paradigm for understanding innovation. In *New Frontiers in Open Innovation*, Chesbrough, H., West, J., & Vanhaverbeke W. (eds.) (Oxford University Press, Oxford), pp. 3–28.

Chesbrough, H. W., & Garman, A. R. (2009). How open innovation can help you cope in lean times. *Harvard Business Review*, 87(12), 68–76.

Chesbrough, H., Vanhaverbeke, W,. & West, J. (2006). *Open Innovation: Researching a New Paradigm* (OUP Oxford, Oxford).

Courbe, J. (2018). Building "Open Banking" on a Platform of Trust. *American Bankers Association ABA Banking Journal*, 110(4), 38.

Dahlander, L., & Gann, D. M. (2010). How open is innovation? *Research Policy*, 39(6), 699–709.

Dahrendorf, R. (2010). After the crisis: Back to the Protestant ethic? Six critical observations. *Max Weber Studies*, 10(1), 11–21.

Dapp, T. F. (2017). Fintech: The digital transformation in the financial sector. In *Sustainability in a Digital World*. Osburg, T., & Lohrmann, C. (eds.), *CSR, Sustainability, Ethics & Governance* (Springer International Publishing, Cham), pp. 189–199.

Davenport, T. H., & Spanyi, A. (2019). Digital transformation should start with customers. *MIT Sloan Management Review*. Retrieved from: https://sloanreview. mit.edu/article/digital-transformation-should-start-with-customers/ (Accessed on 4 June 2021).

Davis, A. (2019). The world turns to open banking. 11:FS. Retrieved from: https://11fs.com/article/world-open-banking (Accessed on 7 July 2021).

Deutsche Bank Innovation Labs (2020). Who we are: Deutsche Bank's commitment to innovation and partnership: Deutsche Bank Innovation Labs. Retrieved from: https://www.db.com/what-we-do/focus-topics/innovation-network (Accessed on 7 July 2021).

Ensor, B. (2012). Innovation Lessons from BBVA. Forrester. Retrieved from: https://go.forrester.com/blogs/12-11-09-innovation_lessons_from_bbva/ (Accessed on 4 June 2021).

Farrow, G. S. (2020). An application programming interface model for open banking ecosystems. *Journal of Payments Strategy & Systems*, 14(1), 75–91.

Finextra (2016). Wall Street messaging outfit symphony looks to raise $100m — WSJ: Retrieved from: https://www.finextra.com/newsarticle/29559/wall-street-messaging-outfit-symphony-looks-to-raise-100m---wsj (Accessed on 4 June 2021).

Finextra (2020). Three Fintechs join Mastercard Open Banking Project: Finextra. Retrieved from: https://www.finextra.com/pressarticle/83135/three-fintechs-join-mastercard-open-banking-project (Accessed on 4 June 2021).

Franke, N., & Piller, F. (2004). Value creation by toolkits for user innovation and design: The case of the watch market. *Journal of Product Innovation Management*, 21(6), 401–415.

Gans, J. S. (2016). Keep calm and manage disruption. *MIT Sloan Management Review*, 57(3), 83–90.

Gassmann, O. (2006). Opening up the innovation process: Towards an agenda. *R and D Management*, 36(3), 223–228.

Gassmann, O., & Enkel, E. (2004). Towards a theory of open innovation: three core process archetypes. R&D Management Conference (RADMA) 2004-Lisbon. Available online at https://www.alexandria.unisg.ch/274/ (Accessed on 4 June 2021).

Gassmann, O., & Enkel, E. (2005). Open Innovation Forschung Forschungsfragen Und Erste Erkenntnisse. University of St Gallen.

Genç, O. (2019). BBVA is once again a leader in terms of profitability: BBVA. Retrieved from: https://www.bbva.com/en/onur-genc-bbva-is-once-again-a-leader-in-terms-of-profitability/ (Accessed on 4 June 2021).

González, F. (2015). Reinventing the company in the digital age. BBVA.

Guibaud, S. (2016). How to develop a profitable, customer-focused digital banking strategy: Open banking services and developer-friendly APIs. *Journal of Digital Banking*, 1(1), 6–12.

Hallsworth, J. R., & Robert, P. I. (2019). Open banking opens opportunities for greater customer value: Reshaping the banking experience. Retrieved from: https://assets.kpmg/content/dam/kpmg/xx/pdf/2019/05/open-banking-opening-opportunities-for-customer-value.pdf (Accessed on 4 June 2021).

Hatch, M. S., Christopher, L., James, M., Varun, B., Tom, C., Sharon, C., & Doina, I. (2019). Global Fintech Adoption Index. Retrieved from: https://www.ey.com/en_gl/ey-global-fintech-adoption-index (Accessed on 4 June 2021).

Hasselwander, M. (2019). Mobility as a Service (Maas) in Deutschland. *Ausblick Und Implikationen Für Den Öffentlichen Verkehr*, 71, 59–63.

Helfat, C. E. (2006). Open innovation: The new imperative for creating and profiting from technology. *Academy of Management Perspectives*, 20(2), 86–88.

Huch, S. (2016). Fallbeispiele Innovativer Fintech-Unternehmen. *Wirtschaftsinformatik & Management*, 8(3), 64–73.

Inauen, M., Carlsson, S., & Schenker-Wicki, A. (2011). The impact of outside-in open innovation on innovation performance. *European Journal of Innovation Management*, 14(4), 496–520.

Innopay (2019). Innopay Open Banking Monitor: Banks moving beyond the PSD2 requirements: Innopay. Retrieved from: https://www.innopay.com/en/publications/innopay-open-banking-monitor-banks-moving-beyond-psd2-requirements (Accessed on 4 June 2021).

King, B. (2018). *Bank 4.0: Banking Everywhere, Never at a Bank* (Wiley).

LaCapra, L. T. (2014). Exclusive: Goldman leads investment by Wall Street in new communications platform. *Reuters*. Retrieved from: https://www.reuters.com/article/us-goldman-communications-investment/exclusive-goldman-leads-investment-by-wall-street-in-new-communications-platform-idUSKCN0HQ 41Q20141001 (Accessed on 4 June 2021).

Laursen, K., & Salter, A. (2006). Open for innovation: The role of openness in explaining innovation performance among U.K. manufacturing firms. *Strategic Management Journal*, 27(2), 131–150.

Lee, I., & Shin, Y. J. (2018). Fintech: Ecosystem, business models, investment decisions, and challenges. *Business Horizons*, 61(1), 35–46.

Lichtenthaler, U. (2008). Open innovation in practice: An analysis of strategic approaches to technology transactions. *IEEE Transactions on Engineering Management*, 55(1), 148–157.

Lichtenthaler, U. (2011). Open innovation: Past research, current debates, and future directions. *Academy of Management Perspectives*, 25(1), 75–93.

Manning, H., & Bodine, K. F. (2012). *Outside In: The Power of Putting Customers at the Center of Your Business* (Houghton Mifflin Harcourt).

McNulty, L. (2020). Symphony doubles hiring plans after 300% user surge among home-bound bankers. *Financial News*. Retrieved from: https://www.fnlondon.com/articles/symphony-doubles-hiring-plans-after-300-user-surge-among-home-bound-bankers-20201023 (Accessed on 4 June 2021).

Nestler, F. (2020). Paydirekt Verschwindet Vom Markt: Frankfurter Allgemeine Zeitung. Retrieved from: https://www.faz.net/aktuell/finanzen/meine-finanzen/geld-ausgeben/bezahldienst-paydirekt-verschwindet-vom-markt-fusion-mit-giropay-16930747.html (Accessed on 4 June 2021).

Noonan, L., & Szalay, E. (2019). Symphony will not go public until it is profitable, says chief. *Financial Times*. Retrieved from: https://www.ft.com/content/603abe2a-ec63-11e9-85f4-d00e5018f061 (Accessed on 4 June 2021).

Nonninger, L., & Mekebeb, T. (2018). Latest fintech industry trends, technologies and research from our ecosystem report. *Business Insider*. Retrieved from: https://www.businessinsider.com/fintech-ecosystem-report?IR=T (Accessed on 4 June 2021).

Nonninger, L. & Mekebeb, T. (2019). The future of Fintech 2019: The five mega-trends reshaping the financial services value chain. *Business Insider*. Retrieved from: https://www.businessinsider.com/future-of-fintech/?r=AU&IR=T (Accessed on 4 June 2021).

Oliveira, P., & Von Hippel, E. (2011). Users as service innovators: The case of banking services. *Research Policy*, 40(6), 806–818.

Paulet, E. (2018). Banking liquidity regulation: Impact on their business model and on entrepreneurial finance in Europe. *Strategic Change*, 27(4), 339–350.

Paydirekt (2020). Paydirekt: Das Sind Wir.: paydirekt GmbH. Retrieved from: https://www.paydirekt.de/ueberuns/index.html (Accessed on 4 June 2021).

PayPal (2020). Paypal about: Who we are: PayPal Holdings, Inc. Retrieved from: https://www.paypal.com/us/webapps/mpp/about (Accessed on 4 June 2021).

Ramdani, B., Rothwell, B., & Boukrami, E. (2020). Open banking: The emergence of new digital business models. *International Journal of Innovation and Technology Management*, 17(05), 2050033.

Reuter, V. G. (1977). Suggestion systems: Utilization, evaluation, and implementation. *California Management Review*, 19(3), 78–89.

Salampasis, D. (2015). Trust-embedded open innovation: Towards a human-centric approach in the financial industry, Lappeenranta University of Technology.

Salampasis, D., & Mention, A-L. (2019). From a-value to value-multiplication: Leveraging outbound open innovation practices for unrelated diversification in the sensor industry. *Technology Analysis & Strategic Management*, 31(11), 1327–1340.

Salampasis, D., Mention, A., & Torkkeli, M. (2014). Open innovation and collaboration in the financial services sector: Exploring the role of trust. *International Journal of Business Innovation and Research*, 8, 466–484.

Satzger, G., & Neus, A. (2010). Principles of collaborative innovation: Implementation of open and peer-to-peer innovation approaches. 10.1007/978-3-642-10823-5_14.

Sawhney, M., & Prandelli, E. (2000). Communities of creation: Managing distributed innovation in turbulent markets. *California Management Review*, 42(4), 24–54.

Schreiber, M. (2019). Paydirekt Ist Vorerst Gescheitert: Süddeutsche Zeitung. Retrieved from: https://www.sueddeutsche.de/wirtschaft/paydirekt-paypal-online-handel-1.4560008 (Accessed on 4 June 2021).

Schueffel, P. (2017). Taming the beast: A scientific definition of Fintech. *Journal of Innovation Management*, 4(4), 32–54.

Schueffel, P. E., & Vadana, I- I. (2015). Open innovation in the financial services sector — A global literature review. *Journal of Innovation Management*, 3(1), 25–48.

Scotchmer, S. (2004). *Innovation and incentives*. (MIT Press, Cambridge, Massachusetts).

Semple, C. (2019). Bbva recognised as a world leader in Open Banking: BBVA. Retrieved from: https://www.bbva.com/en/bbva-recognised-as-a-world-leader-in-open-banking/ (Accessed on 4 June 2021).

Simanis, E., & Hart, S. L. (2009). Innovation from the inside out. *MIT Sloan Management Review*, 50(4), 77–86.

Standaert, W., Muylle, S., & Cumps, B. (2020). Opening the gates: A framework for an open banking strategy. *Journal of Digital Banking*, 4(4), 364–376.

Su, J. (2019). Ceo Tech Talk: Symphony raised $460 million to build the world's corporate social network. *Forbes*. Retrieved from: https://www.forbes.com/sites/jeanbaptiste/2019/08/10/ceo-tech-talk-why-symphony-raised-460-million-to-build-the-biggest-corporate-social-network/?sh=3f57f08f2027 (Accessed on 4 June 2021).

Supervision BCoB (2019). Report on Open Banking and Application Programming Interfaces: BIS — Bank for International Settlements. Retrieved from: https://www.bis.org/bcbs/publ/d486.pdf (Accessed on 4 June 2021).

Van Der Meer, H. (2017). Open innovation? The Dutch treat: Challenges in thinking in business models. *Creativity and Innovation Management*, 16(2), 192–202.

Von Hippel, E. (1986). Lead users: A source of novel product concepts. *Management Science*, 32(7), 791–805.

Von Hippel, E. (1988). *The Sources of Innovation* (Oxford University Press).

Von Hippel, E. (2005a). Democratizing Innovation: The evolving phenomenon of user innovation. *Journal für Betriebswirtschaft*, 55(1), 63–78.

Von Hippel, E. (2005b). *Democratizing Innovation* (The MIT Press).

Von Hippel, E. (2009). Democratizing innovation: The evolving phenomenon of user innovation. *International Journal of Innovation Science*, 1(1), 29–40.

Wadsworth, J. (2020). Readying the open banking system for success. *Journal of Digital Banking*, 5(1), 6–12.

West, J., & Gallagher, S. (2006). Challenges of open innovation: The paradox of firm investment in open-source software. *R and D Management*, 36(3), 319–331.

West, J., Salter, A., Vanhaverbeke, W., & Chesbrough, H. (2014). Open innovation: The next decade. *Research Policy*, 43(5), 805–811.

Williams-Grut, O. (2016). The Goldman Sachs-backed "Bloomberg killer" has 116,000 customers a year after launch. *Business Insider*. Retrieved from: https://www.businessinsider.com/goldman-sachs-symphony-customer-numbers-meetings-webhook-api-fintech-bloomberg-2016-10?r=DE&IR=T (Accessed on 4 June 2021).

Williams-Grut, O. (2019). Inside chat app symphony's battle to break into a $28 billion Wall Street Market — and avoid becoming Bloomberg roadkill. *Business Insider*. Retrieved from: https://www.businessinsider.com/inside-symphonys-battle-to-break-into-a-28-billion-market-for-wall-street-chat-and-avoid-becoming-bloomberg-roadkill-2018-8?r=DE&IR=T (Accessed on 4 June 2021).

Yurcan, B., & Robert, B. (2015). Why more banks will spin off internal tech. *American Banker*. Retrieved from: https://www.americanbanker.com/news/why-more-banks-will-spin-off-internal-tech (Accessed on 4 June 2021).

Zachariadis, M. (2020). How "open" is the future of banking? Data sharing andopen data frameworks in financial services. In *The Technological Revolution in Financial Services King*, R. M., and Nesbitt, W. R. (eds.). (University of Toronto Press, Toronto), pp. 129–157.

Chapter 6

FinTech Innovation Ecosystems

Wajeeha H. Awadh[*]

wajehahussain@gmail.com

Abstract. The FinTech disruption has affected the global financial industry, which required many countries to cater to this disruption by building the right FinTech Innovation Ecosystems. For these types of ecosystems to succeed, they need to be based on open innovation concept, where multiple players in the ecosystem can work together to ensure FinTech innovation. The FinTech industry itself is formed based on various collaborations between different stakeholders to come up with innovative products. However, on a macro level, for countries to become a global FinTech hub, they need to ensure the existence of nine important components of FinTech Innovation Ecosystem. These components are FinTech Start-ups, Traditional Financial Institutions (FIs), Government, Financial Customers, Technology Providers, Human Capital, Supporting Platforms, Associations, and International Profile. These nine components, using an open innovation concept, can play a major role in establishing the right FinTech Innovation Ecosystems, which shall lead countries to become global FinTech hubs.

---

[*] Author has contributed to this edited volume in her individual capacity.

Keywords. FinTech; ecosystem; innovation; start-ups; financial institutions; BigTechs; incubators; accelerators; talent; strategies; governments.

1. Introduction

The financial industry is going through a major disruption due the existence of FinTechs. These FinTechs provide various financial services and products through innovative business models that utilize the concept of open innovation. Therefore, for FinTech industry to grow and further contribute to the economy, it requires a supportive innovative ecosystem that can enable these FinTechs through open innovation. Accordingly, this chapter discusses the ecosystem that need to be in place to support FinTechs through open innovation. Many countries nowadays aim at becoming a Global FinTech Hub, which can only be achieved by creating the right FinTech innovation ecosystem. Such an ecosystem requires supporting open innovation through various collaborations between the components of the ecosystem itself. Accordingly, this chapter identifies these stockholders and their role in FinTech innovation.

2. Changes Lead to FinTech Innovation

It was once said by the Chinese Premier Li Keqiang "Changes call for innovation, and innovation leads to progress." Although there are different stories of how FinTech came to light and disrupted the financial industry, there is no doubt that the changes that occurred during the financial crisis in 2008 had contributed largely to the existence of FinTech[1] innovations. During the financial crisis, banks were busy with compliance and regulations that were imposed on

---

[1]FinTech or Financial Technology firms are those that offer users with a range of financial services and products using technology which once almost exclusively was the business of banks (Chishti and Barberis, 2016).

them and could not pay attention to their customers' needs, which resulted in customers losing trust in them. Consequently, this situation has left behind a large gap in terms of customers' financial needs, where they had to look for alternative financial solutions away from banks.

FinTech start-ups at that time realized the need and turned the situation into a business opportunity by introducing new innovative business models that provide better financial services and products to consumers. These innovative business models were formed using various technologies and existing financial infrastructure. Accordingly, these FinTechs started to disrupt the traditional financial institutions (FIs) and took their business away.

Since then, FinTechs have been getting a lot of attention globally due to the value these new innovations are bringing to customers. In this regard, the value of these FinTechs as well as their potential of profitability have been capitalized by investors globally. This can be noticed clearly in the amounts of investment that are being pumped into this industry by different investors, including traditional banks themselves. Based on a KPMG (2020) report, the global investment in FinTech companies in 2019 has reached US$135.7 billion across 2693 deals.

In the meantime, the impact of FinTech innovations on the economy and its ability to reshape the financial industry have also been realized by different countries globally. Therefore, many of these countries started to declare their interest in becoming the Global FinTech Hub. This of course has resulted in attracting many FinTechs as well as investors globally to these hubs. Even though the FinTech journey is still at its early stages, there are some countries that have started building the right ecosystem that encourages open innovation in the financial industry and embraces the implementation of different technologies.

Initially, market need was the drive behind FinTech innovations, but in order to keep the momentum ongoing and the wheel of innovation evolving, creating ecosystems that support FinTech innovations became a must; in particular, FinTechs require collaborations and support in order to succeed.

3. Building a FinTech Innovation Ecosystem

The first step for building such ecosystem should ideally be setting a FinTech vision for the country, which can be followed by establishing a FinTech Hub (i.e. center). The Hub can act as a FinTech enabler and a collaborative platform for different ecosystem components. Although FinTech ecosystems may vary from one country to another based on the market characteristics, the main components of the ecosystems are almost the same. These components are expected to work in synergy with each other through open innovation to achieve the FinTech vision.

For the FinTech Hub to act as the FinTech innovation ecosystem enabler, it should be directing its focus on filling the existing gaps, enabling open innovation, ensuring collaboration between the components, solving problems, and embracing its strengths. Accordingly, these can only be accomplished by bringing all the ecosystem components to work for the same vision and coordinate the efforts. Figure 1 shows these ecosystem components, which consist of nine different areas that are covered in this chapter.

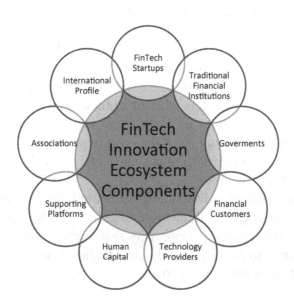

Figure 1.   FinTech Innovation Ecosystem components.

These components are essential for building the right ecosystem by any country wishes to embrace the FinTech innovation:

3.1. *FinTech start-ups*

FinTech start-ups are behind the FinTech revolution, and without the existence of this component in any ecosystem, FinTech innovation cannot take place. These start-ups utilize various technologies to provide innovative financial solutions that can compete with traditional financial services. The technologies used in these innovations vary — e.g. in some cases like M-Pesa in Kenya, they use a basic mobile phone for money transfer through an existing telecommunication service.

Whereas Wahed in the US, for example, have used Artificial Intelligence (AI) for wealth management robo-advisory services that is connected to existing investment instruments. Despite the technologies used, the innovation of this component lies at the opportunities these FinTech start-ups capitalize on to build their business. Using existing telecommunication company services to offer money transfer services through mobile is an example of collaboration that leads to FinTech innovation.

There are five models these FinTech start-ups followed in their way to innovate in the financial industry.

The first model serves the customers that are not attractive enough for banks (including those that are unbanked and underbanked). Usually, the main reason for banks to not serve these customers is due to the low amount of return compared to the investment. An example of this model is Kickstarter, which is a reward-based crowdfunding platform that supports customers with innovative projects that require funding. In return for the funding, the customer provides the investors with a reward from the project which was funded. These types of customers are not interesting for banks despite their need for funding. However, using such platforms gives them the opportunity to access funds and build their projects through directly connecting to investors.

The second model is the one that exploits inefficiencies in banking processes and accordingly provides better financial services.

For example, TransferWise provides a better money transfer service, compared to the high fees charged by banks for overseas transfers, and allows customers to transfer money abroad quickly, easily, and with lower costs using the existing banking system.

The third model of FinTech is used by those that compete directly with banks by providing similar services to the same segment of customers — for instance, Nutmeg, which provides online robo-based investment management services. This FinTech allows customers to build and manage their investment portfolios through a digital platform without the need to have an expensive human fund manager. For such a model to work, it requires using existing investment instruments and connecting it to the platform to provide an innovative financial service.

The fourth model is used by the FinTechs that mainly use the existing infrastructure of banks to provide their financial services and products. For example, Apple has used this model to come up with a credit card through directly partnering with Goldman Sachs. Similarly, Google is planning to offer personal banking account by partnering with Citigroup. All these partnerships are clear representation of open innovation, where the technology company offers its high-tech infrastructure and the bank provides its financial service to come up together with an innovative product.

Last but not least, the fifth model is one where FinTechs offer a totally disruptive product or service that can transform the financial industry, such as Coinbase. This company provides digital currency exchange platform that allows customers to store, buy, and sell digital currencies/cryptocurrencies such as bitcoin using fiat money. This type of business model never existed before as there was no cryptocurrencies in the market. However, with the existence of cryptocurrencies, these types of businesses started to appear in the market and disrupt the financial industry.

3.2. Traditional FIs

Traditional banks are known for being bureaucratic and slow in adopting innovation. However, the fact that FinTechs started to disrupt the financial industry has led many of these banks to move toward building their own FinTech and innovation strategies to deal with the disruption. Despite the strategies formed, most of these banks agree that the best way to deal with FinTechs is through collaboration. This is mainly due to the fact that banks have a large base of customer data and financial knowledge, whereas FinTechs have the technology and innovation. Based on a PwC (2017) report, it was found that 82% of the banks, investment managers, and insurers plan to increase their partnerships with FinTechs. Accordingly, most of the following strategies are built around the collaboration approach.

One strategy some banks have adopted with regard to FinTech is acquisition. This strategy allows the banks to buy a FinTech company that has been already innovating in the financial industry and embed it into their business to further innovate. As an example, BBVA, the Spanish bank, has acquired several FinTech start-ups in the areas of payment, real estate valuation, and online banking. According to CB Insights (2018), BBVA is the most active FinTech acquirer bank in the last five years. Many other banks have followed this strategy, including BNP Paribas, Capital One, JP Morgan Chase & Co., and Goldman Sachs.

Furthermore, partnership is another strategy that has been followed by several banks in order to foster innovation in their products and services. Deutsche Bank, for instance, has chosen FinTech partnership strategy as part of its overall digital transformation strategy. The bank's goal is to become "the contact and collaboration partner of choice in the banking world in Germany and Europe for leading FinTechs." Accordingly, the bank has partnered with a number of FinTech start-ups to embrace digitalization. The partnerships spurred innovation in the areas of digital account opening, mobile app, retail deposit marketplace, multibank aggregation, etc. (Deutsche Bank, 2016).

Additionally, some banks, as a FinTech strategy, have established their own innovation labs, hackathons, incubators, and accelerators to work with FinTech start-ups and various innovations. In this regard, Barclays has established its own accelerator in collaboration with Techstars accelerator. This Accelerator provides a program for FinTech start-ups and entrepreneurs, where it offers mentorships, tools, facilities, and equipment to get their financial products and services to the market. In return, both Barclays and Techstars take small equity stake from each FinTech company (Barclays 2% and Techstars 4%). By this strategy, banks aim at embracing the FinTech innovation internally and create their own FinTech disruptors.

Another form of FinTech strategy followed by banks is establishing a venture capital (VC) that would invest in FinTechs. According to CB Insights (2019), the most active US banks that invest in FinTech going by the number of portfolio companies are Citigroup, Goldman Sachs, and JP Morgan Chase & Co. These banks are using their investment arms for these types of investment. For example, Citigroup has invested in number of FinTech companies through its Citi Ventures. Some of these FinTechs are Jumio, Square, Ayasdi, Chain, and Betterment. Goldman Sachs, on the other hand, has invested in 18 FinTechs in 2019 as part of its strategy (Fintech News Switzerland, 2020).

Finally, banks have the strategy of establishing their own FinTech subsidiary, where they can introduce innovative financial products and services by being agile as a separate entity away from the traditional bank culture. Accordingly, there are several banks that began their own digital bank subsidiaries that operate in new markets. For example, DBS Bank launched "digibank" in India and Al Baraka Turk Participation Bank launched "Insha" digital bank in Germany.

All these FinTech strategies bring new opportunities to the banks and FinTechs alike through fostering innovation in their offerings. In fact, many of these banks, in order to get the most out of FinTech innovation opportunities, adopt mixed strategies, where they can have an accelerator, their own FinTech subsidiary, and partner with FinTechs at the same time. After all, the selected FinTech strategy is largely based on the bank's belief in the importance of innovation and its business priorities.

3.3. *Governments*

The role of governments in the FinTech innovation ecosystem can be seen from two perspectives. First is implementing FinTech solutions and collaborating with FinTech companies to provide innovative governmental financial services to the society. Second is introducing regulations that support FinTech start-ups and encourage innovation in the financial industry. Despite the importance of the first point, the second point has been given more attention globally as it is the driver of innovation in various markets. Accordingly, there are several regulations that have been created specifically for FinTech innovations.

First is the FinTech regulatory sandbox. This regulation intends to keep up with the speed of innovations in the financial industry by providing a testing environment for new business models that are not covered under the existing regulations or supervised by regulatory institutions. Usually, the governments that embrace FinTech innovations start with having these sandboxes as a first step, such as UK, Singapore, Australia, Bahrain, etc. This allows FinTechs to test their innovative products in the market and at the same time allow the regulators to understand the innovative product and build a suitable regulation around it.

In some countries, specific regulations have been introduced to allow the operation of certain types of FinTechs in the market, such as crowdfunding platforms, digital assets, and payment solutions, including electronic wallets (e-Wallet), etc. In this regard, to further support the innovation in the financial industry and encourage FinTechs to come up with better financial services and products, regulations like open banking have been introduced in many countries, including in the European Union, UK, Singapore, Bahrain, and Australia.

Open banking drives innovation in the financial industry through mandating FIs to share their customers data (using open APIs) with other businesses such as FinTechs. This allows the FinTechs to use these data and create new applications (i.e. innovative financial products and services) and come up with new innovative business models.

Eventually, open banking intends to increase competition in the market, foster innovation, and provide better products and services with less cost. The Second Payment Services Directive (PSD2) is an example of open banking regulation in the EU. Today, there are number of banks that have established portals as an API marketplace to allow the FinTechs/third-party developers to directly test their solution. This leads to a win-win situation, where the bank will be able to provide better services to its customers, in addition to creating a new source of revenue for the bank, while the FinTech firm will be able to benefit from its new business model that is built based on different banks APIs.

On the other hand, an initiative called Global Finance Innovation Network (GFIN) was created by UK's Financial Conduct Authority and 11 other regulators globally. This initiative aims at embracing the innovations through creating a global sandbox that will allow FinTechs to test their products and services across multiple jurisdictions. The open innovation in this initiative goes beyond the geographical regulation limitations, which allow FinTechs to further innovate.

GFIN creates network of global regulators to discuss common issues and share experiences related to FinTech innovations, in addition to supporting joint policy work and regulatory trials. Finally, it is expected that more supportive regulations will be created in the near future to support FinTech innovations, as without these types of regulations, some FinTech innovative ideas will not be able to flourish.

3.4. *Financial customers*

Each component plays an important role in the FinTech innovation ecosystem. However, without the adoption of the FinTech innovations by the actual financial customers, all the other components will not add much of a value. That is because the customers are the end-users of these innovations which intend to meet their financial needs. Accordingly, there is no point of having FinTech start-ups, regulations, accelerators, etc., if there is no one (individuals or businesses) to use these FinTech products and services.

With regard to the Diffusion of Innovation (DOI) Theory, every innovation goes through an adoption curve starting with customers that are innovators and pioneers in adopting an innovation, up to customers that are laggards, which means they are the last customers to adopt an innovation. Based on this, EY (2019) in their FinTech Adoption Index for 2019 indicated that the global FinTech adoption is at "Late Majority" stage and has increased to 64%. This indicates that the adoption of FinTech innovations is increasing globally, and more users are going to use these financial services and products. Meanwhile, the same report stated that 16% of global customers are aware of at least one payment and money transfer FinTech service, and 68% of global customers would consider a non-financial services company as a financial institution. These numbers indicate the increasing adoption appetite of global customers to FinTech services and the future of innovative financial services.

Despite the increasing adoption of FinTech by financial customers, it is important to consider that there is a segment of financial customers that are not tech-savvy and they do not want to change even if it is to a better service. Therefore, FinTechs in these cases should be taking some approaches to ensure the adoption of their products and services by the vast majority of customers, including those that are not tech-savvy. These approaches can include creating awareness, building marketing campaigns that highlights the added value of these FinTech innovations compared to the traditional counterparts, and providing training to customers if needed. Last but not the least, some FinTechs, in order to address this issue, have been flexible in their services, where they go visit their clients (such as SMEs in crowdfunding platforms) and help them upload their documents to start their fund-raising campaign on the platform. These types of offline assistance and flexibility are needed to attract those that are not tech-savvy and encourage them to adopt FinTech innovations.

3.5. *Technology providers*

Technology companies play a major role in the FinTech innovation ecosystem. In fact, these companies can be split into two types: BigTech companies like Amazon, Facebook, Alibaba, etc., and Financial Technology Solution providers.

Each type contributes in its own way to the ecosystem. For example, aside from the FinTech start-ups, these BigTechs started to enter the financial industry through the use of the Financial Technology concept. After all, there is no doubt that these BigTechs have a huge potential for FinTech business success due to number of factors. First, they have a large base of customers globally. Second, customers are happy with their services and trust these BigTechs. Third, they have the technology know-how that enables them to innovate in the area of finance. All these factors encourage these BigTechs to obtain financial license and start offering innovative financial products and services, just like what Alibaba did where it established its own FinTech subsidiary called Ant Financial. Likewise, Apple has launched its own payment service Apple Pay, and the list goes on.

On the other side, FinTech solution providers are contributing largely to the speed of financial innovations adoption by various FIs. These companies provide platforms or off-the-shelf solutions to the FIs to help them offer innovative financial products and services to customers in no time; all they have to do is just customizing these solutions. Obviously, these FIs and other organizations that need such solutions are not technology experts and do not have much time to spend on innovation. Accordingly, FinTech solution providers fill this gap through their innovative financial solutions and ensure the speed of innovation adoption. Finally, these solutions can come in different forms such as blockchain, smart contracts, chatbots, AI solutions, robo-advisories, e-Wallets, etc.

3.6. *Human capital*

At the core of FinTech innovations is the human capital or the FinTech talent, although it is one of the main challenges faced by FinTechs and FIs. According to PwC, 80% of these FinTech firms and FIs struggle with hiring the right talent for innovative positions (Bahrain FinTech Bay, 2018). For example, 94% of employers in Singapore stated that there is need for FinTech talent and they have indicated top roles in FinTech as Big Data, FinTech Compliance, and Information Security (MichaelPage, 2019).

There is no doubt that the rise of FinTech industry has led to a growing demand for specific skillsets and expertise, especially as this industry looks into two different areas: finance and technology. These skills can be related to cloud computing, programming, blockchain, robotics, machine learning, cybersecurity, data science, etc. This is aside from soft skills like problem solving, critical thinking, communication, and negotiation.

Therefore, in order to fill the FinTech talent gap, educational systems should be able to equip the students/graduates with these skills to meet the demand in the market. This will require the educational institutions and training centers to work closely with the industry (i.e. FIs and FinTechs) on building the right materials and courses. This shall contribute in having talents in the market that are fit to innovative positions in FinTech firms and FIs.

While it is crucial to have the new generation equipped with the right skillset needed for FinTech innovations, it is also important to reskill the current employees in traditional banks and other FIs as these talents have particularly strong financial background and expertise in the financial industry. Therefore, through upgrading their skills and providing them with the right training and courses, they can add great value to FinTech innovation. However, those current employees that are not willing to upgrade their knowledge and be reskilled will face a tough time staying relevant to the market and being innovative.

3.7. Supporting platforms

This component is about the platforms that provide support to FinTech start-ups and entrepreneurs with innovative FinTech ideas. Incubators serve as one such platform, where they provide co-working spaces for these FinTech start-ups and entrepreneurs. In addition, these incubators offer mentorships, networking opportunities, events, and valuable resources that teaches these start-ups and entrepreneurs how to build their business and make it grow. These incubators can be a great platform for these start-ups to network and be connected directly to the market, thus encouraging open innovation.

Another platform are the accelerators. Once these FinTech start-ups pass the incubator stage and their business is ready, they will be eligible for the accelerator stage. These accelerators provide cohort-based programs, which include tailored mentorships, training, and educational courses that will help early-stage FinTech start-ups grow their business and improve their products. These programs usually take around three to six months, and by completion of the program, these start-ups should be ready and can raise further funds.

These types of platforms contribute in supporting innovative FinTech ideas to become an actual FinTech business that can provide innovative financial solutions to the market. Therefore, aside from the mentorship and programs, these accelerators also provide the FinTech start-ups with pre-seed or seed investment, and in return they take equity stake in the firm. These FinTech start-ups can also raise or get access to funds through other supporting platforms such as angel investors, VC funds, and crowdfunding platforms.

There are several banks globally that have their own FinTech accelerators and incubators that would provide workspace and programs to these FinTechs in order to support flourishing innovative FinTech ideas. These accelerators and incubators include Open Vault by OCBC bank, Al Baraka Garaj by Al Baraka Turk Participation Bank, DBS Accelerator, American Express "Accelerate Me" program, Barclays Accelerator, etc. These accelerators and incubators provide a good platform for both FinTech to grow and banks to innovative in an agile manner using external potentials.

3.8. *Associations*

This component contributes to the FinTech innovation ecosystem in different ways based on the type of the associate. For example, in some countries there are associations of banks that are formed by the central banks or the regulators. These types of associations help in reviewing new financial regulations, including the ones related to FinTech, aside from spreading awareness about the FinTech industry and how it will be shaping the future of banks.

The other type of association is FinTech associations, which represent the FinTech community in the country, including FinTech firms, bankers, academicians, investors, accelerators, incubators, technology companies, etc. The role of these types of associations is to create a platform dedicated to FinTech ecosystem to discuss the current issues, ensure open innovation, and try to find solutions through involving all the stakeholders.

Additionally, it acts as a networking platform that connects the stakeholders with each other and allow them to exchange knowledge and experiences. These types of associations after all can represent the voice of FinTech on a country level and create awareness about the FinTech innovations in the community. There are many associations nowadays for FinTech that play an important role in the FinTech innovation ecosystem such as MENA FinTech Association, Singapore FinTech Association, Financial Innovation & Technology Association of Canada, Fintech Association of Malaysia, etc.

3.9. *International profile*

FinTech is all about collaborations and this concept can be beneficial not only for the FinTechs and banks but also for building the country's FinTech Innovation Ecosystem through collaborating with other countries' FinTech ecosystems. After all, each country has its own unique FinTech innovation ecosystem with its strengths and weaknesses. Accordingly, by collaborating with the international counterparts and being part of the international FinTech community, the existing ecosystem can be strengthened. The opportunities that exist behind collaborations are massive, such as exchanging knowledge and experiences, creating business opportunities for FinTechs to expand into different markets, working on FinTech regulations that encourage the innovation in the financial industry (like GIFA), and many other benefits. In this regard, Singapore is an example of a country that has built an international profile in

FinTech through entering into collaboration agreements with several countries/jurisdictions, including India, China, Denmark, Bahrain, Dubai, etc.

Media is also part of the international profile, especially social media, as it plays a major role in promoting the existing FinTech innovation ecosystem and positioning the country's FinTech ecosystem globally. Accordingly, media activities can result in attracting FinTech innovations, FinTech talents, FinTech investors, FinTech start-ups, and FinTech solution providers from all over the world. This eventually will lead to enriching the local FinTech innovations and open the market for international players to bring their innovations, fill the talent gap, provide better financial services, and fund more FinTech start-ups etc.

4. Conclusion

Globally, there are various FinTech innovation ecosystems that are derived by open innovation concept, where each is unique based on its own market characteristics, market needs, and strategic priorities. However, in order to create a comprehensive FinTech innovation ecosystem that can reap the benefits and opportunities of FinTech through open innovation, there are nine components that should be considered as each one of them contribute in its own way to the ecosystem. These components are: FinTech Start-ups, Traditional FIs, Government, Financial Customers, Technology Providers, Human Capital, Supporting Platforms, Associations, and International Profile.

References

Bahrain FinTech Bay (2018). Bahrain FinTech Talent Report 2018 (Bahrain FinTech Bay, Manama).

CB Insights (2018). More banks are beginning to acquire Fintech startups. Retrieved from: https://www.cbinsights.com/research/top-us-banks-fintech-acquisitions/ (Accessed on 15 December 2018).

CB Insights (2019). Where top US banks are betting on Fintech. Retrieved from: https://www.cbinsights.com/research/fintech-investments-top-us-banks/ (Accessed on 16 November 2019).

Chishti, S. & Barberis, J. (2016). *The FINTECH Book: The Financial Technology Handbook for Investors, Entrepreneurs and Visionaries* (John Wiley & Sons, West Sussex).

Deutsche Bank (2016). *For the Banking of the Future — Deutsche Bank's Digital Factory.* Retrieved from: https://www.db.com/newsroom_news/Digital_Factory_Opening_Presentation_engl._29.9.2016.pdf (Accessed on 15 December 2018).

EY (2019). Global FinTech Adoption Index 2019. Retrieved from: https://fintechauscensus.ey.com/2019/Documents/ey-global-fintech-adoption-index-2019.pdf (Accessed on 16 November 2019).

Fintech News Switzerland (2020). Record year 2019: Fintech deals, mergers and acquisitions study. Retrieved from: https://fintechnews.ch/fintech/record-year-2019-fintech-deals-mergers-and-acquisitions-study/33288/ (Accessed on 18 August 2020).

KPMG (2020). Pulse of Fintech H2 2019. Retrieved from: https://home.kpmg/xx/en/home/campaigns/2020/02/pulse-of-fintech-h2-19-global-trends.html (Accessed on 18 August 2020).

MichaelPage (2019). FinTech Employment 2019 Report. Retrieved from: https://www.michaelpage.com.sg/sites/michaelpage.com.sg/files/16785-sg_fintech_brochure_mp.v6_0.pdf (Accessed on 16 November 2019).

PwC (2017). PwC: 82% of banks, insurers, investment managers plan to increase FinTech partnerships; 88% concerned they'll lose revenue to innovators. Retrieved from: https://www.pwc.com/bb/en/press-releases/fintech-partnerships.html (Accessed on 15 December 2018).

Chapter 7

Reinforcing Value Creation Within a FinTech Cluster

Caroline E. Braastad, Nolwenn Camps-Leysour de Rohello,* Finn C. Arctander,* Omar Abdelhakim* and Magne S. Angelshaug†*

Department of Strategy and Management, Norwegian School of Economics (NHH), 5045 Bergen, Norway
†*magne.angelshaug@nhh.no*

Abstract. In our qualitative study of a newly emerging FinTech cluster, we discuss how different stakeholders can reinforce value creation within the cluster. Focusing on the internal organization of the cluster, we identify the motivations of each stakeholder group, how these diverge, and what challenges these produce. While our case study is limited to Norway, we believe that our recommendations on how to create a common culture for value creation, adapting business models, communicating progress, and developing selection criteria framework, are applicable to FinTech clusters around the globe.

Keywords. Stakeholders; FinTech clusters; internal organization; value creation; business model.

---

*Co-authors have contributed to this book chapter in their individual capacity.

1. Introduction

In what we call the "exponential age," companies across all industries see the need to pool their resources and collaborate to face the threat of disruptive emerging technologies, change in customer demand, and new regulations (Saebi and Angelshaug, 2017). This is particularly true in the banking and financial sectors, where consumer behaviors are moving from long-term, loyalty-driven relationships to immediacy, autonomy, and lower cost. Between tech giants like Amazon and Google pushing the limits of traditional finance and sitting on tremendous amounts of customer data, and FinTech start-ups delivering cheap, innovative financial solutions centered around their customers' experience, financial institutions are sitting at an inflection point (Blackwell, 2018). For many analysts, the rise of these new industry leaders has proven that banks cannot survive this transformation on their own. To cope with these disruptive trends and renew their innovation strategies, companies and financial institutions require access to competencies and resources located beyond their current domain of expertise.

Becoming part of an innovation cluster is one way of establishing these cross-linked collaborations, as actors willing to capitalize on external sources of expertise agree to form an alliance and exchange knowledge to create value jointly. As a result, cluster enterprises have shown a significant growth in value creation (Cappelen *et al.*, 2015). In particular, FinTech clusters have drawn a lot of attention within the industry, as FinTech providers and traditional financial institutions seem to share "complementary strengths and weaknesses in terms of size, speed, regulation, and access to funding" (Cumming, 2016). Nevertheless, reaping the advantages of this type of alliance can be challenging, generally because of a lack of proper internal organization within the cluster and the absence of clearly defined goals among partners.

To address the question of how partners of a cluster can reinforce value creation, we explore the case of an emerging cluster named Finance Innovation. As this particular organization is relatively new, it faces the challenges of ensuring continued momentum of collaboration past the initial excitement of members joining the cluster. Thus, in this chapter we investigate how clusters' management can contribute to building lasting relationships of trust between key actors and organize collaboration activities in a way that captures all potential synergies of sharing resources, while stimulating the actors' creativity process.

2. Background

The key concepts we discuss in this chapter relate to open innovation strategies, innovation clusters, and innovation ecosystems, and FinTech clusters represented by Finance Innovation, as illustrated in Figure 1.

2.1. *Open innovation strategies*

Traditionally, companies have implemented their business strategies in total secrecy, relying on their own individual research and development (R&D) capabilities without much external interaction. They believed sharing information would undermine their competitiveness and weaken their industry positioning. However, with rising R&D

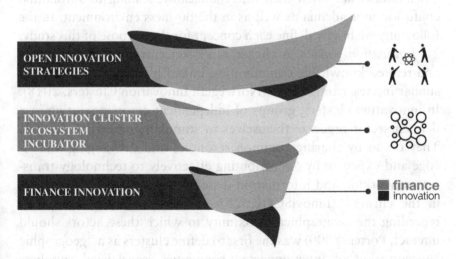

Figure 1. Key concepts in study.

costs and shortening product life-cycles, resources of individual companies remain limited; hence the necessity to diversify their innovation strategies and become more permeable to their external environment (Saebi and Foss, 2015). The process of open innovation englobes multiple types of mechanisms, which can be used either conjointly or separately by an organization, depending on its specific goals and needs. We generally distinguish between two main types of open innovation strategies: (1) "inbound open innovation," which refers to accessing external technical and scientific competences from within a company, and (2) "outbound open innovation," which is the process of commercializing internally developed ideas through the company's external environment (Chesbrough, 2006; Chiaroni *et al.*, 2010). For the purpose of our current study, both inbound and outbound open innovation mechanisms are implied, as we are discussing open innovation in the context of an innovation cluster where the participants partake in both inflow and outflow of knowledge.

2.2. *Innovation cluster, ecosystem, and incubator*

The terms "innovation clusters," "innovation ecosystems," and "incubators" are often used interchangeably, leading to substantial confusion in academia as well as in the business environment. In the following, we briefly define each concept for the purpose of this study.

Innovation cluster. A cluster is a "concentration of enterprises and related knowledge communities, linked by complementarity or similar interests and needs" (Norwegian Innovation Clusters, 2018). In innovation clusters, groups of independent actors operating in a defined sector organize themselves to stimulate innovative activity. They do so by sharing common resources and exchanging knowledge and expertise by "contributing effectively to technology transfer, networking and information dissemination among the partners in the cluster" (InnoviSCOP, 2016). There is limited consensus regarding the geographical proximity to which these actors should interact. Porter (2000) was the first to define clusters as a "geographic concentration of interconnected companies, specialized suppliers and service providers, firms in related industries, and associated institutions in particular fields that compete but also cooperate." Although numerous researchers share the belief that innovative ideas and the process of knowledge creation cannot be spatially controlled (Malmberg and Maskell, 2002), Malmberg and Power (2005) also argue that "spatial proximity seems to enhance processes of interactive learning and innovation." Thus, when using the term "innovation cluster" throughout this chapter, we refer to the local concentration of different sets of actors, organizing themselves to stimulate their innovation process.

Ecosystem. We consider an "ecosystem" to encompass a wider meaning than the cluster. We use the terminology innovation ecosystem to define the quality of the synergies that can emerge out of the cluster, i.e. the intangible relationships, vision and alliances that cross the geographical boundaries of the cluster (Jackson, 2015). Figure 2 represents how the organizational cluster can be embedded into the entire innovation ecosystem (Langkilde, 2014).

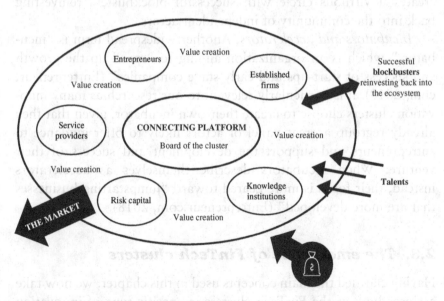

Figure 2. Value creation in ecosystems.

Source: the model for value creation in clusters inspired by Lotte Langkilde's presentation at the 17th TCI Global Conference, Monterrey 2014.

The identified stakeholders (entrepreneurs, established firms, knowledge institutions, risk capital, and service providers) match those we will continue to consider in the current study. Moreover, as we consider the physical gathering of these actors, or their agreement to belong to a common structure, we use the term "cluster" to denominate their formal alliance. When these actors pool resources and work together on common initiatives, which can eventually be commercialized into the market, they create synergies that can have an impact beyond the formal boundaries of the innovation cluster: they form an innovation ecosystem. Thus, the term "ecosystem" denominates all the interactions that take place between the members of the cluster or with other entities outside of its boundaries. Examples of these interactions include the "talents inflow" bringing in creative ideas, research projects, or student entrepreneurs to the ecosystem through local universities, or the "capital inflow" adding new financial resources to the ecosystem to sponsor common initiatives or leverage start-up ideas. When an ecosystem is successful, it creates a virtuous circle with successful blockbusters reinvesting back into the community of independent actors.

Incubators and accelerators. Another widespread term is "incubator," which is an organization aiming to "speed up the growth and success of start-ups and early stage companies" (Entrepreneur. com, 2018). It is particularly relevant to our research as many innovation clusters choose to create their own incubator, given that they already regroup a great panel of actors likely to offer guidance to entrepreneurs and support the development and success of their venture. When incubators describe themselves as accelerators instead, their focus is more geared toward "jumpstarting businesses that are more developed" (Entrepreneur.com, 2018).

2.3. *The emergence of FinTech clusters*

Having clarified the main concepts used in this chapter, we now take a closer look at the FinTech clusters, a specific type of innovation clusters. As a result of changed customer behavior, increased digitalization, and stricter regulation, the banking industry has had to undertake a deep reconversion (Saebi and Angelshaug, 2017). With European banks failing to generate returns above their cost of equity since before 2008, a wave of FinTech companies emerged to exploit the situation, aiming to improve and transform the banking services through technological innovation (Deloitte, 2017a–c). According to PwC (2016), as many as 83% of the financial institutions consider various parts of their businesses to be at risk to FinTech companies. This situation has contributed to a growing interest in open collaboration mechanisms, particularly through FinTech clusters, seeking to develop and nurture a symbiotic relationship between such actor as banks, FinTech companies, consulting groups, investors, and educational institutions. Our case cluster, named Finance Innovation, was established during the summer of 2017 and has stated an ambition to simplify financial services and export new services and technologies globally (Trumpy, 2017). Despite being new, Finance Innovation could already count on more than 50 committed companies at the time of the study, representing a vast array of industries.

3. Framework for the Success of Clusters

In our study, we consider several criteria for success in clusters, many of which have been identified in past research as critical to foster the collaboration between actors. First, prior studies have identified that partnering between different actors may reap several benefits. This includes productivity improvement, cost synergies, and quality enhancement (Naoum, 2003). When teaming up with such partners, achieving incentive alignment and goal congruence among participants is key to ensure that the combined efforts focus upon project objectives (Teece, 2003; Naoum, 2003). In other words, having aligned motivations is of paramount importance to build the collaborative capacity between actors (Hocevar, 2011) needed for achieving the desired benefits.

Second, while understanding the criticality of mutual objectives in the collaboration, actors still need to identify "the potential pitfalls, the points for leverage, and the management strategies that work in bringing different organizations together" (Austin, 2000). In particular, companies choosing to collaborate need to carefully review the different strategic trade-offs, or challenges, associated with the pursued type of relationship. A common mistake made by firms, as underlined by Pisano and Verganti (2009), is to rush into alliances without fully considering their collaborative architecture, defined as the structure and organizing principles. Among these potential challenges in cross-collaboration settings, the resource-constrained environment is identified by several authors as a serious obstacle (Hocevar, 2011; Jackson, 2015). In this regard, Jackson's theory of innovation ecosystems is of great importance in explaining the concept of the "virtuous value creation circle." In particular, she considers an ecosystem to be healthy and thriving when initial R&D or research investments are balanced by increased profits, following the successful implementation of new products and technologies developed within the cluster (Jackson, 2015).

The upper part of Figure 3 illustrates this virtuous circle, while the lower part shows the level of resources that are distributed into activities fostering innovation at the different stages of development. One main issue raised by Jackson (2015) regarding project resource-allocation is that there exists a gap in resources between the "Technology Demonstration" and "Development" phases, which Jackson further qualifies as the "Valley of Death."

Finally, various authors mention the need for a framework or model of collaboration to guide the cross-functional work and incentivize trust and cooperation efforts between participants (Bronstein, 2003; Naoum, 2003). Hocevar (2011), further stresses the crucial role played by the leadership team in ensuring that the collaboration process effectively meets its end goals.

4. Method of Our Case Study

Building on the criteria for success between collaborating actors, we created a three-step approach that allow us to shape propositions on how to best organize clusters. First, it is important to assess the alignment of motivations and expectations between different stakeholders in the cluster. Second, it is crucial to identify the potential pitfalls and challenges that these stakeholders are experiencing. Finally, and based on these insights, we discuss how clusters can

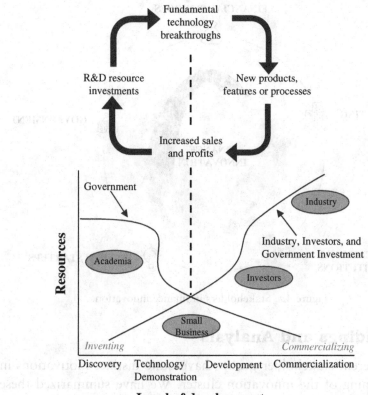

Level of development

Figure 3. Resource allocation at different development stages.
Source: Jackson, 2015.

organize interactions and exchanges of knowledge so that members mutually benefit from their innovation activities.

For the purpose of this single case study, we chose to address the cluster stakeholders based on five main categories as shown in Figure 4. Within Finance Innovation, these are: (1) Financial Institutions, (2) FinTech Start-ups, (3) Educational Institutions, (4) Consulting Groups, and (5) Government Entities (Figure 4).

As part of the data collection, interviews were conducted with different participants in the cluster. Together with archival data, the results of these interviews were analyzed to provide relevant insights regarding current motivations, expectations, and challenges experienced by the members.

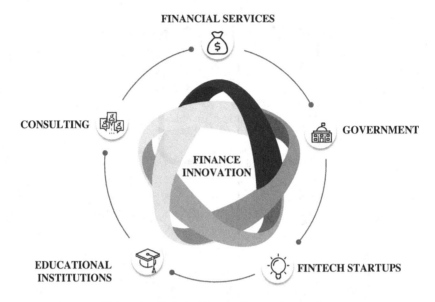

Figure 4.   Stakeholders in finance innovation.

5. Findings and Analysis

The different stakeholder groups have quite distinct motivations in their joining of the innovation cluster. We have summarized these findings in Table 1.

Even if we find there to be a strong degree of alignment between the different actors, we also find two key misalignments: between FinTech start-ups and Consulting groups, and between FinTech start-ups and Financial institutions, as shown in Figure 5.

We find these misalignments to emerge from the differences in size and positioning between the smaller and larger players. The lack of congruence between these actors create obstacles in the cluster's efforts to ensure sufficient space in the collaborative environment for smaller players with less available resources.

Understanding the different stakeholders' intrinsic motivation to join an innovation cluster is key to discern why these actors would be willing to collaborate together in the first place. Nevertheless, the willingness to join forces cannot alone secure the smooth operation of a cluster and a successful innovation process. We identified six key challenges regarding the collaboration, as illustrated in Figure 6.

Table 1. Summary of the main motivations to join Finance Innovation.

Stakeholder				
Financial institutions	Fintech startups	Consulting groups	Educational institutions	Government
Motivation				
• Fear of being left behind • Potential benefits • Improve products and customer experience • Boost innovation • New digitized solutions • Impact on the local community	• Access business • Gain visibility • Utilize other players' current customer base • Receive financial investments • Gain structure • Leverage managerial experience • Legislation compliance	• Be part of the industry changes • Showing relevancy to prospective clients	• Build research/ education • Facilitate the relationship between students and corporate partners.	• Positive economical effect • Increase the employment levels • Create value for the communities

HYPOTHESIS

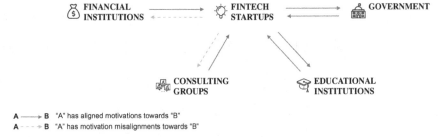

Figure 5. Misalignments between cluster members.

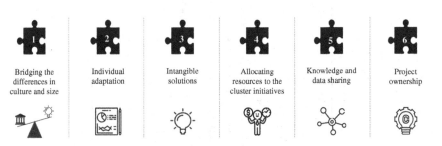

Figure 6. The six main challenges of collaboration.

5.1. *Bridging the differences in culture and size*

This first challenge directly builds on the findings of misalignments of motivation between actors. There is a tendency for FinTech start-ups to be less represented than larger actors in the events organized by the cluster, potentially threatening value creation in areas where these players are crucial. This situation matches our hypothesis of a potential misalignment between FinTech start-ups and larger stake-holders, as shown in Figure 7.

Despite the fact that large corporations and consultancy groups provide valuable contributions, greater participation of these actors might also create some challenges in the long run, where the innovation cluster could turn itself into a "sales channel." WIPO (2011) similarly identifies challenges in negotiations between what they define as "specialized R&D firms" and "vertically integrated R&D

HYPOTHESIS

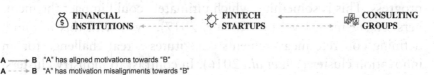

A ———▶ B   "A" has aligned motivations towards "B"
A - - - ▶ B   "A" has motivation misalignments towards "B"

Figure 7. Potential misalignment between smaller and larger stakeholders.

production firms." This derives from the lack of clarification regarding the purpose of each actor in their collaboration activities. Within the case cluster, differences in size and culture between the stakeholders threaten the smooth running of collaborative activities. This situation illustrates that finding the right balance between the different stakeholder groups and creating enough space for each actor are of key importance for cluster organizations.

5.2. *Individual adaptation*

The challenge of individual adaptation relates to the actors' necessity of adjusting their business models to the open innovation strategy. At a firm level, differences in corporate cultures and structural rigidity can further challenge the collaborative benefits of the cluster (Brant and Lohse, 2014). Actors which early on are able to adopt a flexible and open structure could reap more benefits when collaborating with a cluster. However, this entails significant changes to aspects such as corporate strategy and culture, together with the level of commitment and the style of the firm's leadership (Holten and Brenner, 2015). Members that are failing to adopt more flexible structures will also result in additional challenges when growing the cluster, as it is dependent on maintaining connectivity between members in an expanding network (Connell *et al.*, 2014).

5.3. *Intangible solutions*

The challenge of intangible solutions relates to the difficulties of measuring and communicating the impact of the cluster. The nature of innovation activities is to a large extent intangible, making it difficult for clusters to showcase its impact and communicate its progress. This is something which ultimately could impact the members' engagement level (McKinney, 2017). Even with this in mind, defining concrete measurements constitutes a real challenge for an innovation cluster (Oh *et al.*, 2016). In contrast to industry clusters, which most often have measurable feedback and tipping point effects, innovation clusters offer "no ready metrics when it comes to assessing their success" (Oh *et al.*, 2016).

5.4. *Allocating resources*

This challenge relates to the allocation of resources to activities within the cluster. This topic is raising several project management issues that we divide into three sub-challenges. As shown in Figure 8, this includes the initial choice of participants, the maintaining of a sufficient engagement level, and the question of the financing sources at initial project stages.

When a new idea of a project or research topic is being suggested within the cluster, a first challenge encountered before moving forward with the initiative is to choose its optimal participants. Although each stakeholder has something different to contribute, there might be a conflict of interest when it comes to particularly interesting projects. To keep it efficient, each new initiative cannot realistically include all members of the innovation cluster.

Once the allocation phase is handled, an additional challenge can arise in relation to the engagement level of the participants. Ensuring that all members are on board and have aligned

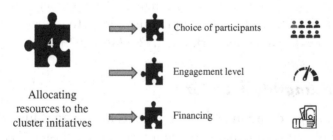

Figure 8.   Allocating resources.

expectations is complex. Members need to agree upfront on the time resources they are willing to provide in order to maintain a healthy dynamic within the group.

5.5. *Knowledge and data sharing*

The challenge of knowledge and data sharing relates to the complexities of sharing data and knowledge between members when collaborating. As open innovation is built on more open channels of knowledge and data, such sharing between cluster members is of key importance. However, this also exposes companies to the risk that their commercial and technological know-how could be misused (Hoecht and Trott, 2006). Considering that it is probable that some of the cluster-members are competitors, it is reasonable to also speculate that some might try to get away with disclosing as little information as possible while still reaping benefits of the knowledge sharing process. This concern is similarly raised in the World Intellectual Property Report published by WIPO (2011), which identifies concepts of free riding and other forms of opportunistic behavior as challenges for a fruitful collaboration. Without specific guidelines addressing the knowledge and data sharing issue, clusters are in risk of failing in their mission.

5.6. *Project ownership*

This final challenge covers the distribution of ownership rights of solutions or processes elaborated within the cluster. When successful initiatives are carried out within the cluster, new solutions, products, or processes may be created conjointly by members. Deciding who should own the proprietary content of such results raises a challenge that needs to be handled by guidelines.

6. Propositions on New Organizational Principles for Clusters

Our findings and analysis ultimately make it possible for us to put forward some propositions regarding new principles for internal organization within an innovation cluster.

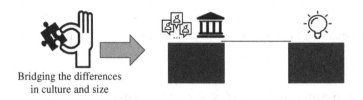

Bridging the differences
in culture and size

Figure 9.   Bridging the differences in culture and size.

6.1. *Creating a common culture for value creation*

To manage the challenge of differences in culture and size, we stress the importance of creating strong relationships between the cluster-members (Figure 9).

As addressed earlier, an innovation ecosystem is bringing together a broad range of actors with the aim of fostering creativity and collaboration. Nevertheless, facilitating the creation of this network of actors is not sufficient for securing success. Jackson (2015) pointed out that a healthy innovation ecosystem must also provide real mechanisms for building both relationships and other intangibles between its members. It is not adequate to solely rely on an assumption that the dynamics of an organizational cluster creates value beyond individual firm.

In terms of knowledge spillovers within the cluster, we propose the establishment of a strong social capital between the members. This implies that by making it a top priority to create not only formal but also informal relationships between partners, these will eventually manage to trust each other enough to capitalize on their connections (Boschma, 2005).

6.2. *Adapt the business model*

To manage the challenge of business models not suited for open innovation, we propose each member of a cluster to take action toward adapting their business model to fully reap the benefits from inbound and outbound collaboration (Figure 10).

Figure 10. Adapt the business model.

For a cluster to function effectively, there exists a need for collaborating firms to ensure a sufficient level of absorptive capacity, i.e. "the ability to recognize the value of new, external information, assimilate it, and apply it to commercial ends" (Cohen and Levinthal, 1990). Member-firms should be able to identify and make use of valuable information from external sources, consolidate it into their business, and adapt their business model accordingly. This is further explained by Viki *et al.* (2017), authors of *The Corporate Startup*, who argue that the best way large companies can innovate is to view themselves as an innovation ecosystem with various products, services, and business models. This allows each firm to become an "ambidextrous organization" that excels both in innovating and executing daily operation (Viki *et al.*, 2017; O'Reilly III and Tushman, 2004). In doing so, firms are better equipped to address the many collaboration challenges that might arise and be ready to implement strategic adjustments when facing new opportunities.

6.3. *Communicate the progress*

To manage the challenge of intangible solutions, we propose cluster-organizations to lay out clear objectives regarding the main strategy of the cluster and identify ways to clearly communicate its achievements. This is important in ensuring that the cluster rightfully capitalizes on its achievements (Figure 11).

Establishing a platform for information sharing is a first step toward enhancing a culture of positive feedback and appreciation within the cluster, further stimulating the sharing of ideas. By enabling

Figure 11.   Communicate the progress.

individual actors to create their own impact and by providing them the right incentives to do so, members feel collectively included while also becoming a vehicle for communicating progress. Outside of its boundaries, organizing events such as hackathons in collaboration with educational institutions can further communicate the achievements and expertise of the cluster.

We further propose clusters to define clear interim goals and celebrate small wins. Measuring the profitability of innovation activities can be difficult and might even be considered as counterproductive, since it could incentivize members to prioritize low-risk projects promising quick gains. Nevertheless, a comprehensive set of quantitative goals balanced with qualitative measures will be of great assistance for clusters to reach their main strategic goals. With this, the cluster will not only stimulate the drive of its members but also maintain own motivation and engagement levels.

6.4. *Allocating resources to the cluster's initiatives*

To manage the challenge of resource allocation, we split our propositions in three parts, as visualized in Figure 12.

6.4.1. *Develop a selection criteria framework*

The challenge of allocating both time-related and financial resources, as well as choosing the participants for each project, could be tackled by incorporating a selection criteria process. These are then criteria making sure that the optimal combination of participants and resources are selected for each initiative. We propose implementing

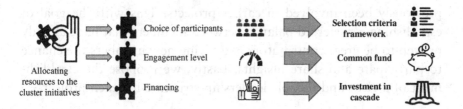

Figure 12.   Allocating resources to the cluster's initiatives.

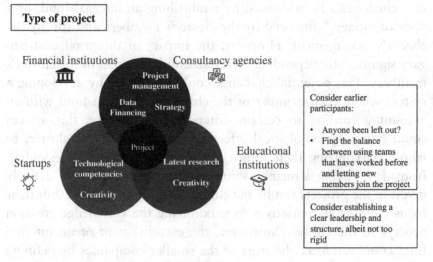

Figure 13.   Outline of selection criteria for projects.

a framework for the selection of participants for each project based on criteria as presented in Figure 13.

We consider the first criteria "type of project" as a fundamental factor for the rest of the selection as process. Indeed, we believe the choice of the participants should depend on the nature of the project itself. For instance, a research initiative centered around a certain technology might require participants with a different skill set than a project defining new guidelines on a specific legislation. Furthermore, to maximize the innovativeness of the project, we propose that participants from different stakeholder groups are chosen, enabling the alignment of the stakeholders' different motivations. Moreover, we propose taking into consideration which of the cluster members have previously been involved in earlier projects. This with the goal of establishing a preferred balance between members that have already proven to be great contributors and giving new members the chance to participate and share insights. Lastly, we propose the establishment of a clear and flexible leadership structure for each project.

6.4.2. *Establishing an internal fund*

The issue relating to the total cost of being a member of an innovation cluster can be addressed by establishing an internal fund, or a "pot of money," financed by the cluster's members and run by the cluster's management. However, the impact of this total cost can vary significantly depending on the size and resources of the cluster's members. This potential challenge could be tackled by developing a system where each member of the cluster invests in a fund with an amount according to certain criteria. Consequently, this system could have a psychological effect on the actors in the cluster, to whom maximizing their return on investment would be essential. Instead of paying a membership fee, members would now actively invest in the projects run by the cluster. A setup that could shift their focus from single initiatives to maximizing the knowledge creation process in the cluster. Moreover, the establishment of an internal fund could reinforce the trust of the smaller companies by defining precisely the level of contribution of each actor and allocating financial resources objectively to different projects or multi-actor teams. By ensuring that smaller organizations such as start-ups do not perceive that a lower investment level induces a weaker position in the collaboration activities, this system could bridge the gap between the larger and smaller players.

6.4.3. *Investment in cascade*

Having an internal fund for investing into projects and initiatives would also represent an opportunity for the cluster members to mitigate their investment risk. Instead of choosing specific project to invest in, partners would now indirectly finance all the initiatives pursued within the cluster, since the initial investments would be taken out of the common "pot of money." This would further reduce the members' exposure to single projects in the event of failure. In Jackson's resource-allocation theory, the author similarly describes a risk-mitigation shift incentivizing corporate actors to invest more into projects at earlier stages, thus reducing the "Death Valley" of start-ups and multi-actor initiatives. Moreover, the cluster needs to find a way to regulate the consumption of its resources, notably by ensuring that resources initially assigned to projects that have failed can be reinvested or "recycled" into other projects (Jackson, 2015). This promotes organizing projects as a "waterfall" or a "cascade" that prevent actors from committing all their resources at once and enabling them to rebound in case of failure.

6.5. *Build knowledge management processes*

To tackle the challenge with knowledge and data sharing, we propose the members of clusters to invest in trust building activities, build knowledge management processes, and incorporate incentives to participate in the cluster (Figure 14). Lastly, we propose the Stage-Gate innovation process model for project management within clusters.

As seen earlier, firms must invest a lot in trust-building activities with other partners of the cluster to ensure an effective process for knowledge sharing over time. Nevertheless, knowledge-sharing processes still need to be handled with caution. As a consequence of facilitating streams of information and expertise between members,

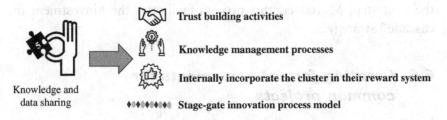

Figure 14. Build knowledge management processes.

Figure 15.   The Stage-Gate product innovation process.
Source: Stage-Gate International (2018).

direct collaboration activities within FinTech clusters might expose firms to the risk of seeing their commercial and technological know-how being misused. Therefore, we propose that member-firms should build knowledge management processes to determine how much they are willing to reveal to their partners, and under which terms. Additionally, to exploit the benefits of open innovation, we propose reward systems within member-firms which favor the employees' achievements within the cluster. This should increase the motivation for participation in the collaborative initiatives. Additionally, we propose clusters to adopt some form of Stage-Gate innovation process (Stage-Gate International, 2018), which breaks up the development of ideas into smaller stages, as illustrated by Figure 15.

In this model, the stages describe the different activities or projects organized within the cluster and the gates represent business evaluations or decisions of whether to move forward or "kill" the project. This process establishes clear objectives for each stage of the project, and enables users to evaluate the achievements made before proceeding. At each gate, members can also decide whether they wish to remain part of the project or to back out. This feature is a way to ensure that all members are fully engaged and on board for the next step. Moreover, this process facilitates the "investment in cascade" strategy.

6.6. Creating formal agreements for common projects

In confronting the last challenge of project ownership, we propose the creation of formal agreements for common projects (Figure 16).

Figure 16. Formal agreements for common projects.

To deal with the challenges of ownership rights, clusters should establish a formal agreement or contract describing the boundaries of each project and their ownership structure. First, this process needs to clarify whether the project is a research initiative or aims at developing a tangible innovation. Further, it should include a specification on what each player is expected to bring to the table in terms of resources, in particular, time and expertise. A project agreement would then provide a basis for the smooth running of the project and clarify the amount and kind of data the different players are agreeing to share. Based on the distinction between a research initiative and a project aiming at developing a tangible innovation, the agreement should also describe the ownership of the project output. We suggest three alternative ownership structures for common projects: (1) Collective (owned by cluster as a whole), (2) Conjointly owned by project partners, and (3) Creation of a new entity (output owned by this new entity).

7. Concluding Remarks

By building on the propositions of this study, we find that clusters can take a large step in enhancing the value creation process through ensuring efficient and inclusive collaboration mechanisms. In turn, this should also create beneficial spillovers effects on all the actors in the ecosystem.

We argue that even if our findings are based on a single case study, the study has some key features that suggest validity of our contribution beyond the current case. First, we are studying the fundamental concepts of cluster organizations, and the current case is not so unique that it should prevent transferability. Second, our propositions are aggregated from detailed case findings to overall patterns that are grounded in existing theory, with limited dependency to the particularity of the case. Still, much is left for us to understand regarding the organization of innovation clusters. Gathering more insight on the development of interactions within clusters and on how clusters are perceived by members could potentially enhance the understanding of our propositions further. Consequently, we suggest that further research should focus on in-depth longitudinal studies, following clusters closely from start to maturity.

References

Austin, J. E. (2000). *The Collaboration Challenge: how nonprofits and businesses succeed through strategic alliances* (Jossey-Bass, San Francisco).

Blackwell, R. (2018). The tech giants are coming for your customers. Be ready. *American Banker,* **128**, 22–23.

Boschma, R. A. (2005). Proximity and Innovation: A Critical Assessment. *Regional Studies,* **39**(1), 61–74.

Brant, J., & Lohse, S. (2014). The open innovation model. Retrieved from International Chamber of Commerce: https://iccwbo.org/global-issues-trends/innovation-ip/ (Accessed on 30 April 2018).

Bronstein, L. R. (2003). A Model for Interdisciplinary Collaboration. Retrieved from Oxford Academic: https://doi.org/10.1093/sw/48.3.297 (Accessed on 30 April 2018).

Cappelen, Å., Fjærli, E., Iancu, D., & Raknerud, A. (2015). *Effect on Firm Performance of Support from Innovation Norway* (SSB, Oslo).

Chesbrough, H., 2006. Open innovation: A new paradigm for understanding industrial innovation. In *Open Innovation: Researching a New Paradigm*, Chesbrough, H., Vanhaverbeke, W., & West, J. (eds.) (Oxford University Press, Oxford), pp. 1–12.

Chiaroni, A., Chiesa, V., & Frattini, F. (2010). Unravelling the process from closed to open innovation: Evidence from mature, asset-intensive industries. *R&D Management,* **40**(3), 222–245.

Cohen, W., & Levinthal, D. (1990). Absorptive capacity: A new perspective on learning and innovation. *Administrative Science Quarterly,* **35**, 128–152.

Connell, J., Kriz, A., & Thorpe, M. (2014). Industry clusters: An antidote for knowledge sharing and collaborative innovation? *Journal of Knowledge Management,* **18**(1), 137–151.

Cumming, H. (2016). Time to partner up? Fintech and banks could complement each other. *Banking Exchange*, November 11.

Deloitte (2017a). A tale of 44 cities: Connecting Global FinTech: Interim Hub Review 2017. Retrieved from: https://www2.deloitte.com/content/dam/Deloitte/uk/Documents/Innovation/deloitte-uk-connecting-global-fintech-hub-federation-innotribe-innovate-finance.pdf (Accessed on 30 April 2018).

Deloitte (2017b). FinTech in the Nordics. Retrieved from https://www2.deloitte.com/content/dam/Deloitte/no/Documents/financial-services/no-fintech-in-the-nordics-2017.pdf (Accessed on 30 April 2018).

Hocevar, S. P. (2011). Inter-organizational collaboration: Addressing the challenge. Retrieved from: https://calhoun.nps.edu/bitstream/handle/10945/37884/Inter-Organizational_Collaboration_2011–09.pdf?sequence=1 (Accessed on 30 April 2018).

Hoecht, A., & Trott, P. (2006). Outsourcing, information leakage and the risk of losing technology-based competencies. *European Business Review*, 18(5), 395–412.

Holten, A.-L., & Brenner, S. (2015). Leadership style and the process of organizational change. *Leadership & Organization Development Journal*, 36(1), 2–16.

InnoviSCOP (2016). Innovation clusters — Definition. Retrieved from: http://www.innoviscop.com/en/definitions/innovation-clusters (Accessed on 30 April 2018).

Jackson, D. J. (2015). *What is an Innovation Ecosystem?* (National Science Foundation, Arlington, VA).

Langkilde, L. (2014). Cluster ecosystem analysis. *17th TCI Global Conference*, TCI Network, Monterrey. 10–13 November 2014.

Malmberg, A., & Maskell, P. (2002). The elusive concept of localization economies: Towards a knowledge-based theory of spatial clustering. *Environment and Planning A*, 34, 429–449.

Malmberg, A., & Power, D. (2005). How do firms in clusters create knowledge? *Industry and Innovation*, 12, 409–431.

McKinney, P. (2017). The economics of innovation: Valuing innovation as an intangible asset. *Phil McKinney Blog*. https://philmckinney.com/the-economics-of-innovation-valuing-innovation-as-an-intangible-asset/ (Accessed on 30 April 2018).

Naoum, S. (2003). An overview into the concept of partnering. *International Journal of Project Management*, 21(1), 71–76.

Norwegian Innovation Clusters. (2018). *Norwegian Innovation Clusters*. Retrieved from: http://www.innovationclusters.no/english/ (Accessed on 30 April 2018).

Oh, D.-S., Phillips, F., Park, S., & Lee, E. (2016). Innovation ecosystems: A critical examination. *Technovation*, 54, 1–6.

O'Reilly III, C., & Tushman, M. (2004). The ambidextrous organization. *Harvard Business Review*, 82(4), 74–83.

Pisano, G. P., & Verganti, R. (2009). Which kind of collaboration is right for you? Retrieved from: http://thismomentintime.wdfiles.com/local--files/collaboration/hbr_what_collab_right.pdf (Accessed on 30 April 2018).

Porter, M. (2000). Location, competition, and economic development: Local clusters in a global economy. *Economic Development Quarterly*, **14**(1), 15.

PwC. (2016). Blurred lines: How FinTech is shaping financial services. Retrieved from: https://www.pwc.com/gx/en/advisory-services/FinTech/pwc-fintech-global-report.pdf (Accessed on 30 April 2018).

Saebi, T., & Angelshaug, M. (2017). The burning platform of retail banking. *The European Business Review*, **5**, 30–35.

Saebi, T., & Foss, N. (2015). Business models for open innovation: Matching heterogeneous open innovation strategies with business model dimensions. *European Management Journal*, **33**(3), 201–213.

Stage-Gate International. (2018). Innovation process. Retrieved from: https://www.stage-gate.com/thought-leadership/ (Accessed on 7 July 2021).

Teece, D. J. (2003). Expert talent and the design of (professional services) firms. *Industrial & Corporate Change*, **12**(4), 895–916.

Trumpy, J. (2017). Bergen samler fintech-miljø. *Dagens Næringsliv*, June 9.

Viki, T., Toma, D., & Gons, E. (2017). *The Corporate Startup: How Established Companies Can Develop Successful Innovation Ecosystems* (Rachel Faulkner, Amsterdam, Netherlands).

WIPO. (2011). World Intellectual Property Report: The Changing Face of Innovation. Retrieved from: http://www.wipo.int/edocs/pubdocs/en/intproperty/944/wipo_pub_944_2011.pdf (Accessed on 30 April 2018).

Chapter 8

FinTech and the Global Wealth Management Industry

Noel Finck,[†,‡] *Meredith Bowden,*[*,§] *Fiona Carter,*[*,¶]
Crag Carttling,[*,**] *Vincenzo Lorefice*[*,††] *and*
Jeffrey Vanderveen[*,‡‡]

[†]*Pitcher Partners, Docklands VIC 3008, Australia*

[‡]*Noel.Finck@pitcher.com.au*

[§]*meredithandtim@bigpond.com*

[¶]*fionaleighcarter@gmail.com*

[**]*crag.carttling@gmail.com*

[††]*chenzosix@gmail.com*

[‡‡]*jeffreyvanderveen@gmail.com*

Abstract. The global Wealth Management industry is changing fast and incumbents need to anticipate and react in order to be successful. Led by a significant rise in wealth in Asia, changing customer preferences, and digital transformation post the global financial crisis, open business models will assist innovative companies in creating tailored solutions for their new customer segments.

---

[*]Co-authors have contributed to this book chapter in their individual capacity.

New customer segments among women, millennials, and cross-border require new services aided by digital technology and are customer-centric and values-based, not just focused on investment returns.

Business models should be underpinned by a hybrid offering of digital services with a strong focus on human relationships. Systems, processes, and structures must ensure agility, innovation, and efficiency in order to continue to compete in this environment and be ready for ongoing technology-led disruption.

Technology-led disruption and involving customers in the value creation process using the Lean methodology and value co-creation can be used in order to understand and increase customer value. FinTech should be simple and responsive and designed to augment human advisors.

Keywords. Digital disruption and transformation; industry consolidation; lean and agile start-up; FinTech; government regulation and compliance costs; business model pivot; innovation value proposition; value chain; co-creation.

1. Introduction

The global wealth management industry has undergone significant change over the last decade following the global financial crisis (GFC). Wealth advisors have been forced and squeezed to adapt to a fast-changing environment to stay on top of client needs, financial technology (FinTech), shareholder expectations, and strong regulatory frameworks. FinTech describes the development and provision of software that facilitate alternate delivery of financial services, including the analysis of information and the automation of processes. FinTech involves computer technology, artificial intelligence (AI), and behavioral science used in banking and financial services.

Having reviewed the wealth management industry, this chapter aims to identify emerging trends, emerging business models, tech-enabled entrepreneurship, the role of lean start-up methodology, and how to be ready for the wave of technology change.

2. Emerging Trends

Four key trends were identified that impact the wealth management industry:

- Industry consolidation
- Asian wealth growth
- Evolving client needs
- Digital transformation

There are other trends, including concerns around cybersecurity. We identified the four key trends due to the speed of the changes in a traditional and large industry and that they were driven by the clients rather than the management of the organizations.

2.1. *Industry consolidation*

The global wealth management industry is highly fragmented. The largest 32 participants control approximately 50% of the market, leaving it ripe for consolidation.[1]

The industry is facing pressure on both revenue and costs. Fees, which are based on a percentage of assets under management (AUM) or on income, are being impacted due to lower asset valuations and income returns, particularly on interest rate products. The ease of financial trading today (with simple transparent products such as exchange-traded funds and index funds) and the competition for funds and clients, places downward pressure on AUM fees. The pressure to deliver "alpha"[2] remains. To stop conflicted investment recommendations, the UK has banned retrocessions, which will impact pricing models and profitability (Kurzo and Jaecklin, 2014).[3]

Following the GFC in 2007–2008, the regulatory burden and costs of compliance have risen. These costs are difficult to pass onto

---

[1]See https://www.ft.com/content/d2c9d58c-6025-11e8-ad91-e01af256df68

[2]Alpha is the value the asset manager brings-that is what they beat their benchmark by after fees.

[3]The Financial Services Authority's Retail Distribution Review bans commissions from fund managers to advisors from 2013.

clients and were introduced to mitigate systemic risks and to protect clients.

Key reasons for the increased regulatory burden include:

- Tax transparency
- Anti-terrorism financing and anti-money laundering initiatives (AML/CTF)
- Financial system stability requirements

Tax transparency is an attempt by governments to stop revenue leakage and support their budgets. The aim is to ensure that taxpayers are reporting appropriate levels of revenue and paying tax where they should. AML/CTF initiatives attempt to monitor transfers of funds and to determine the beneficial owners of funds. This include "know your client" information gathering and reporting obligations. To provide stability to the banking industry, Basel III requirements include higher levels of high-quality liquid assets and capital adequacy for banking subsidiaries. Other regulatory requirements include the European MiFID II[4] requirements that are designed to protect clients by ensuring that the advice given, and products sold, are suitable for the clients' risk profile and financial literacy level.

All these requirements add to the regulatory burden and costs of the market participants. The investment in IT systems and processes and additional staff to monitor compliance will cause organizations to seek greater scale to defray the costs over a larger client base to enable the firm profitability to be maintained. The increased regulatory burden creates a natural barrier to entry for new, smaller market participants.

Following the 2008 GFC, there has been a concentration of service providers. Bear Stearns, Salomon Brothers, Smith Barney, and even Merrill Lynch have all been taken over by larger entities (Stempel, 2008). Increased regulations and reduced margins will contrive to make it harder for smaller independent managers or advisors to compete with larger global entities; as such further

---

[4]Markets in Financial Instruments Directive.

concentration of the market may be expected (Kurzo and Jaecklin, 2014, p. 9).

Surveyed European industry participants anticipate industry consolidation in the market, particularly amongst the small players, who will either merge or be acquired. The cause of this is higher fixed costs and reduced revenue yields, requiring greater scale to be profitable. Increased regulation is also causing business models to be simplified with a focus on core regions and client segments (Kurzo and Jaecklin, 2014, p. 9).

2.2. Asian wealth growth

China has reported US$29 trillion in private wealth, an increase of US$18 trillion over the past decade (Credit Suisse, 2017). China is now in second place with the second highest number of Ultra High Net Worth[5] Individuals (UHNWI), and in 2014 overtook Japan with the most millionaires, behind the US (Shorrocks *et al.*, 2018, p. 2). 2017 was a year of firsts; the first time a Chinese bank had been in the top 10 major global wealth management entities (Selby-Green, 2018) and UBS and PWC found that for the first time that Asian billionaires outnumbered those in the US (Willsher, 2018). In 2008, the Chinese economy was smaller than that of Japan; today it is more than double the size and is bigger than the combined total of the 19 countries using the Euro (*Time*, 2018). Knight Frank Research (2017) reported that the UHNWI population in China and India grew by 281% and 290%, respectively, in the decade to 2016.

Asian wealth growth (the increase in Chinese wealth in particular, and Asian wealth in general, and a shift from the dominant North America and Europe centers of wealth) presents a significant opportunity for global wealth managers to diversify their client base. Increasingly, Asia is now emerging as a market that is willing to pay for professional financial advice. The rise in wealth from new industries presents opportunities from a younger audience.

---

[5]Net wealth above US$50 million.

Stability is offered in Singapore and Hong Kong as both are established trading and financial centers. Wealth-X (2018) reported that, in 2017, Hong Kong had a 31% increase in HNWI and overtook New York as the world's top city for the ultra-rich. Whilst the potential rewards for market participants in Asia are large, there are heightened risk factors in entering any new market and particularly in a region that may be more volatile.

Global wealth has historically been concentrated in Europe and North America, which together account for 64% of total household wealth but contain only 17% of the world adult population (Shorrocks *et al.*, 2017, p. 6). The European Central Bank estimates that half of the wealth in Europe is controlled by people aged over 55 years and that this wealth will transition over the next 20 to 30 years (Kurzo and Jaecklin, 2014, p. 10).

In North America, in 2017, 30% of advisors reduced their fees and advisors struggled to add younger clients to their base (Bol *et al.*, 2018). The region faces similar challenges to Europe. North America is the richest global region in terms of personal wealth with 43% (Zakrzewski *et al.*, 2018).

HNWI in Asia Pacific (excluding Japan) invested with wealth managers saw their investment value increase by 33% in 2016 compared to 24.6% in other regions. However, investor satisfaction remains muted in Asia despite the robust investment performance with fee concerns partly responsible. Business model disruption may be imminent as investors seek value beyond investment returns (Capgemini, 2017a).

Growth opportunities are also emerging from the aging of the population in key markets (facilitating retirement and estate planning) with just 49% of UHNWIs in Asia with a robust succession plan in place compared to 59% in Europe and 62% in North America. (Knight Frank Research, 2018, p. 30).

2.3. *Evolving client needs*

The demographics of clients in the wealth management industry are changing as more young people and women enter the high net worth category (McCrank, 2011). This shift is accompanied by changing attitudes and client needs, which wealth management providers must adapt to in order to remain relevant and viable.

According to Beyer (2017, p. 8), "today's wealthy investors are younger than ever, and do not think like their parents or grandparents." The percentage of the world's HNWI population aged under 45 years increased from 13% in 2008 to 17% in 2010 (McCrank, 2011), and this proportion is predicted to continue to grow as tech entrepreneurs increase their presence in the business environment (Kruger, 2018), older generations retire, and wealth is transferred between generations (Deloitte, 2015).

Affluent women are emerging as a new customer segment in the wealth management industry (Maude, 2006, p. 270) and are set to create significant change in the industry. In 2010, women comprised 27% of the world's HNWI population, an increase from 24% in 2008 (McCrank, 2011). As the number of female entrepreneurs increases, this figure is predicted to rise (McCrank, 2011). Not only is the number of women increasing in this area, but the number of wealthy women is growing at a greater rate than the number of wealthy men. It has been estimated that in North America the number of wealthy women has been growing by 68% compared to only 36% growth in wealthy men (Maude, 2006, p. 270).

Accompanying these demographic changes are significant changes in worldviews and attitudes in the client group. Clients have a broader worldview and are concerned that their "investments have a positive impact on the world around them" (Beyer, 2017, p. 8). Not only do clients have an increasing desire to have a positive impact, such as improving environmental and social outcomes, but they also want to live to see that difference, so the industry is seeing a shift in their clients away from a desire for "dynastic wealth" and the concept of leaving a legacy, to a desire for a "live-acy" (Beyer, 2017, p. 9). Associated with this shift of worldview away from dynastic wealth and creating an easy life for their children is a new client focus on teaching their children "struggle lessons" and developing their resilience to failure and disappointment (Beyer, 2017, p. 9).

Another impact of changing client demographics is that clients are more astute about financial planning and have increased financial awareness (Mehta *et al.*, 2017, p. 3). As this new client group often comprises successful business people and entrepreneurs, many clients have a "do-it-myself" mentality (Beyer, 2017, p. 11) and want to be more actively involved in the management of their investments and have more control (Maude, 2006), demanding greater transparency. As business people themselves, clients expect that their wealth advisers will add significant value and therefore they expect greater productivity and creative ideas from their providers (Maude, 2006). If providers are not performing to their expected standards, clients are more willing to switch providers, and in the case of serious misconduct, they are more prepared to take legal action against them (Maude, 2006). Finally, clients are more price-sensitive (Ernst & Young, 2017) and are interested in lower-cost models, such as automated advisers (Mehta *et al.*, 2017, p. 13).

These changing demographics and associated shifts in worldview and attitudes result in changing client needs occurring along two dimensions (Fischer *et al.*, 2013, p. 35): relationship and solution. Clients tend to follow their wealth managers due to relationship and trust (Mehta *et al.*, 2017, p. 15), however the Capgemini World Wealth Report (2018) found low levels of global client satisfaction and connection with their advisers. Women in particular are often dissatisfied with their providers and can feel "marginalized" in the relationship between themselves, their male partner, and advisor (Beyer, 2017). This poses a serious risk to incumbent providers whose female client group is likely to expand. Younger people might also question their relationship with wealth management advisers, having seen a number of financial crises (McCrank, 2011).

The second dimension of changing client needs is that clients are expecting different solutions. The wealth management industry has traditionally strongly emphasized product-driven support, however as clients seek greater involvement and control, they are now looking for support that is more "advisory" in nature (Ernst & Young, 2017) and is tailored to their individual needs. They want their "wealth viewed and managed holistically" (Ernst & Young, 2017, p. 13) so that they can achieve their often multiple and conflicting goals (Deloitte, 2015), with advice taking into account both their personal as well as their business situations (Maude, 2006).

Clients are also interested in alternative investments such as hedge funds (Maude, 2006, p. 51), and "passion-based investments" (Ernst & Young, 2017, p. 13) such as investment in artwork, wines, or "ethically motivated investments in sustainability and social entrepreneurship" (Ernst & Young, 2017, p. 13). A final and significant change is that clients, having grown up in a technological age, and often having made their wealth in this area, are looking for digital capabilities when it comes to wealth management (Capgemini, 2017b, p. 3). Given this focus on technology, incumbents who do not successfully adopt the newest technology "may not be respected as capable" by clients (Beyer, 2017, p. 11). The following section explores this trend towards technology in greater detail.

2.4. *Digital transformation*

The wealth management industry is being impacted by an "evolution" in information technology, "with the emergence, adoption and importance of cloud, analytics, mobile, social data, distributed ledgers and cognitive computing" (Enness and Graham, 2017, p. 455). The impact of technological developments is not new in the wealth management industry, having previously been disrupted by technologies such the mobile phone, optical glass fibers, and desktop computers (Banziger, 2017). These technological disruptions have "completely transformed how (financial) markets operate" (Bussmann, 2017, p. 473). While advances in information technology have created many business opportunities and efficiencies in the wealth management industry, they have also contributed to "financial turbulence" in the past (Banziger, 2017, p. 426) and will continue to present both opportunities and risks.

Today, the wealth management industry is undergoing evolutionary transformation with the "rise of the internet, mobile technologies, ... cloud computing and big data" (Bussmann, 2017, p. 474). Changing client demographics means that clients are demanding "full use of digital infrastructure capabilities" (Ernst & Young, 2018). Aligned with how they use technologies in other aspects of their personal and professional lives, clients want a "variety of touch-points, 24/7 access and the ability to self-service" (Accenture, 2016, p. 9) with access to online tools and mobility (Schiff and Taylor, 2016).

Bussman (2017, p. 473) argues that the current "catalyst for change" is coming from the FinTechs who are "developing products and services aimed at the financial industry value chain." An important aspect of FinTech is the role of "robo-advisers" (Salampasis *et al.*, 2019, p. 169), or automated wealth advisers, which use AI, big data, and predictive analytics to promote rational decision-making when it comes to financial management and investment. These robo-advisers have the capacity to "monitor public companies, analyse financial, non-financial and supply chain data, and assess risk" (Price Waterhouse Coopers, 2018, pp. 17–18), thus potentially replacing or changing the need for human-provided analysis and advice. However, as wealth management services are "deeply embedded within human-to-human interaction" (Salampasis *et al.*, 2019, p. 168), it is unlikely that robo-advisers will completely replace human advisers. Therefore providing "the right mix of automated analysis and human intervention" (Salampasis *et al.*, 2019, p. 171) in advisory systems and processes is critical for wealth management providers. Rather than being viewed as a solution, technology should be viewed as a tool to improve the relationship between clients and advisers (McKinsey & Co, 2018b).

The introduction of automated wealth advisers has four identified impacts on the wealth management industry. First, digital platforms are "democratising the delivery of financial advice" (Deloitte, 2014, p. 5), thus creating a potential new market as people who do not meet the traditional wealth threshold are able to access advice. Second, by "lowering the barriers to market entry" (Ernst & Young, 2017b, p. 6) there is added competition for incumbent providers

(Bussmann, 2017). Third, incumbents have the potential to use these technologies to manage increasing cost and regulatory pressures (Bussmann, 2017, p 475). According to Price Waterhouse Coopers (2018, p. 18), "RegTech, relying on artificial intelligence, will reduce compliance costs not only through automation but also by alerting firms to regulatory hurdles." This technology also has the potential to improve and reduce the costs of internal processes and make them more efficient, through streamlining the middle and back office (Cebula, 2017, p. 12). Fourth, technology such as big data can assist providers with new client identification (KPMG, 2018).

While it is clear that wealth management incumbents must adapt to this new world in order to retain clients, capture the emerging younger client base, and remain relevant, it is generally thought that the industry is currently not keeping up with these technological changes and has been described as a "digital technology laggard" (Price Waterhouse Coopers, 2018, p. 4). This is a dangerous situation for incumbents who will potentially be competing against automated wealth advisers — one study found that clients of robo-advisers report levels of satisfaction 5 to 10 times higher than clients of traditional wealth managers (Schiff and Taylor, 2016).

3. Emerging Business Models

Business models in the wealth management industry are changing; the main drivers of this are FinTech, which applies big data, robo advice, and wealth management platforms; evolving customer needs; and the regulatory environment (Ernst & Young, 2018). The classic "one bank" model combining investment banking and wealth management has failed to make an impact (Bender, 2018). New business models that link new technology to an emerging market and market needs transform industries (Kavadias *et al.*, 2016). Successful new and emerging business models within the wealth management industry will create stronger linkages between new technological developments, emerging market contextual peculiarities and unmet customer needs in the quest for further innovation, experimentation and disruption.

Ernst & Young (2018) identifies five classic business models in wealth management:

- Diversified product specialists
- Independent wealth advisors
- Traditional wealth managers
- Family offices
- Boutique finance houses

Ernst & Young (2018) also point to a sixth emerging model, which is holistic wealth management, which they project will capture 20%–30% of the market in coming years.

Business model innovation is increasingly recognized as a key approach to success. In order to drive growth and avoid disruption, companies should innovate through their business models, reaching beyond core markets, customer segments and technologies (Bertels *et al.*, 2013). This innovation can be driven by and develop new core capabilities, partnerships, revenue models, and channels. Business model innovation can be cheaper, easier, and more effective and harder for other companies to replicate.

Business model innovation includes adding new activities such as forward and backward integration, linking activities in new ways and structures and new parties performing activities (Amit and Zott, 2012). Indeed, horizontal inclusion of other organizations in the production cycle is now commonplace (Kortmann and Piller, 2016).

As operating costs grow and billions are invested into FinTech, revenue generation no longer drives business models but rather the cost of strategy and service (Bender, 2018). Fees from asset management are the major source of revenue; articulating these fees is a key component of new models. This articulation of fees must be achieved in relation to holistic services (Bender, 2018).

New wealth management business models will be built around networking with fellow investors and links to social and environmental sustainability; generating income from assets is now just a component of the offer. A sophisticated brand and value proposition is crucial to emerging models (Bender, 2018).

Open business models are an important approach for innovation in wealth management. Open business models support innovation by searching for and exploiting outside ideas and allowing unused internal technologies to be shared with others who can unlock their potential. They also allow multiple companies to leverage off those key assets and resource position and off those with whom they share, as well as reducing the cost and time required for R&D (Chesbrough, 2007). An open business model approach will also drive emerging business models in wealth management. This approach of opening up development processes and sharing them with customers and other companies will make it easier for companies to develop a range of FinTech products by sharing capacity and technology and getting it to market quickly while adapting it with greater speed and agility.

To capitalize on open business models, companies need to learn to experiment with their business models, however these experiments can be risky to the company's brand, so it is recommended that granulation, spin-offs, or "white box" companies are developed to reduce this risk (Chesbrough, 2007).

The core components of a business model include (Bertels *et al.*, 2013):

- Customer value proposition
- Profit formula
- Key resources
- Key processes

The business model canvas is a popular tool for business model innovation, which captures these components and assists with identifying and testing assumptions. Companies can use the canvas to define explicit processes for testing these assumptions (Bertels *et al.*, 2013). It is also important to not only test for validation but also dissatisfaction (Moogk, 2012). Bertels *et al.* (2015) include additional fields to the business model canvas to capture internal and external dynamics, including PESTEL analysis and adoption and internal dynamics.

While many suggest that making significant shifts from one's own core business model exposes a company to failure, Bertels *et al.* (2015) posit that this is not the case but rather a failure to constantly test assumptions about the changing model, which leads to failure. More often than not, it is those aspects of the model that are most familiar to the company which require testing.

The value proposition is central to the business model canvas. While most wealth management firms claim to have a customer-centric business model, many are in fact still product-centric (Fischer *et al.*, 2013). Giving advice is at the heart of a client-centric model; it is likely that this will become a major differentiator in the future (Fischer *et al.*, 2013). Customers are demanding real-time digital systems and thus the role of the advisor is decreasing in importance and changing to more of that of coach supported by digital systems (Ernst & Young, 2018).

While FinTech and apps are changing how business models achieve touch points, relationship managers are still important. That said, it is hard to scale using relationship managers due to cost (Fischer *et al.*, 2013). There is also a change in pricing models from commission-based advice to performance-based fee structures (Capgemini, 2017a). How the value proposition and all aspects of the business model delivers value to customers must be carefully addressed.

3.1. *Customer segments*

The wealth management industry has traditionally segmented customers into wealth levels — traditionally starting at US$1 million in liquid assets, not including the family home, whilst some private banks have had a minimum entry point of US$10 million (Baghai *et al.*, 2016, p. 1).

Due to socio-economic, demographic, and technology shifts, new customer segments are starting to become more dominant. With the advancement of technology and low-cost options, the cost of wealth management is more attainable, removing the stigma of just being available to 1% of the population.

There are three key new customer segments that are becoming more prevalent in the industry — millennials, women, and cross-border users.

3.1.1. *Millennials*

Millennials (born between 1980 and 2000) currently hold 10% of global private wealth, which is expected to grow to 16% by 2020 (Beardsley *et al.*, 2016). This customer segment is becoming the largest generation, and their wealth derives from organic growth in income and inheritance (Thompson and Blomquist, 2018). As millennials are extremely technology savvy and engaged in online technology, it is vital that they have a seamless user experience combining both face-to-face interaction with easy-to-use platforms across mobile and online modes.

As the transfer of wealth occurs from baby boomers and World War II generations, this generation will see their wealth significantly increase over the next 15 years. One of the most important focus areas for wealth advisors is to ensure they have strong relationships at all levels of the family hierarchy. For instance, the key relationship contact will be held with the matriarch or patriarch of the family, with little time being invested in getting to know the younger generation — it is vitally important to ensure that appropriate time is invested with the next generation early on, so in the unfortunate event of mum and dad passing, the advisor would be much more likely to maintain the relationship. As the "children" take over the reins of the family wealth, they are typically known to appoint a new advisor who is either a friend or an acquaintance who are a similar age, with a similar lifestyle and values.

Millennials also tend to be more socially aware and are tuned in to the impact they are making on the planet. According to a 2016 BCG survey, nearly 70% of millennials surveyed said they would like to invest in socially responsible products, including sustainable energy, microfinance, and environmentally friendly products

(Beardsley *et al.*, 2016). This presents a real opportunity for wealth advisors as they can focus on portfolios that provide socially conscious options for their millennial investors.

3.1.2. *Women*

Female wealth is on the rise; in 2015, women held 30% of global private wealth, and in Australia, the female workforce participation rate reached 60.5% in 2018 (Australian Bureau of Statistics, 2018; Beardsley *et al.*, 2016; WGEA, 2018b).

As it has become more socially acceptable for females to have a career and work full time, females are starting to earn more and climb the corporate ladder into leadership and executive roles that tend to demand larger salaries. In 2016, it was reported that Australian females made up 57.5% of all higher education enrolments, a figure that is on the rise (WGEA, 2018a).

According to a BCG survey, 30% of women rely on word-of-mouth referrals from trusted friends and family members to help them make financial and investment decisions, whilst only 10% rely on wealth advisors as their most trusted source (Beardsley *et al.*, 2016). This presents an opportunity for wealth advisors to create tailored, relationship-driven customer engagement plans that focus on building long-term relationships that are unique to female customer needs.

3.1.3. *Cross border*

As digital technology becomes more seamless and people become more comfortable with sharing information, the opportunity for cross-border global wealth advisors is huge. By 2019, it is estimated that 2.5 billion people globally will have a smart phone, therefore resulting in them having access to global FinTech and reducing barriers to entry (Statista, 2018). Developing countries who have not been traditionally identified as growth areas will now be accessible with entry points through social media and online marketing.

The real opportunity for cross-border segments is available for the larger global players like Merrill Edge, who have a trusted and strong brand that provides low-cost online options with "best in industry" guidance.

4. Culture and Values

4.1. *Customer centric*

As power to the consumer increases through more transparency and choice, wealth management businesses have been pushed to become more customer centric to retain customer loyalty. It is well known that it is much easier to keep a current customer happy than attract a new one — acquiring a new customer is anywhere from 5 to 25 times more expensive than retaining an existing one (Gallo, 2014).

Fred Reichheld, the creator of the Net Promoter Score (a loyalty metric), states that in financial services, "a 5% increase in customer retention produces more than a 25% increase in profit" (Gallo, 2014). This is mostly because existing customers tend to purchase more products over time and will provide strong word-of-mouth referrals. Customers also get comfortable as they value a person and brand they trust, and moving to a competitor is time-consuming, costly, and unfamiliar. However, this may change over time (the next 5–10 years) with the wealth management industry being forced to be more transparent and with the arrival of open data. "Open data and content can be freely used, modified, and shared by anyone for any purpose" (opendefinition.org, 2018). This would mean that the customer would be able to move between wealth management providers instantly with limited forms and down time.

4.2. *Values*

In the words of Simon Sinek, start with why — why do you do what you do? In the wake of the financial crisis, wealth management firms had to invest time and resources clearly defining their reason and purpose in the industry. Values are extremely important as they help define a company's corporate identity and create guidelines and a framework on how individuals and businesses conduct themselves and can be held to account.

Values are a great way to create team-centric leadership as everyone is in the same boat and striving for the same shared goals. Bad behavior can be called out and good behavior celebrated. One of the key strengths of shared business values is that it allows all team members to be empowered and trusted to do the right thing.

A good example of a well-communicated value proposition is that of Morgan Stanley (2018):

- Putting clients first
- Doing the right thing
- Leading with exceptional ideas
- Giving back

Most business values tend to be quite similar, the difference between good business values and great is the fact that they are embedded in the culture and reinforced as part of business as usual. Recently, the Banking Royal Commissioner Kenneth Hayne (2018) recommended six tenets (values) for Australian banks to follow (Hutchens, 2018):

(1) Obey the law.
(2) Do not mislead or deceive.
(3) Be fair.
(4) Provide services that are fit for purpose.
(5) Deliver services with reasonable care and skill.
(6) And, when acting for another, act in the best interests of that other.

4.3. *Aligned leadership*

Strong leadership is fundamental for the success of any business. Leaders need to be aligned to the strategy of the business and understand the key customer segments. According to Ernst & Young, more than 56% of global wealth advisors are over the age of 50 years, which raises the question: are they truly aligned to the emerging customer segments (Fava *et al.*, 2016, p. 2).

Earlier this month, a spokesperson for Wells Fargo said that "Wells Fargo's wealth and investment management division is in the midst of a number of organisational alignment changes intended to simplify the organisation, create added efficiency, and meet the evolving needs of its diverse client base most effectively" (Piper and Ge Haung, 2018).

4.4. *Training*

Leading wealth management firms have been investing resources and money in training for their wealth advisors to equip them with the right tools to have meaningful client conversations and to help them anticipate needs. For example, Merrill Lynch has a training center in New Jersey that provides a holistic view of the customer needs, including technical training and soft skills (Chishty *et al.*, 2011). They have also engaged in an ongoing implementation plan that requires leaders to mentor team members, resulting in continuous learning and development at all levels.

5. Value Co-creation Through Tech-Enabled Entrepreneurship and the Lean Methodology

5.1. *The Lean methodology*

Lean is a core management idea that revolves around proactive value creation based on direct customer analysis. A Lean organization aims to understand customer value and focus its key processes to continually increase the same. Its goal is to provide perfect value to its customers through perfected value creation processes while creating zero waste.

This methodology is implemented by changing management focus from optimizing separate technologies, vertical departments, etc., to optimizing product and service flow through value streams across all business assets and practices through to customers.

By eliminating waste along entire value streams through overarching refinement of management practices instead of focusing on isolated points, processes can be recursively improved to minimize human and capital requirements and create targeted products and services at much lower costs and higher success rates than through traditional business systems.

The basic principles of Lean as applicable in the wealth management industry are:

(1) Identifying customer needs through customer research;
(2) Designing and producing products or services based on these identified needs;
(3) Implementation and validation of products or services;
(4) Measuring insights and learnings;
(5) Using lessons learned to improve.

This customer-first approach enables companies to leverage their own resources and knowledge and respond to changing customer needs with minimal costs and very fast throughput times (Figure 1).

5.2. *Value co-creation*

With constant connectivity and easy access to a considerable amount of financial research and data, the modern customer demands a better understanding of fees and value provided by wealth managers. Value creation after the onset of the Fourth Industrial Revolution has become value co-creation between wealth management firms and their customers. This new breed of informed, networked, and active customers who become involved in designing and customizing products for their own needs are called prosumers (Prahalad, 2004).

Co-creation grants customers free reign over all resources provided to work with and produce their own value offerings. As they take increasingly active roles in the creation of their own value, the firm is no longer the sole arbiter in value creation. This is enabled by a combination of factors including ubiquitous connectivity, developments in FinTech, rapidly changing markets, and increasingly sophisticated customers.

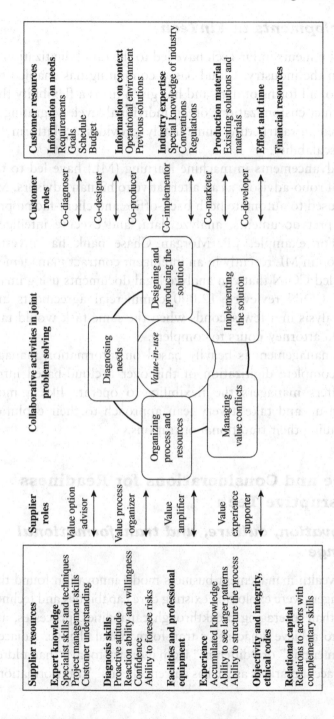

Figure 1. Collaborative activities in joint problem solving.

Source: Aarikka-Stenroos and Jaakkola (2012).

5.3. *Developments in FinTech*

Recent developments in FinTech have led to the rapid digitization of businesses in the industry. Cloud-based computing has enabled the digitization of all forms of data and has given firms a flexibility that enables product customizations on an individual level. Migrating to a cloud-based infrastructure immediately provides a platform for easy future scalability.

Rapid advancements in machine learning (ML) have led to the emergence of robo-advisors as an alternative to human advisors. ML can also be used to automate both back-office and client-facing processes, interpret documents, analyze data, and execute intelligent responses. For example, J.P. Morgan Chase bank has invested US$9.6 billion in ML recently in an intelligent contract management software called COiN that can analyze legal documents using image recognition. COiN reviewed 12,000 commercial agreements and provided analysis in a few seconds when the same task would take over 360,000 attorney hours to complete.

Wealth management is heavily based on information management. The complete digitization of this over a cloud-based infrastructure offers managers the flexibility to operate like a more flexible start-up and take a very lean approach to their evolution while continuing their traditional operations.

6. Advice and Considerations for Readiness to Disruptive Tech

6.1. *Innovation, culture, and transformational change*

A study of wealth management business model innovation found that wealth managers were exploiting existing core capabilities and technology, rather than leveraging breakthrough capabilities, processes, and technology to achieve adjacent or transformational change. Adjacent relates to "emerging" or "different" from industry today "that address clients in adjacent markets as well as current clients." Transformational relates to "new to the industry for brand new client segments addressing completely new client needs" (Kobler *et al.*, 2017).

Transformational change requires innovation, and to achieve greater success with innovation, the leadership group need to adopt the right mindset (one that includes collaboration and open innovation). The leadership team need to accept that their key beliefs and principles of the traditional business model impact the attitude and culture within the organization and therefore needs to be challenged. Industry players are changing, and given the maturity of the industry and the level of disruption occurring within the industry, the leadership team needs to acknowledge the urgency and importance of innovation for their organization (Kobler *et al.*, 2017). Once the leadership team is on board, innovation and the innovation mindset should be integrated and implemented throughout the organization as a discipline and an environment of divergent thinking should be created. Dedicated innovation leaders and in-house capabilities will be required to help drive the process (Kobler *et al.*, 2017).

It is worth considering leveraging underutilized capabilities and assets to expose new innovation, and also explore utilization of "hidden assets." Hidden assets can be found using new combinations of relationships, networks, market position, and new information (Slywotzky and Wise, 2002) and taking advantage of the interconnected ecosystem of partners, digital platforms, customers, and suppliers (Hirt,[6] 2018). On face value, it seems strange to think of competitors as a source of collaboration in the future. However, rather than compete against them, it is better to consider how their strengths and expertise could be leveraged to benefit one's customers (McKinsey & Co, 2018a).

To help explore new innovation, and still maintain/support existing business functions, organizations should be prepared to use small, agile teams to quickly and autonomously develop, iterate, pivot, and test ideas on a continuous basis without fear of failure.

---

[6]Martin Hirt — Senior Partner (Director) McKinsey & Company, Leader of McKinsey's Global Strategy Practice.

The aim is to creatively explore and quickly discover ideas that work and ideas that are viable. Doing so helps to create a culture and environment that is open, transparent, and accountable (McKinsey & Co, 2018a).

6.2. *Technology, AI, and ML*

Contri[7] (2018e) highlights the importance of being able to anticipate change and evolving trends, McKinsey & Co (2018a) advises to be alert and responsive to the environment, and O'Brien (2018) emphasizes the need to be pre-emptive and "become experts at recognising and responding to early indicators." As well as maintaining existing business functions such as financial modeling, portfolio management, etc., additional capabilities are required to obtain "a deep understanding of local markets" and be able to extract and apply the derived insights with analysis to "support strategic decision making" (with the help of AI and ML capabilities). It is important that people within the organization have a familiarity with how the AI and ML algorithms work and what they do, so it may be necessary for re-skilling of employees to become more data literate. After gaining the knowledge, employees will be better able to understand how output is being generated, if any limitations exist, and then also be able to explain the workings to clients, investors, staff, and regulators who may require explanation to feel more at ease (Holly, 2018). Managers will need to be attentive to how staff respond to the ongoing introduction/use of AI and ML and what impact it may have on workplace culture. AI and ML should be used as a complementary tool for people to "make better decisions and be more creative" (Holly, 2018).

Below are some examples of where AI and ML is/could be used

- Day-to-day process automation;
- Customization in creating an investment portfolio through investor profile and preference matching;
- Using virtual agents to autonomously interact with customers;

---

[7]Robert Contri — Global Financial Services Industry Leader at Deloitte.

- Customer service on demand, regardless of customer location;
- Creating new value propositions and custom solutions for customers;
- Real time, up-to-date data access for meetings.

It is advised to take a prioritized approach in deciding which processes should be automated, in what order, and which should remain "performed by humans." Consider resource outsourcing to assist with expediting this strategy (Technavio, 2018).

6.3. *Importance of data and customer focus*

The industry has recognized that data analytics is the best way "to build deeper, more meaningful relationships with. customers. Data will help to customize the offerings for customers and add value through personalized solutions. Organizations risk losing customers if they are not prepared to use data for value-added benefits (Contri, 2018g). Technavio (2018) cautions that with the overwhelming demand for client customization, organizations "must be 100% confident about the accuracy and feasibility of their data" to ensure "repeat business, up-selling and customer loyalties." Accuracy of data and the derived insights are important for survival and growth. What and how the data is gathered, stored, and processed requires careful consideration (Technavio, 2018). Data has typically been stored in silos, in multiple formats, and in a structured and unstructured form. Consider the application of ML and cognitive tools to help synthesize the data. Find ways to standardize, simplify, and optimize "acquisition and analysis" of data to help the whole organization "obtain a single customer view" (Contri, 2018g).

Solutions should be data driven and, ideally, the data should be centralized and therefore available to the whole organization, giving all employees the opportunity to access the data for better all-round decision-making (Contri, 2018a).

Technology should be used to augment and enhance business services. The digital platform is considered the right tool to help advisors/wealth managers develop high-quality, attractive options for clients and make the options available in a customized way (Contri, 2018f). Peter (2018) suggests that a more efficient and enriching experience for clients can be delivered through visual demonstrations and points out that responding to client needs and delivering a solution quickly will become more important in client relationships. Organizations should be aiming to create an environment for advisors/wealth managers that allow them to "generate plans in minutes" and allows them to conveniently interact with clients (Peter, 2018).

6.4. *IoT*

IoT is basically a network of interconnected "devices, networks, platforms and applications or other tools that enable data analytics." IoT Innovation (2018a) believes that IoT will "affect every aspect of how organisations operate" and recommend to "incorporate all aspects of the IoT ecosystem" to "streamline process and gain an advantage over competitors" (see Figure 2).

The basic operation of an IoT system is that a device or module generates data which transfers to a database (cloud) via a network/ gateway. Application software is then used to process data

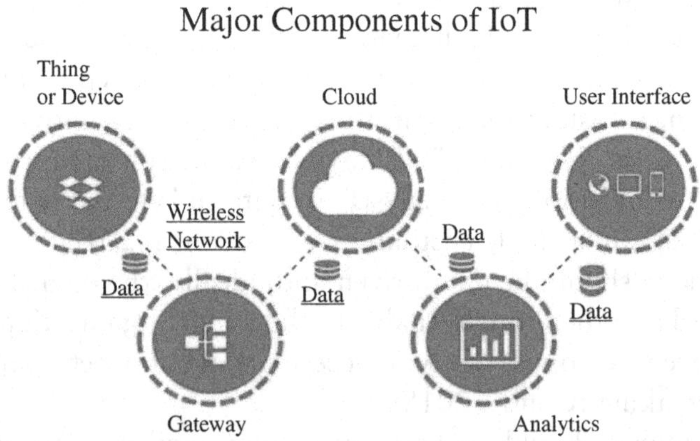

Figure 2.   Major components of IoT.
Source: RF Page (2018).

(analysis). Data can be processed in the gateway or cloud. The user interface helps to visualize the data for the user (RF Page, 2018).

It is important for the network to be secure, and for standardized devices, platforms, and analytics to be used to make the most of the IoT system.

To help organizations consider what is needed for IoT innovation, IoT Innovation (2018b) suggests to

- Understand what goals IoT connectivity has for your organization (this will help decide security, power, and performance requirements);
- Determining what the innovation will communicate and connect to (addresses operability, compliance, and functional considerations);
- Considering devices, connectivity needs, device management platforms, data storage, analytics, and the associated architecture required;
- Considering security design, including encryption, passwords, and other protocols (more devices mean more data).

6.5. *IT infrastructure/assets*

Data is doubling every two years and is predicted to reach 44 zettabytes (44×10^9 terabytes) by 2020 (Larkin, 2018), which is likely to stretch current computing infrastructure. Therefore, an assessment of the usability of existing assets and their suitability with application programming interfaces (APIs) is necessary. It is easier to share data and link software systems using APIs than it is using legacy systems. APIs will make it easier for integration of new technology but also encourage third-party innovation (Contri, 2017b). As an alternative to cloud computing, a new technology called edge computing is available, should you be seeking to expand your infrastructure. Larkin (2018) describes edge computing systems as consisting of "high-performance computer, storage and network resources" that are closer to end-users and devices. For isolated areas (like Australia), edge computing may offer a more attractive proposition particularly as it can help to reduce the burden of data traffic flow to and from the cloud, and hence improve traffic flow, efficiency, and productivity. It is a legitimate alternative to utilizing and relying on cloud centers in distant locations. Both edge and cloud computing technology can co-exist, so organizations should consider which technology is better suited to their circumstances (Larkin, 2018). Supplier partnerships should be considered to help expedite a solution.

6.6. *Digital ID*

For a "purely digital future" to become a reality, physical identifiers, e.g. a driver's license, will need to be replaced with a digital identity. There are already some signs of this happening where Facebook, Google, or similar accounts are required for online sign-in. Although the long-term issues to be resolved focus on standards and security, and privacy versus convenience, there is a growing demand for a more robust solution (Contri, 2017f). A digital identity could help in areas where people verification or legal entities and assets are required. The identity could also help to retrieve assets and transaction history data more readily and also speed up other services (Contri, 2017f).

Below are additional examples of where digital identity could be applied (Contri, 2017e):

- Offer more tailored customer solutions;
- Streamline/automate processes in operations;
- Improve security and authentication and reduce fraud;
- Improve accuracy and ease of identity compliance;
- Provide identity services as an alternative source of income;
- Become more competitive through developing a richer relationship with the customer.

Consideration should be given to partnerships with entities who can help drive the implementation of digital identity, particularly if in-house capabilities are not available or adequate to drive it (Contri, 2017e). Some considerations to be aware of in tackling identity management include user and access permissions; sharing data across users; and online user convenience, control, and privacy (Contri 2017e).

6.7. Regulation/Cybersecurity

Regulators are seeking to deliver uniformity, minimum standards, increase in transparency, and accountability in response to data protection and ownership concerns. It is likely that "compliance demands will multiply worldwide" (Contri, 2018d).

There are six billion Internet users expected by 2022, and with an increased digital and interconnected world, cybercrime becomes more prevalent and identity theft tactics become more sophisticated. Remain vigilant, plan, and commit sufficient resources to address regulation and cyber-risk requirements on an ongoing basis (Merrill Lynch, 2018).

6.8. Talent/Skill retention

Job roles within organizations are changing due to automation of tasks and the increasing requirement to improve customer experiences. Due to the speed of change, organizations will need to critically and honestly evaluate their in-house ability to keep up, implement, and adapt to the changes (Contri, 2016). Being capable and better prepared to more effectively utilize technology in delivering solutions/services to customers will require data modelers and risk experts to help the transition to mobile-based technology and open banking models. Having access to the right talent will be an important requirement for organizations to be able to implement solutions (Contri, 2018c).

Organizations will also need to think about the problem of competing for talent and retaining talent. To compete against external start-ups, consider creating an internal incubation program, partnering/collaborating with other companies or institutions to access qualified talent, or consider acquisition of talent, as required (Contri, 2018d).

6.9. *New markets and opportunities*

Vincent and Dicks (2018) have compared the digital interactive preferences of the following segments:

- Mass market, MM (< US$250K liquid net worth)
- Mass affluent, MA (US$250K–999K liquid net worth)
- HNW and UHNW, HNW+ (≥US$1 mil liquid net worth)

Vincent and Dicks (2018) have broken these segments down further into six sub-segments (below) and suggest that more success will result if digital strategies are customized based on these sub-segments (refer to Appendix, Table A1 for more details and summary)

- Newcomers
- Continued accumulators
- Up-and-comers
- Wealth transfers
- Modestly plateauing
- Top-of-their-gamers

All segments have some desire toward digital capabilities. To "modernise intelligently," organizations need to account for the various segment behaviors, needs, and preferences, particularly for MM and MA segments (Vincent and Dicks, 2018).

"Innovations result from a conscious, purposeful search for innovation opportunities." The following are sources of innovation opportunities, as stated by Kobler *et al.* (2017):

- Changes in industry structure;
- Changes in demographics;
- Changes in perception of an industry;

- Economic incongruities;
- Emergence of new knowledge.

Kobler *et al.* (2017) report that the most successful innovations are centered around

- The profit model (finding new ways to convert an offering into revenue), and
- Client engagement (creating meaningful connections addressing deep seated aspirations).

They suggest focusing innovation on:

- Re-organizing infrastructure (through cloud computing, open APIs);
- Gaining a deeper understanding of clients (through social listening, instant feedback);
- New revenue sources (supplementary client care services, digital security services);
- Refreshing brand (through sub-branding, ingredient branding).

Additional inspiration for opportunity can be found by probing customer inflection points, "a trigger event in a person's life... a point in time," for example, a graduation or first big purchase. Customers may be tempted toward a competing financial product during these moments of inflection, particularly if they are not satisfied with their current financial product, and the alternative is a better option. Be aware that this is a strategy that FinTechs use to acquire customers (Strange and Rampell, 2016).

7. Conclusion

FinTech, including robo-advice platforms along with industry consolidation, evolving client needs, and regulations, is going to continue to drive transformative and disruptive change in the wealth management industry. Successful market participants need to consider the adoption of systems, processes, and structures to ensure agility, innovation, and efficiency in order to continue to compete in this environment.

Business model innovation is key to competing and surviving, and this can be approached in many ways. More open business models, which allow work on adjacent capabilities, processes, and technology, must be pursued. The efforts of other companies to innovate through their business models should also be watched carefully (Amit and Zott, 2012). Business models should be driven by a customer-focused value proposition, provide a holistic service, and be underpinned by a hybrid offering of digital services with a strong focus on human relationships delivered through sound support from advisers with bespoke training in how to engage deeply with all aspects of clients' wealth management needs. The important thing is not to hide your product but to get it out there and experiment with your business model (Blank, 2013). A culture of innovation leadership is crucial to this approach. This should be driven with values, training, and specific processes for innovation, such as the Lean start-up and business model canvas.

Existing market participants should seek merger and acquisitions to defray their increased regulatory costs across a broader client base. These increased compliance costs will also create natural barriers of entry to the wealth management market. It is also recommended that an increasing focus be placed on cross-border segments and the Asian market as it will experience strong growth; Singapore and Hong Kong are particularly stable markets. This broader focus will provide some diversification.

In terms of client segments, it is recommended that focus be placed on millennials and younger family members and women, ensuring intergenerational engagement. These clients must be serviced with low cost, performance-based fees, 24/7 with mobile access providing multiple touch points through offering them engagement and control over their investments while delivering transparency, ideas, and networking opportunities. Values and environmental and social sustainability, along with ethical governance, underline the world views of this emerging group and this should be catered for. This approach allows the business model to also incorporate value correlation which will further engage clients.

FinTech should be simple and responsive and designed to augment human advisors. The use of ML and cognitive tools should be considered, including the use of IoT systems that secure data, reduce costs, and increase growth. This production and use of data can be cloud-based or supported by edge computing and also integrate digital ID systems.

Human capital will be crucial, and diversity of staff trained in emerging FinTech is crucial. This could be supported by an incubator or open innovation system.

All these ideas should be brought together with a customer-centric value identification, creation, and management process through a thorough and complete lean transformation to optimize business processes, minimize costs, and keep up with changing customer needs and market forces.

Appendix

Table A1.   Mass market and mass affluent sub-segments (summarized).

Newcomers	Continued Accumulators
• highly digitally capable • can be served nearly entirely through digital interactive mobile apps and platforms • want ability to digitally review and adjust portfolios 24/7	• have sustained lower levels of financial success • don't trust the system • unfamiliar with technology • have lowest demand for digital
Up-and-comers	**Wealth Transfers**
• want to take ownership of financial lives • want same financial opportunities as HNW+ • demand combination approach (human and digital) • are savvy and confident • want to review and adjust portfolios digitally	• are emotional investors • have high priority on preserving wealth for family and heirs • require a certain level of human involvement • majority would interact digitally with wealth manager

(*Continued*)

Table A1.   (*Continued*).

Modestly Plateauing	Top-of-their-gamers
• less confident in financial ability • rely on human interaction • most want some digital interaction (view and adjust products) • still desire human interaction • want to feel enabled to access their account by themselves	• confident in their financial success • want personalized service combined with digital self-service • would consider using robo-advisor • most desire digital interaction with wealth manager • want ability to digitally adjust portfolios themselves 24/7

Source: Vincent and Dicks (2018).

Summary of Segment findings

• MM and MA segments are "far more open to use digital tools" than the HNW+ segment
• MM and MA are also more open to technology that allows "advisors to serve them effectively"
• MM want control via apps and would rather have others lead decisions
• Most MA find digital helpful
• HNW+ prefer people over robo-advisors, but find digital tracking more helpful than MM and MA segments.

Source: Vincent and Dicks (2018).

References

Aarikka-Stenroos, L., & Jaakkola, E. (2012). Value co-creation in knowledge intensive business services: A dyadic perspective on the joint problem-solving process. *Industrial Marketing Management*, 41(1), 15–26.

Accenture (2016). *Future of wealth management*, Accenture. Retrieved from: https://www.accenture.com/t00010101T000000Z__w__/au-en/_acnmedia/Accenture/Conversion-Assets/DotCom/Documents/Global/PDF/Consulting/Accenture-Future-Wealth-Management.pdf#zoom=50 (Accessed on 6 November 2018).

Amit, R., & Zott, C. (2012). Creating value through business model innovation. *MIT Sloan Management Review*, 53(3), 41–49.

Australian Bureau of Statistics (2018). Female labour force participation reaches all-time high. Retrieved from: https://www.abs.gov.au/ausstats/abs@.nsf/%20lookup/6202.0Media%20Release1Jan%202018 (Accessed on 7 July 2021).

Baghai, P., Gourvitch, D., Ramji, S., & Zucker, J. (2016). A Tale of Two Millionaires: The Best of Times for Private Banks to Look Beyond The Ultra-High-Net-Worth Market. McKinsey & Company, Retrieved from: http://managersofwealth.com/uploads/whitepapers/Private_banking_report_final;_March_14.pdf (Accessed on 10 November 2018).

Banziger, H. (2017). From the end of Bretton Woods to the Global Financial Crisis: 40 years of turbulence. In *Equity Markets in Transition*, Francioni, R. & Schwartz, R. (eds.) (Springer, Cham), pp. 411–427.

Beardsley, B., Holley, B., Jaafar M., Kessler, D., Muxí, F., Naumann, M., Tang, T., Xavier, A., & Zakrzewski, A. (2016). New strategies for non traditional client segments. Retrieved from: https://www.bcg.com/en-au/publications/2016/financial-institutions-asset-wealth-management-new-strategies-for-nontraditional-client-segments.aspx (Accessed on 7 November 2018).

Bender, Y. (2018). Getting to grips with new business models. Retrieved from: https://www.pwmnet.com/Wealth-Management/Business-Models/Getting-to-grips-with-new-business-models?ct=true (Accessed on 30 October 2018).

Bertels, H.M., Koen, P.A., & Elsum, I. (2015). Business models outside the core: lessons learned from success and failure. *Research-Technology Management*, 58(2), 20–29.

Beyer, C. (2017). Evolution and disruption in the wealth management industry. *The Journal of Wealth Management*, Spring, 8–13.

Blank, S. (2013). Why the lean start-up changes everything. *Harvard Business Review*, 91(5), 63–72.

Bol, K., Kennedy, P., & Tolstinov, D. (2018). The state of retail wealth management in North America, May 2018. Retrieved from: https://www.mckinsey.com/industries/financial-services/our-insights/the-state-of-retail-wealth-management-in-north-america (Accessed on 4 November 2018).

Bussmann, O. (2017). The future of finance: FinTech, tech disruption, and orchestrating innovation. In *Equity Markets in Transition*, Francioni, R., & Schwartz, R. (eds.) (Springer, Cham, Switzerland).

Capgemini (2017a). Asia Pacific Wealth Report, p. 5.

Capgemini (2017b). Top 10 trends in global wealth management. Retrieved from: https://www.capgemini.com/wp-content/uploads/2017/12/wealth-managment-trends-2018.pdf (Accessed on 14 October 2018).

Capgemini (2018). World Wealth Report 2018 (infographic). Retrieved from: https://www.capgemini.com/wp-content/uploads/2018/06/Capgemini-World-Wealth-Report.pdf (Accessed on 6 July 2021).

Cebula, J. (2017). How AI is shaping the wealth management industry. *Investment Week*, 7 August, p. 12.

Chesbrough, W.H. (2007). Why companies should have open business models. *MIT Sloan Management Review*, 48(2), 1–13.

Chishty, S., Erasmus, M., & Oberstein, J. (2011). Winning in wealth management. Retrieved from: https://www.bain.com/insights/winning-in-wealth-management (Accessed on 10 October 2018).

Contri, R. (2016). Digital innovation is upending the financial services talent model, LinkedIn, 26 January. Retrieved from: https://www.linkedin.com/pulse/digital-innovation-upending-financial-services-talent-robert-contri (Accessed on 3 November 2018).

Contri, R. (2017a). Types of RegTech Innovation. LinkedIn, 3 February. Retrieved from: https://www.linkedin.com/pulse/types-regtech-innovation-robert-contri (Accessed on 3 November 2018).

Contri, R. (2017b). APIs signal mainstream adoption of financial services blockchains. LinkedIn, 25 January, Retrieved from: https://www.linkedin.com/pulse/apis-signal-mainstream-adoption-financial-services-robert-contri/ (Accessed on 3 November 2018).

Contri, R. (2017c). Financial services: Three principles to jumpstart blockchain. LinkedIn, 19 January. Retrieved from: https://www.linkedin.com/pulse/financial-services-three-principles-jumpstart-robert-contri/ (Accessed on 3 November 2018).

Contri, R. (2017d). Five strategies financial institutions can take to unleash AI. LinkedIn, 27 October. Retrieved from: https://www.linkedin.com/pulse/five-strategies-financial-institutions-can-take-unleash-robert-contri (Accessed on 3 November 2018).

Contri, R. (2017e). How to get started with digital identity. LinkedIn, 18 January. Retrieved from: https://www.linkedin.com/pulse/how-get-started-digital-identity-robert-contri (Accessed on 3 November 2018).

Contri, R. (2017f). What will digital identity look like in financial services? Here are three possible scenarios. LinkedIn, 11 January. Retrieved from: https://www.linkedin.com/pulse/what-digital-identity-look-like-financial-services-here-robert-contri (Accessed on 3 November 2018).

Contri, R. (2018a). Front and center: Placing the customer at the heart of financial services. LinkedIn, 18 July. Retrieved from: https://www.linkedin.com/pulse/front-center-placing-customer-heart-financial-services-robert-contri (Accessed on 3 November 2018).

Contri, R. (2018b). Governments are ushering in a new era of regulation. AI is helping to make it happen. LinkedIn, 8 November. Retrieved from: https://www.linkedin.com/pulse/governments-ushering-new-era-regulation-ai-helping-make-robert-contri (Accessed on 9 November 2018).

Contri, R. (2018c). In financial services, technology is reshaping the front office. LinkedIn, 11 January. Retrieved from: https://www.linkedin.com/pulse/financial-services-technology-reshaping-front-office-robert-contri (Accessed on 3 November 2018).

Contri, R. (2018d). Three trends that are redefining the back office. LinkedIn, 23 January. Retrieved from: https://www.linkedin.com/pulse/three-trends-redefining-back-office-robert-contri (Accessed on 3 November 2018).

Contri, R. (2018e). Why the middle office is about to get a lot more attention. LinkedIn, 19 January, Retrieved from: https://www.linkedin.com/pulse/ why-middle-office-get-lot-more-attention-robert-contri (Accessed on 3 November 2018).

Contri, R. (2018f). Learn to walk, then learn to run: Unleashing the true potential of technology in financial services. LinkedIn, 31 July. Retrieved from: https:// www.linkedin.com/pulse/learn-walk-run-unleashing-true-potential-technology-financial-contri (Accessed on 3 November 2018).

Contri, R. (2018g). The currency of the future? How data is becoming the lifeblood of financial institutions. LinkedIn, 25 July. Retrieved from: https://www. linkedin.com/pulse/currency-future-how-data-becoming-lifeblood-financial-robert-contri (Accessed on 3 November 2018).

Credit Suisse (2017). The Continuing Rise of Private Wealth, *CNBC*. Retrieved from: https://www.cnbc.com/advertorial/2017/12/11/the-continuing-rise-of-private-wealth-in-china.html (Accessed on 6 November 2018).

Deloitte (2014). Digital disruption in wealth management: Why established forms should pay attention to emerging digital business models for retail investors. Retrieved from: https://www2.deloitte.com/content/dam/Deloitte/us/Documents/ strategy/us-cons-digital-disruption_061114.pdf (Accessed on 6 November 2018).

Deloitte (2015). 10 disruptive trends in wealth management. Retrieved from: https://www2.deloitte.com/content/dam/Deloitte/us/Documents/strategy/us-cons-disruptors-in-wealth-mgmt-final.pdf (Accessed on 6 July 2021).

Enness, P., & Graham, A. (2017). IT in transition. In *Equity Markets in Transition*, Francioni, R., & Schwartz, R. (eds.) (Springer, Cham, Switzerland), pp. 455–471.

Ernst & Young (2018). Ernst and Young Wealth Management Outlook 2018. Anticipating and seizing global growth potential in a challenging environment. Retrieved from: https://www.ey.com/publication/vwluassets/ey-wealth-management-outlook-2018/%24file/ey-wealth-management-outlook-2018.pdf (Accessed on 17 October 2018).

Ernst & Young (2017). Digital disruption in wealth management: Are you supporting tomorrow's wealth management with yesterday's technology? Ernst & Young. Retrieved from: https://assets.ey.com/content/dam/ey-sites/ey-com/en_gl/ topics/wealth-and-asset-management/wealth-asset-management-pdfs/ey-digital-disruption-in-wealth-management.pdf?download (Accessed on 7 July 2021).

Fava, M., Boersema, J., & Hamaloglu, U. (2016). The next generation of financial advisors. Ernst & Young. Retrieved from: https://leadingresponse.com/wp-content/uploads/2017/12/ey-the-next-generation-of-financial-advisors.pdf (Accessed on 6 July 2021).

Fischer, R., Jorge, M., Ko, D., & Toepfer, O. (2013). Wealth Management in New Realities- From defends to off-licence: How to realign business models for opportunities resulting from structural change. Retrieved from: https://www. rolandberger.com/en/Publications/Wealth-Management-in-New-Realities.html. (Accessed on 1 November 2018).

Gallo, A. (2014). The value of keeping the right customers. *Harvard Business Review*. Retrieved from: https://hbr.org/2014/10/the-value-of-keeping-the-right-customers (Accessed on 15 October 2018).

Hayne, K. (2018). Final Report: Royal Commission into Misconduct in the Banking, Superannuation and Financial Services Industry. Volume 1. Available online at https://www.royalcommission.gov.au/royal-commission-misconduct-banking-superannuation-and-financial-services-industry (Accessed on 6 July 2021).

Hirt, M. (2018). The 3 technological forces your strategy can't ignore. LinkedIn, 5 April. Retrieved from: https://www.linkedin.com/pulse/3-technological-forces-your-strategy-cant-ignore-martin-hirt (Accessed on 02 October 2018).

Holly, T.J. (2018). Five trends to watch in asset and wealth management in 2018. LinkedIn, 1 March 2018. Retrieved from: https://www.linkedin.com/pulse/five-trends-watch-asset-wealth-management-2018-thomas-j-holly/ (Accessed on 7 july 2021).

Hutchens, G. (2018). Banking royal commission told 90% of financial advisers ignored clients' best interests. *The Guardian*. Retrieved from: https://www.theguardian. com/australia-news/2018/apr/16/banking-royal-commission-told-90-of-financial-advisers-ignored-clients-best-interests (Accessed on 7 July 2021).

IoT Innovation (2018a). Defining the IoT ecosystem for enterprises. Retrieved from: https://internet-of-things-innovation.com/insights/the-blog/defining-iot-ecosystem-enterprises (Accessed on 14 November 2018).

IoT Innovation (2018b). Top considerations for enterprise IoT innovation. Retrieved from: https://internet-of-things-innovation.com/insights/the-blog/top-considerations-enterprise-iot-innovation (Accessed on 14 November 2018).

Kavadias, S., Ladas, K., & Loch, C. (2016). The transformative business model. *Harvard Business Review*, **94**(10), 91–98.

Knight Frank Research (2017). The Wealth Report. 11th edition, p. 14.

Knight Frank Research (2018). The Wealth Report. 12th edition, p. 30.

Kobler, D., Schlotmann, J., & Grampp, M. (2017). Innovation in private banking & wealth management: Embracing the business model change, Deloitte.

Kortmann, S., & Piller, F. (2016). Open business models and closed-loop value chains: Redefining the firm-consumer relationship. *California Management Review*, **58**(3), 88–108.

KPMG (2018). Refocus on the customer: How customer experience is shaping the future of wealth management. KPMG. Retrieved from: https://assets.kpmg. com/content/dam/kpmg/xx/pdf/2018/06/Customer-experience-V9.pdf (Accessed on 6 November 2018).

Kruger, C. (2018). A new wave of tech entrepreneurs are changing the wealth tide. *The Sydney Morning Herald*. Retrieved from: https://www.smh.com.au/technology/a-new-wave-of-tech-entrepreneurs-are-changing-the-wealth-tide-20180928-p506nd.html (Accessed on 3 November 2018).

Kurzo, C., & Jaecklin, S. (2014). The Future of European Wealth Management: Imperatives for Success — Joint J P Morgan Asset Management and Oliver Wyman report. November, p. 12. Retrieved from: https://www.oliverwyman.com/content/dam/oliver-wyman/global/en/2015/jan/The_Future_of_European_Wealth_Management.pdf (Accessed on 6 July 2021).

Larkin, S. (2018). Edge vs cloud computing: Which is the best investment? Retrieved from: https://www.afr.com/personal-finance/edge-vs-cloud-computing-20181031-h17bn7 (Accessed on 8 November 2018).

McCrank, J. (2011). Wealth advisers urged to adapt to demographic shifts. *Reuters*. Retrieved from: https://www.reuters.com/article/wealthreport-merrill-demographics/wealth-advisers-urged-to-adapt-to-demographic-shifts-idUSN1E75J1JU20110622 (Accessed on 3 November 2018).

McKinsey & Co (2018a). From start-up to scale: A conversation with Box CEO Aaron Levie. Retrieved from: https://www.mckinsey.com/industries/high-tech/our-insights/from-start-up-to-scale-a-conversation-with-box-ceo-aaron-levie?cid=podcast-eml-alt-%E2%80%A61/10 (Accessed on 01 November 2018).

McKinsey & Co (2018b). Transforming customer experience in wealth management. Retrieved from: https://www.mckinsey.com/business-functions/digital-mckinsey/how-we-help-clients/transforming-customer-experience-in-wealth-management (Accessed on 10 November 2018).

Maude (2006). *Global Private Banking and Wealth Management: The New Realities* (John Wiley & Sons, West Sussex).

Mehta, H., Acharya, A., Arora, P., & Govil, A. (2017). Top 10 trends in wealth management 2018: What you need to know, Capgemini. Retrieved from: https://www.capgemini.com/wp-content/uploads/2017/12/wealth-managment-trends-2018.pdf (Accessed on 5 October 2018).

Merrill Lynch (2018). 10 powerful, positive trends shaping our world. Merrill Lynch, Bank of America. Retrieved from: https://www.ml.com/articles/10-powerful-positive-trends-shaping-our-world.html#financial-research-and-insights (Accessed on 15 October 2018).

Moogk, D. (2012). Minimum viable product and the importance of experimentation in technology startups. *Technology Innovation Review*, 2(3), 23–26.

Morgan Stanley (2018). Overview. Retrieved from: https://www.morganstanley.com/im/en-us/liquidity-investor/about-us/overview.html (Accessed on 10 October 2018).

O'Brien, J. (2018). 7 disruptions CIOs may not see coming: Gartner, CIO. Retrieved from: https://www.cio.com.au/article/648428/7-disruptions-cios-may-see-coming-gartner (Accessed on 01 November 2018).

Opendefinition.org (2018). Defining open in open data, open content and open knowledge. Retrieved from: http://opendefinition.org (Accessed on 15 October 2018).

Oxford Dictionaries English (2018). Fintech | Definition of fintech in English. Retrieved from: https://en.oxforddictionaries.com/definition/fintech (Accessed on 15 October 2018).

Peter, A. (2018). Top 5 wealth management trends in 2018. Advicent Solutions blog. Retrieved from: https://www.advicentsolutions.com/en/resources/blog/top-5-wealth-management-trends-in-2018 (Accessed on 9 October 2018).

Piper, N., & Ge Haung, V. (2018). The bank is to create new leadership positions reporting to the head of wealth and investment management. *City Wire*. Retrieved from: https://citywireusa.com/professional-buyer/news/wells-fargo-to-reorganize-private-bank-and-abbot-downing/a1174257 (Accessed on 10 November 2018).

Prahalad, C.K., & Ramaswamy, V. (2004). Co-creating unique value with customers. *Strategy & Leadership*, 32(3), 4–9.

Price Waterhouse Coopers (2018). Asset and wealth management revolution: Embracing exponential change. Retrieved from: https://www.pwc.com/gx/en/asset-management/asset-management-insights/assets/awm-revolution-full-report-final.pdf (Accessed on 06 November 2018).

RF Page (2018). What are the major components of Internet of Things, 10 January, Retrieved from: https://www.rfpage.com/what-are-the-major-components-of-internet-of-things (Accessed on 12 November 2018).

Salampasis, D. Mention, A.-L., & Kaiser A. (2019). Age of Discovery: Navigating the Balance Between Human and Machine. In *WealthTech: Wealth and Asset Management in the FinTech Age*, Schueffel, P. (ed.) (Information Age Publishing), pp. 167–174.

Schiff, D., & Taylor, A. (2016). Key trends in digital wealth management — and what to do about them, McKinsey. Retrieved from: https://www.mckinsey.com/business-functions/mckinsey-digital/our-insights/key-trends-in-digital-wealth-management-and-what-to-do-about-them (Accessed on 6 November 2018).

Selby-Green, M. (2018). The 15 biggest wealth managers in the world. *Business Insider*. Retrieved from: https://www.businessinsider.com.au/the-15-biggest-wealth-managers-in-the-world-2018-6?r=US&IR=T#3-morgan-stanley-1045-billion-13 (Accessed on 5 November 2018).

Shorrocks, A., Davies, J., & Lluberas, R. (2018). Credit Suisse Research Institute Global Wealth report. p. 6

Slywotzky, A., & Wise, R. (2002). The growth crisis-and how to escape it. *Harvard Business Review*, 80(7), 72–83

Statista (2018). Number of smartphone users worldwide 2014-2020. Retrieved from: https://www.statista.com/statistics/330695/number-of-smartphone-users-worldwide (Accessed on 15 October 2018).

Strange, A., & Rampell, A. (2016). Using 'inflection points' to overcome FinTech startup distribution challenge. Andreessen Horowitz, 6 May. Retrieved from: https://a16z.com/2016/05/06/inflection-points-fintech-distribution/ (Accessed on 15 November 2018).

Stempel, J. (2008). TIMELINE: History of Merrill Lynch, Reuters, September 15. Retrieved from: https://www.reuters.com/article/us-merrill/timeline-history-of-merrill-lynch-idUSN1546989520080915 (Accessed on 15 October 2018).

Thompson, K., & Blomquist, E. (2018). Future of wealth management, Accenture. com. Retrieved from: https://www.accenture.com/t00010101T000000Z__w__/au-en/_acnmedia/Accenture/Conversion-suets/DotCom/Documents/Global/PDF/Consulting/Accenture-Future-Wealth-Management.pdf#zoom=50 (Accessed on 15 October 2018).

Time Magazine (2018). The view opener. 1 October, p. 18.

Technavio (2018). Top-5 global trends in wealth management in 2018. Technavio blog, 24 April. Retrieved from: https://www.technavio.com/blog/2018-trends-wealth-management (Accessed on 9 October 2018).

Vincent, G., & Dicks, R. (2018). Retooling wealth management for the digital age, Deloitte. Retrieved from: https://www2.deloitte.com/us/en/pages/consulting/articles/retooling-wealth-management-for-the-digital-age.html (Accessed on 20 October 2018).

Wealth-X (2018). Ultra Wealthy Analysis: World Ultra Wealth Report.

Willsher, R. (2018). The growth of ultra-high-net-worth individuals will also bring rewards to finance professionals. Accounting and Business (October 1st 2018). Available online at https://www.accaglobal.com/hk/en/member/member/accounting-business/2018/10/insights/finance-professionals.html (Accessed on 6 July 2021).

Workplace Gender and Equality Agency (WGEA) (2018a). Higher education enrolments and graduate labour market statistics. Retrieved from: https://www.wgea.gov.au/sites/default/files/graduate-labour-market-statistics.pdf (Accessed on 10 November 2018).

Workplace Gender and Equality Agency (WGEA) (2018b). Gender workplace statistics at a glance. Retrieved from: https://www.wgea.gov.au/sites/default/files/Stats_at_a_Glance.pdf (Accessed on 10 November 2018).

Zakrzewski, A. *et al.* (2018). Global wealth 2018: Seizing the analytics advantage. Retrieved from: http://image-src.bcg.com/Images/BCG-Seizing-the-Analytics-Advantage-June-2018-R-3_tcm87-194512.pdf (Accessed on 18 November 2018).

https://doi.org/10.1142/9789811239731_0009

Chapter 9

The Open Banking Era: Surfing the Australian Data Wave

Leila Fourie[*,†,§] and *Thomas K. Bennett*[‡,¶]

[†]*Johannesburg Stock Exchange, Johannesburg, South Africa*
[‡]*Cambridge Centre for Alternative Finance, Cambridge, United Kingdom*
[§]*leilafourie1@gmail.com*
[¶]*tmcm8738@uni.sydney.edu.au*

Abstract. Open banking regulatory regimes represent an attempt by regulators to take advantage of a wave of digitalization and its associated sea of data to encourage more dynamic and efficient financial services sectors. This chapter explores Australia's Consumer Data Right regime and how its planned expansion beyond financial services could propel fundamental changes to large sectors of Australia's economy and society. We explore why these regimes are being put into place now and what these changes could look like, including potential consequences. Lastly, we provide recommendations on how regulators should build data sharing regulatory regimes. In order to best achieve the goals of encouraging data leveraged social economic development, financial inclusion, and furthering innovation through data sharing requirements, we make

---

[*]Author has contributed to this edited volume in her individual capacity.

three recommendations. First, regulators must ensure the burdens and benefits of these regimes are consistent and fair, as it is very easy to replace one asymmetry with another. Second, consumers must be at the center: their benefits and safety are paramount to adoption and success of an economy that properly leverages consumer data. Third, open banking regimes must consider other technological developments, regulations, and trends to be incorporated as part of a larger national data strategy if they are to be effectively adopted.

Keywords. Open banking; data sharing; digital platforms; open innovation; data regulation.

1. Introduction

Open innovation, underpinned by a co-creative and open systems approach, is fueling a paradigm shift in the financial services industry and particularly open banking. The pace and scale of change in the digital economy is shifting the competitive landscape and reconfiguring financial services (Zachariadis and Ozcan, 2017). The recent regulatory reforms mandating open banking introduce the potential to further transform the structure of the rapidly digitizing financial economy. The Productivity Commission's (2017) influential report into data availability and use stated: "Increased data collection and use is a tidal wave that is already upon us." Open banking is part of a broader transformation in the sector whereby financial services are becoming increasingly digitized, and this sweeping change is rewriting the competitive landscape. Open banking and the emergence of neo-banks suggest that we are moving to a world where financial services are delivered exclusively over digital platforms. There is a shift to digitally based innovation and customer inclusion, underpinned by digital-only open platforms. Unconstrained by the need to employ physical capital, digital platforms such as Alipay and Tenpay in China have experienced nearly unchecked, exponential growth, leveraging the power of network effects. Open banking provides for a competitive landscape that is much more aligned with open innovation, as industry players must take greater concern of how other players will interact with their products. This chapter investigates the impact of open banking on the financial services sector and the economy at large and asks what factors Australians need to consider in order to effectively surf this new wave of data.

The former Governor of the Bank of England, Mervyn King, maintains that banks pre-date contemporary capitalism and "owes a great deal to the technologies of an earlier age" (King, 2017). There is no reason, however, why banks will not adapt and renovate their technologies to take advantage of digital transformation and open banking.[1] Moreover, the future of payments is big enough for both established banks and FinTechs. There is no reason for us to conceptualize the future of finance as a battle between established players and disruptive newcomers. More likely, banks will co-exist with FinTechs. One should not assume there are attributes that every large bank lacks that every FinTech possesses, or that the relationship between banks and FinTechs is necessarily adversarial. The institutions who "win" will be the ones that adapt to the era of digital platforms, remain at the front of their customer relationships, and position themselves to take advantage of developments such as open banking (Fourie, 2017).

This research investigates the potential disruptive effect that open banking might introduce to the financial economy. The chapter provides qualitative analysis and evaluation to address three questions. First, how will open banking affect the structure of the economy and reshape business models? Second, what are the potential pitfalls and unintended consequences of open banking? Third, what are the principles to ensure responsible and safe innovation? This analysis provides industry participants and regulators with a comprehensive overview of the properties of an open banking regime that must be considered to ensure the success of a financial sector that employs more open innovation.

The chapter is set out as follows. A review of the contextual factors leads to a comprehensive explanation of APIs and how they function. This review is followed by a discussion on the economic

---

[1] David Birch (Consultation 2018).

effect of open banking explored through two lenses: financial-economic and socio-economic considerations. Pitfalls and potential unintended consequences are exposed, and the chapter concludes with critical enabling factors for successful open banking.

2. Background

The large-scale adoption of open banking regulatory frameworks began in earnest with the implementation of open banking regimes by the European Union and the UK in January 2018. After many Government Inquiries into the use of data,[2] the Australian Government announced it would legislate an economy-wide Consumer Data Right (CDR) regime, beginning with open banking.[3] In February 2018 the Review into Open Banking, also known as the Farrell Report, was released, which gave the first insight into how the open banking landscape will emerge in Australia (The Treasury, 2017). The CDR launched in July 2020.

Despite open banking regulatory origins being European, Australia's unique intention to expand a data right across all industries significantly expands the potential effects and even the purpose of the regime. CDR provides consumers with the right to share their data with accredited third parties. In Australia, this is currently limited to "read only" access, creating a legal obligation to provide consumer data, but not requiring banks to provide so called "write" access to third parties to authorize transactions from the account. This is less scope than European open banking, which also facilitates "write" access and the creation of accredited Payment

---

[2]In 2014, the Financial Services Inquiries recommended a further review into the benefits and costs of increasing access to data, leading to the Productivity Commission's *Data Availability and Use* and the *Review Into Open Banking*.

[3]The Financial System Inquiry, Competition Policy Review, The Review of the Four Major Banks, and Independent Review into the Future Security of the National Electricity Market all recommended the use of data rights improve outcomes for customers.

Initiation Service Providers (PISPs) who can authorize an account transaction.

Regulation is not necessary for the sharing of consumer financial data to occur. Other jurisdictions have begun private-sector data sharing without the use of formal regulatory regimes, e.g. Singapore and New Zealand (Gilbert + Tobin, 2018). Moreover, the US hosts one of the largest open-style banking systems using screen scraping,[4] in which a customer enables a third party to access their data by providing them with their username and password; the third party is then able to login to a given account on behalf of the customer. This type of data sharing is often perceived to be less secure because it does not use standardized Application Programming Interfaces (APIs), nor do entities need to be accredited as they do in many mandated open banking regimes. Rule 2.2 of the Australian Competition and Consumer Commission's (ACCC) Consumer Data Right Rules Framework requires relevant organizations to provide consumers with the ability to transfer their own data to an accredited third party via APIs (Australian Competition & Consumer Commission, 2018). But what is an API and why are they useful?

3. Decoding APIs

APIs facilitate the secure sharing of data between different software applications. Berlind (2015) explains APIs by comparing them to electricity sockets, but instead of transporting electricity, they transfer data. Electricity sockets are the gateway that allow consumers to access the electricity service and use it to power other products like vacuum cleaners, computers, and mobile phones. A standardized electricity interface allows people to control the flow of electricity to whichever third-party devices can plug into the socket in a secure manner. Similarly, an API acts as a plug-and-play–styled standard interface but to data, allowing people to easily transmit data from one software application to another in a standardized, safe, and

---

[4]Luis Uguina (Consultation 2018).

secure manner (Euro Banking Association, 2016). Open APIs contrast with screen scraping, which requires unique programs to be built to access the data on different webpages and "scrape" it from the page. APIs are not the only architectural approach to creating a data sharing interface, but they are designed to be easy for developers to use and are more secure, stable, and scalable than screen scraping (Euro Banking Association, 2016).

APIs have been around for quite some time. Non-bank tech and platform companies such as Amazon, Facebook, Apple, and Google would not have expanded as rapidly were it not for growth-accelerating APIs (Euro Banking Association, 2016). One of the most famous examples is Google Maps, releasing open API access to their data in 2005, just four years before Uber was founded in 2009 (Taylor, 2005). Uber used the API to move Google Maps data to their own application. By 2013, more than a million websites were using Google Maps APIs for some feature of their service (Hoetmer, 2013).

APIs are not new in financial institutions. Financial institutions have long utilized private APIs to transfer data between different systems within the organization. In recent years, with a burgeoning FinTech landscape, many banks have also introduced partner APIs, which facilitate the transfer of data to the bank's partners. Open banking requires the development of public APIs by financial institutions, which allow for third parties to plug in, without a partnership with the bank. Currently there are 112 distinct categories of Bank API functionalities (INNOPAY, 2018), and the World Economic Forum estimates financial services to be the second fastest growing category of APIs (World Economic Forum, 2018).

Figure 1 represents a global view of API functionality provided by banks. Geographical weightings reflect differences in the development of open banking across regions. European banks represent 79%, Asian Banks 7%, Oceanian Banks 7%, and American banks 7% (INNOPAY, 2018). About 36% are related to payment data and functionality, which is unsurprising due to the importance of payments in Europe's Revised Payment Service's Directive, (PSD2).

Policy commentators, regulators, and independent reviews maintain that, in the aftermath of the Global Financial Crisis, Australia's

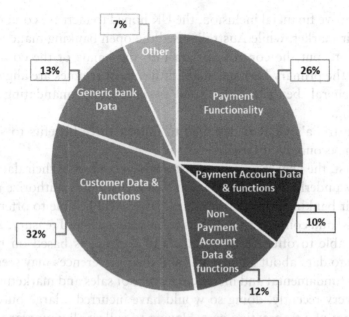

Figure 1. Financial services API categories.

financial regulatory regime has prioritized stability over competition and innovation (Productivity Commission, 2018). The Productivity Commission argues that a low propensity to switch providers has led to considerable dissatisfaction with the level of competition in the banking sector. Open banking regimes seek to improve these market outcomes through the regulation of information and information flows. The challenge of open banking is to create these data flows, via APIs, that will provide the most value to consumers. The question becomes how can a regulator design and build an effective API economy, where data is most effectively leveraged as a tool for development?

3.1. *Why open banking? Theoretical underpinnings*

The genesis and primary motivation for mandating open banking varies across regulatory regimes. Mexico introduced open banking to improve financial inclusion, the UK hoped to increase competition in their market, while Australia used the open banking mandate primarily to put the control of data into the hands of the consumer. While the primary heritage might differ, most regimes are aligned on the general benefits they seek to enable by mandating open banking.

Australia's CDR is designed to unlock three benefits to society and the economy at large.

First, the new regime puts customers in control of their data. The theory underling the CDR is that when customers authorize access to their banking information, third parties will be able to offer more tailored and convenient products to customers (The Treasury, 2017). Being able to offer better products to consumers based on having access to data about a consumer and their preferences may seem like a very fundamental and historical feature of sales and marketing, but until very recently, doing so would have incurred a large burden in the form of a transaction cost. Having to collect all your transaction and financial product history to provide to a competitor, who would then have to find a way of efficiently processing it, will incur a burden that neither side is often unwilling to incur. However, digitalized data and standardized APIs allow us to overcome this transaction cost. The data can exist, already collected automatically, and can be easily called and provided in a useful structured form. It can then be put into a machine learning program which can automatically assess the data to make a decision. This lowers transaction costs to the point where consumers can easily express their preferences and firms interpret them, improving market efficiency.

Second, the CDR argues that by considering the consumer's actual account history, they will be able to access better and more personalized price comparison services, which should lead to savings for the customer (The Treasury, 2017). Recent developments in machine learning have made it possible to consume large amounts of information about a consumer and make appropriate decisions, culminating in a level of personalization that previously was left only to those who could afford to hire a human to analyze their financial situation.

Third, more personalized prices with better comparisons should lead to broader benefits, including improved competition and data-driven economic growth. If firms are forced to stop competing based on information asymmetries, and instead focus on providing a better service, that should spur the development of a higher level of competition in the field of digital financial services. The logical argument is that this new demand for data science skills will drive the creation of new jobs in Australia as ecosystems emerge (The Treasury, 2017).

4. Economic Impact

The CDR will not be limited to facilitating greater consumer choice, but rather drive and accelerate fundamental changes in the economy that are being brought about more generally by digitization. Open banking is driving a shift that is replacing the classical asset-based value with data-based value (Gilligan, 2018). Gilligan (2018) draws the analogy of the new value that can be found in data to a similar shift that occurred unlocking value in money. Historically, money itself provided limited leverage for promoting economic activity, but as technology and institutions changed to allow the effective movement and management of money, we have been able to use it for significantly more value creation. Bank credit has become an enormous stimulus for growth, creating the attendant increase in the liquidity of money. Data has the same potential — by improving its management, our societies can leverage greater benefits. However, as Gilligan (2018) notes, the difference between money and data is that data as a liquid mobile asset is uncapped in its use.

4.1. *Data will be the root of most progress*

In his book *The Ascent of Money*, Niall Ferguson (2008) claimed that "Money is the root of most progress." The condensing of transactional information into a single standardized form allowed for economic efficiencies that powered the progress of the rest of the economy, argues Ferguson. Every leap in improving the management of money has fueled subsequent advances in economic activities.

As Australia's API economy expands from the initial implementation of open banking to data sharing across other sectors such as energy and telecommunications (The Treasury, 2017), a multiplier effect comes into play. The CDR aims to support data enabled economic growth by fostering the development of a data sector (The Treasury, 2017). The Productivity Commission (2017) found the combination of rapid digitization across the economy, improving data analytics techniques, and falling costs of data storage were making it possible for small- and medium-sized enterprises (SMEs) to create value based on data. This finding is contrasted with around 22% of the global digital data generated in 2013 being useful in some analytical use cases, with less than 5% of that data being analyzed (The Productivity Commission, 2017). The *Review into Open Banking* specifically states that as "the connections increase, and participants come to rely on the customer-directed flow of data between them, a data ecosystem should emerge" (The Treasury, 2017). It is hoped that by encouraging the sharing of data across sectors, it will catapult industry initiatives on unlocking the value of data. As new technologies facilitate the better management and use of data, we will find that, as money has done in the past, it will make us better at coordinating human activity and data will become the root of most progress. Consumer data must be shared across sectors and ecosystems to achieve the goal of a data economy. The effects of data sharing for the new economy are wide reaching. This section explores two areas of impact to the economy — financial economics and socio-economics.

5. Impact on Financial Economics

Open banking will challenge the orthodox economic assumptions that underpinned the old world of financial services. Moreover, open banking will transform competition dynamics and introduce a shift in power. This section on financial economic impact investigates how open banking changes firm competition and its place as part of a larger shift in supply and demand economics.

5.1. *Different business models are emerging*

The growth in the digital financial services sector, and open banking is increasingly underpinned by digital platforms, a business model that orchestrates the exchange of value between two or more groups. According to platform experts Parker *et al.* (2016), "Practically any industry in which information is an important ingredient, is a candidate for the platform revolution," and financial services are all about information. The World Economic Forum (2018) takes this further, arguing that "Platforms that offer the ability to engage with different financial institutions from a single channel will become the dominant model for the delivery of financial services." Digitization has started the unbundling of financial services and a journey toward digital convergence where there are fundamental differences in the sources of value (Omarini, 2018). However, the final form that the economics of these future business models will take is far less certain. How will the move toward platforms fit with financial services and payments?

New business model opportunities are likely to challenge traditional value creation to form along the lines of manufacturing (involving curation of products) and distribution of those products (Euro Banking Association, 2016). The management of co-creating value is a major new challenge for some incumbent financial institutions. APIs create the potential for the decoupling of product curation and distribution (Euro Banking Association, 2016). Standardized APIs create the possibility of combining different forms of data to develop novel products or services and unique distribution channels (Euro Banking Association, 2016). While financial services incumbents currently own the full product curation and distribution value chain, this bundled role is unlikely to persist in its current form. Incumbents and new entrants will need to address three key questions to create a strategic response to open banking. First, is there a role I could play in distributing competitor products exposed via competitor APIs? Second, what products might I create from data exposed in competitor APIs? Solutions might take the form of dynamic credit risk services. And third, should I build a two-sided platform that connects product manufacturers to consumers? Here, solutions will take the form of aggregation platforms or digital eco-systems. Starling Bank in the UK launched a platform bank which connects third-party services via API technology. Customers with a Starling transaction account will be able to view all other financial products in one place, including products such as superannuation, motor vehicle loans, home loans, insurance, and investment. In addition to the API-enabled platform, Starling also provides third parties with a white label banking solution that enables non-banks to offer banking services to customers by leveraging Starling Bank's back office services and banking license. Starling Bank charges service fees and an interest fee for white label services. Alipay and WeChat Pay provide similar platform solutions to customers, with deposits held with licensed banks. The platform model is perhaps most entrenched in the Chinese payments system. The exponential growth of Alipay and WeChat Pay and their integrated nature are archetypal of successful platform or API strategies. Outside of China we also see examples of platform models beginning to be utilized in many ways across financial services. While these platforms open opportunity, they also introduce threats and challenges.

There is a paradigm shift underway in payments processing and business models toward platforms, as payments move from a single-sided system (bank to customer) to a multi-sided system (provider to provider with the customer at the center). Technology networks are transforming the way markets develop, and Australia's payments system is no different. The API economy is modifying competition dynamics and the power construct is changing.

5.2. *The move toward exponential value creation*

The change in business models to which open banking contributes is part of a broader shift in the economy to a digital form underpinned by an exponential growth curve. As we shift toward a more digitized and networked economy, the fundamental supply and demand principles upon which competition has been based in the past are being challenged (Scopelliti, 2018). Open banking is part of a wider drive away from a product-centric economy toward an "experience" economy. According to Scopelliti (2018), the product-centric economy is founded on the basis of linear value creation. In this linear value chain, products such as wine are part of a chain of value that is incremental, whereby value is added linearly at each step of the chain. Value is added linearly when the soil is prepared; vines are tended; the grapes are harvested and crushed; and the wine is created, distributed, marketed, and sold. Each of these discrete activities add value on a linear basis, and each value chain process can be discretely measured in a supply and demand curve. In the linear model, each activity measures marginal cost of production. The new experience economy moves away from product curation where value attribution is linear and toward an exponential value creation model which has its roots in the platform economy. Moreover, competition based on linear assumptions underpinning linear value creation in supply and demand curves are challenged in the exponential value creation economy (Scopelliti, 2018). Exponential models differ from linear models in that they capture a network effect at each stage of value creation on a non-linear and exponential path. Value in this exponential model is derived from multisided experiences rather than linear experiences in a discrete value chain. Take Apple as an example. The new "experience economy" develops and grows when an application developer builds an application by capturing network effects based on crowd-sharing data while simultaneously coding the application. Apple was able to provide its customers access to over 1,600 new apps a day and expand into new segments of consumers' lives (World Economic Forum, 2017). This is far beyond what would be possible if building apps took a linear product curation approach and were restricted to Apple employees. The sheer speed of value creation is possible because platforms invert the firm, allowing the value to be derived from a community, rather than internally. In this new world, a linear model cannot compete against an exponential model as the marginal cost of new products or services are virtually zero in the exponential world (Figure 2).

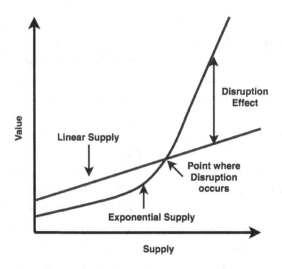

Figure 2.   Exponential vs linear supply.

Source: Singularity University, cited in Scopelliti, R. (2018). *Youthquake 4.0* (Marshall Cavendish International (Asia) Private Limited).

These exponential models are possible because of the feedback loops present in the business models of companies that are dependent on data. As Schönberger and Ramge (2018) put it, "Teslas literally gets better with every mile somebody drives them." By generating massive amounts of data about their car's performance including on features such as self-driving, Tesla is able to keep improving the performance of their cars using machine learning. Each car they sell is not a single unit of value they have created, but instead is also another building block on their infrastructure of data, that itself will keep adding new value as long as the car is in use.

Scopelliti (2018) contends that at the point at which an exponential supply curve crosses a linear supply curve, disruption occurs. Those who are successful in this new exponential world will think about transformation earlier in the industry competitive cycle. Scopelliti (2018) also notes that those incumbents that are not able to transform their business typically try to delay the point of disruption. It is anticipated that open banking will enable an "experience economy" with exponential growth curves. Multiple new products are likely to evolve using the underlying data exposed via APIs.

5.3. *Incongruent value drivers*

As non-traditional players begin to enter the financial services market, a new challenge is emerging as these non-banks march to an entirely different beat. According to Birch, non-traditional players providing "experiences" that cut across financial services do not share the same value drivers as incumbents.[5] Birch contends, "for non-banks, it's different. It may not make a difference if they make money from financial services. Tech and social media companies' primary aim is to keep customers on their platform. Payments are secondary. Amazon's business driver is focused on keeping you on the platform. Those business models will be very different" (Birch, 2018). The banks' ability to compete on this basis is difficult as banks have a very different business model. Banks earn revenues by charging fees to take deposits, lend, and process payments. There is a fundamental change in the motive of financial services provision, which will be rapidly expanded due to open banking.

These incongruent value drivers risk destroying the incumbent revenue model. Birch says, "I would tend to assume that the profit in payments is tending towards zero."[6] Downward pressure on interchange rates and the PSD2 requirement for "write access" to be made freely available will only further accelerate this shift. While Birch puts forward an extreme view on the future of payments, alternative perspectives have challenged this thinking. Many technology and social media companies maintain they do not have an appetite to enter the highly regulated banking sector as constraining bank regulation would threaten their non-payments business (Wozniak, 2017).

6. Socio-economic Reform or Retreat?

According to Gilligan, data will become the single biggest lever for microeconomic and social reform.[7] The Australian Payments Council

---

[5]David Birch (Consultation 2018).
[6]*Ibid.*
[7]Danny Gilligan (Consultation 2018).

Figure 3.   emFUND App — P2P donations for natural disasters.

held a hackathon in 2017. The theme was "using transaction data to improve the lives of Australians." In less than 48 hours, apps were created that could create microeconomic benefits that go beyond the basic provision of credit or payments in the financial system. Solutions ranged from mental health applications that use payments profiles to predict mental stress to crowdfunding apps that assist survivors to source funds after being caught up in a natural weather disaster or fire (Figure 3).

The socio-economic effect of data and the evolving reliance of financial services on a richer and wider variety of data appears to be a double-edged sword for consumers. On the one hand, data has been utilized to improve financial inclusion amongst societies' most vulnerable. One of the most famous examples of the power to bring financial services to the underserved is Ant Financial's operations in China. Ant Financial gathered 190 million users between 2014 and 2017 under its Sesame Credit service, which compiled non-traditional data sources to provide a credit rating to consumers who previously did not have access to one, providing 400 billion yuan in microloans (Carney, 2017). The CDR will effectively foster the use of even more non-traditional data points to be utilized and supplement traditional financial data sources in the provision of credit. It will also allow alternative finance providers to observe greater scope of consumers' financial history and possibly improve their offerings. Benefits may also arise not only for the unbanked but for the less financially literate, as clearer value propositions through comparison websites may allow consumers and SMEs to make more optimal decisions.[8]

However, there are also concerns that the increased sharing of data between industries comes with the risk of financial exclusion and creating a privacy premium. First, by making these new data points the norm in financial services provision, it will have an exclusionary effect on the people who do not provide such data points, the "non-swimmers" who do not wish to enter the sea of data (Stigler, 1980). These can be split into two categories of excluded consumers — the "non-digital" and "privacy concerned." Both consumer types have the potential to be negatively impacted in this new data world as providers may assume that those unwilling, or unable, to share such data points are more likely to exhibit negative characteristics. Access to information for credit assessment is especially important considering recent inquiries into Australian financial services and the importance of responsible lending. Exclusionary effects on the non-digital are only likely to be exacerbated due to the changes in business models described above. The modularization of financial services can lead to many new and dynamic products, but it could also kill many products that are cross-subsidized and unprofitable, but essential for some consumers. That said, a mitigating factor in the exclusionary effect is Australia's relatively high number of digitally active citizens. Research indicates that 9 out of 10 Australians own a smartphone (Australian Payments Network, 2018). As digital exclusion increasingly becomes financial exclusion, potential mitigants would include ensuring that government policy

---

[8]Martin McCann (Consultation 2018).

encourage Internet availability to traditionally underserved areas like rural communities.

A more direct ramification of these data-based services will be the dominance of algorithms that may price and distribute services to people based on data points that people may consider unethical, especially with the increasing use of Artificial Intelligence. These so-called "Weapons of Math Destruction" (O'Neil, 2016) will force governments to develop further policy responses around the CDR in the form of legislating which data should not be utilized. Kemp and Vaile (2018) note these concerns are heightened by the potential for companies to develop a "god-view" of the consumer, which the consumer is not aware of and cannot observe. This would run counter to the purpose of providing consumers with more power over their consumption of financial services by potentially making their bargaining position worse.

Whilst this may be mitigated by Australia's adoption of a consent-driven model, consent can be blurred, and consumers often misunderstand where their data is going and how it is being used by companies. The EU's PSD2 comes concurrently with the General Data Protection Regulation (GDPR). This regulation provides consumers with significantly more power over what a company can do with their data, including the "right to be forgotten" — a right that is not embedded in Australian open banking. This privacy and data regulation could provide the much-needed security consumers require to desire to share their data often and with many providers.

Socio-economic benefits of open data are not limited to individual consumers and will extend to SMEs. Open banking could be the catalyst for increasingly sophisticated cashflow services by providing access to meaningful data points that might be used as dynamic variables to improve the existing measurement of SME credit worthiness. SMEs depend on working capital facilities as a vital lifeline to keep the enterprise liquid and to fund operations. The predictive power of classical credit rating models is currently not fully exploited in traditional credit-granting organizations. Consequently, SMEs often struggle to qualify for loans and particularly for working capital facilities due to the inability to accurately forecast risk, and therefore banks default to preconceived high risk of the SME. In China,

Ant Financial and Tencent have used dynamic data as alternative credit rating variables to create powerful credit rating algorithms using data that will be made available in an open banking regime (Sheng *et al.*, 2017; Kapron and Meertens, 2017). Improved access to credit by SMEs will create jobs and significantly boost economic growth and uplift socio-economic welfare.

7. Potential Pitfalls and Unintended Consequences

Open banking regulation has significant potential to improve consumer outcomes and market efficiency, but it also risks introducing considerable potential pitfalls that policy-makers, consumer rights groups, and industry players must watch carefully. The unintended consequences that may arise from open banking can be split into two broad categories. First, issues that arise from implementing an open banking regime that is not part of a cohesive national data strategy, and second, the asymmetries and disincentives created by the design of data sharing regulation.

7.1. *Regulating open banking requires a more holistic view*

First, Gilligan (2018) notes that the success of Australian open banking and building a data economy may be at risk from a lack of a "comprehensive, connected and cohesive data sharing and privacy legislative framework." In line with the original intent of the Productivity Commission's report, to achieve the most leverage from open banking, it is necessary to view the regulation as part of a national data approach.

7.1.1. *Security and digital ID as complimentary products*

The open innovation ecosystems that will arise out of open banking regulation will change the nature of what financial institutions must consider during their innovation process, and this will have implications for digital identity and accompanying products. Open innovation systems increase the importance of businesses coordinating their own innovation strategies with other ecosystems, increasing the weight of interdependence risk and interconnection risk in an innovation ecosystem (Ardner, 2018). This requires an assessment of what other products need to succeed and who needs to adopt them before a product can take off. In open banking, it is worth considering what complimentary products are necessary to ensure successful adoption. Digital identity services are a rapidly developing field with both private and public sector initiatives being developed (Digital Transformation Agency, 2018). Many consumers cite privacy and fraud concerns as a reason to refrain from participating in open-banking–powered data transfers (Eyers, 2018). Digital identity and other security services may prove to be the complimentary product required for consumers to embrace data sharing and the business services that may come out of open banking. Gilligan (2018) asserts that governance around data flows is not sophisticated enough yet and that Australia's data-sharing system should be moving toward "privacy by design," involving a design that is privacy-centered and minimizes the raw data flows across the economy and associated creation of data honey pots. The use of digital identity services to validate assertions online, such as age, may prove useful in reducing the risk associated with raw data flows. Yet it is equally important to consider where we are starting, with the current security of consumer data sharing. Scott Farrell, the author of the *Review into Open Banking*, notes that we should evaluate open banking against the far less secure alternative that was already emerging, and states: "There is a need for urgency and there is a risk of being too late. In fact, we might be barely catching this issue in time, in the sense of providing a safer alternative to people before they get too used to sharing data in a less safe way."[9] Rather than asking if swimming in this data sea is dangerous, it may be better to ask, does the regulation provide red and yellow flags to allow consumers to find the best place to swim and lifesavers in the form of regulators in case some-

---

[9]Scott Farrell (Consultation 2018).

thing goes wrong. The degree to which consumers and organizations trust the sharing of data may significantly affect the success of open banking, yet these solutions may not yet have advanced sufficiently. Unexpected catalysts can also encourage consumer adoption, with the COVID-19–related recession causing many Britons to increasingly use money management tools via open banking as they see greater value in sharing their data (Open Banking Implementation Entity, 2020). Regardless of how, consumers must be able to clearly see the value in sharing their financial data, and coordinating open banking implementation with other innovation that enhances data sharing value is a serious challenge.

7.1.2. *Systemic risks in the financial sector and financial stability*

The process of modularization brought about by open banking and the general digitization of financial services will potentially alter the nature of systemic risk present in the financial sector. This is a potential ramification of the new business models that will enter financial services. Carney (2017) notes the role of customer loyalty in bank funding stability. Wiggins and Retimana suggest open banking could move deposits out of the core system into other stores of value, similar to products like WeChat's wallet, which has become tremendously popular in both China and Kenya.[10] According to Brett King (2017), the value of deposits in prepaid wallets in Kenya exceeds that held in ordinary bank accounts. The systemic risks of deposits becoming fragmented and moving to a less regulated or shadow banking environment may be somewhat lower in Australia because there is no regulatory requirement to enable third parties to transact on customers' accounts since the CDR mandates "read" access and not "write" access.[11] The creation of a "gray financial economy" as financial services become increasingly intertwined into other sectors may pose a challenge for financial systems regulators in monitoring activity,

---

[10]Steve Wiggins and Jane Retimana (Consultation 2018).
[11]Martin McCann (Consultation 2018).

and their view may become limited.[12] We may decide that we do want people swimming between the flags, but do the lifesavers have the goggles required to see what is happening beneath the water?

7.1.3. *Standardization and global inconsistencies*

One of the touted benefits of open banking is the ability to better compare products, but the standardization necessary to achieve this may prove beyond the capabilities of a regulatory body. Data-rich markets require effective ontologies so that data can be compared in effective ways. An interest rate charged on a credit card is only one aspect of the costs/benefits of using that financial product. Many credit cards come with associated benefits such as charge back rights, travel insurance, or loyalty points, yet it is unclear whether or how this data would have to be made available or how it could be made available in a standardized format. The importance of standardization is apparent, because open banking is not the first attempt at using data to improve market outcomes. The Australian Treasury's *Review into Open Banking* (2017) specifically calls out a previous attempt to use data sharing in the energy sector, which was ultimately unsuccessful due to insufficient standards development. The standardization of data and product descriptions may prove increasingly challenging as the sector moves closer to contextual and personalized banking. The success of data sharing across ever more intertwined and interdependent industries will rest on the successful ontology creation so that data can be effectively classified and analyzed.

The absence of a global standards setting organization has led to a variety of standards being created by countries implementing open banking. Australian open banking standards are being developed by CSIRO's Data 61. The standards can be classified into transfer standards, data standards, and security standards (The Treasury, 2018). Recommendation 5.2 of the *Review into Open Banking* is that Australia's standards should use the UK's technical specification as a starting point of development, though there is currently much debate

---

[12]*Ibid.*

about the degree to which Australia should follow the UK's model (The Treasury, 2017). Singapore has released its own "API playbook" (The Association of Banks in Singapore and Monetary Authority of Singapore, 2017). Global standardization is also difficult to achieve because open banking is not being used to achieve the same policy outcomes in each jurisdiction, but rather is a function of the state of their domestic banking landscape, and the nations' key priorities. As mentioned earlier, Mexico is using an open banking regime to spur financial inclusion amongst its large impoverished community (Llanos-small, 2018), the UK to increase competition, and Australia to build a national data right. The divergence in purposes could make standardization complex. A lack of standardization will place a significant burden on international financial institutions, not just in terms of increased costs of building API-compatible systems, but also in potentially conflicting requirements.

7.1.4. *Geopolitical impact of data — A world with no borders?*

As open banking becomes more widely accepted, it may lead to an even more globalized financial services industry with more regulatory convergence and a global world of data with no borders. We could plausibly see how technology with no borders enables a more global financial services system as a direct result of open banking (Gilligan, 2018). The exploitation of data will not only cross geographic borders but will occur across industry lines. The geopolitical implications of data and the emerging data economy should not be underestimated. We go back to the principle we discussed at the outset of the discussion on the economics of data, to reiterate that shifts in value are evident. The economy is replacing the classical asset-based value with data-based value (Gomart *et al.*, 2018). Industry data experts argue that global tech giants are stripping assets from national economies by transmitting and/or storing valuable data outside of the borders of the country from which the data was sourced. The implication of these new global data lakes is profound in that sovereign states are constrained in their ability to exert legislative or regulatory control over data. This loss of control over data extends to oversight on how data is transmitted and stored, the purpose for which data is used, and consumer protection in the case of a data breach. India places a high priority on data sovereignty and views data as a national resource (Gomart *et al.*, 2018). Gomart *et al.* (2018) find that the flow of data has moved from being a commercial and regulatory issue to a subject of international relations, with many countries including India looking at data localization to achieve what they call "digital decolonization." Moreover, leadership in the race to manage and control data could affect trade relationships or even establish new corridors of data-based trade between countries with powerful technology companies and those that supply data. Those countries with advanced technology, platform, and social media sectors are likely to be net gainers in this data trade race. There have been calls in the past for international economic cooperation facilities to be created or updated to consider the changing nature of business, including Jack Ma's call for an Electronic World Trade Organization (Alibaba Group, 2016). A new World Data Organization that operates like a World Trade Organization for the trade and governance of data would add tremendous value to the establishment and oversight of data trading, privacy, security, and jurisdiction considerations.

7.2. Fixing competition by distorting competition?

Second, there are concerns around the design of the data sharing regulation possibly creating new competitive unfairness and disincentives. The primary policy reason for implementing open banking in the UK was unsatisfactory levels of competition in the financial sector (Open Data Institute and Fingleton Associates, 2014). The requirement of open APIs was initiated to foster both FinTech competition with incumbent banks, and competition among incumbent banks. However, according to the Chair of Santander Bank, Ana Botin, and David Birch, this appears to be a miscalculation by the Competition and Markets Authority; instead of creating a flourishing environment of small financial services players, it may reinforce the "tech giant oligopoly" (Birch, 2018).

7.2.1. *Asymmetrical competitive landscapes*

The UK regulation requires banks to make available their customer data to whichever registered third party with which the customer wants to share it. However, there is no requirement for many of these third parties to make their customer data available in a reciprocal manner. For example, if Google registers as a third party, it could ask consumers to ask their banks to share their data with them and banks would have an obligation to provide that data. If the reverse situation occurs, and a customer asks Google to share their data with their bank, as Google is not a bank, it is not legally compelled to oblige. Effectively, financial institutions will have everything to give, and nothing to gain. Tech giants will have access to everything banks can see about customers when making the assessment about selling them financial products, but banks will have no ability to see everything the tech giants can see. This asymmetrical information landscape effectively creates an uneven playing field that promotes the provision of financial services by tech companies over incumbent, and even challenging, financial institutions.

Australia's CDR, through expansion to other sectors of the economy, mitigates this effect in comparison to the UK but remains open to potentially unfair regulated information asymmetries. The Australian Treasury has accepted that the CDR will eventually be economy-wide, which should eliminate regulated information asymmetries between sectors. However, the right's implementation is being phased sector by sector. Therefore, Recommendation 3.9 of the *Review into Open Banking* (The Treasury, 2017) seeks to deal with reciprocal obligations, stating:

> *"Entities participating in open banking as data recipients should be obliged to comply with a customer's direction to share any data provided to them under open banking, plus any data held by them that is transaction data or that is the equivalent of transaction data."*

There are multiple practical implications for this recommendation. First, the tech giants do not have anywhere near as much valuable data on customers financial activity as financial institutions do, making the additional data that would be made available to them under Recommendation 3.9 inconsequential. Furthermore, in the current environment banks are "data rich insights poor," and adding data to them in the short term would have little to no measurable benefit until they improve their data insight management capabilities. It should be noted that this point does not advocate their comparatively poor insights capability as a reason for restricting access, but rather that this should be taken into consideration for the speed with which the regulatory regime will be implemented. A data-sharing requirement, when applied to limited sectors, will potentially harm those sectors. Even when it will apply to all sectors, as is the case in Australia, at the very least it will create a transitionary issue where some sectors have an informational advantage over other sectors for an unknown period. In the age of networks and accelerated consumer adoption, a small window is all that is needed for markets to change and new barriers to entry be set up.

7.2.2. Asymmetric regulatory landscape

However, the reach of tech giants into financial services may be limited due to a desire to avoid the considerable burden that comes with operating under financial services' licenses (Carney, 2017). Financial services, due to their unique externalities on the rest of the economy, are one of the most heavily regulated industries. The additional requirements may mitigate the effects of the informational advantage tech giants are given above as they are kept at bay by their primary business models (King, 2018).

However, it is not necessary to have a financial services license to have a considerable influence and control over financial services, and in some cases, their lack of regulatory burden will be an advantage. Stephen King (2018) argues that regulation may strangle some of the potential open banking benefits due to constraining factors such as capital requirements under the Basel Accords, which employs a one size fits-all to the capital requirements for SME lending. This is representative of possible constraints that may arise from existing regulation which may disproportionately affect the financial services firms of the past, rather than where the risk has moved to in the future.

7.2.3. *Fixing incentives by distorting incentives?*

Data regulation not only affects the information economics between different industries but also within industries. Specifically, open banking, and a broader CDR, has the potential to create perverse incentives for firms in their collection of data and alter the points of competition (King, 2018). Depending on the data that is required to be transferred, it will effectively create a free rider problem. Data, unlike physical assets, can be replicated infinitely and is non-rivalrous. Therefore, when it is compelled to be shared by law, it can undertake the qualities of a public good. This perverse incentive is less of an issue where the data generated is a natural by-product of services, which will be the case for most financial services data — e.g. transaction accounts produce data by their very nature. The problem arises with the second objective of the Consumer Data Right, to build a data economy and the use of non-traditionally associated data points to enhance economic insights. Companies often undertake "pure data plays," undertaking the provision of a service for the primary reason of gathering data on an individual. If they do not have proprietary ownership over this data, they may not be incentivized to collect it.

The *Review into Open Banking*'s attempt at mitigating the implications of potential free-rider problems is covered under Recommendation 3.3 to restrict the data that is required to be transferred to not apply to "value-added customer data." Value-added data is defined as data that results from "material enhancement by applications of insights analysis or transformation by the data holder." It should be noted that this value-added data does not include what would be considered "creative sources" of data, rather only the data that is generated through the firm's data analysis.

The restriction to value-added customer data solves one free-rider problem but fails to solve the other. A pricing mechanism could potentially ensure incentives remain, and such a mechanism was placed in the Exposure Draft of the *Treasury Laws Amendment (Consumer Data Right) Bill 2018*, with what will be Section 56BC(d) of the amended *Competition and Consumer Act 2010,* which gives the ACCC the power to regulate the fees charged for data sharing under the CDR[13]. However, since then, regulators have been going in the opposite direction, with a narrower power provided to the ACCC in the finalized *Treasury Laws Amendment (Consumer Data Right) Act 2019*, containing limited circumstances where fees may be allowed, and the ACCC's release of the Consumer Data Right Rules Framework Section 2.3 specifying that sharing must not attract a fee (Australian Competition & Consumer Commission, 2018).[14] It will be necessary for the Australian regulators to carefully analyze how the application of certain data sets will affect incentives in industry.

8. Cornerstones for Success and Conclusions

Open banking is a cornerstone in the development of open innovation in financial services. It is vital for policy-makers to build an open banking regime that improves consumer outcomes and unleashes the economic potential of data. The following principles for responsible and safe innovation will ensure that the Australian CDR meets the benefits it sets out to achieve.

(1) *Consistency and industry fairness* — The sharing of consumer data will foster a greater degree of open innovation in financial

---

[13]*Treasury Laws Amendment (Consumer Data Right) Bill 2018, Exposure Draft,* Retrieved from: https://static.treasury.gov.au/uploads/sites/1/2018/08/Consumer_ Data_Right_ED_T316972.pdf

[14]*Treasury Laws Amendment (Consumer Data Right) Act 2019,* Retrieved from: https://www.legislation.gov.au/Details/C2019A00063/751bd321-0ce9-430c-8b63-e095d764c730

services. There must be consistent standards for data sharing between sectors, and data sharing must be regulated in a way that avoids asymmetries. Industry regulation must be adjusted to be appropriate for the functions of a business rather than applied to sectors. Parties that control consumers and are at the forefront of the customer relationship must be appropriately regulated.

(2) *Customer education and a social license are paramount* — Regulators and market participants should undertake ongoing educational campaigns to make consumers aware of what open banking means for them. A lack of consumer awareness is often considered one of the mistakes of the UK's regime. Consumers must see the value proposition and understand privacy and security if they are going to participate in sharing their data. This also has implications for how open banking is marketed generally. Many propositions in the UK were about how it would help FinTechs to enable consumer benefits necessary in the Australian regime. Consumers need to feel safe and in control.

(3) *Open banking must be part of a national data strategy* — Regulation must be a subset of policy that takes into consideration the wide range of implications of increased data sharing. Standards must be developed beyond technical standards. This includes the development of an environment that is supporting investment in financial technology in Australia. Open banking must not be a one-off push but rather constantly develop according to changes in technology and industry. The ability for banks to improve their offerings based on more dynamic risk assessment must not be constrained by inflexibility of regulatory requirements.

Australia's open banking implementation has the potential to contribute to developments in open innovation, and moreover, it will improve outcomes for consumers in financial services. Beyond these consumer outcomes, Australia's unique step of creating an economy-wide CDR could effectively contribute to a change toward a data-based economy. Nevertheless, there may be significant pitfalls and unintended consequences if policy-makers fail to design and implement a framework that accounts for consistency and industry fairness, customer education, and a social license that is part of a national data strategy. These factors will determine whether we stand up and surf, or fall and flounder, in our new sea of data.

Acknowledgments

We would like to acknowledge the individuals who were consulted for this chapter. They provided many thought-provoking insights and an understanding of how industry was reacting to open banking. Thank you to Scott Farrell, Danny Gilligan, Steve Weston, Luis Uguina, Ellen Broad, Steve Wiggins, Jane Retimana, Imran Gulamhuseinwala, Alistair Milne, Martin McCann, David Birch, David Beardmore, Rocky Scopelliti, and Jamie Campbell.

References

Alibaba Group (2016). Electronic World Trade Platform, *Alibaba*, Retrieved from: https://www.alizila.com/wp-content/uploads/2016/09/eWTP.pdf?x95431 (Accessed on 8 February 2019).

Ardner, R. (2006). Match your innovation strategy to your innovation ecosystem. *Harvard Business Review*, Retrieved from: https://hbr.org/2006/04/match-your-innovation-strategy-to-your-innovation-ecosystem (Accessed on 13 December 2018).

Australian Competition & Consumer Commission, (2018). *Consumer Data Right Rules Framework*, Canberra, Australia. Retrieved from: https://www.accc.gov.au/system/files/ACCC%20CDR%20Rules%20Framework%20%28final%29.pdf (Accessed on 16 November 2018).

Australian Payments Network (2018). The Digital Economy, Ninth Report, Retrieved from: https://www.auspaynet.com.au/sites/default/files/2018-06/AusPayNet_Digital-Economy-Report-June18%20.pdf (Accessed on 15 November 2018).

Berlind, D. (2015). What is an API, Exactly? *Programmableweb*. Retrieved from: https://www.programmableweb.com/news/what-api-exactly/analysis/2015/12/03 (Accessed on 11 December 2018).

Birch, D. (2018). Open banking: A remedy Against monopolies in data? http://www.dgwbirch.com/library/pdf-library/pfl-june-2018-p13-14.pdf (Accessed on 17 November 2018).

Carney, M. (2017). The Promise of Fintech — Something New Under the Sun? [Transcript] Bank of England, 25 January. Retrieved from https://www.bankofengland.co.uk/-/media/boe/files/speech/2017/the-promise-of-fintech-something-new-under-the-sun.pdf (Accessed on 18 November 2018).

Euro Banking Association (2016). Understanding the business relevance of Open APIs and Open banking for Banks. Information Paper. Retrieved from: https://www.abe-eba.eu/media/azure/production/1380/understanding-the-business-relevance-of-open-apis-and-open-banking-for-banks.pdf (Accessed on 16 November 2018).

Eyers, J. (2018). Stronger privacy needed for "open banking" to avoid Facebook style scandal. *Australian Financial Review*, 27 March. Retrieved from: https://www.afr.com/business/banking-and-finance/financial-services/stronger-privacy-needed-for-open-banking-to-avoid-facebookstyle-scandal-20180327-h0y0h5 (Accessed on 16 November 2018).

Ferguson, N. (2008). *The Ascent of Money* (The Penguin Press, London, United Kingdom).

Gilbert + Tobin (2018). Open banking regimes across the globe. Retrieved from: https://www.gtlaw.com.au/insights/open-banking-regimes-across-globe (Accessed on 15 November 2018).

Gilligan, D. (2018). Global data wars: Building a thriving data economy for Australia, *Reinventure*. Retrieved from: http://reinventure.com.au/wp-content/uploads/2016/10/GlobalDataWarsReportReinventure.pdf (Accessed on 17 November).

Gomart, T., Nocetti, J., & Tonon, C. (2018). Europe: Subject or object in the geopolitics of data? Institut Francais des Relations Internationales. Retrieved from: https://www.ifri.org/sites/default/files/atoms/files/gomart_nocetti_tonon_europe_geopolitics_data_2018.pdf (Accessed on 10 December 2018).

Hoetmer, K. (2013). A fresh new look for the Maps API, for all one million sites. Google. Retrieved from https://mapsplatform.googleblog.com/2013/05/a-fresh-new-look-for-maps-api-for-all.html (Accessed on 7 February 2019)

INNOPAY (2018). Open banking Monitor. July. Retrieved from: https://www.innopay.com/themes/apis/openbankingmonitor/ (Accessed on 19 November 2018).

Ismael, S., Malone, M., & Van Geest, Y. (2014). *Exponential Organisations: Why New Organisations are Ten Times Better, Faster and Cheaper Than Yours* (Diversion Books, New York, United States).

Kapron, Z., & Meertens, M. (2017). Social networks, e-commerce platforms and the growth of digital payment ecosystems in China: What it means for other countries. Better Than Cash Alliance. Retrieved from https://btca-production-site.s3.amazonaws.com/documents/283/english_attachments/Better_Than_Cash_Alliance_China_Report_April_2017_%281%29.pdf?1492605583 (Accessed on 7 July 2021).

Kemp, K., & Vaile, D. (2018). Joint Submission to Treasury, Final Report of the Review into Open Banking in Australia. University of New South Wales Law Research Series 23, February 9.

King, B. (2017). *Bank 4.0: Banking Everywhere, Never At A Bank* (Marshall Cavendish International Asia, Chichester, United Kingdom).

King, M. (2016). *The End of Alchemy: Money, Banking, and the Future of the Global Economy* (WW Norton & Company, London, United Kingdom).

King, S. (2018). Data, technology and competition: The uncertain future for banking and regulation. *23rd Melbourne Money and Finance Conference 2018*, Retrieved from: https://australiancentre.com.au/wp-content/uploads/2017/12/Dr-Stephen-King-Data-technology-and-competition.pdf (Accessed on 17 November 2018).

Llanos-small, K. (2018). Mexico fast tracks open banking rules. *Iupana*, June 18. Retrieved from: http://iupana.com/2018/06/18/mexico-fast-tracks-open-banking-rules/?lang=en (Accessed on 15 November 2018).

Mayer-Schönberger, V., & Ramge, T. (2018). *Reinventing Capitalism in the Age of Big Data* (John Murray, London, United Kingdom).

Megaw, N., & Toplensky, R. (2018). Santander chair calls EU rules on payments unfair. *Financial Times*, April 17. Retrieved from https://www.ft.com/content/d9f819f2-3f39-11e8-b7e0-52972418fec4 (Accessed on 16 November 2017).

Open Data Institute and Fingleton Associates (2014). Data sharing and Open Data for Banks. A report for HM Treasury and Cabinet Office. December 3. Retrieved from: https://assets.publishing.service.gov.uk/government/uploads/system/uploads/attachment_data/file/382273/141202_API_Report_FINAL.PDF (Accessed on 15 November 2018).

Omarini, A. (2018). The retail bank of tomorrow: A platform for interactions and financial services. Conceptual and managerial challenges. *Research in Economics and Management*, 3(2), 110.

O'Neil, C. (2016). *Weapons of Math Destruction* (Crown Books, New York).

Parker, G., Van Alstyne, M., & Choudary, S. (2016). *Platform Revolution* (W.W. Norton & Company, United States).

Productivity Commission (2018). Competition in the Australian Financial System, Report No. 89, Canberra Australia, Commonwealth of Australia. Retrieved from: https://static.treasury.gov.au/uploads/sites/1/2018/02/Review-into-Open-Banking-_For-web-1.pdf (Accessed on 13 November 2018).

Productivity Commission (2017). Data Availability and Use: Overview & Recommendations, Report No. 82, Canberra Australia, Commonwealth of Australia. Retrieved from: https://www.pc.gov.au/inquiries/completed/data-access#report (Accessed on 13 November 2018).

Scopelliti, R. (2018). *Youthquake 4.0* (Marshall Cavendish International (Asia) Private Limited, Singapore).

Sheng, C., Yip, J., & Cheng, J. (2017). Fintech in China: Hitting the Moving Target. *Oliver Wyman*. Retrieved from: https://www.oliverwyman.com/our-expertise/insights/2017/aug/fintech-in-china-hitting-the-moving-target.html (Accessed on 7 July 2021).

Stigler, G. J. (1980). An introduction to privacy in economics and politics. *The Journal of Legal Studies*, 9(4), 623–644.

Taylor, B. (2005). The world is your JavaScript-enabled oyster. Google. Retrieved from: https://googleblog.blogspot.com/2005/06/world-is-your-javascript-enabled_29.html (Accessed on 18 December 2018).

The Association of Banks in Singapore and Monetary Authority of Singapore (2017). Finance-as-a-service: API Playbook. Retrieved from: https://abs.org.sg/docs/library/abs-api-playbook.pdf (Accessed on 7 July 2021).

The Treasury (2017). Review into Open Banking, Canberra Australia, Australian Government. Retrieved from: https://static.treasury.gov.au/uploads/sites/1/2018/02/Review-into-Open-Banking-_For-web-1.pdf (Accessed on 16 November 2018).

The Treasury (2018). *Consumer Data Right*, The Treasury, 9 May. Retrieved from https://static.treasury.gov.au/uploads/sites/1/2018/05/t286983_consumer-data-right-booklet.pdf (Accessed on 16 November 2018).

Treasury Laws Amendment (Consumer Data Right) Bill 2018, Exposure Draft. Retrieved from: https://static.treasury.gov.au/uploads/sites/1/2018/08/Consumer_Data_Right_ED_T316972.pdf (Accessed on 17 November 2018).

Treasury Laws Amendment (Consumer Data Right) Act 2019. Retrieved from: https://www.legislation.gov.au/Details/C2019A00063/751bd321-0ce9-430c-8b63-e095d764c730 (Accessed on 2 October 2020).

White & Case LLP (2018). Mexican Fintech Law Becomes Effective. Retrieved from: https://www.jdsupra.com/legalnews/mexican-fintech-law-becomes-effective-83452/ (Accessed on 17 November 2018).

World Economic Forum (2018). The new physics of financial services, August. Retrieved from: http://www3.weforum.org/docs/WEF_New_Physics_of_Financial_Services.pdf (Accessed on 13 November 2018).

World Economic Forum (2017). Beyond Fintech — A pragmatic assessment of disruptive potential in financial services, August. Retrieved from: http://www3.weforum.org/docs/Beyond_Fintech_-_A_Pragmatic_Assessment_of_Disruptive_Potential_in_Financial_Services.pdf (Accessed on 13 November 2018).

Wozniak, S. (2017). Steve Wozniak at the AI deep dive stage. *Money2020*, https://www.youtube.com/watch?v=FQbsvLQTFxI&feature=youtu.be (Accessed on 3 February 2019).

Zachariadis, M., & Ozcan, P. (2017). The API economy and digital transformation in financial services: The case of open banking. SWIFT Institute Working Paper No. 2016-001.

Chapter 10

Making Sense of Blockchain as a Digital Technology for Open Innovation: A Review Exploring Blockchain Business Applications, Start-Up Business Models, and Blockchain Services Ecosystem

Suraj Bhattarai, [*] *Harry Fulgencio* [†,§]
and Hans LeFever [‡,¶]

[†] *Center for Social Impact, Swinburne University Technology,*
Hawthorn VIC 3122, Australia

[‡] *Leiden Institute of Advanced Computer Science,*
Leiden University, Niels Bohrweg 1 Leiden, the Netherlands

[§] *hfulgencio@swin.edu.au*
[¶] *H.t.le.fever@liacs.leidenuniv.nl*

---

[*] Co-author has contributed to this edited volume in his individual capacity.

Abstract. Performing open innovation within a company should also consider the potential of new and disruptive digital technology such as blockchain. In the plethora of business models of digital technology, blockchain seems to be the most disruptive versus social media, cloud computing, and big data. Blockchain is a digital ledger where transactions are chronologically recorded, and a copy of the ledger is distributed across a network. Initially used by financial technology companies to provide cryptocurrency services, major financial institutions, technology firms, and other non-financial companies are investing in understanding the business application of blockchain. Similarly, a lot of technology start-ups have emerged in the past years who have businesses capitalizing on blockchain-based services. In this chapter, we ask: how can we make sense of blockchain, by asking two questions that relate to the business applications of blockchain and the possible start business models. Our systematic review extended the conception and understanding of a financial technology as a way to pursue open innovation through the lens of a business model. We do this by analyzing blockchain various business applications, identifying the business models used by existing start-ups, and then proposing the ecosystem of blockchain business application.

Keywords. Blockchain; technology start-up; business model; systematic literature review; blockchain services; blockchain application ecosystem; ecosystem; review; open innovation; technological innovation; innovation.

1. Introduction

Advancements in digital technology will bring new opportunities, challenges to adapt and bring about changes to both incumbent and start-up companies (Matt *et al.*, 2015). While incumbent companies may have extensive investments and processes for exploring new ideas and technologies, they often have little if any ability to innovate the business models through which these inputs will pass (Chesbrough, 2003). Open innovation is inherent within technology start-up's businesses practice (Alberti Fernando, 2017; Di Pietro *et al.*, 2018; Spender, 2017; Usman, 2017), but rather than follow the mainstream literature of studying the open innovation practices, networks, and knowledge flows, our research wants to understand the digital technology that gave rise to a technology start-up. In doing this, researchers, managers, and policy-makers that a particular digital technology that can play a key role in the emergence of technology start-ups that are openly innovating by finding opportunities to exploit the digital technology (e.g. blockchain [Eyal, 2017; Kannan and Li, 2017]).

Studying blockchain may enhance our understanding of open innovation within blockchain-based technology start-ups by using the Business Model Canvas (Osterwalder and Pigneur, 2010) to understand various applications. Blockchain is a new digital technology that promises to be extensively used in future company operations and processes (White, 2017).The adoption of new technology involves the transformation of critical company operations, which often leads to changes in the products, services as well as the entire business model of the company (Matt *et al.*, 2015). However, as a digital technology taken to market through two different business models will yield two different economic outcomes, it makes good business sense for companies to understand the possibilities offered by the digital technology and perform open innovation (Chesbrough, 2010). Changes in the business model lead to new company offerings that affect the technology start-ups business models (Teece, 2010; Zott *et al.*, 2011), e.g. the influence of social media as digital technology in the business model (Hanna *et al.*, 2011). However, without understanding, new technology brings about uncertainties, and often the possibilities of the new technology are identified as it gets adapted and reaches a certain maturity level (Teece, 2010). This understanding becomes even more crucial for start-up as well as established companies who lack a basic framework to follow in their venture into blockchain.

Whereas previous research focused on existing industry themes and topical implementations of blockchain (White, 2017; Zeadally and Abdo, 2019) or the theoretical blockchain offers, our study builds on the conception that blockchain applications need to be understood by exploring the various business application (through business models) of blockchain start-up companies and their characteristics based on the nine components of their business model and characteristics. The findings can help future start-ups, venturing into blockchain applications, to understand the different business aspects to consider in order to develop their business. It will also provide a reference point for future research of business models exploiting blockchain.

1.1. *Technology start-ups and open innovation*

In the study of open innovation, large companies have been well researched in the topics such as the dynamics of open innovation (Brunswicker and Chesbrough, 2018; Brunswicker and Vanhaverbeke, 2015; Huang *et al.*, 2015), the role of technology played in open innovation (Yun *et al.*, 2016) and importance of business models (Robaczewska *et al.*, 2019). Although company size has not been conclusive in determining the success of open innovation practices (Greco, 2015), start-up companies have the potential as builders of future innovation ecosystems (Valkokari *et al.*, 2017). The role of start-up companies in harnessing technological innovations and generating wealth has been evident and instrumental to big technology and data-driven companies (former start-ups) like Apple for personal computing, Facebook and Instagram for social media, and Google for web search (Del Vecchio *et al.*, 2018). The idea that "open innovation is even more important for start-ups than for large companies" (Usman, 2017) is more evident for technology start-ups as they have been observed to rely on technological relations with large companies (Segers, 2015). Hence studying technology start-ups (mainly digital technology start-ups) practice in open innovation (finding business opportunity) through their business model (Teece, 2010) may provide insight as to how non–start-up companies can perform open innovation using new technology (Chesbrough, 2003). One such technology that is seen is influencing the creation of new blockchain technology start-ups and at the same time affecting existing business models (Nowiński and Kozma, 2017).

1.2. *Business model*

A new business model helps companies gain competitive advantage and build stronger customer relationships (Lindgardt *et al.*, 2009), create value to customers and partners, maintains relationships with customers, supports differentiation from competitors, and is constructed with products and services (Schallmo and Brecht, 2010). There are two well-known specifications of a business model: a seven-element Activity System Design Framework (Zott *et al.*, 2011) and the nine-element Business Model Canvas (Osterwalder and Pigneur, 2010). The seven-element activity-based system design framework elements are content, structure and governance, novelty, lock-in, complementarities, and efficiency (Zott *et al.*, 2011). Focusing on the first three elements, the content element relates to the selection of the actual business activities to be carried out by the firm while the structure defines how these activities are linked to each other and their importance to the firm, and finally the governance relates to who performs these activities (Zott and Amit, 2009). The nine elements of the business model are customer segments, value propositions, channels, customer relationships, revenue streams, key resources, key activities, key partnerships, and cost structure (Osterwalder and Pigneur, 2010). The latter has been used extensively researched and has become the legitimate reference when referring to the business model, so this research will apply to the Business Model Canvas in order to form a systematic and well-defined basis for investigation. The connection of business model with business strategy and innovation management states that businesses explicitly or implicitly employ a business model (Teece, 2010).

Although the innovation of a business model may allow companies to overcome intense competition, products and processes can be easily imitated and competitor's strategies can converge, therefore the sustained advantage is elusive (Lindgardt *et al.*, 2009). Business model innovation applied in existing companies who employ blockchain may be an interesting topic of study. However, this is not within the scope of this study. Our study only focused on start-up companies who are undertaking business model innovation by starting a new company using blockchain. The firm's capacity to capture value will be compromised if it does not have the ability to create new business models (Teece, 2010). Obtaining value implementing change in the business model may be as guided by three steps (Giesen *et al.*, 2007)

2. Digital Technologies

Digital technology (e.g. social media, cloud computing, big data, and blockchain) can be an accelerator for generating new business models, and current digital trends have been topics of significant investigation in the field of digital technology-powered business transformation. The three digital technology that has been extensively discussed and investigated for their potential to disrupt business models across organizations and industries are social media (Hanna *et al.*, 2011), cloud computing (DaSilva *et al.*, 2013), and big data (Schroeder and Halsall, 2016).

Big data technology is disruptive, and the impact of cloud computing on the business model has been studied (Sultan and van de Bunt-Kokhuis, 2012). Some researchers proposed a big data framework to reduce the impact of big data on the business model (Brownlow *et al.*, 2015). There are even more comprehensive studies about business models of social media, and the first research comes up with an actual framework for salesperson or marketer usage and value creation (Agnihotri *et al.*, 2013); while the second suggests the need for a proper framework for salesperson or marketer and manager to understand value creation (Agnihotri *et al.*, 2013); and finally the third mentions the different value propositions created and revenue streams generated (Pihl and Sandström, 2013).

Paving the way to digital transformation research on business models (Berman Saul, 2012) and embracing digital technology may lead to significant business improvements (Fitzgerald *et al.*, 2014).

In general, the number of studies we just mentioned about the digital technologies — big data, cloud computing, and social media — shows the partial investigations on a digital technology's potential and opportunity of digital technology from a holistic business perspective. Another limitation of previous research is in its general approach in terms of existing companies and start-ups. Digital technology start-ups may be more agile and innovative in applying new technology, whereas existing companies would be reluctant, and it takes a while before they perform open innovation and build business models on new digital technology. To add to this complexity, a new digital technology is becoming popular called blockchain. Blockchain is purported to be a disruptive technology; this then leads us to the subject of this chapter investigating business models of blockchain and utilizing a more holistic and widely known framework called Business Model Canvas to cover most of the aspects of the business model. At the time of research, there was minimal research done about business models of blockchain. The various components of a Business Model Canvas are interconnected (Osterwalder and Pigneur, 2010). By adopting a holistic perspective, this research will be able illustrate the business models of blockchain and propose an ecosystem model for blockchain. This study would be significant to business and digital transformation researchers and practitioners.

2.1. *Blockchain*

Blockchain is the latest digital technology that has been steadily growing in its implementation by established companies and start-ups alike. Its appeal to companies may lie in its technical features such as enhanced security, anonymity, and data integrity without any third-party interference. These technical features of blockchain create new research (Crosby *et al.*, 2016) as it will affect our lives (Boucher *et al.*, 2017) and the world around us (Tapscott and Kirkland, 2016). Blockchain is an open ledger of business transactions that have ever occurred, which is recorded in chrono-logical order (Swan, 2015). Blockchain is the "decentralized manag-ing technique of Bitcoin, designed for issuing and transferring money for the users of the Bitcoin currency" by maintaining a public ledger of all bitcoin transactions independent of a third-party organization (Yli-Huumo *et al.*, 2016). The advantages of blockchain are faster, reliable, immutable, and transparent transactions with the elimina-tion of any third-party involvement (Crosby *et al.*, 2016; Yli-Huumo *et al.*, 2016). The blockchain started with the advent of an alternative cryptocurrency called bitcoin. Bitcoin is a cryptocurrency used for an online payment system that uses encrypted techniques to generate units of currency and verify the transfer of funds while operating independently of a central bank (Swan, 2015). Cryptocurrency, also known as virtual currency, is decentralized peer-to-peer payment systems that are digital representations of value and can be transferred, stored, and traded electronically (Ong *et al.*, 2015). Although there are other cryptocurrencies around, bitcoin is the most prominent one. Blockchain is said to reshape business processes, empower technological development, and accelerate their adoption in our day-to-day lives (Pilkington, 2016). Within banking and finance, it simplifies the business processes of creating safe, and trustworthy transactions (Treleaven *et al.*, 2017).

2.2. *Business applications of blockchain in financial technology*

Today the concept of blockchain is finding a range of applications and has moved beyond the idea of bitcoins. Companies like Microsoft, IBM, and Amazon, as well as major Wall Street banks, including JPMorgan Chase and Citigroup, are investing in blockchain while Infosys, Tata Consultancy Services, Hindustan Computers Limited (HCL), Accenture, and Deloitte are working on blockchain-based products and services (Breitman, 2017). The implementation of the blockchain has been broadly categorized into financial and non-financial areas, with a majority of the study finding its primary use and impact in the financial sector (Crosby *et al.*, 2016; Swan, 2015). Financial institutions and banks do not see blockchain as a threat to their traditional business models, and in fact, the world's biggest banks are looking for opportunities in this area by investing in innovative blockchain applications (Crosby *et al.*, 2016). New financial technology companies have been capitalizing on the use of technology (Nguyen, 2016). There are three application categories of blockchain, namely Blockchain 1.0, Blockchain 2.0, and Blockchain 3.0 (Swan, 2015). Blockchain 1.0 refers to the use of cryptocurrency and its transfer, while Blockchain 2.0 refers to extensive economic and financial transactions. Finally Blockchain 3.0 refers to "non-financial applications," i.e. applications in non–business-oriented areas such as health, science, literacy, culture, and art (Swan, 2015).

2.3. *Beyond financial technology application of blockchain*

In the financial technology domain, blockchain finds its major use in the area of cryptocurrency, where bitcoin has been the main application, which is followed by Ether, a currency used by smart contract platform Ethereum (Breitman, 2017). Similarly, past literature mentions many other emerging platforms that use the technology for cryptocurrency transactions. The other significant financial use of blockchain is smart contracts. Smart contracts are facilitated by computer programs that can automatically execute the terms of a contract where, when conditions are met, payments can be made automatically between them (Crosby *et al.*, 2016). There are three distinct characteristics of smart contracts, namely, autonomy, self-sufficiency, and decentralization (Swan, 2015). Autonomy refers to smart contracts being independent of a person initiating the contract; self-sufficiency refers to its ability to be able to gather the required resources by itself; and finally decentralization applies to smart contracts being distributed among networked nodes and not residing in a central server (Swan, 2015). Smart contracts also give rise to another related application called smart property. Smart property may give rise to centralized trust-less asset management systems as well as cryptographically activated assets, and this would have implications for the entire field of property law (Swan, 2015). Smart property relates to the control of ownership of a physical or non-physical property. Properties such as car, house, or company share via the technology using smart contracts. The critical concept in smart contracts and the smart property is the control of ownership and access to an asset by having it registered as a digital asset on the blockchain (Crosby *et al.*, 2016). Blockchain-enabled crowdfunding removes the need of an intermediary third-party enabling start-ups to raise funds by creating their own digital currencies and selling "cryptographic shares" to their investors and early backers (Swan, 2015).

There are a wide range of non-financial domain applications such as proof of existence, performance improvement, automation, and decentralization. Proof of the existence of an entity is one major application. Proof of the existence of all legal records, legal documents, health records, loyalty payments in the music industry, notary, private securities, and marriage licenses can be envisioned to be put inside the blockchain (Crosby *et al.*, 2016). This can be achieved through hashing and timestamping, where hashing provides a unique identifier to the document and timestamping provides the time it was authored (Swan, 2015). Proof-of-existence blockchain application demonstrates document ownership, and the time it was authored without revealing the document content (Swan, 2015).

Another application is in the performance improvement in business and management (White, 2017) and of another digital technology such as big data and the Internet of Things (IoT). Blockchain "could be joined with big data, layered onto the reactive-to-predictive transformation that is slowly underway in big data science to allow the automated operation of large areas of tasks through smart contracts and economics" (Swan, 2015). Blockchain may also facilitate the implementation of decentralized IoT platforms such as secured and trusted data exchange as well as record-keeping where the blockchain serves as the general ledger, keeping a trusted record of all the messages exchanged between smart devices in a decentralized IoT topology (Crosby *et al.*, 2016). Another application is in the decentralized storage of electronic data. Blockchain-based storage allows users to transfer and share data without relying on any third-party cloud storage applications, thus allowing them to share unused Internet bandwidth and spare disk space in their personal computing devices to others in return for bitcoin-based micropayments.

Blockchain enables the efficient organization and effective collaboration between people and machines and may lead toward a very fast, reliable, transparent, and secure interaction and dealings among people and organizations (Swan, 2015). More blockchain applications are underway as companies and governments become aware of the applications and technology, and the resistance stance is transforming into opportunity-seeking behavior of companies. However, blockchain as a disruptive and revolutionizing digital technology comes with its own challenges and risks that need to be understood as organizations globally get more and more involved.

Investigations carried out on the impact of digital technology in creating new business models lack depth. Hence, we used the Business Model Canvas in this study. Each of the digital technology opportunities — i.e. big data, cloud computing, and social media — can be best understood through the Business Model Canvas. Hence, to contribute to the digital business model research, we explored the start-up business model applications of blockchain. Start-up blockchain companies are an ideal context for this study because start-up business models are centered on the blockchain. In addition, there are various write-ups comprising mainly non-scholarly articles about the companies. The objective of this chapter is to explore the business applications and provide some initial analysis of the business models currently being implemented by blockchain start-ups. The research would allow business and digital transformation researchers and practitioners to think and perform open innovation about blockchain as a disruptive technology that needs to be understood.

3. Methodology

Blockchain is a relatively recent technological innovation, and much of the established and existing business start-ups around blockchain are inaccessible due to sensitivity or would not attend to our request to divulge their business model. We studied the blockchain start-ups using Osterwalder and Pigneur's Business Model Canvas. Due to the sensitivity of the topic, and novelty of the services provided by blockchain start-up, we opted for a research design that triangulates our data from the systematic literature review, analysis of Factiva articles, and two interviews conducted with blockchain experts. There are four significant results of this study: blockchain applications, start-ups, business models, and an ecosystem of block-chain services.

This study is using qualitative approach of triangulation (Flick, 2004; Thurmond, 2001) relying on secondary data such as (1) scholarly articles, (2) non-scholarly articles (Factiva), and (3) interviews for the theoretical understanding of the business applications of blockchain through the various blockchain start-up business models. We opted to gain understanding by mapping the business models using secondary data sources in reliable industry article sources such as scholarly repositories, Factiva, and two subject-expert interviews. This study was conducted around March 2017–September 2017. The research design of this chapter draws on the Design Science in Information Systems Research (Hevner *et al.*, 2004), we designed a three-step process.

3.1. *Data preparation*

A systematic literature review (SLR) can be defined as a means of identifying, evaluating, and interpreting all available literature relevant to a particular research question (Kitchenham, 2009) to inform future research activities. An effective review creates a firm foundation for advancing knowledge while facilitating theory development and closing areas where a substantial amount of research exists and uncovering areas where research is needed (Webster and Watson, 2002). Relating this to our study, the objective is to explore and understand the different business applications and their corresponding start-ups venturing into the blockchain.

The SLR steps are as follows; first, a review protocol was developed (Kitchenham *et al.*, 2006) where process to be undertaken is specified to reduce the possibility of researcher bias (Kitchenham *et al.*, 2006).Second, creating a search strategy where a number of scholarly databases were chosen from, and keywords were identified in order to do the search. The journal databases and publisher aggregator are Academic Search Premier, ACM Digital Library, IEEE Computer Society Digital Library, Informaworld — Taylor &

Francis, National Center for Biotechnology Information (NCBI), ProQuest: Business Collection, ScienceDirect, Scopus, Social Science Research Network, Springerlink, and Web of Science. Third, selecting the primary studies according to certain filtering criteria keywords were used separately in each database namely: "blockchain," "public ledger," and "distributed ledger." The following inclusion criteria were applied to the final articles for SLR — language: English; journal type: scholarly articles; content type: a comprehensive discussion of the various business applications of the blockchain; and full-text availability. The language needed to be was set to English as the research was carried out in English, and non-English articles were excluded due to the time and resources involved in translating such articles. The type of journal chosen was scholarly articles as the research itself is carried out in a scientific methodology, and therefore the primary papers were desired to be scholarly as well. The type of content of the articles was chosen to be containing a comprehensive discussion about the various applications of the blockchain as it was necessary for fulfilling the objective of the SLR to explore and understand the different business applications and their corresponding business models of blockchain start-ups. Finally, thematical data were extracted and synthesized in order to record the necessary information from the SLR studies that will form part of the conceptualization and the validation of the findings

The SLR results are shown below. It generated 1,694 papers, 685 were included as they were related to blockchain, and these papers were downloaded and saved in the Mendeley citation manager. The selection was made by looking into the title and abstract of the papers. Finally, 102 duplicates were found out of 583 relevant publications (Table 1).

Having read the title and abstract of 583 articles, 30 articles were qualified for contained information on blockchain business applications. Further analysis showed only four articles to be fully relevant. These four articles (Crosby *et al.*, 2016; Kane, 2017; Pilkington, 2016; Swan, 2015) were chosen for the final review.

Table 1.   Shows the results from the SLR.

Database	# of articles	Keywords			Included	Excluded	Total	Search date 2017
		Blockchain	Distributed ledger	Public ledger				
Academic Search Premier	174	13	1	4	18	158	16	25 April
ACM Digital Library	82	53	12	4	57	25	45	1 May
IEEE Computer Society Digital Library	124	42	9	19	70	73	51	25 April
Informaworld — Taylor & Francis	84	3	2	2	7	81	3	2 May
NCBI	36	3	2	2	7	33	3	3 May
ProQuest: Business Collection	91	64	6	3	73	19	72	1 May
Sciencedirect	86	28	6	6	40	53	33	1 May
Scopus	281	213	12	18	227	58	223	20 March
Social Science Research Network	273	84	13	38	135	182	91	2 May
Springerlink	342	18	7	10	35	310	32	25 April
Web of Science	121	11	3	2	16	107	14	25 April
Total	1694	532	73	108	685	1099	583	

3.2. *Conceptualization*

In the data preparation, using the four articles about blockchain business models, we conceptualized blockchain applications and listed some blockchain start-ups; to supplement the lack of scholarly articles discussing the various business models of the employed by blockchain start-ups, the researcher gathered additional data through Factiva. Factiva covers articles that are not scholarly reliable but are essential sources of information. Both the SLR of scholarly and non-scholarly themes were used to conceptualize the blockchain ecosystems.

3.3. *Validation*

To validate the blockchain applications business model and blockchain application ecosystem, two subject-expert professionals working in the field of blockchain development and related services were interviewed. The blockchain experts were provided with the conceptualized (1) blockchain applications business model and (2) blockchain application ecosystem (Table 2).

4. Results

4.1. *Business applications of blockchain*

The business applications of the blockchain are — (1) cryptocurrency services: (a) cryptocurrency generation, (b) cryptopayment, (c) cryptotrade; (2) other financial services: (a) private equity exchange; (3) contract management services: (a) smart contracts; (b) smart property; (c) online identity verification; (d) crowdfunding; (e) blockchain development, and (f) traceability.

4.1.1. *Cryptocurrency services — Generation, payment, trade*

Cryptocurrencies are alternate forms of money that are virtual and independent of any government-regulated monetary authority, and

Table 2.   Research method and expected result.

#	Research method			
	SLR 01 — scholarly		SLR 02 — Factiva and Interview	Interview
	Blockchain application	Blockchain startups	Blockchain business model	Blockchain ecosystem model
1	Crypto-currency generation	Bitcoin, Ethereum, Ripple	Crypto-currency generation	Crypto-currency generation
2	Crypto-payment	Remitsy, BitPay	Crypto-payment	Crypto-payment
3	Crypto-trade	Bitpay, CoinBase, Kraken, TeraExchange	Crypto-trade	Crypto-trade
4	Private equity exchange	Chain.com, Medici, BitShare	not covered	Equity exchange
5	Smart contracts	Ethereum	Smart contracts	Smart contracts
6	Smart property	Swan Coin, Ownage	not covered	Smart property
7	Online identity verification	OneName, BitId, BitHandle	not covered	Online identity verification
8	Crowd-funding	Funder-Growth, Swarm	not covered	Crowdfunding
9	Blockchain development	Blockchain.info, Stellar, Chain	not covered	Blockchain development
10	Traceability	Everledger, BlockVerify	not covered	Traceability

blockchain is the underlying technology that supports cryptocurrency transactions. Cryptocurrency defines a new type of economy which, for now, is not constrained by geographic location, political structure, or the legal system (Pilkington, 2016). Cryptocurrency on the blockchain acts as a decentralized ledger, allowing for the peer-to-peer transfer of funds without the need of a third party such as a bank (Kane, 2017). The major application of the blockchain in cryptocurrency transactions has been in the generation of authentic cryptocurrency that can be traded legally, like Bitcoin, Ethereum, Ripple, and Gridcoin (Kane, 2017; Pilkington, 2016).

4.1.2. *Other financial technology services — Private equity exchange*

A prime area for the applications of the blockchain is in relating to cryptocurrencies with traditional banking and financial markets (Swan, 2015). Financial services are empowered by the use of the blockchain in providing fast international fund transfers, and with low transfer costs (Kane, 2017). The major financial service application of the blockchain has been in providing fast and cheap cryptocurrency payments across the blockchain between various companies. For example, Ripple allows banks to transfer funds and foreign exchange transactions directly between themselves (Swan, 2015). Another start-up providing similar service is Remitsy, which provides international transfer of funds using the blockchain (Kane, 2017). Other start-ups are providing the facility of cryptocurrency payment to other traditional financial and market payment solutions like Paypal, as in the case of bitcoin payment processors are Bitpay, Coinbase, and GoCoin (Swan, 2015). Another application is the cryptocurrency trade, which deals with accepting cryptocurrency from consumers and trading them with others according to the current value of the currency, as in the case of Bitpay and Coinbase (Swan, 2015). A banking facility for digital currency savings, as in the case of the start-up Kraken, that allows direct savings and lending services for the bitcoin users (Swan, 2015). Other start-ups providing similar services are BTCjam and TeraExchange. Another application is in private equity exchange (e.g. Chain.com, Medici, Bitshare, and Blockstream). Chain.com is working with NASDAQ to allow a fast, traceable, and efficient way compared to traditional means of trading stocks (Crosby *et al.*, 2015).

4.1.3. *Contract management services — Smart contracts*

Contract management services such as smart contracts are a method of making agreements with people via the blockchain (Swan, 2015). These contracts are specific programs used in order to decide whether a specific blockchain operation, such as payments, should be permitted (Pilkington, 2016). The smart contracts allow users to create self-evaluating and self-regulating codes of the contract, thus displaying a certain level of autonomy after being placed in the blockchain (Kane, 2017). The application of the blockchain in contract management services is smart (Kane, 2017). Ethereum is an innovative blockchain-based virtual machine featuring stateful user-created digital contracts (Pilkington, 2016). Ethereum is a fundamental underlying infrastructure platform and programming language for building and publishing distributed applications that can run all blockchains and protocols, much like a unified development platform (Swan, 2015). Ethereum is already powering a wide range of early applications in areas such as governance, autonomous banks, keyless access, crowdfunding, financial derivatives trading, and settlement using smart contracts (Crosby *et al.*, 2015).

4.1.4. *Asset management services —* *Smart property*

Asset management services in the form of smart property are the concept of controlling the ownership of a property or asset (physical such as cars, house, or non-physical such as company shares) via blockchain using smart contracts (Crosby *et al.*, 2015). Blockchain-encoded property becomes smart property via smart contracts, thus enabling trustless lending and trading of property (Swan, 2015).The application of the blockchain in asset management has been in managing smart property using smart contracts, e.g. SwanCoin, where 121 physical-world artworks, crafted on 30 × 30 cm varnished plywood, are available for purchase and transfer via the bitcoin blockchain (Swan, 2015). Another start-up is Ownage, an Ethereum-based platform to distribute, collect, and trade digital game content (Kane, 2017). Smart property can be used with other blockchain applications such as digital identity, in order to allow access to use it as in the case of a smartphone or to open the doors of physical assets like cars and homes (Swan, 2015).

4.1.5. *Digital identity services — Online identity verification*

Blockchain, due to its security and permanence, makes a great technology to use for verifying and securing a person's digital identity (Kane, 2017). It benefits from the fact that all cryptocurrency users have a personal e-wallet, and therefore a wallet address that can be used to verify the users (Swan, 2015). The main application of blockchain in digital identity services has been in online identity verification. This includes verifying an individual's identity to a website using blockchain verification; two start-ups providing these services are OneName, BitId, and BitHandle (Swan, 2015). These start-ups provide a trustless and decentralized service so that one's digital identity cannot be controlled by a central institution or company; therefore, its more secure for authenticating to websites than using social media sites (Pilkington, 2016). Another application is in insurance, where any property/asset that can be registered inside a blockchain (e.g. smart property) becomes useful to provide and verify the digital authentication of the ownership (Crosby *et al.*, 2015). The other application is in using the digital identity services for verifying other blockchain transactions such as cryptocurrency, smart contracts, and smart property alike for securely verifying the parties involved in the transactions (Swan, 2015).

4.1.6. *Crowdfunding services*

Blockchain-based crowdfunding platforms make it possible for start-ups to raise funds by creating their own digital currencies and selling "cryptographic" shares to early backers, where the investors receive a token that represents the shares of the start-up they support (Swan, 2015). The main application of the blockchain in crowdfunding services has been to gather funding for blockchain-based projects through the blockchain. FunderGrowth is a start-up that allows people to invest their money in blockchain start-ups (Kane, 2017). Another start-up is Swarm, an incubator of cryptocurrency-focused start-ups that gave rise to several funded projects ranging from the development of smart personal drone networks to a decentralized cryptocurrency workplace (Swan, 2015).

4.1.7. *Blockchain development services*

There are many blockchain protocol development projects for enabling their own blockchain processes and applications.Some of them seek out help in creating their own private blockchain applications (Kane, 2017; Swan, 2015). The main service of blockchain development services is in providing new opportunities and catering to growing demands for new protocol development projects (Kane, 2017). This demand would rise up as the blockchain gets increasingly popular. Examples of start-ups involved in protocol development for their own blockchain and corresponding application are Ripple and Ethereum, while start-ups like NXT and Open transactions develop for bitcoin blockchain overlay. Some of the start-ups like Blockchain.info, Stellar and Chain offers interfaces and Application Programming Interfaces (APIs) seeking out for protocol development for them (Swan, 2015).

4.1.8. *Traceability services — Anti-counterfeiting*

Blockchain helps in anti-counterfeiting and ensuring the authenticity of an entity by building a shared consensus-based and immutable ledger that helps track the origin and the transformations undergone by the entity, by creating a formal registry enabling the identification and the tracking of possession of the entity (Pilkington, 2016). The main application of the blockchain in traceability services is in providing traceability for various business operations, and the most prominent one is in SCM. The start-up Everledger is involved in creating permanent ledger of diamond certification and the transaction history of the diamond using blockchain (Crosby *et al.*, 2015). Another start-up involved in proving blockchain-based anti-counterfeit solutions is BlockVerify that is finding its applications in pharmaceutical, luxury, diamond, and electronics industries (Crosby *et al.*, 2015). Another application of blockchain in traceability services is in proof-of-existence. Putting all legal documents, health records, notary, private securities, etc., in the blockchain can be envisioned (Crosby *et al.*, 2015).

4.2. *Blockchain applications business model*

The thematic analysis identified 10 blockchain applications. Let us now take a look at four blockchain applications, with the first three being a financial technology blockchain-based services: (1) cryptocurrency generation, (2) cryptopayment, (3) cryptotrade, and (4) smart contracts. These four blockchain applications were chosen due to their popularity and the readily available information in Factiva, whereas the others are still under development and have minimal information available. At the time of the research, Table 3 shows the business model of the various business applications.

(1) **Cryptocurrency**: Start-ups generally reserve 20% of the cryptocurrency and float the rest 80% in the market. The business value generated by 80% gives value to 20%, which is the income. A venture capitalist invests through direct crowdfunding and initial coin offering (ICO). Miners solve complex computer algorithms attached to each block of transaction to validate the blocks and mint digital currency. They are paid for the computing resources. Start-ups venturing into providing cryptocurrency mainly benefit from the rise in the prices of the value of these currencies. Most of the currencies are offered as ICO and tokens by new start-ups to fund themselves. Others provide it for serving other blockchain applications in making payments for transactions in the blockchain.

(2) **Cryptopayments**: Cryptopayment processors have consumers paying transaction fees for payments as well as merchants paying subscription fees for using the processors through API. Every block of transactions is validated in the public network by validators. Cryptopayments mainly benefit from the transaction cost for the payment processing services they offer. The payment services are generally required by all start-ups and other business firms, including general users intending to benefit from its efficiency in making digital payments.

Table 3.   Blockchain applications business model.

Business Application	Business model canvas components								
	Value proposition	Revenue streams	Cost structure	Customer segment	Channels	Customer relationship	Activities	Resources	Partners
Crypto-currency generation	• autonomous currency • fixed & transparent supply	• digital currency reserve • crowd-funding	• network cost • miner fees • R&D cost • marketing cost	• crypto-consumers • crypto-investors • blockchain start-ups	• website/app • ICO • partner programmes • direct marketing	• availability & merchant acceptance	• marketing • product & process dev. (mining algorithms, rules, tec.)	• s/w protocols • R&D team (s/w dev., system adm., business dev., etc.)	• network providers • miners • crypto-exchanges • investors
Crypto-payment	• real-time • secure • autonomous • cheap & fast	• transaction fees • merchant subscription fees • crowd-funding	• conversion fees • miner fees • R&D cost	• crypto-consumers & merchants • crypto-exchanges • ICO(start-ups & investors)	• website/app • e-commerce platforms • partner programmes • direct marketing	• online account • e-wallet • debit card • API & plugins	• payment processing • product & process dev. (API, plugins, etc.)	• s/w protocols • R&D team (s/w dev., system adm., business dev., etc.)	• network providers • miners • crypto-providers • investors

Crypto-trade	• secure • cheap & fast • binding • transparent	• trading commission • crowd-funding	• miner fees • R&D cost	• crypto-investors • crypto-merchants • ICO (start-ups & investors)	• website/app • partner programmes • direct marketing	• online account • e-wallet • debit card	• exchange processing • product & process dev.	• s/w protocols • R&D team (s/w dev., system adm., business dev., etc.)	• miners • crypto-providers • crypto-processors • investors
Smart contracts	• real-time • autonomous • unforgeable • binding • transparent	• transaction fees • platform usage fees • service fees • crowd-funding	• network cost • platform maintenance • miner fees • R&D cost	• business firms • blockchain start-ups • DAO (distributed autonomous organisations)	• website/app • partner programmes • direct marketing	• online platform • scripting language • API • apps	• product & process dev. (platform, API, script, etc.) • support services	• s/w protocols • R&D team (s/w dev., system adm., business dev., etc.)	• miners • crypto-providers • network providers • investors

(3) **Cryptotrade:** Cryptoexchanges benefit from the intention of consumers to buy and sell while taking commissions from between. Miners validate the transactions using their computing resources and get paid for the transactions. Miners give priority to higher transaction fees as that can offset expenses. Cryptotrading services also benefit from transaction fees the users pay. These business models sustain due to the consumer's intentions of buying, using, and selling cryptocurrency, and therefore, all start-ups, business firms, and general users benefit from it.

(4) **Smart contracts:** These start-ups provide smart contract services tools for contract development and charge for the usage fees and other service charges. They use miners to validate the transactions and pay them for the transaction fees. Smart contract services companies mainly benefit from usage and transaction fees while using their platform and related service. The automation of the transactions generated by other blockchain business applications is the primary use of smart contract services.

4.3. *Business application ecosystem of blockchain*

Using the thematic results in the previous sections, an interrelated and layered ecosystem was conceptualized. The model shows an ecosystem (Figure 1) that may exist in the near future of the blockchain-based on business model. Each layer is defined by the possible role in relation to the different blockchain application(s) within the overall blockchain ecosystem.

The top of the figure indicates a close proximity to the end-users or customers whereas bottom of the figure indicate that it's away. These layers indicate an interrelationship among the companies — those in the top level of the ecosystem model could avail the services of the companies dealing with the lower levels, making them potential customers, hence business-to-business and business-to-customer services may exist in this layered ecosystem. Similarly, companies dealing with blockchain applications in the bottom levels could serve and support the business activities of the companies dealing with the

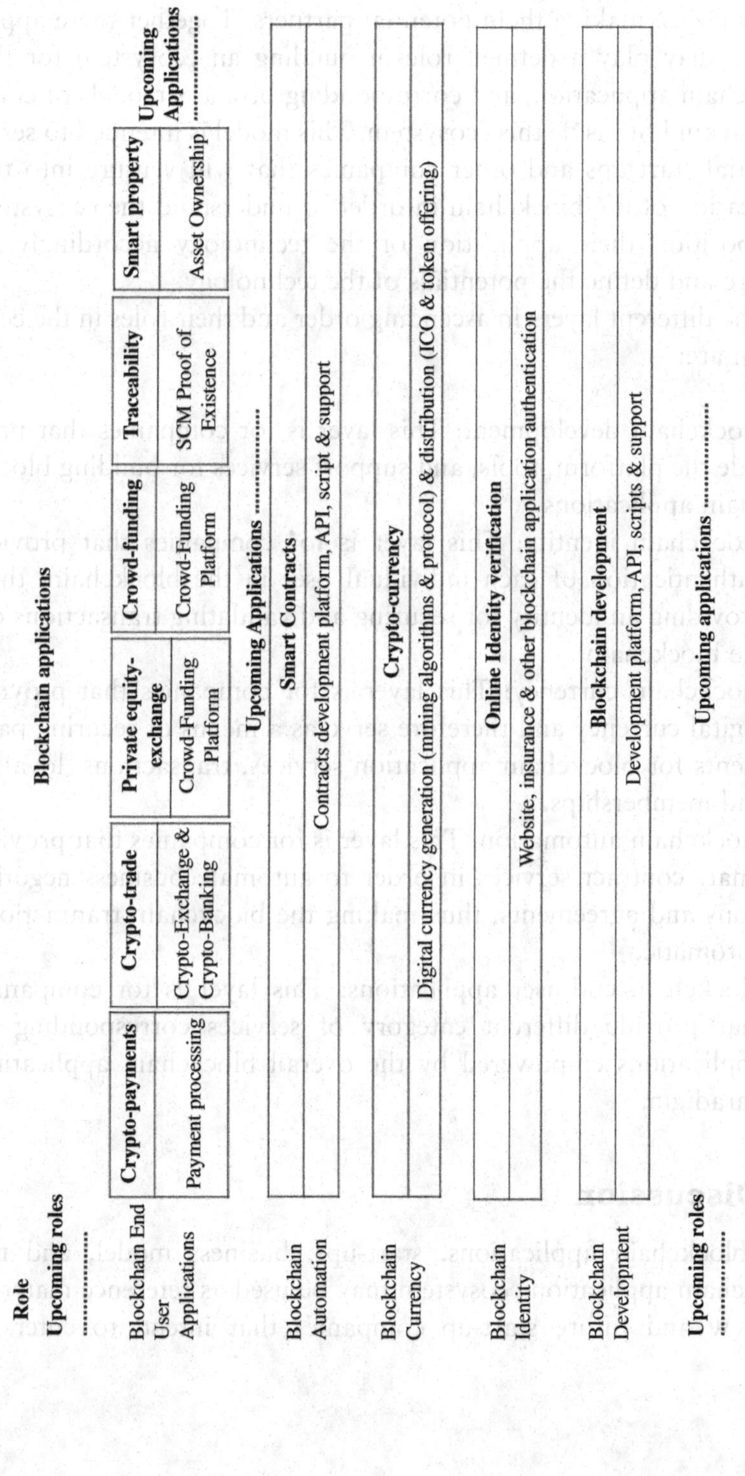

Role Upcoming roles	Blockchain applications							
	Crypto-payments	**Crypto-trade**	**Private equity-exchange**	**Crowd-funding**	**Traceability**	**Smart property**	**Upcoming Applications**
Blockchain End User Applications	Payment processing	Crypto-Exchange & Crypto-Banking	Crowd-Funding Platform	Crowd-Funding Platform	SCM Proof of Existence	Asset Ownership	

Upcoming Applications

Smart Contracts

Blockchain Automation — Contracts development platform, API, script & support

Crypto-currency

Blockchain Currency — Digital currency generation (mining algorithms & protocol) & distribution (ICO & token offering)

Online Identity verification

Blockchain Identity — Website, insurance & other blockchain application authentication

Blockchain development

Blockchain Development — Development platform, API, scripts & support

Upcoming applications

Upcoming roles

Figure 1. Blockchain applications ecosystem.

higher levels, making them potential partners. Together these applications may play a defined role in building an ecosystem for the blockchain application, and corresponding business models of companies could fit inside this ecosystem. This model is intended to serve potential start-ups and other companies that will venture into the application of the blockchain in order to understand the ecosystem and position their application of the technology accordingly to explore and define the potentials of the technology.

The different layers in ascending order and their roles in the ecosystem are:

(1) Blockchain development: This layer is for companies that provide the platform, tools, and support services for building blockchain applications.
(2) Blockchain identity: This layer is for companies that provide authentication of each individual user in the blockchain, thus providing an identity for securing and validating transactions on the blockchain.
(3) Blockchain currency: This layer is for companies that provide digital currency and therefore serve as a means of securing payments for blockchain application services, transactions, loyalty, and memberships.
(4) Blockchain automation: This layer is for companies that provide smart contract services in order to automate business negotiations and agreements, thus making the blockchain transactions automatic.
(5) Blockchain end-user applications: This layer is for companies that provide different category of services corresponding to applications empowered by the overall blockchain application paradigm.

5. Discussion

The blockchain applications, start-ups, business model, and the blockchain application ecosystem may be used as reference material for new and future start-up companies that intend to enter or diversify their business models using blockchain. The research proposed to come up with an understanding of the business models of the blockchain from a holistic perspective by exploring the different business applications and focusing on four blockchain applications to depict the interrelational or linked aspect of the business application of the blockchain and is depicted in the blockchain application ecosystem. These findings will be useful to further understand the technology and its business model impact to realize new business opportunities. Start-ups will be able to understand their position in the overall blockchain application paradigm.

Our study limitations were that only a few blockchain companies were willing to talk about their business models. This may be due to the sensitivity of the topic. The blockchain application, start-ups, business models, and ecosystems presented in this study will be increasing over time as more and more companies take their initial steps in creating blockchain-related business models. Due to time and resource constraints, only 4 business models out of 10 blockchain applications were explored in this chapter, new articles published after May 2017 were not covered, and only few interview participants could be included. Future researchers (especially financial technology researchers) may extend our findings by exploring the business models on private equity exchange, smart property, online identity verification, crowd-funding, blockchain development, and traceability and expand the analysis of the blockchain applications to include the rest of the categories and analyze the layered ecosystem, as we did not take into account existing companies wanting to incorporate blockchain in their business models. Also the "dark side" of the blockchain was not discussed in this chapter — apart from the technical limitations in scaling, throughput, latency, size, and bandwidth, and security difficulty in bootstrapping for migrating into the new technology, one of the significant risks of block technology is seen in fraudulent activities, such as industry thefts and fraud, fraudulent activities like money trafficking (Crosby *et al.*, 2016; Swan, 2015), and possibly legal dimensions to prevent such activity (Dion, 2013). The future of blockchain may also depend on government regulations, which could slow down the adoption due to new industry regulation and compliance (Crosby *et al.*, 2016; Swan, 2015). Finally, one major concern by researchers of blockchain is coming up with a viable business model for blockchain adoption; henceforth, we refer to blockchain application (Swan, 2015). Existing companies with traditional business models may benefit from knowing that blockchain removes intermediaries, thus disrupting the existing business models (Swan, 2015).

As the blockchain has moved beyond the financial technology application of cryptocurrency, there has been keen interest from academicians and business firms alike in trying to discover and understand the possibilities that can be realised using this digital technology. An increasing amount of financial and non-financial applications have been observed in this study, and the business models of each of these applications are under development. These developments may open up new areas and scope for future research. The different business models of these applications can be studied in-depth separately. Blockchain can be integrated with other digital technologies like big data, cloud computing, and social media.

6. Conclusion

We identified the prominent blockchain applications and found a lack of well-defined business models of the active blockchain start-ups. The different blockchain applications, indicating that most of the business applications of blockchain are seen in the financial sector, private and public record-keeping, and asset management, and that there are new business applications in other domains. One of the recent developments in financial technology is the concept of ICO, where increasing number of start-ups are offering their own tokens in order to fulfill funding needs, akin to crowdfunding. As mentioned above, the various aspects, depending on the business applications, may affect managers, policy-makers, regulators, financial technology researchers, and others. For example, contract management may be of interest to regulators who want to enforce rules and regulations while at the same time working closely with the entities involved in the contract. Managers of existing companies (utilizing technology or not utilizing blockchain) can benefit from our study by gaining knowledge of the various services that can be developed using blockchain. This research contributes toward understanding the business applications and the accompanying business models. The findings of this study can be used as part of the ongoing research in the field of disruptive digital technology, and it is through the relations of start-ups and open innovation that financial technology practitioners, managers, and policy-makers may be able to exploit blockchain. As blockchain becomes more prominent, it may become a significant part of our daily lives and almost completely change the way we live.

Acknowledgments

The current chapter was expanded from the original thesis research stored in the thesis repository of LIACS, Leiden University (Bhattarai, 2017). We would like to thank the editors and reviewers who took their time and effort in providing feedback.

References

Agnihotri, R., Kothandaraman, P., Kashyap, R., & Singh, R. (2013). Bringing "social" into sales: The impact of salespeople's social media use on service behaviors and value creation. *Journal of Personal Selling & Sales Management*, 32(3), 333–348. doi:10.2753/pss0885-3134320304

Alberti Fernando, G. (2017). Oops, I did it again! Knowledge leaks in open innovation networks with start-ups. *European Journal of Innovation Management*, 20(1), 50–79. doi:10.1108/EJIM-11-2015-0116

Berman Saul, J. (2012). Digital transformation: Opportunities to create new business models. *Strategy & Leadership*, 40(2), 16–24. doi:10.1108/10878571211209314

Bhattarai, S. (2017). Business models with blockchain: "Exploring the business models of the applications of blockchain technology in start-up enterprises." Master Thesis. Leiden University Institute of Advanced Computer Science. Retrieved from: https://theses.liacs.nl/854

Boucher, P., Nascimento, S., & Kritikos, M. (2017). How blockchain technology could change our lives: In-depth analysis (9284605490). Retrieved from: https://www.europarl.europa.eu/RegData/etudes/IDAN/2017/581948/EPRS_IDA(2017)581948_EN.pdf

Breitman, K. (2017). What's next for blockchain and cryptocurrency. *TechCrunch*. Retrieved from: https://techcrunch.com/2017/01/23/whats-next-for-blockchain-and-cryptocurrency/

Brownlow, J., Zaki, M., Neely, M., & Urmetzer, F. (2015). Data and analytics — Data-driven business models: A blueprint for innovation. Working Paper, Cambridge Service Alliance.

Brunswicker, S., & Chesbrough, H. (2018). The Adoption of Open Innovation in Large Firms: Practices, Measures, and risks: A survey of large firms examines how firms approach open innovation strategically and manage knowledge flows at the project level. *Research-Technology Management*, **61**(1), 35–45.

Brunswicker, S., & Vanhaverbeke, W. (2015). Open innovation in small and medium-sized enterprises (SMEs): External knowledge sourcing strategies and internal organizational facilitators. *Journal of Small Business Management*, **53**(4), 1241–1263. doi:10.1111/jsbm.12120

Chesbrough, H. (2003). *Open Innovation: The New Imperative for Creating and Profiting From Technology* (Harvard Business Press).

Crosby, M., Pattanayak, P., Verma, S., & Kalyanaraman, V. (2016). Blockchain technology: Beyond bitcoin. *Applied Innovation*, **2**, 6–10.

DaSilva, C. M., Trkman, P., Desouza, K., & Lindič, J. (2013). Disruptive technologies: A business model perspective on cloud computing. *Technology Analysis & Strategic Management*, **25**(10), 1161–1173. doi:10.1080/09537325.2013.843661

Del Vecchio, P., Di Minin, A., Petruzzelli, A., Panniello, U., & Pirri, S. (2018). Big data for open innovation in SMEs and large corporations: Trends, opportunities, and challenges. *Creativity and Innovation Management*, **27**(1), 6–22. doi:10.1111/caim.12224

Di Pietro, F., Prencipe, A., & Majchrzak, A. (2018). Crowd equity investors: An underutilized asset for open innovation in startups. *California Management Review*, **60**(2), 43–70. doi:10.1177/0008125617738260

Dion, D. A. (2013). I'll gladly trade you two bits on Tuesday for a byte today: Bitcoin, regulating fraud in the e-conomy of Hacker-cash. *Journal of Law, Technology & Policy University of Illinois*, **2013**, **Spring**(1), 165–202.

Eyal, I. (2017). Blockchain technology: Transforming libertarian cryptocurrency dreams to finance and banking realities. *Computer*, **50**(9), 38–49. doi:10.1109/MC.2017.3571042

Fitzgerald, M., Kruschwitz, N., Bonnet, D., & Welch, M. (2014). Embracing digital technology: A new strategic imperative. *MIT Sloan Management Review*, **55**(2), 1.

Flick, U. (2004). Triangulation in qualitative research. In *A Companion to Qualitative Research*, Flick, U., von Karoff, E., & Steinke, I. (eds.) (SAGE Publications, London), pp. 178–183.

Giesen, E., Berman, S., Bell, R., & Blitz, A. (2007). Three ways to successfully innovate your business model. *Strategy & Leadership*, **35**(6), 27–33. doi:10.1108/10878570710833732

Greco, M. (2015). Open innovation actions and innovation performance. *European Journal of Innovation Management*, 18(2), 150–171. doi:10.1108/ EJIM-07-2013-0074

Hanna, R., Rohm, A., & Crittenden, V. (2011). We're all connected: The power of the social media ecosystem. *Business Horizons*, 54(3), 265–273. doi: https://doi. org/10.1016/j.bushor.2011.01.007

Hevner, A., March, S., Park, J., & Ram, S. (2004). Design science in information systems research. *MIS Q.*, 28(1), 75–105.

Huang, F., Rice, J., & Martin, N. (2015). Does open innovation apply to China? Exploring the contingent role of external knowledge sources and internal absorptive capacity in Chinese large firms and SMEs. *Journal of Management & Organization*, 21(5), 594–613.

Kane, E. (2017). Is blockchain a general purpose technology? Available at SSRN 2932585.

Kannan, P. K., & Li, H. A. (2017). Digital marketing: A framework, review and research agenda. *International Journal of Research in Marketing*, 34(1), 22–45. doi: https://doi.org/10.1016/j.ijresmar.2016.11.006

Kitchenham, B., Brereton, O.P., Budgen, D., Turner, M., Bailey, J., & Linkman, S. (2009). Systematic literature reviews in software engineering — A systematic literature review. *Information and Software Technology*, 51(1), 7–15.

Lindgardt, Z., Reeves, M., Stalk, G., & Deimler, M. (2009). *Business Model Innovation. When the Game Gets Tough, Change the Game* (The Boston Consulting Group, Boston, MA).

Matt, C., Hess, T., & Benlian, A. (2015). Digital transformation strategies. *Business & Information Systems Engineering*, 57(5), 339–343.

Nguyen, Q. (2016). Blockchain — A Financial Technology for Future Sustainable Development. Paper presented at the *2016 3rd International Conference on Green Technology and Sustainable Development* (GTSD), 24–25 November.

Nowiński, W., & Kozma, M. (2017). How can blockchain technology disrupt the existing business models? *Entrepreneurial Business and Economics Review*, 5(3), 173–188.

Ong, B., Lee, T. M., Li, G., & Chuen, D. L. K. (2015). Evaluating the potential of alternative cryptocurrencies. In *Handbook of Digital Currency*. David Lee Kuo Chuen (ed.). (Academic Press, Cambridge, Massachusetts, United States), pp. 81–135.

Osterwalder, A., & Pigneur, Y. (2010). *Business Model Generation: A Handbook for Visionaries, Game Changers, and Challengers* (Wiley, New York).

Pihl, C., & Sandström, C. (2013). Value creation and appropriation in social media — The case of fashion bloggers in Sweden. *International Journal of Technology Management*, 61(3/4), 309. doi:10.1504/ijtm.2013.052673

Pilkington, M. (2016). Research handbook on digital transformations. In *Blockchain Technology: Principles and Applications*, Xavier Olleros, F., & Zhegu, M. (eds.) (Edward Elgar, Northampton, MA).

Robaczewska, J., Vanhaverbeke, W., & Lorenz, A. (2019). Applying open innovation strategies in the context of a regional innovation ecosystem: The case of Janssen Pharmaceuticals. *Global Transitions*, 1, 120–131. doi: https://doi.org/10.1016/j.glt.2019.05.001

Schallmo, D., & Brecht, L. (2010). Business model innovation in business-to-business markets–procedure and examples. Paper presented at the *Proceedings of the 3rd ISPIM Innovation Symposium: "Managing the Art of Innovation: Turning Concepts into Reality."*

Schroeder, R., & Halsall, J. (2016). Big data business models: Challenges and opportunities. *Cogent Social Sciences*, 2(1). doi:10.1080/23311886.2016.1166924

Segers, J. (2015). The interplay between new technology based firms, strategic alliances and open innovation, within a regional systems of innovation context. The case of the biotechnology cluster in Belgium. *Journal of Global Entrepreneurship Research*, 5(1), 16. doi:10.1186/s40497-015-0034-7

Spender, J.-C. (2017). Startups and open innovation: A review of the literature. *European Journal of Innovation Management*, 20(1), 4–30. doi:10.1108/EJIM-12-2015-0131

Sultan, N., & van de Bunt-Kokhuis, S. (2012). Organisational culture and cloud computing: Coping with a disruptive innovation. *Technology Analysis & Strategic Management*, 24(2), 167–179. doi:10.1080/09537325.2012.647644

Swan, M. (2015). *Blockchain: Blueprint for a new economy* (O'Reilly Media, Inc. Sebastopol, CA, USA).

Tapscott, D., & Kirkland, R. (2016). How blockchains could change the world. *McKinsey Q*, 3, 110–113. Available online at https://www.mckinsey.com/industries/technology-media-andtelecommunications/our-insights/how-blockchains-could-change-the-world (Accessed on 16 June 2021).

Teece, D. J. (2010). Business models, business strategy and innovation. *Long Range Planning*, 43(2), 172–194. doi: https://doi.org/10.1016/j.lrp.2009.07.003

Thurmond, V. A. (2001). The point of triangulation. *Journal of Nursing Scholarship*, 33(3), 253–258. doi:10.1111/j.1547-5069.2001.00253.x

Treleaven, P., Gendal Brown, R., & Yang, D. (2017). Blockchain technology in finance. *Computer*, 50(9), 14–17. doi:10.1109/MC.2017.3571047

Usman, M. (2017). How start-ups successfully organize and manage open innovation with large companies. *European Journal of Innovation Management*, 20(1), 171–186. doi:10.1108/EJIM-07-2016-0066

Valkokari, K., Seppänen, M., Mäntylä, M., & Jylhä-Ollila, S. (2017). Orchestrating innovation ecosystems: A qualitative analysis of ecosystem positioning strategies. *Technology Innovation Management Review*, 7(3), 12–24.

Webster, J., & Watson, R.T. (2002). Analyzing the past to prepare for the future: Writing a literature review. *MIS Quarterly*, pp. xiii–xxiii.

White, G. R. T. (2017). Future applications of blockchain in business and management: A Delphi study. *Strategic Change*, **26**(5), 439–451. doi:10.1002/jsc.2144

Yli-Huumo, J., Ko, D., Choi, S., Park, S., & Smolander, K. (2016). Where is current research on blockchain technology? A systematic review. *PLoS One*, **11**(10), e0163477. doi:10.1371/journal.pone.0163477

Yun, J., Won, D., & Park, K. (2016). Dynamics from open innovation to evolutionary change. *Journal of Open Innovation: Technology, Market, and Complexity*, **2**(2), 7.

Zeadally, S., & Abdo, J. B. (2019). Blockchain: Trends and future opportunities. *Internet Technology Letters*, **2**(6), e130. doi:10.1002/itl2.130

Zott, C., & Amit, R. (2009). The business model as the engine of network–based strategies. In *The Network Challenge-Strategy, Profit, and Risk in an Interlinked World*. Paul R. Kleindorfer, Yoram R. Wind & Robert E. Gunther (eds.) (Wharton School Publishing, Upper Saddle River, New Jersey), pp. 59–275.

Zott, C., Amit, R., & Massa, L. (2011). The business model: Recent developments and future research. *Journal of Management*, **37**(4), 1019–1042. doi:10. 1177/0149206311406265

Chapter 11

Who Invests in FinTech, Artificial Intelligence, and Blockchain? Evidence from the Wealth Management Industry

Percy Venegas

Economy Monitor, King's College London, King Business School,
London WC2B 4BG, UK

percy.venegas_obando@kcl.ac.uk

Abstract. An asset class can be considered truly mature until family offices are investing in it. Family offices are private wealth management advisory firms that serve ultra-high-net-worth investors. They are different from traditional wealth management shops in that they offer a total outsourced solution to manage the financial and investment side of an affluent individual or family. Having built their fortune with the purpose of wealth preservation across generations, families are notoriously risk-averse. This is, therefore, the perfect "canary in the mine" set up to understand if FinTech is a real category beyond simply speculative investments, and if its applications in artificial intelligence (AI) and blockchain have already crossed the boundary of trust among investors concerned with capital preservation. The book chapter begins by summarizing relevant statistics from private markets investment activity and then moves into using a predictive analytics (evolutionary cognitive algorithm) approach to describe the relevant patterns that are in process of formation. The coverage is global and the period of study spans over a decade, from January 1st, 2007 to November 5th, 2018.

Keywords. FinTech AI start-ups; FinTech AI companies; FinTech AI blockchain; AI-based FinTech; FinTech AI investment; family office FinTech; trustworthy AI.

1. Introduction

Authors have studied the relationship between innovation and FinTech (Salampasis and Mention, 2018) in the early stages of the vertical. However, an asset class can be considered truly mature until family offices are investing in it. Family offices are private wealth management advisory firms that serve ultra-high-net-worth investors. They are different from traditional wealth management shops in that they offer a total outsourced solution to managing the financial and investment side of an affluent individual or family. In addition, having built their fortune with the purpose of wealth preservation across generations, families are notoriously risk-averse. This is, therefore, the perfect "canary in the mine" set up to understand if FinTech is real, and its close applications in artificial intelligence (AI) and blockchain have already crossed the boundary of trust (Venegas, 2018a, 2018b) among investors concerned with capital preservation. In other words, an increasing and sustained level of investment by family offices and similar wealth managers provide the validation to affirm that FinTech is moving from the realm of open innovation alone to a consolidated asset class. This chapter begins by summarizing relevant statistics from private markets investment activity and then moves into using a predictive analytics approach to describe the relevant patterns and drivers in the process of formation of the asset class. The coverage is global and the period of study spans over a decade.

2. State of the Industry

We present the descriptive statistics that characterize the industry from the perspective of family office investors. First, we focus solely on the FinTech vertical (excluding deals not explicitly marked as AI, blockchain, and cryptocurrency investments), although some of the underlying technology used by FinTech start-ups is based on machine learning — a branch of AI. The overlaps with those other categories will be discussed toward the end of the chapter. The data is from Morningstar and Pitchbook and spans 12 years, from January 1, 2007 to November 5, 2018. This long period sheds light on when FinTech started: beyond the neobanks, chatbots, and banking Application Programming Interface (APIs) popular today, financial technology has been around for a while.

3. Companies

3.1. *Capital invested and deal count*

FinTech has come of age among family offices, which in 2018 invested over US$8.55 billion in the space. By November 5, 2018, the total number of deals had already matched that of 2017 — but the total capital invested was five times that of the previous year (Figure 1).

3.2. *Median pre-money valuation and deal count*

Expectations remain high, as shown by the pre-money valuations of the past three years — there has been little change in valuations and deal count when comparing 2015 (US$66.8 million, 60) and 2018 (US$70 million, 61) (Figure 2).

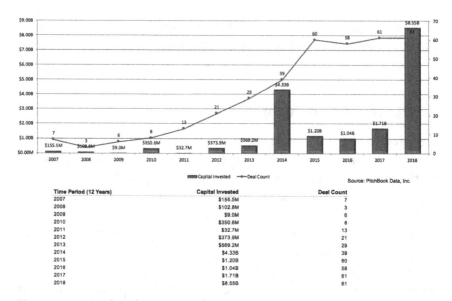

Figure 1. FinTech industry, capital invested, and deal count (by Family Office (FO)).

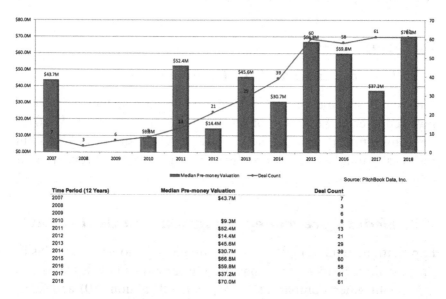

Figure 2. FinTech industry, median pre-money valuation, and deal count (by FO).

3.3. *Median post-money valuation and median deal size*

Post-money valuations are also up, except by an anomaly in 2008: a deal in the National Stock Exchange of India (which is categorized under the FinTech umbrella because of its approach to trading services, clearing and settlement services, market data feeds, technology solutions, and financial education offerings — perhaps the broader definition of what are FinTech companies). The company received development capital of US$100.3 million (INR4.8 billion) from Premji Invest on October 15, 2008. The investment represented a 3% stake in the company. According to the *Economic Times* (Talgeri and Chanchani, 2018), Premji Invest is the largest family office in India (Figure 3).

4. Funds

4.1. *Total capital raised and fund count*

In 2018, family office funds specializing in FinTech raised the most capital of the last 12 years. The largest fund, ICG Europe VII,

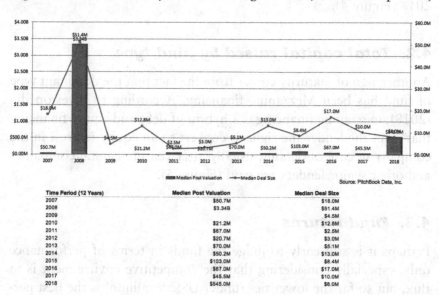

Time Period (12 Years)	Median Post Valuation	Median Deal Size
2007	$50.7M	$18.0M
2008	$3.34B	$51.4M
2009		$4.5M
2010	$21.2M	$12.8M
2011	$67.0M	$2.5M
2012	$20.7M	$3.0M
2013	$70.0M	$5.1M
2014	$50.2M	$13.0M
2015	$103.0M	$8.4M
2016	$67.0M	$17.0M
2017	$45.5M	$10.0M
2018	$545.0M	$8.0M

Figure 3. Fintech industry, median post-valuation, and median deal size (by FO).

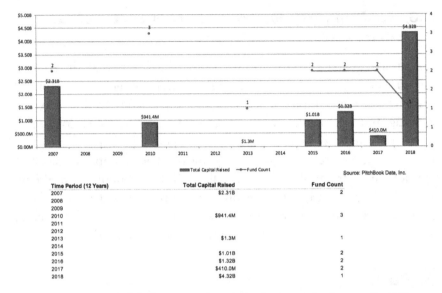

Time Period (12 Years)	Total Capital Raised	Fund Count
2007	$2.31B	2
2008		
2009		
2010	$941.4M	3
2011		
2012		
2013	$1.3M	1
2014		
2015	$1.01B	2
2016	$1.32B	2
2017	$410.0M	2
2018	$4.32B	1

Figure 4.   FinTech industry, total capital raised, and fund count (by FO).

amassed a dry powder of US$4,324.75 million and closed in July 2018 (Figure 4).

4.2. *Total capital raised by fund type*

Another sign of maturity comes from the fact that the dominant type of fund has been Mezzanine financing. According to Investopedia (2018), mezzanine financing is a hybrid of debt and equity financing that gives the lender the right to convert to an equity interest in the company in case of default, usually after venture capital companies and other senior lenders are paid (Figure 5).

4.3. *Fund returns*

Perhaps it is still early to judge the funds in terms of performance only, especially considering that the competitive environment is in flux, but so far the lower tier (under US$99 million) is the best performing (Figure 6).

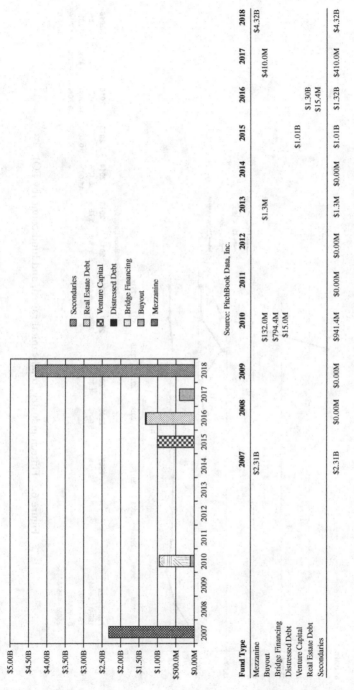

Source: PitchBook Data, Inc.

Fund Type	2007	2008	2009	2010	2011	2012	2013	2014	2015	2016	2017	2018
Mezzanine	$2.31B											
Buyout				$132.0M			$1.3M				$410.0M	$4.32B
Bridge Financing				$794.4M								
Distressed Debt				$15.0M								
Venture Capital									$1.01B			
Real Estate Debt										$1.30B		
Secondaries										$15.4M		
	$2.31B	$0.00M	$0.00M	$941.4M	$0.00M	$0.00M	$1.3M	$0.00M	$1.01B	$1.32B	$410.0M	$4.32B

Figure 5. Fintech industry, total capital raised by fund type (by FO).

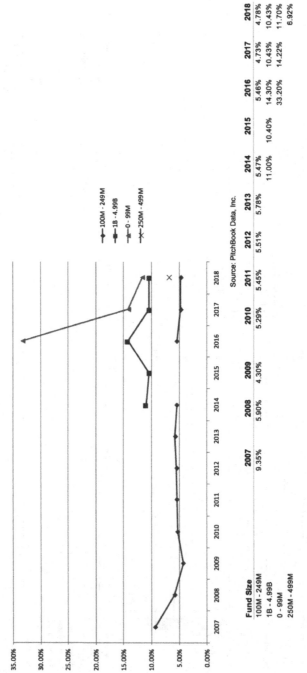

Figure 6.   Fintech industry, total capital raised, and fund count (by FO).

5. Predictive Models

It might be still early to be able to generate robust predictive models, but some general patterns emerge that describe investor behavior. We use a symbolic regression approach (Evolved Analytics LLC, 2018) and Mathematica (Wolfram Research, 2018) to create the models. The details of the model setup are included in the Appendix section of the chapter.

5.1. *Last investment size*

5.1.1. *Drivers*

When predicting the last investment size, we find the strongest driver to be the investment of the past five years. This shows that family offices tend to gradually build expertise in FinTech before making larger commitments in the vertical (Figure 7).

However, "total active portfolio" is also a strong driver: it appears 34 times in 8.5% of the models (Table 1).

One of the benefits of the symbolic regression method is that it allows to generate a multitude of models with different error/complexity profiles. The optimal models present the best combination of lowest error at a given level of complexity, or of the lowest complexity at a level error. Complexity is usually a good measure of the difficulty of computation, an important consideration if the algorithm has to be deployed at an industrial scale (Figure 8).

In Table 2, we see the family of models that likely explain the "last investment size" in family office investments into FinTech. We see that, generally, it is a function of the number of active portfolio investments, the number of investments in the last five years, the likelihood that the fund is currently fundraising, and the total investment in the last five years.

Those variables have high prevalence across models, as we can see in the variable presence map (Figure 9).

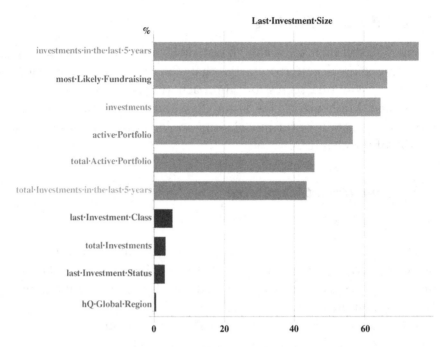

Figure 7.   Variable presence chart.

Table 1.   Model basis set table.

last•Investment•Size

Rank	Count	ModelBasisSet	% of models	% of ModelBasisSets
1	37	investments•in•the•last•5•years	9.2	11.8
2	34	total•Active•Portfolio	8.5	10.8
3	27	investments	6.7	8.6
4	19	active•Portfolio	4.7	6.1
5	17	total•Investments•in•the•last•5•years	4.2	5.4
6	16	active•Portfolio^2 most•Likely•Fundraising total•Investments•in•the•last•5•years	4.0	5.1
7	16	investments^4	4.0	5.1
8	15	active•Portfolio$^2 \sqrt{\text{most•Likely•Fundraising}}$ total•Investments•in•the•last•5•years	3.7	4.8
9	15	most•Likely•Fundraising	3.7	4.8

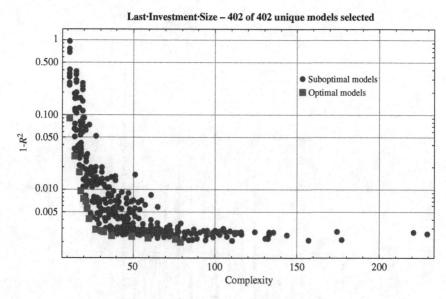

Figure 8. Pareto front context log plot.

5.1.2. *Deal size*

We would like to understand the determinants of the deal size as well. The dataset contains 423 deals and 109 variables. We being by studying the linear correlation among variables.

5.1.3. *Correlation*

We find that most variables are somewhat correlated with deal size, particularly Implied EV/EBITDA, Debt Raised in Round/EBITDA, Debt Raised in a Round, and Total Invested Equity. Strongly uncorrelated variables include Implied EV/Net Income and Debt Raised in Round/Equity (Figure 10).

It is important to note that not always family offices go in alone, they sometimes have co-investors in the deals. This is positive because it provides insight into how FinTech is shaping financial services: institutional investors that are co-investors in these deals

Table 2.   Model selection report.

	Complexity	1−R^2	Function last*Investment*Size
1	11	0.091	$-71.01 + 24.34$ total*Active*Portfolio
2	14	0.028	$16.79 + 0.83$ investments total*Active*Portfolio
3	17	0.018	$20.68 + (3.65 \times 10^{-2})$ investments investment*in*the*last*5*years total*Active*Portfolio
4	18	0.010	$12.57 + (2.16 \times 10^{-3})$ investments*in*the*last*5*years^3 total*Active*Portfolio
5	20	0.008	$8.82 + (2.03 \times 10^{-3})$ active*Portfolio investments investments*in*the*last*5*years^3 total*Investment*in*the*last*5*years
6	21	0.007	$19.00 + (2.16 \times 10^{-3})$ investments*in*the*last*5*years^3 most*Likely*Fundraising total*Active*Portfolio
7	22	0.006	$16.39 + (9.49 \times 10^{-5})$ investments*in*the*last*5*years^4 total*Active*Portfolio
8	23	0.004	$16.54 + (2.03 \times 10^{-3})$ active*Portfolio investments investments*in*the*last*5*years most*Likely*Fundraising total*Investment*in*the*last*5*years
9	27	0.003	$18.82 + (8.91 \times 10^{-5})$ active*Portfolio investments investment*in*the*last*5*years^2 most*Likely*Fundraising total*Investment*in*the*last*5*years
10	31	0.003	$19.76 - (2.44 \times 10^{-3})$ active*Portfolio (5 − investments) investments*in*the*last*5*years investment*in*the*last*5*years total*Investment*in*the*last*5*years
11	32	0.003	$39.39 - 12.04$ active*Portfolio $+ (9.58 \times 10^{-5})$ active*Portfolio investments investment*in*the*last*5*years^2 total*Investment*in*the*last*5*years
12	37	0.002	$25.80 - 14.78$ active*Portfolio $+ 11.36$ investment*in*the*last*5*years $+ (7.33 \times 10^{-2})$ active*Portfolio^2 most*Likely*Fundraising total*Investment*in*the*last*5*years
13	49	0.002	$32.58 - 22.16$ last*Investment*Class $+ \dfrac{0.10\ \text{most*Likely*Fundraising} \left(-\text{investments}^2\ \text{total*Active*Portfolio}\right)}{\text{investments*in*the*last*5*years}}$
14	59	0.002	$32.43 - 19.60$ last*Investment*Class $- \dfrac{0.13\ \text{most*Likely*Fundraising} \left(-\text{investments}^2\ \text{total*Active*Portfolio}\right)}{-6.51\ \text{investments*in*the*last*5*years}}$
15	76	0.002	$17.36 + (1.42 \times 10^{-3})$ investments*in*the*last*5*years^2 $(-4 + 0.43$ investments*in*the*last*5*years$)^2$ most*Likely*Fundraising $(6.91 +$ last*Investment*Class $- 2$ most*Likely*Fundraising $+$ total*Active*Portfolio$)$
16	79	0.002	$32.67 - 18.49$ last*Investment*Class $+ (1.42 \times 10^{-3})$ investments*in*the*last*5*years^2 $(-4 + 0.43$ investments*in*the*last*5*years$)^2$ most*Likely*Fundraising $(5.61 +$ last*Investment*Class $-$ most*Likely*Fundraising $+$ total*Active*Portfolio$)$

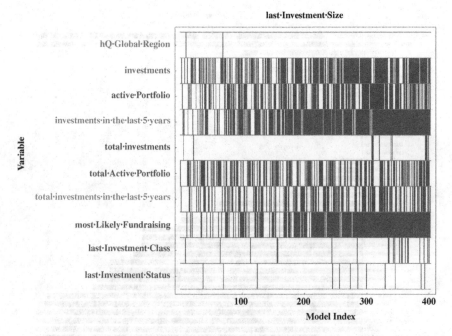

Figure 9. Variable presence map.

usually maintain interests in financial services and financial infra-structure at large, and probably this alignment of objectives is one of the reasons why FinTech is changing the face of banking. However, to avoid pathologies in the model development, we do not include the outliers (deals for the amount of US$3,500 million, $1,752.81 million, $1,557.62 million, $1,398.20 million), in which the family offices participated as co-investors (Figure 11).

5.1.4. *Model diversity*

We created an ensemble of 23 diverse models. A representative model is shown in Figure 12. Specifically, we investigate the relation-ship between deal size and business status (Generating Revenue, Profitable, and so on), amount raised to date, number of deals, and

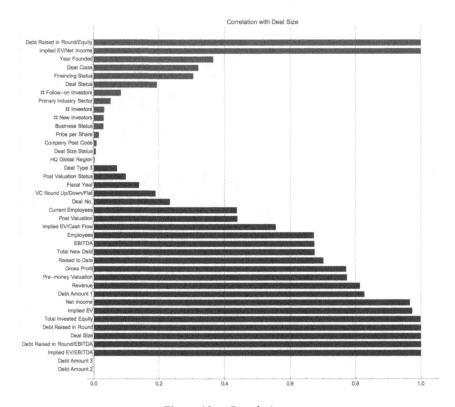

Figure 10.   Correlations.

Figure 11.   Data distribution plot.

total invested equity. Although the model tends to underpredict for large deal sizes, it provides a good summary of the main drivers. Interestingly, neither fundamentals such as the number of employees, investors, or new investors nor other financials such as Post Valuation, Post Valuation Status, % Acquired, or Raised to Date, appear to have a major impact on deal size.

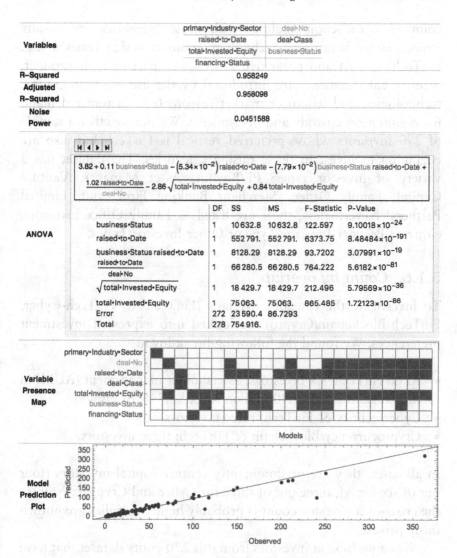

Variables	primary·Industry·Sector	deal·No
	raised·to·Date	deal·Class
	total·Invested·Equity	business·Status
	financing·Status	
R–Squared	0.958249	
Adjusted R–Squared	0.958098	
Noise Power	0.0451588	

$$3.82 + 0.11 \, \text{business·Status} - \left(5.34 \times 10^{-2}\right) \text{raised·to·Date} - \left(7.79 \times 10^{-2}\right) \text{business·Status raised·to·Date} +$$

$$\frac{1.02 \, \text{raised·to·Date}}{\text{deal·No}} - 2.86 \sqrt{\text{total·Invested·Equity}} + 0.84 \, \text{total·Invested·Equity}$$

ANOVA

	DF	SS	MS	F-Statistic	P-Value
business·Status	1	10 632.8	10 632.8	122.597	9.10018×10^{-24}
raised·to·Date	1	552 791.	552 791.	6373.75	8.48484×10^{-191}
business·Status raised·to·Date	1	8128.29	8128.29	93.7202	3.07991×10^{-19}
$\frac{\text{raised·to·Date}}{\text{deal·No}}$	1	66 280.5	66 280.5	764.222	5.6182×10^{-81}
$\sqrt{\text{total·Invested·Equity}}$	1	18 429.7	18 429.7	212.496	5.79569×10^{-36}
total·Invested·Equity	1	75 063.	75 063.	865.485	1.72123×10^{-86}
Error	272	23 590.4	86.7293		
Total	278	754 916.			

Variable Presence Map

primary·Industry·Sector
deal·No
raised·to·Date
deal·Class
total·Invested·Equity
business·Status
financing·Status

Models

Model Prediction Plot

Predicted

Observed

Figure 12. Deal size model.

5.1.5. *Cross-investments*

Finally, we studied the emerging categories of AI, cyber risk, crypto-currency, and blockchain. When one thinks about FinTech companies, the commonalities with those categories are usually strong, either because of technology solution design reasons (e.g. FinTechs use AI and predictive analytics as part of their product, security enhancements are introduced by the use of cryptographic technologies, and so on) or market reasons (e.g. customer demand for digital asset custody and investment). We put together a sample of 270 investors whose preferred vertical is FinTech but also are beginning to invest in those raising categories. The dataset has a variety of investor types: PE/Buyout, Asset Manager, Venture Capital, Family Office, Merchant Banking Firm, and, Limited Partners. Nevertheless, these are listed as Family Office investors, either as Primary Investor Type or Other Investor Types.

5.1.6. *Count by overlap*

To investigate the category overlaps (FinTech-AI, FinTech-Cyber, FinTech-Blockchain/Crypto) we looked into expressed investment preferences. We found the following breakdown:

- AI & FinTech: six investors, assets under management (AUM) in the range of US$149.40 million to US$3,748.70 million.
- Cybersecurity & FinTech: three investors.
- Cryptocurrency/Blockchain & FinTech: three investors.

In all cases, they are predominantly venture capital investors (four out of six for AI, three out of three for Cyber and Crypto). Even so, the cross-over investor count is probably higher: families are notoriously private.

When we look at investors from this 270-entity dataset that have invested in FinTech (regardless of whether they also invested in the other categories or not), an interesting picture emerges. The values of the active portfolio investments by country headquarters are 7–8 for Switzerland, 3–5 for the US, 3 for Canada and Ireland, and 1–2 for Brazil, Germany, Monaco, Norway, and, Singapore. Since 2010, the total investments by headquarters global region shows 289 investments in the Americas and 305 in Europe (Asia is just starting to pick up activity more recently). This answers the question of where FinTech companies are located, and where is FinTech innovation is happening: the phenomenon is truly global.

The values of total investments for each year (last closed fund close date) shows an increasing trend: US$220 million in 2016, US$454 million in 2017, US$811 million in 2018, and US$4663 million in 2019. The breakdown of other investment preferences is: Prefers minority stake, will syndicate (15); Prefers majority stake (6); Long-term investor (2); Seeks Environment, Social, Governance (ESG) investments (2). The minimum preferred investment amount is US$0.05M. At least 71 family offices had an exit, another indication of growing maturity.

5.1.7. *Idiosyncratic factors*

When looking at the relationship between total active portfolio and the number of funds closed in the last two years by numbers of investment professionals, we find an interesting data point: 118 investment professionals overseeing a total 49 active investments (with two and three funds closed in the last two and five years, respectively); this speaks for the high concentration of expertise in the industry, very few professionals in the whole of the financial industry possess the practical knowledge to work on these types of deals (Figure 13).

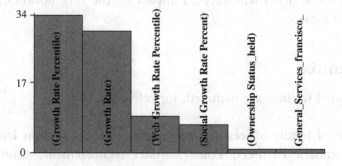

Figure 13. Number of models each variable appears in.

Moreover, in the case of these FinTech companies, there is a material relationship between growth and visibility. Performing model development again using symbolic regression, we find that variables such as web and social presence are predictors of the growth percentile that a company has achieved. Interestingly, the effect of particular investment professionals shows up again in the modeling, which is a sign of how important it is (there are only a handful of persistent variables in the model). This is remarkable considering that the model search begins with dozens of variables (as shown in the Appendix section (Table A1) of this chapter).

6. Conclusions

We found that FinTech is reaching a new point of maturity as an investment vertical, as demonstrated by the shifting preferences of risk-averse investors (family offices) that are increasingly allocating capital into those companies. However, not only financial and fundamental factors play a role: soft factors from social and web growth to the money managers behind the deals have predictive power to assess revenue growth. The final point to be noted is the emergence of convergence: slowly but surely, the entanglement of adjacent categories, such as AI, cybersecurity, cryptocurrencies, and blockchain, is manifested by money flows from investors that have built expertise in FinTech over the past few years. In the long run, those cross- and co-investments will have an impact on the very notion of what FinTech means.

Appendix

The model settings are included, for reference.

The list of family offices and multi-family offices with at least one exit: Graham Partners, Point72 Asset Management, Cambridge Information Group, The Stephens Group, MSD Capital, G. Scott Capital Partners, Cincinnatus Partners, Ziff Brothers Investments,

Table A1.   Model settings, last investment size.

Control	Count $\Rightarrow$ Settings
	last·Investment·Size
Searches	**4 Independent Evolutions Contribute 402 models**

Model Age (distribution plot, x-axis 0 to 60)

Control	Count $\Rightarrow$ Settings
TimeConstraint	402 $\Rightarrow$ 180
FunctionPatterns	402 $\Rightarrow$ $\{$Plus, Times, Divide, Subtract, x^2, $\sqrt{x}$, $\frac{1}{x}$, Minus$\}$
MetaVariables	402 $\Rightarrow$ None
CategoryThreshold	402 $\Rightarrow$ {3, 0.95}
ConvertedForms	402 $\Rightarrow$ All
BinaryFormat	402 $\Rightarrow$ PlusMinus
ResponseMapping	402 $\Rightarrow$ {}
InputMapping	402 $\Rightarrow$ {{24, Categorical, {Americas → −1, Asia → 0, Europe → 1}}, {25, Categorical, {North America → −1, Southeast Asia → 0, Western Europe → 1}}, {32, Categorical, {Actively Seeking New Investments → −1, Not Making New Investments → 0, Out of Business → 1}}, {33, Categorical, {Affiliated Managers Group → −1, Citigroup → 0, HSH Nordbank → 1}}, {44, Categorical, {}}, {48, Categorical, {}}, {49, Categorical, {}}, {58, Categorical, {No → 0, Yes → 1}}, {66, Categorical, {}}, {82, Categorical, {2.00 − 10.00 → 0, 5.00 − 30.00 → 1}}, {83, Categorical, {}}, {84, Categorical, {}}, {91, Categorical, {}}, {97, Categorical, {Actual → 0, Estimated → 1}}, {100, Categorical, {Add-on → 0, Corporate Divestiture → 1}}, {101, Categorical, {Corporate → −1, Private Equity → 0, Venture Capital → 1}}, {102, Categorical, {Loan → 0, Revolving Credit Line → 1}}, {105, Categorical, {Announced/In Progress → 0, Completed → 1}}, {111, Categorical, {01–Jun–2016 → 0, 20–Nov–2015 → 1}}}
OptimizeLinearModel	402 $\Rightarrow$ False
RobustModels	402 $\Rightarrow$ False
BasisSetLimit	199 $\Rightarrow$ 10
	104 $\Rightarrow$ 3
	99 $\Rightarrow$ 6
RescaleData	402 $\Rightarrow$ None
NumberOfVariables	402 $\Rightarrow$ 14
PowerLimit	402 $\Rightarrow$ 4
TemplateTopLevel	402 $\Rightarrow$ Automatic
AllowedVariables	402 $\Rightarrow$ {active·Portfolio, aUM, dry·Powder, exits, hQ·Global·Region, hQ·Global·Sub·Region, hQ·Post·Code, investments, investments·in·the·last·12·months, investments·in·the·last·2·years, investments·in·the·last·5·years, investments·in·the·last·6·months, investor·Status, last·Closed·Fund·Open·Date, last·Closed·Fund·Size, last·Closed·Fund·Vintage, last·Investment·Class, last·Investment·Debt·Type, last·Investment·Size, last·Investment·Status, last·Investment·Type·3, last·Investment·Valuation, last·Investment·Valuation·Status, max·Fund·Size, median·Fund·Size, min·Fund·Size, most·Likely·Fundraising, parent·Company, preferred·EBITDA, preferred·EBITDA·Max, preferred·EBITDA·Min, preferred·Investment·Amount·Max, preferred·Investment·Amount·Min, total·Active·Portfolio, total·Exits, total·Funds·Closed, total·Funds·Closed·in·the·last·2·years, total·Funds·Closed·in·the·last·5·years, total·Funds·Open, total·Investments, total·Investments·in·the·last·12·months, total·Investments·in·the·last·2·years, total·Investments·in·the·last·5·years, total·Investments·in·the·last·6·months, year·Founded, ·Funds·Closed, ·Funds·Closed·in·the·last·2·years, ·Funds·Closed·in·the·last·5·years, ·Funds·Open, ·of·Investment·Professionals}
ExcludedVariables	402 $\Rightarrow$ Complement
ModelingObjective	402 $\Rightarrow$ $\{$ModelComplexity[‡1], 1 − AbsCorrelation[‡2, ‡3]$^2\}$ &
ModelingObjectiveNames	402 $\Rightarrow$ $\{$Complexity, 1−$R^2\}$
CreateBasisSetModel	402 $\Rightarrow$ False
ActiveGenomeSimplification	402 $\Rightarrow$ False
AlignModel	402 $\Rightarrow$ OptimizeLinearModel
NumericInputRequirement	402 $\Rightarrow$ 0.75
NumericPredictionRequirement	402 $\Rightarrow$ 1.
ProjectName	402 $\Rightarrow$ investors
RoundName	402 $\Rightarrow$ Round1
TargetColumn	402 $\Rightarrow$ 94
TargetLabel	402 $\Rightarrow$ last·Investment·Size

Viburnum Funds, Hunt Capital Group, Palisade Capital Management, Banque Pictet & Cie, Everwatch, Hamilton Investment Partners, Mousse Partners, Fremont Group, Souter Investments, Stephens Investment Management, Black Coral Capital, Calibrium (Pfäffikon), Ping Identity, Green Brook Capital Management, King Capital Partners, Kestrel Investments, Palm Ventures, BHS Verwaltungs, Sands Brothers Asset Management, China Asset Management (Hong Kong), Baron Capital Management, Loring Wolcott & Coolidge Office, U.S. Trust, Bank of America Private Wealth Management, Cascade Investment, Dolby Family Ventures, ESAS Holding, Zen Investments, Arbor Ventures (London), Hill Creek Holdings, SKion, B Cinque, De Hoge Dennen Capital, RLB Holdings, Nedvest, FFP Group (PAR: FFP), Samson Investment Partners, Jado Investments, Aqton, Zimmermann Investment, Wicklow Capital, Crown Predator Holdings, Pontos Group, New Sparta, Premanco Ventures, Orfin Ventures, Clarke Capital Partners, Gullspång Invest, Dasym, LSG Holdings, Keeler Investments Group, Nima Capital, Lepercq, de Neuflize & Co., Wasson Enterprise, Acacia Asset Management, GFO Companies, Wu Capital, Perscitus, Curran Companies, Burtzloff Family Trust, La Tourelle Capital, Ott Properties, Prometheus Capital (Shanghai), 3G Capital Investments.

A partial list of features describing FinTech companies where family offices invested in: Company Name, Company Former Name, Company Also Known As, Primary Industry Sector, Primary Industry Group, Primary Industry Code, All Industries Verticals, Keywords, Company Financing Status, Total Raised, Business Status, Ownership Status, Universe, Employees, Exchange Ticker, Year Founded, Parent Company, Daily Updates, Weekly Updates, Revenue, Gross Profit, Net Income, Enterprise Value, EBITDA, Fiscal Period, Primary Contact Title, HQ Location, HQ City, HQ State/Province, HQ Country, HQ Global Region, HQ Global Sub Region, Financing Status, # Active Investors, Acquirers, Former Investors, Other Investors, General Services, Services on a Deal, First Financing Date, First Financing Size, First Financing Size, Status First Financing, Valuation First Financing, Valuation Status, First

Financing Deal Type, First Financing Deal Type 2, First Financing Deal Type 3, First Financing Deal Class, First Financing Debt Type, First Financing Debt Type 2, First Financing Debt Type 3, First Financing Status, Last Financing Date, Last Financing Size, Last Financing Size Status, Last Financing Valuation, Last Financing Valuation Status, Last Financing Deal Type, Last Financing Deal Type 2, Last Financing Deal Type 3, Last Financing Deal Class, Last Financing Debt Type, Last Financing Debt Type 2, Last Financing Debt Type 3, Last Financing Status Growth Rate, Growth Rate Percentile, Growth Rate Change, Growth Rate %, Change Web Growth Rate, Web Growth Rate Percentile, Social Growth Rate, Social Growth Rate Percentile, Twitter Growth Rate, Twitter Growth Rate Percentile, Size Multiple, Size Multiple Percentile, Size Multiple Change, Size Multiple %, Change Web Size Multiple, Web Size Multiple Percentile, Social Size Multiple, Social Size Multiple Percentile, Twitter Size Multiple, Twitter Size Multiple Percentile, Change Twitter Followers, Twitter Followers, Change Twitter Followers % , Last Known Valuation, Last Known Valuation Date, Last Known Valuation Deal Type, Facebook Likes, Change Facebook Likes, % Change Facebook Growth Rate, Facebook Growth Rate, Percentile Facebook Size Multiple, Facebook Size Multiple, Percentile Facebook Likes.

Acknowledgments

We thank the Opal Group for its hospitality at the Newport Family Office & Private Wealth Management Forum in July 2018. The exchanges and input from professional money managers and families greatly contributed to refining the scope of this research.

References

Evolved Analytics LLC. (2018). "DataModeler," Version 9.3. Midland, MI, USA.

Family Offices. Retrieved from: https://www.investopedia.com/terms/f/family-offices.asp. (Accessed on 1 October 2018).

Mezzanine Financing. Retrieved from: https://www.investopedia.com/terms/m/mezzaninefinancing.asp. (Accessed 1 October 2018).

Salampasis, D., & Anne-Laure, Mention (2018). FinTech: Harnessing innovation for financial inclusion. In *Handbook of Blockchain Digital Finance, and Inclusion,* Volume 2 (Elsevier), pp. 451–461. Retrieved from: https://doi.org/10.1016/b978-0-12-812282-2.00018-8

Talgeri, K. & Chanchani, M. (2018). How Premji Invest became the top investment co from a quiet family office. *The Economic Times* (January 18th 2018). Available online at: https://economictimes.indiatimes.com/industry/banking/finance/how-premjiinvest-became-the-top-investment-co-from-a-quiet-family-office/articleshow/62500500.cms (Accessed on 7 July 2021).

Venegas, P. (2018a). Asymmetric trust and causal reasoning in blockchain-based AIs. Morales, A. (ed.), New England Complex Systems Institute Cambridge, USA, July (STEM Academic Press and Authorea Inc). IX International Conference on Complex Systems, STEM Academic Press (online), pp. 44–55. Retrieved from: https://doi.org/10.22541/au.152770370.07988377

Venegas, P. (2018b). Trust asymmetry. In *Unifying Themes in Complex Systems IX* (Springer International Publishing), pp. 467–475. Retrieved from: https://doi.org/10.1007/978-3-319-96661-8_48

Wolfram Research, Inc. (2018). "Mathematica," Version 11.3. Champaign Illinois.

Chapter 12

FinTech Firms and the Exploration and Exploitation of Financial Landscapes

Tamer Khraisha[*]

Budapest 1051, Hungary
tamer.khraisha@gmail.com

Abstract. A problem is said to be complex if it comprises many parts or dimensions with various interactions. In such a case, it is reasonable to assume that the problem admits a multidimensional solution space, which comprises all candidate solutions. Different solutions can have different goodness score, which can be called *fitness*. Innovators and problem solvers interested in solving a complex problem are assumed to be located somewhere in the solution landscape. Ideally, a searching agent would be interested in finding the solution with the highest fitness possible, and in doing so, employing a *search heuristic*. Financial problems such as investment, payment, risk management, and fraud detection are all examples of complex problems that have complex landscapes of solutions. In searching for solutions to financial problems, firms often engage in financial innovation. A particular type of financial innovation

---

[*] Author has contributed to this edited volume in his individual capacity.

is developed by FinTech start-ups, which introduce innovations in the backend and customer-face financial services. FinTech firms are thought to follow a unique approach to change characterized by agility and unconstrained search for new solutions. So far, little has been done to understand the nature of the search behavior of FinTech firms; this, therefore, is still an open gap in the literature that requires further investigation. In this theoretical chapter, I first propose to use the theory of fitness landscapes to model the solution space of financial problems, and second, I adopt an open innovation perspective to model the search heuristics of FinTech firms who look for solutions in such landscapes.

Keywords. Fitness landscape; open innovation; complexity; search heuristic; exploration and exploitation; local optima; platform economics; experiential vs cognitive search; FinTech.

1. Introduction

Following the financial crisis of 2008, a new wave of financial innovations, known as FinTech, has been transforming and disrupting the financial industry landscape (Philippon, 2016, Gomber *et al.*, 2018). FinTech firms emerging after the 2008 crisis have attracted attention due to their original and disruptive approach to innovation (Anagnostopoulos, 2018). More specifically, the FinTech approach is mainly characterized by two aspects. First is the agility and flexibility in exploring alternative and non-conventional solutions to financial problems This has been enabled thanks to the employment of the latest software and computing technologies and data mining techniques in solving financial problems. Traditional and well-established financial institutions might lack this flexibility due to factors such as organizational inertia, security concerns, and regulatory constraints. Second, instead of engaging in a competition war, several FinTech companies and traditional financial institutions have adopted an open innovation approach by engaging in mutual collaborations, where big banks act as a platform through which FinTech firms can explore and test new solutions and interact with the final clients (Hornuf *et al.*, 2020; Hendrikse *et al.*, 2018; Mohan,

2016). Given the agile and collaborative approach of FinTech inno-vations, an important question might arise as to how the actual process of innovation by FinTech firms is being conducted. Despite the increasing interest in the phenomenon of FinTech, there is insuf-ficient literature explaining the nature and dynamics of FinTech innovations. This chapter is a contribution in this direction, where I suggest using the theory of fitness landscapes as a tool to model the innovation process of FinTech firms within an open innovation paradigm. The open innovation aspect of FinTech innovation is mainly justified by the notable collaborations between the FinTech firms and the traditional financial system. This chapter does not intend to discuss how to classify FinTech innovations and will sim-ply assume that FinTech firms aim at developing new and better solutions for *existing* rather than *new* problems (Arner *et al.*, 2016). For a more detailed discussion of how to classify FinTech innova-tions, see Gomber *et al.* (2018).

Explaining the development process of FinTech innovations would involve understanding their emergence, diffusion, and evolu-tion. As claimed in Khraisha and Arthur (2018), financial innova-tions emerge, diffuse, and evolve for factors that are often specific to the problem at hand. These driving factors can be institutional, economic, technological, and/or historical. Different innovations in the financial sector are likely to have their unique combination of stimulating factors that lead to their development. Therefore, a good theory of innovation development would ideally identify the particu-lar economic, institutional, and evolutionary factors behind innova-tions (Khraisha and Arthur, 2018).

The existing literature on FinTech has primarily focused on explaining the problem of emergence (Cojoianu *et al.*, 2020; Haddad and Hornuf, 2019; Buchak *et al.*, 2018; Arner *et al.*, 2016). In this regard, a common justification for the emergence of FinTech states that, following the crisis of 2008, the traditional banking system has shifted focus from innovation to compliance and regulatory conformity, leaving an innovation gap that has been exploited by FinTech firms (Buchak *et al.*, 2018). Another point of view seeks to explain FinTech innovations as the result of economic factors. This last claim is often justified by referring to the success of financial innovations in several underdeveloped countries in Africa and Asia. In many of these countries, FinTech solutions are developed due to the lack of well-established financial institutions, weak financial inclusion, and the increasing demand for financial services (Arner *et al.*, 2016). Another economic factor that explains the emergence of FinTechs is the availability of venture capital and high levels of IT investments in the financial sector (Haddad and Hornuf, 2019; Gombet *et al.*, 2018). Last but not least, from a technological point of view, given the data-driven aspect of FinTech firms, factors such as advances in information technology, the increasing availability of data from old and new sources, and progress in data analytics techniques have all been considered as drivers of FinTech innovations (Cojoianu *et al.*, 2020; Goldstein *et al.*, 2019).

Besides the problem of emergence, little attention has been devoted to understanding the actual FinTech innovation process itself. Generally speaking, the financial industry is not known for having traditional R&D departments and, therefore, the task of theorizing and understanding the innovation process in financial firms might be non-trivial and remains an essential gap in the literature. In order to make progress along this gap, the present chapter introduces a theoretical framework to explain the process of FinTech innovation as a search process that happens on what I would call the fitness landscape of financial problems. The fitness landscape is a concept borrowed from evolutionary biology that is often used to model solution spaces and optimal/adaptive search behavior (Khraisha, 2019). Each financial problem is assumed to have its fitness landscape. A solution in the fitness landscape has a measure of goodness assigned to it, which I shall call *fitness*. The better is a solution, the higher its fitness. In the presence of fitness landscapes, agents might choose from a variety of search strategies to explore solutions in search for (the) optimal one (Lopez-Vega *et al.*, 2016). Very often, it is assumed that searching agents are faced with a trade-off between *exploration*, which involves choosing and trying solutions that are far apart from each other in the landscape, and *exploitation*, which refers to making small and incremental steps without long jumps (March, 1991).

The rest of the chapter proceeds as follows: Section 2 presents the concept of complex problems, their fitness landscapes, and the nature of search heuristics. Section 3 offers a discussion of how the concept of fitness landscapes and search heuristics might be used to model the innovation behavior of FinTech firms. Finally, Section 4 provides a short conclusion with some recommendations for theoretical and empirical extensions.

2. Innovation as a Complex Problem

2.1. *What is a complex problem?*

A problem is said to be complex if it is composed of interconnected components or dimensions. For example, constructing a jet fighter might present the innovator with complementary dimensions such as speed, weight, maneuverability, firing power, and armor. Dimensions are complementary in that improvement along one dimension might lead to a lower performance in another. For instance, increasing the firing power of the jet fighter might reduce its speed. If dimensions were independent, then the optimal solution to the jet fighter problem would be to optimize each one independently (e.g. make it as fast as possible, as heavy as possible, and so on). Since complementarity characterizes most complex problems, this implies that there are many possible combinations of candidate solutions, which if listed would constitute a solution space whose dimensionality is equal to the dimensionality of the problem. If we can assign a measure of goodness or fitness to each one of the candidate solutions, then we arrive at what is often called *Fitness Landscape* of a problem. Figure 1 shows an illustrative example of a one-dimensional fitness landscape. Moving in the landscape (along the x-axis in Figure 1), several solutions with different fitness values can be encountered.[1]

---

[1]The use of one-dimensional landscapes is intended for illustrative purpose. Most problems are likely to have more than one dimension.

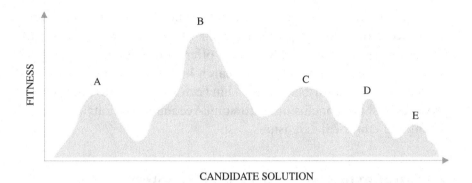

Figure 1. One-dimensional fitness landscape. Point B is a global optimum, while points A, C, D, and E are local optima. The figure is constructed by the author and was inspired by a chart produced by Claus Wilke in 2001 for Nupedia.

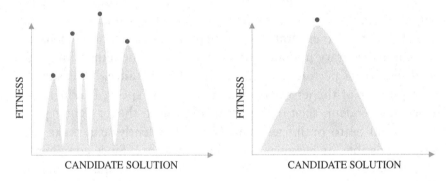

Figure 2. Rugged landscape with several local optima (left), and a smooth landscape with one local (or global) optimum.

A solution in the fitness landscape of a problem is said to be a *local optimum* if its fitness value is higher than the fitness of all solutions in its local neighborhood. In Figure 1, points A, B, C, D, and E are local optima: being at any of these points, a move to the left or right will always result in solutions with lower fitness. A solution is said to be a *global optimum* if its fitness value is higher than the fitness of all other solutions in the landscape. In Figure 1, point B can be treated as a global optimum.

Fitness landscapes characterized by a high number of local optima are called *rugged* landscape, while landscapes with one or a small number of local optima are called *smooth*.[2] Figure 2 illustrates this concept. The more rugged a fitness landscape is, the more complex is the problem being modeled and the more challenging is the search for the optimal solution. If a problem admits a smooth fitness landscape like in Figure 2 (right), then starting from any point in the landscape, an agent can simply choose the direction going uphill and reach the local optimum. This is because neighboring solutions tend to have similar fitness values such that it is trivial to decide the direction of higher fitness. If instead, a problem has rugged landscape, then the fitness of neighboring solutions might be significantly different, therefore making it more challenging to decide the direction and search strategy that would lead to the most optimal solution. The reason why neighboring solutions might have very different fitness values is due to complementarity (Kauffman and Levin, 1987). When complementarity between the dimensions of a problem is high, then the changing of the value of one dimension might induce a non-linear effect on the total evaluation of the fitness of such a solution.

2.2. *Search on rugged landscapes*

When faced with a rugged landscape, agents such as organizations or people can adopt a search heuristic to find the optimal solution. In the presence of rugged landscape, a typical search strategy would mainly aim at avoiding situations of sub-optimal lock-ins. A sub-optimal lock-in is a scenario whereby an agent or a group of agents arrive at a local optimum that has lower fitness value than other local optima, thus overcoming the chance of finding better solutions (Cecere *et al.*, 2014). The more agents in the system adopt the same sub-optimal solution, the stronger is the lock-in. Sub-optimal lock-ins occur mainly because of path dependency, which implies that the current location determines the set of potential solutions at the next

---

[2]In addition to local and global optima, fitness landscapes can be characterized by several other features that are not discussed in this chapter. For a comprehensive review on this topic, see Pitzer and Affenzeller (2012).

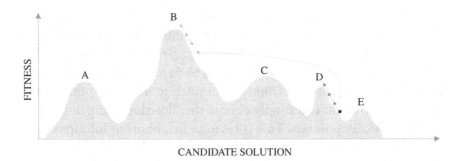

Figure 3. Illustration of the concepts of exploration and exploitation. Starting from an arbitrary point (the round dot), exploitation consists of making small steps to reach the nearest local optimum (location D), while exploration consists in making long jumps in order to discover distant high-fitness solutions (location B).

step. If an agent performs a sequence of steps that form a trajectory leading to a sub-optimal solution, then she is likely to end up locked into that solution.

To overcome the problem of sub-optimal lock-in, organizational theorists sustain that searching agents strive to achieve a balance between exploration and exploitation of a landscape (March, 1991). Exploitation consists of making small incremental steps in one of the directions near the current location in the landscape. Instead, exploration involves making long jumps to explore distant solutions (see Figure 3 for an illustration). Achieving a balance between exploration and exploitation is non-trivial because too much exploration is costly and would waste the opportunity of exploiting and benefiting from what has been discovered, while too much exploitation is likely to lead the agent to overcome significantly better solutions, thus increasing the risk of sub-optimal lock-in. The exploration–exploitation dilemma is often used to address questions like "where do agents look for solutions?" Besides this question, understanding search behavior might involve the dimension of "how to search?" According to Lopez-Vega *et al.* (2016), the "how" dimension can be classified as either experiential or cognitive. Experiential search is a *learning-by-doing* process, where solutions are tried and evaluated, and the outcome of the experiment is used to decide on the next step. In cognitive search, solutions are evaluated before testing them, therefore making it more of a *learning-before-doing* process. In Section 3.2, I will explore the search heuristics topic more in detail and illustrate how it relates to the problem of FinTech innovation.

3. The Complexity of FinTech Innovations

3.1. *Dimensionality of FinTech problems*

In order to understand the search behavior of FinTech firms, we first need to understand the types and complexity (dimensionality) of the problems being tackled. According to Sironi (2016), FinTech firms are developing innovations in a large variety of financial areas, which can be aggregated into five categories: (1) *payments* such as mobile and digital payments; (2) *retail lending* such as P2P; (3) *personal finance* such as robo-advisors; (4) *big data analytics*; and (5) *residual models* such as scientific research, cloud computing, and analytics platforms. Crucially, this categorization shows that the problems being tackled by FinTech firms are in the majority of cases already existing financial problems (e.g. payments, transfers, investment, risk management, fraud detection, and insurance). Therefore, we might be able to assume that FinTech firms and traditional financial institutions are located on the same fitness landscape of a financial problem, with the main difference being the approach used to navigate the landscape.

Listing the complete number of dimensions and sub-dimensions of financial problems might not be possible, and it is beyond the scope of this chapter. However, regardless of the financial problem being developed, many FinTech problems can be thought as having four core and common dimensions: security and privacy, data and analytics, and information technology infrastructure. Security and privacy are perhaps the most critical of these dimensions (Gai *et al.*, 2016). Any innovation in the financial industry involves working with confidential data, and therefore, privacy and security are a primary constraint in the innovation process. The increase in cyberthreats and the demand for data protection make it essential for a FinTech firm to address security and privacy to gain trust among (potential) customers. Optimizing this dimension could be non-trivial for at least two reasons. First, it might hard to anticipate the kind of threats that a firm could be exposed to or the ways privacy can be compromised. Second is the fact that attackers and hackers are adaptive in that they tend to adjust their strategy based on the security measures adopted by the firm. This implies that the firm needs to monitor and adjust their security and privacy measures constantly.

The second dimension of the FinTech innovation problem is data and data analysis techniques. Given that most financial products are data products, the emergence and success of many FinTech companies would not have been possible without the availability of large and various sets of financial data as well as the advancements in data mining and machine learning algorithms (Puschmann, 2017; Van Liebergen, 2017). The data and analytics dimension can be challenging to optimize due to factors such as data collection, quality, storage, processing, and model training. Machine learning approaches, which are often used by FinTech solutions, are known for the so-called *cold start* problem. The cold start problem refers to the fact that it is hard to get sufficient and good-quality data in order for a machine learning model to produce satisfying results. Additionally, machine learning models might very quickly reach a performance plateau where it is very hard to improve the accuracy of the model or engine being developed.

Finally, the third dimension concerns hardware and infrastructure. Deploying and maintaining an advanced, efficient, and scalable data storage and computing infrastructure is critical for the functioning and growth of FinTech firms. Several solutions can be adopted for this dimension, for example, FinTech firms might decide to acquire and maintain their own physical infrastructure or they can make use of third-party cloud-based solutions. Physical resources give more control, but they are costly and hard to scale, while cloud-based solutions are scalable but might entail control and security issues.

Crucially, the three dimensions discussed in the previous paragraphs are highly complementary, therefore producing trade-offs and constraints for the innovating FinTech firm. For example, the more data-driven the FinTech firm is, the more reliant it will be on customer data, and this might increase the risks of data security and privacy. Similarly, the use of cloud-based solutions might increase performance and solve scalability and reliability issues, but at the same time, it reduces the control over the data and makes security and privacy dependent on the measures adopted by the service provider (Gai, 2018).

The multidimensional nature of financial problems and the presence of conflicting constraints between them can be used as an indicator that the financial landscape of FinTech problems is rather complex, meaning that there are many local optima whose fitness might vary significantly. The fitness of a solution to a financial problem might refer to different things. For example, a money transfer or payment might be evaluated based on the speed of execution, a fraud detection solution might be evaluated based on its accuracy, a robo-advisor might be evaluated based on how well they match customer preferences.

Faced with a complex landscape of candidate solutions, FinTech firms would need to make use of a search heuristic to explore such landscape in search of the optimal solution. In the next section, I give a brief discussion of how a theoretical approach of FinTech innovation might be constructed.

3.2. *Search behavior of FinTech firms*

Due to the complex nature of financial landscapes, FinTech firms that adopt better search strategies are likely to obtain better results and therefore achieve a competitive position in the market. This is clear, for example, by observing the fact that banks are more likely to enter into alliance with a FinTech firm if the firm has a clear digital strategy (Hornuf *et al.*, 2020).

FinTech firms are often distinguished by their unconventional and flexible approach to innovation. Crucially, little has been done to explore in detail the nature of the search process of FinTech firms. In order to do so, I rely on the framework proposed by Lopez-Vega *et al.* (2016), which combines the two dimensions of *how* and *where* to search in order to explain firm search behavior. Before exploring these two search dimensions, I would assume that FinTech firms operate within a specified *technological paradigm*. According to Dosi and Orsenigo (1988, p. 16), a technological paradigm entails "a definition of the relevant problems that must be tackled, the tasks to be fulfilled, a pattern of inquiry, the material technology to be used, and the types of basic artifacts to be developed and improved."

There can be several candidates for describing the specific technological paradigm of FinTech solutions; however, a good candidate is that of an *open innovation* paradigm. The main idea behind open innovation is that firms seek and share knowledge with actors outside their organizational confines (West *et al.*, 2014). Numerous observations might indicate that FinTech firms operate within an open innovation paradigm. Perhaps the most important one is the fact that FinTech firms need to find partners from the traditional financial system to be able to gain access to the marketplace and offer their products (Hendrikse, 2018). A good example in this regard is open banking, which refers to the use of financial APIs[3] that allow a FinTech firm to access a traditional financial institutions' internal data or infrastructure in order to build applications and solutions around the financial institution. Traditional banks increasingly realize the need to adopt an open innovation approach to benefit from the innovations of FinTech firms (Chishti and Barberis, 2016). For instance, in 2016, the US bank JP Morgan Chase announced a program called "IN-RESIDENCE" where the bank invites FinTech firms, "to sit 'side by side' with its businesses in order to develop innovations that could revolutionize the sector, enabling banks to operate faster, safer and at a lower cost." Additional factors such as collaboration with universities and

---

[3] API stands for Application Programming Interface, which in computer science refers to the set of protocols and procedures used to allow one software to communicate with another.

regulators and use of open-source technologies might also be considered indicators of the open innovation nature of FinTech innovations.

Moving to the question of what characterizes the search process of FinTech firms, the first dimension mentioned above concerns the *where* to search. Assuming that a FinTech firm wants to search in the fitness landscape of a financial problem, the question is how to decide where to search next? In Lopez-Vega *et al.* (2016), the authors distinguish between *local* search, where the firm identifies the solutions in the proximity of its current location, and *distant* search, which involves solution at a considerable distance from the current position. Local search might be treated as equivalent to what is often called exploitation, while distant search is equivalent to exploration. Although FinTech firms use a unique innovative approach, it is still an unanswered question whether these firms are performing incremental, short-distance search, or long-range exploration. One possible hypothesis could be that existing solutions to financial problems are located near a local optimum, and FinTech firms do nothing more than climbing from that position to the nearest optimum. Several reasons might support this short-distance-search hypothesis. For instance, short-distance (incremental) innovations are easier to implement in the already existing infrastructure, mainly if the FinTech firm is operating within the platform of a traditional financial institution. Additionally, assessing the security and privacy risks of solutions near the existing solution might be much easier than distant solutions. Finally, clients might be more likely to adopt a solution that is better but at the same time close enough to what they are used to. On the other hand, some arguments might be provided to justify the long-distance hypothesis of FinTech search. Solutions such as cryptocurrency, blockchain, and robo-advisors, often developed by FinTech firms, can be considered as long-distance solutions for already existing problems such as payment and investment. If one can prove that the solution adopted by traditional financial system to a problem is actually a local optimum, then it is reasonable to assume that FinTech innovations result from long-distance search for other local optima. The short- vs long-distance dilemma of

FinTech search remains an important research question that requires further investigation.

Moving to the other dimension discussed by Lopez-Vega *et al.* (2016), i.e. *how* to search, two views are offered: *experiential* and *cognitive* search. In experiential search, a solution is first tried, and then feedback from the experiment is used to decide on the next step. In other words, experiential search resembles a learning-by-doing process. Here it worth mentioning that financial innovations might be hard to experiment in real time for two main reasons: first, a financial firm would risk its reputation if it tests its product on its clients should the product fail or compromises client privacy (Haliassos, 2013). Second, the outcome of some financial innovations, such as the estimated risk or number of frauds, is to be obtained in a future time, therefore making it hard to get immediate feedback to decide on the next steps. Nevertheless, the availability of large datasets and the digital nature of FinTech firms can allow for data-driven experiments using a variety of training sets and data mining methods. The second option in deciding how to search, i.e. cognitive search, involves a learning-before-doing process, where abstract and theoretical representations of the solution space are obtained, and decisions regarding how to find a solution are made based on such representations. One of the arguments that might sustain the cognitive hypothesis in FinTech search is the fact that these firms might rely on scientific discoveries (or conduct scientific research) before developing a new financial solution. This might be especially the case when the solution found to a financial problem is a breakthrough one.

Lopez-Vega *et al.* (2016) showed that all four search heuristics (local, distant, experiential, and cognitive) could be combined to understand the nature of search paths followed in an industry. For this reason, it would be a significant extension of this chapter to collect data and investigate the nature of search paths that are followed by FinTech firms. Answering the question of how and where FinTech firms search for solutions to financial problems can help understand and predict the future of this industry. A vital prediction that can be made concerns the likelihood of a *technological plateau* of FinTech innovation, where new and better solutions to existing problems can hardly be found anymore. A report by Skan *et al.* (2016) showed, the FinTech industry is actually showing signs of maturity and this might suggest that we are reaching a technological plateau. This, however, might simply mean that the system has reached a local optimum and got locked in there. On the other hand, some retain that the FinTech approach will significantly contribute in shaping the financial services landscape (Gomber *et al.*, 2018; Nicoletti *et al.*, 2017).

4. Conclusion and Possible Extension

This chapter is intended to provide a brief discussion of a theoretical approach that can explain the nature of the search process by FinTech firms. In doing so, I propose to use the approach of fitness landscapes to model both the space of solutions to a financial problem and the search heuristics that can be adopted by FinTech firms to explore such space.

Practitioners and policy-makers might derive useful insights from a fitness landscape view of FinTech solutions. For policy-makers, a landscape view of the financial system might increase the awareness of the complexity of FinTech innovations and the risks that the system might get locked in a sub-optimal solution. This can guide policy-makers to incentivize more exploration in the search for better solutions to financial problems, and FinTech firms might be the key to discover such solutions. Additionally, understanding how FinTech firms innovate can help policy-makers decide on the right amount of regulation for the FinTech industry. The right number of regulatory requirements should guarantee the minimum exploratory freedom that FinTech firms need in order to innovate. Finally, regulators who understand the open innovation nature of the collaboration between FinTech firms and traditional financial institutions will be able to introduce regulations that foster such collaborations.

As for industry practitioners, a landscape view of financial problems can help them decide on the search strategy they should pursue to find optimal/better solutions. Achieving a trade-off between exploration and exploitation is perhaps the most challenging task in this regard. Performing both experimental and cognitive search can also increase the understanding of the landscape of financial problems, therefore giving FinTech firms information on how to search. Finally, FinTech firms might avoid the complexity of search by forming collaborations and alliances with traditional financial institutions. By working with financial institutions, FinTech firms can gain access to an already established platform to test their product and gain knowledge that will help them explore the fitness landscape.

The investigation offered in this chapter is on the fundamental level, and therefore there is potential for both theoretical and empirical extensions. On the theoretical level, it would be essential to investigate how to model the fitness landscapes of a financial problem. It would also be interesting to understand how to operationalize and develop an understanding of the concept of fitness when it comes to financial problems. It is also of high importance to try to model the search behavior of FinTech firms following a framework such as the one offered by Lopez-Vega et al. (2016). On the empirical level, it would be essential to collect/analyze data on the solutions developed by FinTech firms and their main features of such solutions. Additionally, it is an essential task to collect data on the nature of problems being tackled by FinTech firms. Obtaining data and analyzing the search behavior of FinTech firms would also be a significant contribution that can help predict the future of the FinTech industry.

References

Anagnostopoulos, I. (2018). Fintech and Regtech: Impact on regulators and banks. *Journal of Economics and Business*, 100, 7–25.

Arner, D. W., Barberis, J., & Buckley, R. P. (2016). The evolution of fintech: New post-crisis paradigm. *Georgetown Journal of International Law*, 47(4), 1271–1320.

Bogers, M., Chesbrough, H., & Moedas, C. (2018). Open innovation: Research, practices, and policies. *California Management Review*, 60(2), 5–16.

Buchak, G., Matvos, G., Piskorski, T., & Seru, A. (2018). Fintech, regulatory arbitrage, and the rise of shadow banks. *Journal of Financial Economics*, 130(3), 453–483.

Cecere, G., Corrocher, N., Gossart, C., & Ozman, M. (2014). Lock-in and path dependence: An evolutionary approach to eco-innovations. *Journal of Evolutionary Economics*, 24(5), 1037–1065.

Chishti, S., & Barberis, J. (2016). *The FinTech Book: The Financial Technology Handbook for Investors, Entrepreneurs and Visionaries* (John Wiley & Sons, New York, United States).

Cojoianu, T. F., Clark, G. L., Hoepner, A. G., Pažitka, V., & Wójcik, D. (2020). Fin vs. tech: Are trust and knowledge creation key ingredients in fintech start-up emergence and financing? *Small Business Economics*, 1–17.

Dhar, V., & Stein, R. (2016). FinTech platforms and strategy. MIT Sloan Research Paper, United States.

Dosi, G., & Orsenigo, L. (1988). Coordination and transformation: An overview of structures, behaviours and change in evolutionary environments. In *Technical Change and Economic Theory*, Dosi, G., Freeman, C., & Nelson, R., *et al.* (eds.) (Pinter Publishers Limited, London, UK), pp. 13–37.

Gai, K., Qiu, M., & Sun, X. (2018). A survey on FinTech. *Journal of Network and Computer Applications*, 103, 262–273.

Gai, K., Qiu, M., Sun, X., & Zhao, H. (2016). Security and privacy issues: A survey on FinTech. In *International Conference on Smart Computing and Communication* (Springer, Cham), pp. 236–247.

Goldstein, I., Jiang, W., & Karolyi, G. A. (2019). To FinTech and beyond. *The Review of Financial Studies*, 32(5), 1647–1661.

Gomber, P., Kauffman, R. J., Parker, C., & Weber, B. W. (2018). On the fintech revolution: Interpreting the forces of innovation, disruption, and transformation in financial services. *Journal of Management Information Systems*, 35(1), 220–265.

Haddad, C., & Hornuf, L. (2019). The emergence of the global fintech market: Economic and technological determinants. *Small Business Economics*, 53(1), 81–105.

Haliassos, M. (ed.) (2013). *Financial Innovation: Too Much or Too Little?* (MIT Press).

Hendrikse, R., Bassens, D., & van Meeteren, M. (2018). The Appleization of finance: Charting incumbent finance's embrace of FinTech. *Finance and Society*, 4(2), 159–180.

Hornuf, L., Klus, M. F., Lohwasser, T. S., & Schwienbacher, A. (2020). How do banks interact with fintech startups? *Small Business Economics*, 1–22.

Kauffman, S., & Levin, S. (1987). Towards a general theory of adaptive walks on rugged landscapes. *Journal of Theoretical Biology*, 128(1), 11–45.

Khraisha, T. (2019). Complex economic problems and fitness landscapes: Assessment and methodological perspectives. *Structural Change and Economic Dynamics* (Accepted manuscript).

Khraisha, T., & Arthur, K. (2018). Can we have a general theory of financial innovation processes? A conceptual review. *Financial Innovation*, 4(1), 4.

Lopez-Vega, H., Tell, F., & Vanhaverbeke, W. (2016). Where and how to search? Search paths in open innovation. *Research Policy*, 45(1), 125–136.

March, J. G. (1991). Exploration and exploitation in organizational learning. *Organization Science*, 2(1), 71–87.

Mohan, D. (2016). How banks and FinTech startups are partnering for faster innovation. *Journal of Digital Banking*, 1(1), 13–21.

Nicoletti, B., Nicoletti, & Weis. (2017). *Future of FinTech* (Palgrave Macmillan, Basingstoke, UK).

Philippon, T. (2016). The fintech opportunity. National Bureau of Economic Research No. w22476.

Pitzer, E., & Affenzeller, M. (2012). A comprehensive survey on fitness landscape analysis. In *Recent Advances in Intelligent Engineering Systems*, Fodor, J., Klempous, R., Suárez, A., & Carmen, P. (eds.) (Springer, Berlin, Heidelberg), pp. 161–191.

Puschmann, T. (2017). Fintech. *Business & Information Systems Engineering*, 59(1), 69–76.

Sironi, P. (2016). *FinTech Innovation: From Robo-advisors to Goal Based Investing and Gamification* (John Wiley & Sons, New York, United States).

Skan, J., Dickerson, J., & Gagliardi, L. (2016). Fintech and the evolving landscape: Landing points for the industry. Accenture. Retrieved from: https://www. accenture.com/t20161011T031409Z__w__/pl-en/_acnmedia/PDF-15/Accenture-Fintech-Evolving-Landscape.pdf (Accessed on 24 March 2019).

Van Liebergen, B. (2017). Machine learning: A revolution in risk management and compliance? *Journal of Financial Transformation*, 45, 60–67.

West, J., Salter, A., Vanhaverbeke, W., & Chesbrough, H. (2014). Open innovation: The next decade. *Research Policy*, 43(5), 805–811.

Index